MAGICAL
BRITAIN

650 Enchanted and Mystical Sites

Rob Wildwood

WILD
THINGS
PUBLISHING

Dun Taimh, p322

MAGICAL
BRITAIN

Roche Rock, p84

CONTENTS

REGIONAL OVERVIEW

Fairy Church, p204

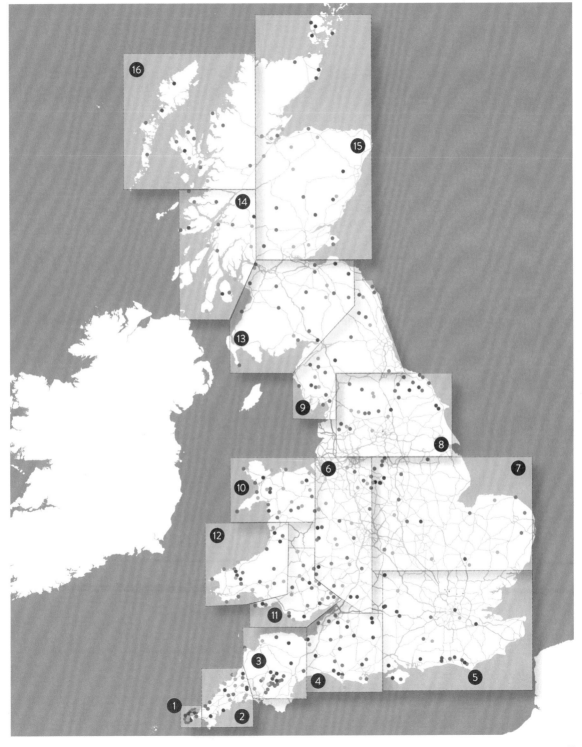

Callanish Stones, p329

BRITAIN'S MAGICAL HISTORY

The folklore of the British Isles evolved out of the unique cultures of its inhabitants and their connection to the land and its supernatural beings and spirits.

The earliest visitors to these isles, once the ice sheets had receded, were Mesolithic hunter-gatherers. These nomadic people almost certainly followed an animist religion as many indigenous people still do today, seeing all of nature – animals, plants, rocks, elements and heavenly bodies – as alive and imbued with spirit, a spirit they felt themselves to be an integral and inseparable part of. It is also likely that these early people honoured Mother Earth, the Great Goddess, as one of the most powerful of spirits. They would have followed long hunting tracks through the wilderness, mapping out their journeys in songs and legends, each location along the way infused with meaning by their stories.

Later, the more settled farming cultures of the Neolithic and Bronze Age left behind their enigmatic monuments of stone and earth, including stone circles, dolmens, standing stones and barrows, many of which are aligned to the cycles of the sun and moon. Given the absence of written records the purpose and meaning of these structures were as much of an enigma to those who came after as they are to us, and some thought them the work of an ancient race of giants.

During the Iron Age, Celtic peoples inhabited the British Isles. Spread over numerous tribes they are collectively referred to as Ancient Britons. They spoke a version of the Celtic tongue known as Brythonic – the ancestor of today's Welsh, Cornish and Breton languages – and were ruled over by tribal chieftains and a scholarly elite known as the Druids, the keepers of ancient wisdom and arcane knowledge. These Druids wrote down none of their knowledge and they worshipped in sacred groves in the forest, so almost nothing survives of their temples or religion. All that remains are offerings cast into sacred springs and pools, and later stone carvings consisting of a number of basic inscriptions in their linear ogham script.

What little knowledge we do have of the beliefs and practices of the Ancient Britons comes down to us through the literature of the Romans, who were to become their conquerors. After invading the British Isles, the Romans set about eradicating the Druids who they saw as rivals, completely dismantling their power structures. However, the Romans were tolerant of Celtic beliefs, gods and religious sites, identifying the Ancient Britons' gods as aspects of their own pagan deities. So for example the Celtic goddess Sulis at Bath (Aquae Sulis) became the Roman goddess Sulis Minerva. The Romans, too, made offerings at sacred springs and forest shrines, honouring the nymphs of the waters and the dryads of the woods, but they also worshipped their gods in dedicated stone temples.

Dunadd, p287

Iona, p290

During the Roman occupation of Britain, which lasted almost 400 years, Christianity arrived in the British Isles, and by the early medieval period it had evolved into a unique form known as 'Celtic Christianity'. Yet after the Romans departed, Britain was plunged into a 'Dark Age' as government structures collapsed, Roman towns and fortifications were abandoned, and the written historical record came to an end. Out of this darkness emerged some of Britain's most colourful and enduring myths – tales of King Arthur and his knights, the wizard Merlin and the Welsh bard Taliesin.

The Romano-British Celts, Romanised successors to the Ancient Britons, were at this time being assailed from all sides. From the east came the Angles, Saxons and Jutes, later to be referred to collectively as the Anglo-Saxons. The Scots-Gaels from Ireland advanced from the west and from the north came the Picts –these two would later amalgamate to become the Scottish Highlanders.

A desperate rearguard action was being fought by the new Romano-British kingdoms against these savage invaders. Warlords like Arthur would achieve some victories and stem the tide for a while, but their fate was sealed and the Anglo-Saxons would eventually overrun the whole of the land that would become known as England. Only in Wales and Cornwall did the Ancient Britons endure and they also held onto the Lowlands of Scotland for some time until these were finally relinquished, going down in Welsh legend as the lost lands of the 'Hen Ogledd' the Old North.

It is these Brythonic Celtic peoples who retained the original *lore* of the land of Britain and so were keepers of its ancient wisdom and folk knowledge. The Anglo-Saxon newcomers had less of a relationship with this new land and so imprinted upon it far fewer stories and legends than their Celtic neighbours. This is one of the reasons why there is such a dearth of folklore in the southeast of the country compared to the riches of the Celtic west. The flatter, more arable landscape in the east, its closer ties to the continent and its earlier modernisation are also likely to be contributory factors.

Cornwall is renowned for its wealth of unique folklore about giants, piskies, spriggans and knockers, for its abundance of holy wells and prehistoric sites, and for the birthplace of King Arthur at Tintagel. Wales, too, has its own fairy folk, the Tylwyth Teg and the shining beings known as Ellyllon. It is also the home of Myrddin Emrys (the Welsh Merlin), and produced an abundance of Celtic saints – itinerant priests who travelled through Britain establishing hermitages and performing miraculous acts.

In the Old North, the Brythonic speaking Britons carried their own versions of the Merlin and Arthur stories. They occupied the land between the two Roman walls (Hadrian's Wall and the Antonine Wall), but were eventually defeated by the incoming Angles and so Lowland Scotland became 'Anglicised'. Their mythology became linked to that of the Anglo-Saxons and they retained Anglo-Saxon terms such as the word elf, found in Scots phrases such as *elfhame*.

The Scots-Gaels in the Highlands of Scotland had very different mythology and folklore to the Lowland Scots further south. These Gaelic speaking Celts had no tales about King Arthur or Merlin, instead their heroes were Fingal (Fionn mac Cumhaill) and the warrior-poet Ossian, and their fairy folk were known as the sith (sidhe) who lived in fairy hills called sitheans. They also had a whole host of other supernatural beings unique to the Highlands, such as the glaistig, the urisk and the each-uisge (water horse). Of the ancient Picts, the original Brythonic inhabitants of Highland Scotland, we know almost nothing as they left no written record. Only their enigmatic carved, picture-stones remain, hinting at a lost mythology and belief system.

During the period referred to as the Dark Ages, Christianity and the old Romano-Celtic paganism existed side by side in a patchwork of small kingdoms, some following the new religion and some the old. Pagan figures such as Myrddin Wylt (the Scottish Merlin) interacted with Christians including St Kentigern, and legendary saints St Columba and St Aidan established missions on the holy islands of Iona and Lindisfarne. Celtic Christianity would eventually win the hearts and minds of the remaining Celtic peoples as paganism slowly faded back into the mists of time.

During this period the Anglo-Saxons remained firmly wedded to their old gods: Woden, Thunor and Frigga. But over time they too would ultimately succumb to the new religion, as Celtic Christian missions spread south from Lindisfarne and Roman Catholic missions spread north from Kent. These two versions of Christianity disagreed on many points of Christian theology and practice however, and so the inevitable confrontation came to a head in 664 at the Synod of Whitby. Roman Christianity won the day and so Celtic Christianity and the age of the magical Celtic saints would eventually fade into memory. Yet with the approval of the Roman Catholic Church veneration of the old Celtic saints would continue, especially in Cornwall and Wales. Right up to the present day the numerous holy wells and shrines dedicated to them are still believed to have miraculous healing powers. The old pagan ways were not entirely forgotten either. Many pagan shrines became Christian churches, sacred springs became holy wells, the fairies and the elves were still believed to inhabit the mounds, and people's lives were filled with magic and ritual. Yet Britain was now a largely Christian land, with close ties to the Church of Rome.

The triumph of Christianity was to be short-lived, however, as from the end of the 8th century the heathen Norsemen, known later as Vikings, started to ravage these shores. Coming first as raiders, then invaders and finally as settlers, they still followed their old gods Odin, Thor and Freya. They worshipped in sacred groves and wooden temples where they sometimes made blood sacrifices. Their religion was very similar to that of the Anglo-Saxons who had arrived centuries before them and they worshipped a similar pantheon of gods, albeit with slightly different names.

The Norse, and then the Danish Vikings, very nearly succeeded in conquering the whole of England until they were eventually defeated by the Saxon kings of Wessex. The subsequent treaty still gave the Vikings control of more than half of the country, roughly north of the line of the rivers Thames and Severn. This is why many towns, villages and landscape features in the north of England still have Viking names and a unique character distinct from those in the South. The Vikings were the last pagan peoples to invade Britain and they left the names of their pagan gods imprinted upon the landscape, but within a generation or two of settling this land the Vikings too would be converted to Christianity, merging with the English to become the Anglo-Danes. It is not known when, or even if, paganism eventually died out, but we do know that many centuries later kings were still issuing edicts banning many specific details of pagan practice – evidence that it was indeed still being practised!

The Vikings also settled around the coasts of Scotland, particularly in the far north where they established 'The Kingdom of the Isles'. Orkney still retains its Viking heritage and its own unique folklore about trows, finfolk and dwarves. Other attempts were made by Viking kings to conquer the British Isles but the ultimately successful invasion came not from Scandinavia but from the south. These were the Normans, former Vikings themselves who had settled in Northern France and adopted French customs and language. They brought with them many French ideas, including the introduction of the French word *fée* (fairy) into the English language, which largely displaced the Old English concept of elves.

Castell Dinas Bran, p226

Allied to the Norman French were the Bretons, descendants of Brythonic-speaking Celts who had fled the British Isles for Northern France during the 'Dark Ages', taking their Celtic heritage with them. It was the influence of these Bretons that probably led to a renewed interest in British (Celtic as opposed to English) history, culminating in Geoffrey of Monmouth's epic History of the Kings of Britain, appearing in 1136. He covered the whole of British history, starting with the battles between men and giants when people first arrived on these shores; but he is mainly remembered for writing extensively about the exploits of King Arthur and Merlin. His hugely successful book prompted more authors from France and Germany to write their own versions of the Arthurian romances, and so began the whole genre of Arthurian myth that is still popular today.

From the medieval period we also have the chronicles of such notables as Gerald of Wales, Gervase of Tilbury, Ralph of Coggeshall and Walter Map whose writings are filled with supernatural tales and observances, as well as Britain's first recorded fairy tales. William Shakespeare would later draw

Eildon Hills, p272

extensively on these medieval tales from Britain's semi-legendary past. It was also during this period that many ancient Welsh bardic tales were finally committed to paper, tales that would later be compiled into a celebrated collection, the Mabinogion. They tell of Welsh heroes, journeys to the Otherworld, magical cauldrons, perilous quests and the exploits of Arthur and his band of warriors, all set in a mythical Welsh past.

During the Protestant reformation, old Roman Catholic 'superstitions' such as the veneration of saint's relics and rituals at shrines and holy wells were actively banned. Many ancient traditions, which had been given a thin veneer of Christian acceptability under Roman Catholicism, were lost, culminating in the fundamentalist Puritan movement of the 17th century when ancient monuments, sacred sites and anything 'popish' were actively being destroyed. Fortunately, antiquarians such as William Stukeley, John Aubrey and William Camden were recording local folklore, customs and details about ancient monuments which would otherwise have been lost. William Stukeley, however, was also mainly responsible for the unfounded belief that stone circles and other prehistoric sites were places of Druid worship. It was also during this time that witches were persecuted, making people terrified to have any connection with magic or ancient superstitions. Fairies and other supernatural beings were cast as demons and those who consulted them were seen as consorting with the Devil himself. During this period, it is likely that many folk tales involving the old gods, giants or fairies were recast as the exploits of devils, demons and imps.

One of the most influential, and fanciful, of antiquarians was Sir Walter Scott, who at the beginning of the 19th century published his Minstrelsy of the Scottish Border, which popularised such enduring tales as Tam-Lin and Thomas the Rhymer, describing their journeys into Elfland. The antiquarian movement continued into the Victorian period and beyond when folklore and customs from almost every part of the country were being recorded in detail. These records were to prove invaluable as most traditions would soon die out with the coming of industrialisation, surviving only in the remote western and upland regions of the country. The Victorians, however, were responsible for the twee depictions of fairies with wings.

In the early 20th century, many traditional storytellers, particularly in Wales, Cornwall and the Highlands and islands of Scotland, preserved the old tales and folklore spoken in the original Celtic languages. But with the coming of radio and then television, storytelling as a form of entertainment rapidly died out and many of the tales not written down have been lost to us.

Today most people have largely forgotten their ancient connection to the land and its stories, seeming to prefer a sanitised version of fairy tales that are no longer rooted in the landscape and its web of supernatural beings and spirits. Myths and legends are more than just stories; they are a way for us to remember our magical relationship with the land. It is through restorying the landscape that we may one day regain this ancient respect and reverence for the land. Indigenous people know what we perhaps no longer remember: that only through respecting its sacredness will the land endure and sustain us for centuries to come.

HOW TO USE THIS BOOK

SYMBOLS

	Creation stories		Merlin
	Giants		Legendary heroes
	Songlines		Celtic saints & miracles
	Goddess		Christianised pagan sites
	Animate stones		Norse & Anglo-Saxon
	Portals		Wild hunt
	Fairies		Dragons
	Pixies		Wishes & divination
	Mermaids		Healing
	Water spirits		Rituals & shrines
	Hobs & brownies		Magic

LISTINGS

Sites fall under one or more categories denoted by symbols (see above and as described in the following pages). The site description then gives a brief overview of the site along with its magical properties, followed by a brief summary of the folklore of the site (for more information see Bibliography at the back of the book or look up the story online. Most folklore tales are available online for free). The site description will also include some indication of what it is like to visit the site today and what can be experienced there. No stars means worth a detour. One star then it's worth a trip. Two stars then it's worth stay-ing over. Sub-locations are also mentioned followed by GPS co-ordinates and UK grid ref. A visit to those highlighted in bold is recommended and most include a photo. For other sub-locations GPS co-ordinates and UK grid ref are given for reference purposes only. These sites may still be visited (unless listed as 'private') but might only be of interest to those who wish to delve deeper into the stories and folklore.

FINDING YOUR WAY

GPS co-ordinates can be typed directly into any map app or website or into a Sat Nav (GPS unit) by setting the Coordinate Format to h ddd.dddddd°. The UK grid ref refers to the National Grid as shown on Ordinance Survey (OS) maps. Available either in paper or digital format, the large-scale 1:25,000 maps are highly recommended and show detail including footpaths and public rights of way, springs and streams, contours and minor prehistoric and historic sites such as holy wells and burial mounds. When purchasing a paper map you also get a free digital version. Unless the site is beside the road, GPS co-ordinates and UK grid ref are given for the trailhead. This is the nearest point reachable by road for access to the site on foot, or the nearest parking area. Trail-heads without parking will require you to look for a parking space nearby. The approxi-mate walking distance in metres follows the UK grid reference.

ACCESS TO SPECIFIC LOCATIONS

Some locations are on private land in which case this will be clearly stated after the UK grid ref. In England and Wales, you are only permitted to walk on public footpaths and other permissive paths, and on open access land. All other areas are considered private and the landowner should be contacted first to seek permis-sion. In Scotland the 'right to roam' allows access to most land except for areas around private dwellings as long as you

Malvhina Spring, p154

act responsibly. For Scottish sites marked 'private' you must get permission from the owner. Some locations require an entry fee to be paid, shown in multiples of £. Each £ = up to £6; e.g. ££ = £6.10 to £12. Parking fees are shown in the same fashion. Coastal sites only accessible when the tide is out are clearly marked 'low tide only'. Always check the tides before walking to these sites and preferably set off when the tide is falling to avoid being cut off by the rising tide. Some sites are marked 'secret/ secluded'. These are generally off the beaten track and not well known. Expect to have these sites to yourself if you manage to find them! Other sites marked 'popular' will usually be busy unless visited out of season or at dawn/dusk. Visiting sites marked 'no paths' will involve walking across country with a GPS unit or compass to find them. If there are paths only part of the way, this is indicated by 'no paths at end'.

VISITING A MAGICAL PLACE
RESPECT, REVERENCE & INSIGHT

When you visit any of the magical sites in this book, remember that to our ancient ancestors the land was sacred, filled with a spirit and a mystery that deserved both honour and respect. If you want to show your reverence by leaving an offering at a site then please make sure it is made from biodegradable organic material. Plastic ribbons kill trees and modern coins pollute well water. It is better just to sit in silence, quieten the mind and take time to tune into the energy of the place. Let the stories and folklore guide you to the true 'spirit of place' and what it has to offer in terms of insight and wisdom for our future relationship with the land.

St Issui's Well p243

THE CELTIC WHEEL OF THE YEAR

The Celts had four main festivals to mark the seasons. These 'sabbats' were held on the cross-quarter days that marked the halfway point between the solstices and equinoxes, thus ushering in the new season. Beltane and Samhain in particular are often referred to in folklore as nights when the veil between worlds is thin, fairy doors open and otherworldly beings can be seen out riding.

The four main Celtic sabbats are:

Samhain
Winter, dying/ancestors, goddess Cailleach, 1st November ★ (Hallowe'en ★★)

Imbolc
Spring, new growth, goddess Bride, 1st February ★

Beltane
Summer, fertility, god Bel, 1st May ★ (May Day)

Lughnasadh
Autumn, harvest, god Lugh, 1st August ★ (Lammas)

They occur halfway between the solstices and equinoxes:

**Midwinter solstice,
Ostara equinox
Midsummer solstice
Maben equinox**

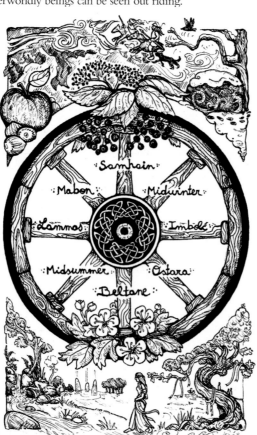

★ Dates given are modern equivalents; originally the festivals would have been determined astrologically or by seasonal changes.
★★ Note that Celtic days began in the evening. They reckoned by nights not days, therefore Hallowe'en (All Hallows Eve) is the start of the old Samhain and is even today associated with the dead. Likewise, the Celtic year begins at the start of winter on Samhain.

Stonehenge, p131

CREATION

Ancient myths to explain the creation of the earth exist worldwide and indigenous cultures developed their own interpretations of how the landscape and its features came into being. In British folklore, an ancient race of giants formed the landscape before the advent of human beings. These representations of the primal forces of nature could be seen to embody the glaciers and floods that gouged out valleys and deposited huge boulders, earthquakes that raised and shook the land, and winds and erosion that created all the diverse forms in the landscape.

Strangely shaped natural features, as well as more mundane ones, were once giants, gods or ancestor beings who were turned to stone, forming huge boulders and rocky pillars or even whole islands such as Steepholm and Flatholm in the Bristol Channel. A handful of tales survive of these great primeval beings, even if the details of the stories themselves have been altered beyond all recognition.

As well as tales about giants we also hear about legendary heroes, grown to giant size, who shaped the land by hurling boulders around or creating causeways. In later, Christian times when belief in giants was seen as ungodly, any earth- or stone-moving moving activity was attributed to the Devil.

Occasionally there are stranger creation stories, such as landmasses being created by wizards or by fairies, or of rocks and buildings being sculpted by supernatural beings. These stories probably arose to account for the unusual location or shape of certain structures in the landscape.

GIANTS

Before the arrival of the first human settlers, the island of Britain was inhabited by a race of legendary giants. Thought to have been quite dim-witted, these giants liked to show off their strength by hurling rocks around and in the process they created many of the landscape features that we see today. Stories of two giants on adjacent hilltops throwing rocks at each other are common, as are those of giants flinging a shared hammer back and forth between them. The giants usually lived in fortified hilltop dwellings and the remains of these legendary locations are still in evidence, especially in Cornwall where some were the sites of Iron Age hillforts and others date back to the Neolithic period.

When humans came onto the scene, they easily outwitted and defeated the giants, as did the early Celtic saints. Stories of legendary giant killers such as Jack the Hammer or Jack the Giant Killer may go back to the Iron Age, or to the time of mythical Celtic heroes and gods. The exploits of these giants sometimes become conflated with those of legendary heroes, so in some stories King Arthur himself or Fingal (the Irish Finn mac Cumhail) acquire the stature and strength of giants, enabling them to throw rocks around or carve out valleys.

As Christian teachings became more widespread, our pagan past and its supernatural beings were considered taboo. Tales were revised and the giants of legends were replaced by devils or the Devil himself. Later still, stories of folk heroes of giant status became popular but their protagonists were not the giants of old but rather humans of extraordinary size whose stature increased as the tales grew in the telling.

BEST SITES

SONGLINES –
MYTHIC ROUTES

The term songlines refers to the ancient, sacred pathways that criss-cross Australia. They came into being in the Dreamtime, when the ancestral spirits of Indigenous Australians created life and formed the landscape. The course of these tracks, taking in landscape features and sacred locations, was passed down in songs and stories that serve to re-enforce cultural bonds and function as navigational and teaching aids.

The ancient Britons also had stories that linked several locations, such as the hunt for the giant boar Twrch Trwyth and his piglets. The pursuit took King Arthur and his men across the landscape of South Wales, stopping at many significant landscape features along the way. Most surviving British songline stories, however, are much shorter, consisting of just two or three linked sites. Common themes are landscape features that were dug up in one place and deposited or hurled to another, sites where giants and other magical beings would leap from one place to another or share a hammer by throwing it back and forth between them. Such themes combine in stories of Wade the giant and his wife Bel, associated with several sites across the North York Moors.

Sacred sites were sometimes linked by causeways, tunnels or fairy paths, echoing the idea of ancient songlines or spirit routes and as stories evolved, an ancient connection between two places could be recalled in a simple folk tale about a giant's leap. Just as in Chinese geomancy, currents of energy called dragon lines connect prominent landscape features, so our ancient ancestors might have tuned into these subtle earth energies that are now remembered only in stories. In the 1920s, British photographer and antiquarian Alfred Watkins coined the term ley lines – a network of straight lines that connected sites of ancient significance, including megaliths, mounds and churches built on pre-Christian sites. These lines, now perceived as more fluid, can be sensed by dowsers using dowsing rods or pendulums and the same instruments are also employed to detect earth energies – those hidden lines of power that seem to connect sacred sites.

MOTHER GODDESS

Female figurines found all over Europe from the Mesolithic period onwards are evidence of the most ancient religion in Europe, the cult of the Mother Goddess. These sacred females are symbols of the earth itself and places where the form of the goddess (such as twin hills) was represented in the shape of the landscape were especially venerated. Sacred springs, representing the lifeblood of Mother Earth, were also associated with goddess worship.

To the ancient Celts, the Mother Goddess had many names such as Anu, Danu or Annis, and the sites of her sacred springs and wells would later become associated with Christain saints, such as St Anne. Another Celtic Mother Goddess, Bride, was associated with fire, water and childbirth. Many wells were named after her or her Christian counterparts St Bridget or St Ffraid / Fride (Welsh).

In the Highlands of Scotland, the powerful Mother Goddess was known to the Scots-Gaels as the Cailleach-Beara and her appearance changed with the seasons, from a young woman in spring to a crone in winter. The Cailleach formed the landscape of Scotland, creating lochs with her feet or mountains out of piles of rocks. In later times, she was perceived primarily as a fearsome old crone (like Black Annis or Mother Darkly in English folklore) who dwelt in the mountains. Invading Saxons and Norse tribes also brought their own incarnations of the Mother – the goddesses Frigga and Freya, whose names persist in some landscape locations.

With the coming of Christianity, sacred goddess sites were co-opted and became associated with female saints. As well as St Anne and St Bridget there were more obscure Celtic saints such as St Milburga and St Melangell. Some see the Christian Mary as a version of the Mother Goddess and the name of her mother, Anna, echoes that of the original Celtic Anu.

BEST SITES

ANIMATE STONES

Folk tales concerning stones that come to life and move, or people who were turned to stone forming stone circles and other stone monuments, are widespread. In these stories, stones were not simply inanimate objects but part of a natural world that, according to animist religions, was alive and populated by spirits. Besides animals and plants, the four elements, rocks and celestial bodies, were all seen as imbued with a living, conscious spirit. Animism underpinned the belief system of the ancient Celts, pagan Anglo-Saxons and Norse peoples, whose gods were originally personifications of natural forces.

In Britain, our tribal ancestors would have viewed at least some stones as living beings, or 'stone people' and folk tales developed from this belief. In a common folk tale, stone circles were once maidens who were punished for dancing on the sabbath (possibly a Christianisation of witches dancing on the *sabbat*). Often there is an outlying stone, sometimes known as the piper, who played the music and could be the Devil himself.

Another curious and yet common folk tale is of stones that come to life at certain times of the day or year. Some stones spin around while others go down to a nearby water source, such as a river or pond, to drink. In these stories, the stones are somehow kept in suspended animation until the time is right for them to come to life. Other stones are said to be immovable, while those that are removed from their rightful place will bring down a curse that will be lifted only when they are returned. Attempts to count the stones in many stone circles may never yield the same result twice, perhaps because the stones will move around and deceive the counter! Finally, there are tales of 'living' stones that will bleed if they are scratched or chipped.

PORTALS – ENTRANCES TO THE OTHERWORLD

The Otherworld, a place of magic and the abode of spirits, co-exists alongside our mundane world but at certain locations the boundaries between the two realities were flimsy. These 'thin places' contained portals that gave access to the Otherworld, the most celebrated being the land of faerie, also known as *annwn* in Welsh and elfhame in Scotland. Portals to the Otherworld were often found in mounds and hollow hills, or *sithean*, where fairies were known to dwell. Other access points included certain enchanted lakes, caves, fairy glens and ancient stone *brochs*.

On auspicious nights of the year such as Beltane and Samhain, fairies ventured forth and might be glimpsed in the twilight. Sometimes the fairy door remained open for a while, allowing humans access, or the door could be opened by magical means. Gaining entry into fairyland, however, was fraught with danger and the unwary, especially those who accepted food or drink, could never return. The spirits of these trapped souls might be seen riding with the fairies, hoping to find a way back home. Some did but they were offered just a single opportunity to escape.

Time was perceived very differently in fairyland: after a single night of revelry a whole year might have elapsed in the realm of mortals and those who tarried even longer might return to find many decades had passed and their friends and relatives were all dead. The experience had profound physical and emotional effects on humans, ranging from the gift of poetry, magic or prophesy to illness or insanity.

Other magical gateways, often set into in mountains or hills, led to a cavern where knights and their horses slumbered. The knights and their leader, often King Arthur or another legendary hero, were awaiting the call to battle and must on no account be disturbed before the appointed time.

FAIRIES

The fairies of folklore bear little in common with the cute, winged fairies of popular imagination. Devoid of wings, they were represented as tall, shining beings similar to Tolkien's elves or little people in brightly coloured but old-fashioned caps, coats and gowns. In the former category are the *shee*, (Irish *sidhe*), known in Scots-Gaelic as *sith* who inhabited *sithean* – usually small hills or mounds containing hidden doors that offered portals to the Otherworld.

In Wales, the fairies were the *tylwyth teg* (fair family) or *ellyllon* (shining beings), while to the Norse and Anglo-Saxons they were *alfar* or elves. Only later was the word *fairy* (from the French *fée*) incorporated into the English language. However, naming the fairies directly risked offending them so they were referred to as the 'good people' or the 'fair folk'.

These magical beings were glimpsed only fleetingly at twilight sometimes dancing, feasting or making merry. Humans who encountered the fairies felt compelled to join them and, unable to stop dancing, found themselves trapped in fairyland. The pure in heart or those with exceptional musical talent were rewarded with precious gifts.

The shee occasionally traversed the land in processions (*rades*). Sometimes mounted on horseback, these 'trooping fairies' were most often seen on Beltane or Samhain when they left their *sitheans* to roam. Fairies belonged to different courts often ruled by a fairy king or queen such as the Welsh Gwynn ap Nudd or the Welsh/English Queen Mab.

Some fairies interacted directly with mortals. Fairy women might take human lovers, some called on mortal women to act as their midwives and others stole human babies and replaced them with changelings. Fairies might, at best, tolerate humans but to our ancestors they were a mysterious race and treated with extreme caution and respect.

PIXIES & PISKIES

There's piskies up on Dartymoor
An' tidden gude you say there b'aint

Pixies are a race of supernatural beings with strongholds in Devon and Cornwall where they are more commonly referred to as 'piskies'. Although similar to their fairy cousins, they are a distinct race and once did battle against the fairies at Buckland St Mary, Somerset. The river Parrett marks the border between the two warring factions.

Piskies are generally small in stature and mischievous by nature. Fond of gifts, they are easily offended if not properly propitiated. Like hobs and brownies, they wear shaggy clothes or none at all and visit farms at night to help out with chores. They also live in wild places, such as their heartland, Dartmoor, where they inhabit caves, remote river valleys and the windswept moors. Lone travellers might spy them dancing and capering in their moorland domain.

Country folk often became 'pixie led', losing their way and getting hopelessly lost while travelling over once-familiar land. A regular journey might last for hours as the traveller became completely disorientated, trudging down unfamiliar lanes or across open moors until the fairy spell was broken with the coming of dawn. Turning your pockets or coat inside out, or reaching running water at certain streams or springs could also dispel the enchantment. Piskies' intentions, however, were rarely malicious; they simply delighted in causing mischief. Some, known as 'colt pixies' liked to steal ponies and ride them at night until the animals were worn out.

The most celebrated piskie lived at Carn Kenidjack in Cornwall. Known simply as 'The Piskie', this powerful and mysterious figure presided over a court of supernatural beings. Just two other piskies, also from Cornwall, are known by name: Jack o' the Lantern and Joan the Wad. Today, the South West's piskies, usually wearing bright green clothes and little pointed hats, adorn a range of lucky charms and souvenirs.

BEST SITES

MERMAIDS & OCEAN SPIRITS

Legendary mermaids, more usually associated with the western coast of the British Isles, are depicted as beautiful young women with long flowing hair and fishy tails, often like a salmon's but without scales. They might also appear in inland pools thought to be connected to the sea by underground tunnels. Occasionally seen swimming in the water, mermaids were more often encountered by chance while basking on rocks by the shore. In some stories, onlookers cause the creatures to flee, but the classic tale features a mermaid with a human lover – a man who has fallen for her or who the mermaid has enticed down to her undersea realm. In these tales the mermaid assumes human form: her tail is replaced by legs and she is able to bear human children, yet she retains a salty odour and a wayward, non-conformist character.

Mermaids also possessed magical powers. If treated well they warned fishermen of impending storms but if wronged they cast terrible curses, summoning tempests that caused harbours to silt up or be blocked by sandbars, ruining the economy of a whole fishing community. Curiously, representations of mermaids can be found in some churches, such as Zennor in Cornwall. Carved on a bench end with a comb and mirror as symbols of her vanity, the Mermaid of Zennor fell in love with Matthew Trewhella who followed her into the ocean.

In the Orkney Islands, tales of mermen are traditional. Known as 'finfolk', they would emerge from the water at night to raid isolated farms. Better known are the selkies or seal women of the Scottish Northern Isles. These ocean spirits could discard their seal skins and walk about on land in human form, but only in remote locations where they wouldn't be spotted. A man lucky enough to spy a selkie in this form could steal her seal skin and hide it, forcing the beautiful selkie to become his bride. Once she had recovered her seal skin, however, the selkie immediately escaped back to the sea.

WATER SPIRITS OF RIVERS, LAKES & SPRINGS

In myth and legend, fresh water has long been the realm of female spirits. For the Romans, the water nymphs who inhabited sacred springs must be propitiated with offerings placed into the waters. The Celts, too, followed a similar practice as evidenced by the huge number of votive offerings found in springs and pools. Female fairies who dwelled in enchanted lakes often appear in tales from British folklore. Some fell in love with mortal men, set up home and raised children while others were accompanied by fairy cattle that brought their husbands prosperity. If treated badly or struck with iron, however, the fairy bride would disappear back into the water, leaving the farmer heartbroken. The most famous water spirit is perhaps the Lady of the Lake of Arthurian legend who receives the sword, Excalibur, back into her watery depths.

Jenny Greenteeth and Peg Prowler were wicked spirits who dwelt in rivers. These old hags, with pondweed in their hair and sharp teeth, delighted in grabbing children from the banks and drowning them. The sources of rivers were particularly venerated as were the spirits of the river who might be appeased and prevented from taking human lives with offerings. At waterfalls, ethereal, sorrowful figures known as white ladies could be glimpsed and these spirits were generally harmless. In Scotland, many rivers and lakes were haunted by water spirits known as kelpies. These shape-shifting beings mostly assumed the form of a horse and would entice people onto their backs, only to drown them in the water. Less malevolent were water bulls that emerged to mate with mortal cattle, producing enchanted offspring. Of the monsters that inhabit certain lakes, the most famous still resides in Loch Ness. Several other lochs in Scotland boast similar inhabitants as does Llyn Tegid (Bala Lake) in Wales, thought to be the dwelling place of the monster Teggie. Stories from several other locations in Wales also feature the afanc, a fearsome water monster that could be subdued and then banished only by Arthur or a similarly heroic figure.

HOBS, BROWNIES & OTHER HOUSEHOLD SPIRITS

Hob Hole Hob! Me bairn's gotten t'kink cough.
Tak it off, tak it off!

Rhyme traditionally spoken at Hob Holes, Runswick Bay

Belief in household spirits, once common worldwide, led people establishing new dwellings to make offerings or sacrifices, which then continued on a regular basis to ensure good luck and prosperity. Such ancient and universal beliefs found their way into folk tales from all over the British Isles, which feature household spirits who help out on the farm at night, churning butter or threshing corn. In Scotland these spirits are known as brownies, in the North of England they are hobs, while in the South West this role is assigned to pixies.

In appearance, household spirits tend to be short, hairy men who wear ragged clothes or no clothes at all. In return for their overnight help, the family left an offering such as a bowl of cream or milk in a special location, for example on a 'brownie stone'. Leaving no offering was considered insulting but the worst offence was to see the spirit's naked form, take pity on him and attempt to provide him with new clothes. At this, some spirits vanished while others became malevolent boggarts who caused milk to sour or hurled objects around at night, like a poltergeist. Much feared, some boggarts attached themselves to unfortunate families and even followed them when they moved home.

Hobs and brownies lived in unseen corners of the house by day, or in nearby hollow trees or ruins. Some were solitary and resided in remote caves or valleys. In northern England, they go by the name of Hobthrush or variations including Hob Thirst, as in Thirst House Cave. Some had healing powers, such as the spirit at Hob Holes who could cure children of whooping cough (see quote above), while others including bogles and bogies, were mischievous and best avoided. In Scottish folklore, female household spirits known as 'glaistigs' haunted castles, houses and cattle folds, while lonesome, goat-footed land spirits called 'urisks' inhabited remote Highland glens and waterfalls.

MERLIN

Wizard, druid or prophet of great renown, who was Merlin? The Merlin of Medieval romance who served at the court of King Arthur is well known, but early British history and folklore reveal some very different versions. Originally Merlin was a figure from Brythonic Celtic mythology, and known as Myrddin. In what is now the Scottish borders region, he became Myrddin Wyllt (Merlin the Wild) after being on the losing side at the battle of Arderydd (near Arthuret). There, the pagan king Gwenddolau and his Druid advisor Myrddin were heavily defeated by the Christian, Rhydderch Hael. Fleeing north to Hart Fell, Myrddin blamed himself and went insane and uttered his prophecies.

Myrddin later confronted Rhydderch's ally St Kentigern near Stobo. Some say that he was baptised there, but shortly afterwards Myrddin died a druidic triple death by falling from a cliff, being impaled on a stake and drowning in the river Tweed. In Merlindale, the valley where he died, are the remains of his grave.

In North Wales, where he was known as Myrddin Emrys, the young Merlin was taken to King Vortigern in Snowdonia to be offered as a sacrifice to appease the spirits who destroyed the foundations of the king's fortress daily. Myrddin Emrys amazed the king's magicians by telling them to dig down and release the two dragons that were trapped there. His life was spared and the fortress became known as Dinas Emrys.

In South Wales and Cornwall are familiar sites associated with the Merlin of Arthurian tales. Born in Carmarthen, Merlin was later trapped by Vivien in Merlin's Hill, just to the east, after teaching her his magic. Merlin is also said to be buried on Bardsey Island, where he guards the thirteen treasures of Britain. At Tintagel Castle in Cornwall, Merlin helped Uther Pendragon seduce Igerna (Igraine) and conceive Arthur, who was hidden at birth in Merlin's Cave below.

Merlin's mythical status continues to grow. Some see him as a spiritual guide and teacher of wisdom for the New Age, while for others he is the spirit of Albion and an embodiment of ancient Brythonic Celtic culture.

ARTHUR AND OTHER LEGENDARY HEROES

The ancient cultures of the British Isles each had legendary heroes: the Brythonic Celts had Arthur, the Scots-Gaels had Fingal and the Anglo-Saxons had Wade and Wayland. The Brythonic Celtic lands once extended all the way from Cornwall to the Scottish borders and locations bearing Arthur's name are widespread over this area including Arthur's Seat, Arthur's Stone and Arthur's Table. The Arthur of folklore and Celtic myth, however, was very different to the King Arthur of popular medieval romance. He was a warlord who led a band of warriors across the land, performing great deeds and undergoing quests such as the hunt for the great boar the Twrch Trwyth.

The Scottish borders were once part of the *Hen Ogledd* (The Old North), composed of Brythonic kingdoms whose inhabitants were eventually driven out by the invading Anglo-Saxons, Norse and Scots-Gaels. Some consider this area Arthur's original home and that refugees carried his legends south to Wales and then to Cornwall.

Today those seeking sites from Arthurian legend flock to the South West to visit both Arthur's birthplace, Tintagel Castle in Cornwall, and his court, Camelot, at Cadbury Castle in Somerset, where Arthur and his knights are said to lie sleeping. Also significant are Camelford, the site of the battle of Camlan, and Dozmary Pool on nearby Bodmin Moor where the Lady of the Lake resided and Arthur's sword Excalibur was finally laid to rest. Arthur, in common with other legendary heroes, was also perceived to be of giant stature, and powerful enough to hurl huge boulders around. Scots-Gaelic Fingal is a version of the legendary Irish hero Finn mac Cumhail, whose stories were brought to Scotland by immigrant Gaels. He also assumed giant stature and his legends and exploits are associated with several locations in the Scottish highlands and islands. In Anglo-Saxon myth, Wayland the smith was revered as the son of the god/giant Wade who is remembered at several locations around the North York Moors.

CELTIC SAINTS & MIRACLES

The period covering the early fifth and sixth centuries, after the departure of the Romans from Britain was perhaps the darkest period of Britain's 'Dark Ages'. Few written historical records exist but what endures are the extraordinary legends of King Arthur and the miraculous tales associated with the early Celtic missionaries, especially St Columba of Iona, St Aidan of Lindisfarne, St Piran of Cornwall and St David of Wales. There are hundreds of lesser-known or obscure saints, some of whom are remembered only at a single shrine or holy well, including some female saints such as St Winefride of Holywell, St Melangell of Pennant Melangell and St Bega of Cumbria.

This earlier form of Christianity, which incorporated pagan beliefs connected to the land and to nature, was pluralistic and egalitarian, lacking the control structures and hierarchy of the Roman Catholic Church. Some believe it evolved from druidic beliefs, while for others it arose from a very early, pure form of Christianity introduced by such legendary figures as Joseph of Arimathea at Glastonbury.

Tales of the Celtic saints include all kinds of fabulous beasts and miraculous occurrences. Springs spontaneously erupted at a place where a saint was martyred, and decapitated saints' heads could be reattached. Some saints were guided by beams of light, could produce light from their hands or consorted with shining beings (interpreted as angels). Others subdued fearsome dragons and wild animals or fought with pagan wizards. Almost all these saints have at least one dedicated holy well, often a place of healing or possessing some other miraculous property. Many of them are located in the West of Britain, particularly Wales and Cornwall where you can barely travel a few miles without coming across one.

CHRISTIANISED PAGAN SITES

The temples of the idols in England should not on any account be destroyed. Augustine must smash the idols, but the temples themselves should be sprinkled with holy water and altars set up in them in which relics are to be enclosed. For we ought to take advantage of well-built temples by purifying them from devil-worship and dedicating them to the service of the true God.

The above quote is taken from a letter written by Pope Gregory in 601 to Abbot Mellitus. The abbot was about to travel to Britain to meet with Augustine (later St Augustine) who, only four years previously had been sent to England to convert the Saxons to the Roman Catholic faith. The letter provides clear evidence that well-built churches were to be consecrated upon existing sites of spiritual and ritual significance within the landscape – places that pagans already considered sacred.

What started as an attempt to convert the pagans would eventually become a complete takeover of the spiritual landscape of Britain. The pagan network of sacred sites was to be shut down and replaced by places of Christian worship. Eventually, churches would be built on all the principal places of power once venerated by the pagans and sacred hills including Glastonbury Tor, Brent Tor and St Michael's Mount would all be surmounted by churches.

Surprising examples of churches built on pagan sites include Knowlton in the centre of a prehistoric henge monument, Rudston sited next to the tallest standing stone in Britain, and Ysbyty Cynfyn where the churchyard walls incorporate parts of a prehistoric stone circle.

Legends concerning the siting of churches, especially those in unusual locations away from the village, may be attempts to Christianise a site of pagan veneration. Sometimes fairies or other supernatural beings moved the building overnight, while the location of other churches was auspicious and magically divined. To ignore the sacred Christian landscape of Britain is to ignore its pagan roots. Many places of the deepest spiritual significance are now occupied by churches, and by visiting them it is still possible to tune into that ancient power.

NORSE & ANGLO-SAXON MYTHOLOGY

"There were excessive whirlwinds and lightening storms, and fiery dragons were seen flying in the sky. These signs were followed by a great famine, and shortly after in the same year the ravaging of heathen men did most miserably destroy God's church at Lindisfarne with rapine and slaughter."

Anglo-Saxon Chronicle, 793 AD

When Norse invaders arrived towards the end of the 8th century, they battled with the Anglo-Saxons for control of Britain. In pre-Christian times, the two worshipped the same gods: the Norse Odin was Woden, Thor was Thunor and the fertility goddess Freya was Frig. The invaders left their mark upon the landscape and its place names but traces of their gods were harder to find once the Norse settlers had, like the Anglo-Saxons before them, converted to Christianity.

Legends and sites associated with the Anglo-Saxons include Wayland's Smithy, a Neolithic long barrow in Oxfordshire haunted by the legendary smith. Sites associated with his giant father Wade are also found all across the North York Moors. Norse mythology, too, persists in place names. When the god Odin travelled in disguise he was known as Grim and is remembered at Grimspound on Dartmoor and Grimsbury Castle in Berkshire. Odin's Anglo-Saxon namesake Woden built the Wansdyke (Woden's Dyke) all the way across Wiltshire, where you can also find Woden's Barrow (now Adam's Grave). In Christianised versions of the story, the Devil was substituted for Odin so Grimsdyke became Devil's Dyke – a name change that may have affected many other locations named after Norse gods.

Traces of Norse belief also survive in tales of supernatural beings such as dwarves. The Simonside Hills in Northumberland were inhabited by dwarves and in Orkney there is a rock-cut chamber known as the Dwarfie Stane. Also in Orkney, where Norse ancestral connections remain strong, there are tales about trows (trolls) and oaths were made at a holed-stone known as the Odin Stone.

THE WILD HUNT & OTHERWORLDLY HOUNDS

A pack of spectral hounds led by ghostly huntsmen on horseback charging through the night sky is a phenomenon common to European folklore and to see the wild hunt pass by, hounds baying and horns blowing, was an ill omen. On auspicious nights, such as Samhain Eve (Hallowe'en), the huntsmen awoke and emerged from the Otherworld to round up and reclaim lost souls or the souls of the dead. The lead huntsman was a legendary hero or supernatural being, such as King Herla (Germany), Charlemagne (France), the Roman goddess Diana or the Norse god Odin. In Britain King Arthur, the fairy king Gwyn ap Nudd, and semi-legendary figures including Wild Edric or Herne the Hunter led the chase.

These visitations from the Otherworld could also take other forms, as in the tale of Welsh prince Pwyll's encounter with Arawn, the lord of the Otherworld realm of Annwn. Accompanied by a pack of white hounds with red ears – colours that indicated their otherworldly status – Arawn was pursuing a stag that Pwyll stole for himself. In recompense, Pwyll agreed to change places and spent a year in Arawn's realm. Packs of ghostly hounds also haunted certain mystical locations, such as Wistman's Wood on Dartmoor. These Wisht Hounds, led by Dewar the Huntsman, lured people to their deaths over the cliffs of the Dewarstone. In the north of England these unearthly hounds were known as Gabriel Hounds or Gabriel's Ratchets, while in Somerset they were the Yeth Hounds.

Encountering a single spectral hound, usually black in colour and often with glowing red eyes the size of saucers, was often a portent of death. These 'black dogs' go by many names in different parts of the country, from Black Shuck in East Anglia and the Gurt Dog of Somerset to the fearsome Barghest of Yorkshire. They often haunt lonely country lanes, crossings and pathways as well as old ruins and open moors. Hearing their loud panting and the padding of their feet, then seeing two huge red eyes loom out of the darkness would be truly terrifying.

DRAGONS

I wyrd ye to become a laidly worm
And borrowed shall ye never be
Until Childe Wynd, the king's own son
Do come and thrice kiss thee

'The Laidly Worm of Spindleston Heugh', *Northumbrian ballad*

Mainly Anglo-Saxon or medieval in origin, tales about dragons or 'worms' (from the Anglo-Saxon *wyrm*) occur all over England and into the lowlands of Scotland. Wales has its own version of the dragon, similar to the English worm, known as a *wiber* or *gwiber* ('viper').

Usually snakelike, with or without legs, and more rarely with wings, these troublesome beasts would emerge from their lairs at night and rampage around the countryside until some brave knight, hero or saint was found to dispatch them. Unusual ploys to defeat the dragon included armour covered in blades, burning pitch thrust down its throat, or fooling the beast into coiling itself around a stone pillar covered in spikes. Some lived underground or in caves where they could hoard treasure, while others wrapped themselves around conical hills, leaving the imprints of their snakelike bodies. Others, sometimes called *knuckers*, made their lairs in magical springs or pools.

Belief in dragons was so widespread that in medieval England there was a brisk trade in selling dragon parts for medicinal or magical use. Indeed, if you fed milk to a snake it could grow into a dragon, and dragons were said to be placated with regular offerings of milk as in the ballad above about a woman turned into a dragon by a witch's curse.

Dragons have also become associated with the earth energies represented by ley lines in Europe and *lung mei* or dragon lines in Chinese feng shui. In Welsh, this life force flowing through the earth was known as *nwyfre* and harnessed by the Druids. Such lines connected powerful places, such as Cadbury Castle and Dolbury Hill in Devon, where a dragon would fly back and forth between the two, guarding the treasure buried in each.

BEST SITES

WISHES & DIVINATION

Making a wish at the archetypal circular wishing well complete with a little roof is the stuff of fairy tales but also an old tradition that echoes the ancient Celtic practice of dropping offerings into natural springs and pools. The Romans continued this tradition and at sites such as the hot springs in Bath (Aquae Sulis) they wrote down their wishes (or curses) on small lead tablets that make for interesting reading! From medieval times people have visited a variety of springs to take part in a simple ritual and make a small offering in return for the granting of a wish. Such offerings, often of metal pins, were made to the fairy, pixie or other supernatural spirit or guardian of the well. At Christian holy wells, by contrast, the ritual involved prayers, usually to a saint, in return for healing.

Some sacred springs and holy wells were places of divination, usually frequented by young women who were keen to know who they would marry and when. Rituals included throwing a small object into the water and the number of bubbles that rose to the surface indicated how many years until marriage. A visit to a spring was also likely to summon a vision of a future husband when the woman was asleep that night.

Wishes could also be made at certain magical stones, either by standing on them or circling around them a number of times, and some were places of divination. At the holed stone of Men-an-Tol in Cornwall, rituals included placing two pins on its top and then interpreting their movement. In the sea cave at Tresilian Bay, South Wales, young men and women would attempt to throw pebbles over its inner arch to find out how many years would pass before they married. In addition to springs, wells and magical stones, one of the more unusual places to make a wish is on the eye of the Uffington White Horse in Oxfordshire.

PLACES OF HEALING

Visiting holy wells and sacred springs were, alongside folk medicine, the most common forms of healing available to ordinary people, especially those who had sick children. The practice dates back to pagan times when offerings would be made to the spirit of the well. With the coming of Christianity, many were 'rebranded' and dedicated to saints. The healing rituals continued and could include immersion in the well, bathing the affected area, drinking the water, reciting certain verses, walking around the well a certain number of times, or leaving an offering. Some wells had a guardian who performed the ritual, often an old woman who inherited the position. She wouldn't accept money for her service, just a small offering of food or drink.

Leaving of strips of fabric – called *clooties* in Scotland – at a well was common. These would first be dipped in the well water and then either hung from a tree or hidden in a cleft in the rocks. People believed that their illness would retreat as the natural material of the rag rotted away.

Most wells were associated with a specific ailment, such as an eye well for curing sore eyes but for really intractable problems, the sufferer may have had to travel a considerable distance to one of the principal shrines, such as Holywell in North Wales or Walsingham in Norfolk – both still visited by pilgrims. To banish warts, the cure was to stick a pin in the wart and then throw it in the wart well, often a natural bowl-shaped depression in a rock filled with rainwater. At larger, deeper 'bowsenning' wells, the cure for those with mental health problems included a forced immersion.

Less common places of healing were certain stones with natural features, such as holes, that the afflicted person had to pass through. Examples include the Tolmen on the river Teign, Dartmoor, and the Drake Stone in Northumberland. Healing was also attributed to certain supernatural beings such as the hob at Hob Holes in Yorkshire or the piskie of Men–an–Tol in Cornwall.

RITUALS & SHRINES

In certain locations, a ritual must be performed in order to activate the magic of the place. At holy wells, people performed a simple ritual such as throwing a metal pin into the water for healing, wish fulfilment or divination purposes then left an offering or a tied ribbon. The procedure at other sites, such as St Beuno's shrine in North Wales, was more complex. After bathing in the well, the afflicted person had to spend the night stretched out on the cold slab of St Beuno's tomb. At St Tecla's Well, where people sought a cure for epilepsy, the ritual involved bathing in the well at dusk, leaving an offering, then walking three times around the well carrying a chicken. The sufferer then took the chicken to the nearby church where the two spent the night under the communion table and if the chicken died, he or she would be cured!

Pagan rituals for summoning the fairy folk included running nine times widdershins (anti-clockwise) around a fairy mound – a practice that, in the Christian era, was repurposed into a way of invoking the Devil. At other auspicious locations, such as at magically charged stones, rituals for good luck, to aid fertility or to ease childbirth were performed. Placing a stone on a cairn would ensure good weather for those going out to sea or would simply bring good luck.

From the 18th century through to the Victorian era some antiquarians associated prehistoric sites, such as stone circles, with druidic rituals, and so many sacred sites became known as 'places of druidic worship'.

At many current spiritual and magical locations there is still some kind of altar where people leave offerings, light a candle or burn some incense. These simple acts of reverence are themselves a kind of ritual, whether they are to honour the spirits of the place or to make prayers, wishes or intentions for the future.

MAGIC

Many places said to have magical properties or associated with supernatural occurrences are difficult to fit into a specific category. These include those that conferred good fortune or were protected by animal guardians or supernatural beings. Sometimes treasure lay buried in these sites but huge storms erupted when anyone attempted to dig it up. By contrast, there were places devoid of life that remained eerily silent, as if put under a curse. At certain magical locations strange music could be heard emanating from below the earth, produced either by fairies or by pipers who had long ago become trapped in underground realms. Tales of another eerie sound, the ringing of ghostly bells rising up from drowned villages, are associated with particular lakes while other pools are said to be bottomless.

Magical stones imprinted with the fingermarks or footprints of legendary figures including saints, giants, mythological heroes (or the hoofprint of the hero's horse), abound and some footprints had the ability to confer sovereignty upon a potential king who placed his foot there. Other stones were benign but, according to an ancient prophecy, doom and disaster would follow if they were to split apart or sink. Standing in some locations conferred magical powers, such as the ability to see fairy islands or perform witchcraft. At other places, a supernatural spirit could be summoned by performing a ritual – such places tended to become associated with witches or the Devil once Christianity took hold.

Today, there are locations where miraculous occurrences take place, such as the bleeding yew tree at Nevern or the petrifying well at Knaresborough, and there is, of course, the famous prophecy attached to the ravens at the Tower of London.

BEST SITES

WEST CORNWALL

Sitting at the tip of Cornwall, the Penwith Peninsula is one of the most intensely magical places in the British Isles. Like Dartmoor and Bodmin Moor, the peninsula is composed almost entirely of granite and its ancient and eroded granite tors dominate the Penwith skyline.

In ancient times Penwith was occupied by a race of legendary giants, many making their homes on its rocky hilltops where they built defensive enclosures. Their tendency to hurl boulders around helped to form the present landscape. Rocky outcrops, cairns and boulders were also the dwelling places of the fairy folk, who in Penwith were often known as spriggans. Particularly malevolent and grotesque in appearance, these spriggans caused trouble by terrifying travellers, blighting crops and hoarding stolen loot, hence their reputation as guardians of hidden treasure. Penwith also has a number of immense boulders known as logan stones that can be rocked back and forth by standing on them. Some of these stones were thought to have magical and healing properties.

In contrast to the stark, rocky uplands, Penwith's wooded valleys conceal holy wells and hidden watercourses, and its small stone-lined fields are traversed by impossibly narrow lanes and trackways that lead to stone circles and dolmens (quoits). At the centre of all this magical activity and dominating the surrounding moorland known as the Gump, is Carn Kenidjack, a strangely shaped and haunted rock outcrop steeped in legend. Other supernatural beings who inhabited the ancient mines in Penwith were known as knockers and would lead the miners to new seams of ore.

Most impressive of all is Penwith's coastline of dark, jagged cliffs sheltering hidden coves with white sandy beaches. The jutting headlands were giants' strongholds, while hidden bays were home to mermaids who were often seen sitting out on the rocks. This towering coastline is broken only by the sweep of low-lying Mounts Bay where a tidal causeway leads to St Michael's Mount. This iconic feature of Penwith, its conical outline crowned by an imposing church dedicated to Archangel Michael, was once home to the legendary giant Cormoran and his giantess wife.

WEST PENWITH

1 Alsia Well, St Buryan

Tucked away in the corner of a field behind the small hamlet of Alsia Mill, Alsia Well is secluded and little visited. A few ribbons and offerings are left there by others who have been lucky enough to discover its hidden location. Like **Madron Well** and **St Euny's Well**, parents and children visited Alsia Well on the first three Wednesdays in May to seek a cure for their sick and disabled offspring. Divination rituals, often concerning marriage prospects, included counting the bubbles after a pin or stone was thrown in the water

50.0691, -5.6446; SW392251; Secret / Secluded; Trailhead: 50.0705, -5.6428; SW394252; 300m

2 Boscawen-ûn Stone Circle, Crows-an-Wra *

The 19 stones of this circle are, according to legend, the petrified forms of young women who were turned to stone while dancing on the Sabbath. Reached by a narrow trackway, the circle is contained within a network of small fields and high hedgerows and, uniquely, has a central stone set at a sharp angle. The trackway is said to be an ancient processional route of the Druids who performed rituals at Boscawen-ûn, one of the few stone circles in the country with a recorded history. It was mentioned in the Welsh triads as one of the three British gorsedds (bardic or druidic meeting places). Step back in time and follow in the footsteps of the druids as you take the ancient track to the stone circle, hidden within its hedged enclosure. This powerful centre of ley energies has many mysteries, including one stone made entirely of white quartz. On a nearby outcrop of rock just north of Boscawen-ûn, known as **Creeg Tol** (50.0916, -5.6217; SW410275) are indentations said to be a giant's footprints. Its proximity to Boscawen-ûn, which can clearly be seen on the slopes below, may indicate some ancient ritual connection between the two.

50.0898, -5.6192; SW412273; Trailhead Parking: 50.0934, -5.6124; SW417277; 900m

3 Bosence Chapel, Sancreed

Tiny Bosence Chapel now lies in ruins but legends of hauntings and unearthly lights hovering above it survive, such as the tale of Uter Bosence. One midsummer's night Uter was crossing a field when thick fog suddenly descended. He made his way to the familiar gap in the hedge, but unable to find it he tried to climb the hedge, which seemed to grow higher and higher. In desperation he got down and followed the hedge towards the old chapel where he saw the most frightful apparition of 'sprites and spriggans'. Terrified, he tried to flee but an unseen presence like a powerful wind sent him rolling down the field, tossing him over a hedge and pushing him through brambles, furze and bogs. Today, the chapel is a tranquil place, its ruins hidden by trees and wildflowers. Enjoy the peace there and commune with spirits of nature and ancient Celtic spirituality, but be aware that the location retains a sinister edge, especially at night!

50.1177, -5.6293; SW406304; Private Land; Secret / Secluded; Trailhead: 50.1135, -5.6247; SW409300; 1km

4 Carn Galver, Porthmeor

The rocky tor known as Carn Galver overlooks the ocean and contains an ancient Neolithic tor enclosure that was once home to a friendly giant called Holiburn. He protected the local people by launching rocks at the troublesome giants of **Trencrom**

Hill. Many local landscape features are said to be his handiwork including piles of boulders and logan stones that he used for rocking himself to sleep. Holiburn befriended a local lad and the two liked to play quoits but their games came to an end when the giant patted the boy on the head and his skull caved in like a pie crust.

50.1707, -5.6061; SW425363; Trailhead Parking: 50.1717, -5.6127; SW421364; 600m

5 Castle-an-Dinas, Nancledra

Some say the old giant Denbras made his home at Castle-an-Dinas before he was killed by Long Tom in single combat. Long Tom was transporting ale in his cart from Marazion to St Ives when he disputed Denbras' right to block the roads with his hedges. After his victory, Tom took possession of the stronghold but continued to keep the roads blocked so was challenged in turn by Jack the Hammer. When the battle resulted in stalemate, the two decided to live together at Castle-an-Dinas. Jack eventually married Tom's eldest daughter on the feast of Lughnasa and moved away to build **Chûn Castle**. In other stories, fairies were said to hold their fairs inside the enclosure. The remains of this Iron Age ring fort, which had two concentric stone ramparts, are now so overgrown with vegetation that the original stonework is hardly visible. Much more prominent are a turreted, ruined folly on the edge of the fort called Rogers' Tower and the working quarries situated nearby.

50.161637, -5.522961; SW484350; Trailhead: 50.1696, -5.5270; SW482359; 1.5km

6 Chûn Quoit, Bojewyan

A remarkable survival from the early Neolithic period, Chûn Quoit is a dolmen with a mushroom-shaped capstone that has sat completely undisturbed for over 5,000 years. Dolmens were thought to have been created by legendary giants and one made this chambered tomb his home.

On a hilltop 300m away is **Chûn Castle** (50.1487, -5.6338; SW405339), a circular Iron Age hillfort. Like Castle-an-Dinas, it has two concentric stone walls and these are still visible. According to folklore, the castle was built by Jack the Hammer, a local giant killer who first had to rid the hill of the troublesome giant who dwelt there. Chûn Quoit was erected to mark the giant's grave.

50.1486, -5.6377; SW402339; Trailhead Parking: 50.1430, -5.6496; SW393333; 1.2km

7 Gwennap Head, Porthgwarra

This rocky headland, also known by its old Cornish name, Tol-Pedn-Penwith, features a stack of stepped rocks known as Madgy Figgy's Chair Ladder. Having climbed to the top, a legendary witch of the same name would launch herself into the air on a broomstick fashioned from a stem of ragwort. From her rocky perch, Madgy Figgy could also summon up storms that caused ships to be wrecked in Porth Loe.

According to local folklore, a woman's body once washed up there after just such a shipwreck and Madgy, sensing there was something special about this female, buried the corpse at Porth Loe then hid the woman's jewels in a chest at her home in nearby Raftra. Afterwards a strange light would emerge from the grave at night and then pass over the cliffs, settling over the Chair Ladder before moving off to Maggie's hut and hovering over the chest. Three months later a mysterious stranger arrived from abroad, found the grave and then followed the light to Madgy's hut where he reclaimed the jewellery and then departed, leaving gifts in return.

50.0366, -5.6811; SW365216; Trailhead Parking: 50.0380, -5.6730; SW370217; 850m

8 Madron Well *

One of Cornwall's most renowned healing wells, Madron Well is set in marshland and reached via a woodland path. Cures were sought there for a variety of ailments from aches, pains and stiffness to lameness, skin diseases, wounds and colic.

In the usual ritual for a sick child, the parents would stand facing the sun and then plunge the naked child into the water three times. After they and the child had run around the well clockwise nine times, the child had to rest on a mound at the nearby chapel known as St Maddern's Bed. Small pieces of cloth could be torn from the child's clothing and then stuffed under a rock or hung on a nearby thorn tree to ensure healing and good fortune. The whole ritual, however, had to be performed in silence or the cure would not be effective and the procedure would have to be repeated. Presiding over these rituals, performed only on the first three Wednesdays in May, was the custodian. This was a local wise woman to whom the title had passed – the last was known as An' Katty. She would accept no money but balls of yarn or other useful items could be left. Pious people who visited the well preferred to ascribe its cures to St Maddern.

The well water was reputed to give protection from witchcraft and the evil eye, and the well itself was used for divina-

tion. Pins, stones or straw crosses were dropped into the water and the resulting bubbles showed the number of years until a particular event (most often a marriage) would take place. If no pins were available, then sometimes just jumping beside the well and counting the bubbles would suffice. Also, if two pins dropped into the water landed close together, this indicated a successful relationship.

Access to the original well, deep in marshland surrounded by alder and willow, is slippery and very difficult but the waters flow out nearer to the path into a shallow pool. Here, visitors leave brightly-coloured clooties (ribbons) and other offerings tied to the trees.

A little further along the enchanted woodland pathway lie the ancient ruins of **Boswarthen Chapel** (50.1402, -5.5751; SW447328), into which the waters of another well flow. The disabled came to this Christian holy well for a healing ritual that involved leaving a small offering on the altar, drinking the water, and then sleeping there overnight.

50.1397, -5.5765; SW445327; Popular, Trailhead: 50.1367, -5.5756; SW445324; 400m

9 Mên-an-Tol, Morvah *

Nestled in a gorse enclosure up on the Penwith moors, the holed stone of Mên-an-Tol, with a standing stone at either end, has been renowned since ancient times for its magical cures. It was once known locally as the Crick Stone and, according to custom, crawling through the hole naked three times against the sun (i.e. anti-clockwise) would cure pains in the neck and back, as well as rheumatism. Children were passed through the hole to ensure good health, and the friendly pixie who inhabited the stone could help parents whose baby had been stolen and replaced by a changeling. Visitors could also ask questions of the pixie by placing two brass pins in a cross shape on the top of the stone and interpreting their movements. Mên-an-Tol continues to exert its power and visitors still dutifully clamber through its central hole.

Continuing along the network of moorland paths you eventually reach the well-preserved **Nine Maidens or Boskednan Stone Circle** (50.1605, -5.5938; SW434351; 1.5km from Mên-an-Tol). Here, young women who danced on the Sabbath were turned to stone.

50.1586, -5.6044; SW426349; Popular, Trailhead Parking: 50.1535, -5.6149; SW418344; 1km

10 Merry Maidens Stone Circle, Lamorna

This large and well-preserved circle of stones stands in a grassy field surrounded by farmland. These fun-loving 'merry maidens' were turned to stone while dancing on the Sabbath, as were the musicians who accompanied them then tried to flee the scene. The two huge stones nearby are **The Pipers** (50.0674, -5.5859; SW434247 / 50.0681, -5.5851; SW435248; private land) and some sources say the **Blind Fiddler** (50.0979, -5.6016; SW425281; private land) was another musician who met the same fate. The Merry Maidens are thought to be unmovable and cattle who have been harnessed to dislodge them are said to have collapsed and died. Less than a kilometre away, in the gardens of Rosemerryn House, lies a mysterious tunnel lined with megalithic blocks. This is **Boleigh Fogou** (50.0715, -5.5829; SW437251; private land) an enigmatic structure which, according to folklore, was a gathering place of witches. The local squire was out hunting near Lamorna when a hare he was chasing disappeared into Boleigh Fogou. There he found a coven with witches dancing around a fire and recognising one as 'Bet of the Mill' concluded she had taken the form of the hare he'd pursued. The fogou can be visited by calling the number on a

sign located by the driveway to Rosemerryn House at (50.0699, -5.5835; SW436250). The fishing village of Lamorna was also once home to a mermaid who sat on a rock in Lamorna Cove, either luring unsuspecting fishermen or warning them of storms. Mermaid Rock, now known as Half-Tide Rock (50.0609, -5.5579; SW454239), is submerged at high tide.

50.0651, -5.5887; SW432245

11 St Euny's Well, Brane *

At this magical well with a stone arch, the waters are accessed by walking down a short flight of stone steps. Overhanging trees are adorned with clooties and other offerings that enhance the magical atmosphere of the place. A sacred well since pre-Christian times, its waters could heal wounds and cure sick children, who were immersed there on the first three Wednesdays in May. In one folk tale, Jenny Trayer who lived just to the west of Carn Brea had her baby stolen and replaced by the spriggans of Bartinney with a fairy changeling. To get back her own child, Jenny took the changeling to St Euny's Well and after immersing him in the water three times, she ran with him around the well three times widdershins (anti-clockwise). In some versions of the story, she was reunited with her own child but he always suffered from ill-health.

Nearby **Carn Brea** (50.0950, -5.6563; SW385280. Trailhead parking: 50.0976, -5.6526; SW388283; 450m), also called Chapel Carn Brea, is the most westerly hill in Cornwall and a prominent feature of the landscape. Pagan fires used to burn on its summit before it became a Christian site with a chapel dedicated to Archangel Michael (now ruined and barely visible). Many ancient barrows along the coast are aligned with Carn Brea, signifying that this was once a sacred hill.

On the other side of St Euny's Well, **Carn Euny** (50.1030, -5.6342; SW402288; popular) is a remarkably well-preserved Iron Age village with a large underground fogou reached by a curving passage. The fogou was probably used for ritual purposes and it certainly feels like a mysterious portal to the underworld. To the east of Carn Euny is the ring fort of Caer Brân (50.1047, -5.6269; SW407290), which has both Bronze and Iron Age remains and was also a ceremonial site. Known to be an abode of the fairies, it was said that nothing evil could pass through there.

50.1033, -5.6375; SW399289

12 St Levan's Stone, St Levan

A large cleft boulder in the village churchyard is known as St Levan's Stone and was reputed to have been split when St Selevan,

an early Cornish saint, struck it with his fist or his staff. A prophecy, said to have been uttered by Merlin, is associated with the rock
"When a horse can ride
with panniers astride
though St Levan's stone
the earth will be done."
St Levan's Holy Well (50.0398, -5.6594; SW380219) where people went to cure their toothache, is a short distance away on the cliff top with stunning views over Porth Chapel bay.

50.0422, -5.6601; SW380221

13 St Michael's Mount, Marazion **

Iconic St Michael's Mount is accessible only at low tide via a long cobbled causeway. When the tide is high, like a mystical Isle of Avalon it can only be reached by boat. Its conical shape, topped by a church dedicated to Archangel Michael, is clearly visible from the hills and coastline all around.

When sea levels were much lower, Mounts Bay was part of the legendary sunken kingdom of Lyonesse that extended all the way to the Isles of Scilly. At that time, St Michael's Mount lay hidden in a forest and was known as *Karrek Loos yn Koos,* 'grey rock in the wood'. This pale rock was transported from **Trencrom Hill** by the giantess Cormelian on the instructions of her fierce husband Cormoran, who was building their home on the Mount while stealing cattle from local farmers. Cormelian tried to substitute some local green-coloured stone but Cormoran found out and forced her to drop it where she stood. It formed the small rocky outcrop known as **Chapel Rock** (50.1225, -5.4757; SW516305; low tide only). Cormoran shared tools with the giant Trecrobben who

lived on **Trencrom Hill**. They would fling the tools back and forth as and when they were needed. But one day Cormoran called to Trecrobben for a cobbler's hammer and just as he threw it Cormelian came out of her cave. Blinded by the sun, she didn't see the hammer which hit her straight between the eyes and killed her outright. Cormoran mourned Cormelian and buried her under Chapel Rock, which subsequently became the site of an early 15th-century chapel to St Katherine where pilgrims would halt before making the crossing to ascend the Mount. Local people eventually grew tired of Cormoran's stealing and a local hero lured him into a huge pit and finished him off. He became known as Jack the Giant Killer. On the Mount, you'll find memorials to Cormoran – the **Giant's Well** (50.1171, -5.4776; SW514299), source of the Mount's water supply where local people made wishes, and a rock beside it known as the Giant's Heart. After fishermen at sea saw a vision of Archangel Michael on the Mount, it became a holy shrine and a site of pilgrimage. A monastery may have existed there and later a castle and church were built on its summit. On top of the tower of St Michael's Church is a stone structure known as St Michael's Chair. In local folklore, when a couple have just been married, the first one to make it up to the chair will have the

14

upper hand. Just by the church, the exposed bedrock of the mount's summit can be seen, and it is said that a truly romantic wish made there will always be granted.

St Michael's Mount is also a place of power where two of the most significant ley lines in Britain – the Michael/Mary and the Apollo/Athena lines – cross. The Michael line runs from the tip of Cornwall to East Anglia, following the alignment of the Beltane and Lughnasa sunrise, passing through many other churches along the way that are also dedicated to Archangel Michael, including **Brent Tor**, **Glastonbury Tor** and **Burrow Mump**. All of these may have been the sites of pagan temples dedicated to Bel or Lugh, the gods of light. The Apollo line runs all the way from Skellig Michael off the west coast of Ireland, through Cornwall, to France, Italy, Greece and Israel, again passing through many ancient shrines dedicated to Archangel Michael and to the sun god Apollo. One of these is Mont Saint Michel, the French counterpart to St Michael's Mount. The similarities between these two sites are remarkable – each is a conical tidal island topped by a church dedicated to Archangel Michael.

St Michael's Mount Castle & Church £££: 50.1165, -5.4781; SW514298. Parking in Marazion; Very Popular

14 Sennen Cove

The popular village of Sennen Cove lies at the southern end of stunning Whitesand Bay, just above Land's End, on the western tip of Cornwall. Although mermaids visited the waters around Sennen Cove, a better-known local legend is that of the Sennen Whooper. When mist started to descend over Cowloe Rocks (50.0805, -5.7076; SW348266) out in the bay, the villagers sometimes heard a strange sound and interpreted it as a warning not to go out to sea. One day two fishermen ignored the Whooper and set out through the mist, never to be seen again. Sennen was

also home to a local wise woman who could control the winds, sending a west wind to blow the Danish fleet away when they were about to invade. Fairies, too, were seen in Sennen Cove. According to one story, two young sisters went to a well one night to fetch water and saw the little people dancing there, their skins white as snow and dressed in white muslin. Walk out from the village to the rocky headland and you may still sense the ancient spirits of the ocean as you gaze out over Cowloe Rocks.

A little further along the South West Coast path heading west is **Maen Castle** (50.0727, -5.7083; SW347257; 800m from Sennen Cove), an Iron Age promontory fort, its ruins rooted in a rocky headland.

14

Semi-circular banks and ditches, as well as an ancient stone gateway, guard a grassy mound that was once the home of a family of legendary giants. They were in conflict with the giants of **Treryn Dinas,** who had abducted one of their children.

Sennen Cove Parking £: 50.0778, -5.7048; SW350263; Very Popular

15 **Treryn Dinas, Treen** *

This stunning natural cliff-top fortress dominates a rocky headland and is the perfect giants' lair. You can almost see the faces of these ancient petrified giants etched into the stone of the seaward-facing cliffs, forever gazing out to sea. One of the occupiers was Den an Dynas, a deaf and dumb giant who protected the coast by hurling huge boulders at approaching ships. His giantess wife An' Venna built its huge landward defences, while the headland itself was created by a sorcerer who summoned it up from the ocean and locked it in place by dropping a boulder into a deep hole. Another story tells of a giant couple who lived at Treryn Dinas but were unable to conceive a child so they stole one from their enemies, a family of giants at **Maen Castle**. When the giantess grew tired of her husband, she began a rela-

tionship with her adopted son and threw her husband off the cliff. In his dying moments, the giant called out for vengeance and his wife was turned into the famous Logan Rock at the top of the cliffs.

The logan stone, which weighs over 90 tons and is the largest in Cornwall, was reputed to cure sick children who, in spite of the dangerous climb, were taken to be rocked on it. Local people made a sport of trying to

tip the stone over, though it wouldn't budge more than an inch until a group of Royal Navy sailors tipped the stone off the cliff! They were made to put it back in place, at considerable expense and effort, but unfortunately the stone now no longer rocks. Treryn Dinas was also considered an enchanted place. Fairies inhabited the seaward side of the cliffs where they tended their flower gardens and played sweet-

sounding music that could be heard by passing fishermen. At midsummer, fairy lights twinkled in the darkness of the enchanted gardens and a sweet perfume wafted in on the breeze.

Climb over the huge rocky outcrops then lie among the pink sea thrift in spring and feel the magic of this ancient fairy realm.

50.0412, -5.6365; SW397220; Popular, Trailhead Parking: 50.0499, -5.6409; SW394229; 1km

16 Twelve O'Clock Stone, Cripplesease

Sitting atop a stack of huge boulders on the southern flank of Trink Hill, this magical stone is said to rock like a cradle at midnight. Children would be placed on it at this propitious time to be cured of rickets and other diseases. From the stone, you have a clear view of **Trencom Hill** and **St Michael's Mount**, the homes of the giants Trecobben and Cormoran. Trink Hill also has its own giant associations: a rock known as the Giant's Chair once stood here.

50.1812, -5.4957; SW505370, Secret / Secluded; Trailhead Parking: 50.1787, -5.5026; SW500368; 1km

17 Zennor *

Celebrated for its famous mermaid, Zennor is a clifftop village steeped in legend and its church contains an ancient wooden panel carved with the mermaid's image. According to the story, young Mathey (Matthew) Trewella was singing in Zennor church when he was entranced by a beautiful woman called Morveren who was occasionally seen at services. The two fell in love and one day they set off walking towards the cliffs but were never seen again. People whispered among each other that Morveren was one of the sea people and had abducted Mathey. Years later some fishermen were anchored out at sea near **Pendour Cove** (50.1955, -5.5774; SW447389; 800m from Zennor) when they heard the cry of a mermaid from the waves. She asked them to haul up their anchor as it was blocking the entrance to her house and she was anxious to get back to her husband Mathey and their children. The terrified captain quickly obliged and returned to Zennor, where he related the tale. It confirmed the villagers' long-held suspicions that Morveren was a mermaid who had enticed Mathey down to her underwater realm. Sometimes Mathey's wailing could be heard at Pendour Cove – a

19 Carn Kenidjack, Pendeen *

The eerily shaped rocky outcrop of Carn Kenidjack stands like a fortress on Woon Gumpus Common. This wild expanse of moorland, also known as the 'Gump', is one of the most spirit-haunted places in Cornwall where fairies and all kinds of otherworldly beings have been seen singing and cavorting. Carn Kenidjack seems to have been at the centre of all this supernatural activity and people avoided it, especially at night, for fear of being either pixie-led and abducted by the fairies or encountering the wild hunt (see quote). It was also known as the Hooting Cairn owing to an eerie sound that sometimes emanated from the rocks on dark nights. *"Few go near that wisht place, about the turn of night, without hearing, if not seeing, the Old One and his hounds, hunting among the rocks for any restless spirits that may have strayed so far from the churchyard."*

warning of bad weather to come.
Just outside the village of Zennor is the **Giant's Rock** (50.1942, -5.5690; SW453387; 300m from Zennor; private land), a huge logan stone that now barely moves but was once the rocking chair of the legendary giant of **Carn Galver**. It must have been a very sensitive stone because anyone who climbed up without it rocking would become a powerful witch. Also, on Zennor Hill just to the southeast of the village, there is a finely balanced **Logan Stone** (50.1890, -5.5559; SW462381; 1km from Zennor). The huge weight of the boulder concentrated on a tiny area of crystal-rich rock causes the quartz crystals to release an electrical charge, said to produce healing and magical effects.
Further along the hill is **Zennor Quoit** (50.1880, -5.5474; SW468380; 1.6km from Zennor), a collapsed Neolithic dolmen

said to have been constructed by a giant. According to local tradition, if the stones are removed they will always find their way back, leaving a curse upon the perpetrators.
50.1918, -5.5674; SW454385

ST JUST

18 Ballowall Barrow, St Just

Also known as Carn Gluze, Ballowall Barrow is an amazingly well-preserved Bronze Age chambered stone tomb with a circular arrangement of stone walls. Cornish miners returning home in the evenings reported seeing lights glowing on the barrow and fairies dancing all around it.
50.1225, -5.7015; SW355312

19

Wisht means 'ill-wished' or 'cursed' and the Old One refers to Arawn, lord of the underworld, leading the wild hunt while on the lookout for lost souls. The Gump was also haunted by Old Moll, the spirit of a terrifying witch who lived nearby. She is sometimes seen in the mist, wearing a red shawl and seated by an old well.

One moonlit night, a foolish man set out alone across the Gump, intent on stealing the fairies' gold. Soon, he began to hear music that was so beautiful it made him both laugh and cry, then out of a door in the hillside poured hundreds of tiny spriggans carrying sparkling lamps. They set up a huge feast and began to dine from golden plates, luring the greedy man ever closer until he was so near he tried to scoop up the fairy prince and princess and all their gold in his hat. Immediately a shrill sound whistled through the air, all the lights went out and the man felt spriggans crawling all over him, like insects, before he was tied down with fine threads. When dawn finally arrived the spriggans had disappeared and he was alone on the Gump – cold, frightened, wet and covered in gossamer threads. Two miners also had a ghostly encounter on the Gump as they lost their way one dark and starless night. Finding themselves wandering near Carn Kenidjack, they heard a low, moaning sound and saw an unearthly glow above the rocks. The miners sensed that other beings were passing in the darkness, all making their way towards the cairn, and soon they too felt drawn to it. On arrival, they

witnessed a large crowd of supernatural beings watching a brutal wrestling match. One of the miners, who was also a lay preacher, felt compelled to say a prayer for the unfortunate loser. This had an immediate and startling effect. Everything went dark and all the beings turned into spots of light, like will o'wisps, then disappeared into the night. Despite all the dark and sinister tales, Carn Kenidjack has a magical atmosphere (at least when visited in the daytime) and feels like a place of real power in the landscape. Another power spot in close proximity to Carn Kenidjack is Tregeseal Stone Circle (50.1337, -5.6585; SW386323) where many ley lines are said to cross.

50.1389, -5.6571; SW387329. Trailhead Parking: 50.1430, -5.6496; SW393333; 1km

ST IVES

20 Rosewall Hill Mines, St Ives

Tin has been mined in Cornwall since the Bronze Age when it was traded all over Europe to make bronze weapons and artefacts. Rosewall Hill near St Ives is riddled with these ancient mines whose supernatural inhabitants were known as 'knockers' on account of the strange, knocking sounds they made. While deep underground, miners would go to where the sounds were

20

21 Trencrom Hill, Lelant *

Originally the site of a Neolothic tor enclosure, then an iron Age hill fort, this grassy hill crowned with rocky outcrops was once home to a legendary giant called Trecobben. He shared his tools with the giant Cormoran of **St Michael's Mount** – visible in Mounts Bay to the south – and was said to have buried treasure in the labyrinthine passages under Trencrom Hill. One man went to look for it but as he dug, a terrible storm erupted and hundreds of tiny spriggans appeared from the rocks, growing to giant size and threatening him until he fled in terror. Another story relates how an old woman came upon some Trencrom spriggans counting their treasure in a house near Carbis Bay. She stole some of the gold from them but suffered from mysterious pains thereafter.

On the summit of the hill beneath one of the many rocky outcrops is a natural stone well (50.1742, -5.4786; SW517362) under a shelf of rock, while on the east side of the hill, hidden in the bracken, a stone structure known as the Giant's Well (50.1747, -5.4747; SW519362) has now been capped.

loudest and sometimes they were led to new veins of ore. In return for this valuable guidance, miners would leave offerings but any who didn't acknowledge the knockers or disrespected them might fail to find any more tin or be lured to their deaths. Decaying stone chimneys, overgrown with ivy, are now all that remains of the tin-mining industry on Rosewall Hill, but by sitting quietly and listening you may still connect with the spirits dwelling deep within the maze of tunnels and caverns far below.

50.2006, -5.5102; SW496392. Trailhead Parking: 50.2017, -5.5223; SW487394; 1km

At the bottom of the hill, beside a stream that flows along its northern edge, a huge rounded boulder known as **Bowl Rock** (50.1789, –5.4712, SW522367) was said to have been used by Trecobben in a game of bowls.

50.1739, –5.4775; SW517362. Trailhead Parking: 50.1716, –5.4776; SW517359; 300m

22 Venton Uny Fairy Well, Carbis Bay

Tucked away in the wooded cliffs above St Ives Bay, this magical little wishing well is an ancient rock-cut basin that still fills with clear, fresh water before the flow cascades over the cliff edge to the sands far below. Local people left bent pins here for the fairies when they made wishes, and visitors still tie ribbons and other offerings to the branches all around the well. Hidden in the cliff-side foliage, the well receives relatively few visitors. Follow the South West Coast Path east from the railway bridge in Carbis Bay until you see a tiny turning to the left, just before the well.

50.1954, –5.4540; SW535385. Secret/ Secluded; Trailhead: 50.1975, –5.4637; SW529388; 1km

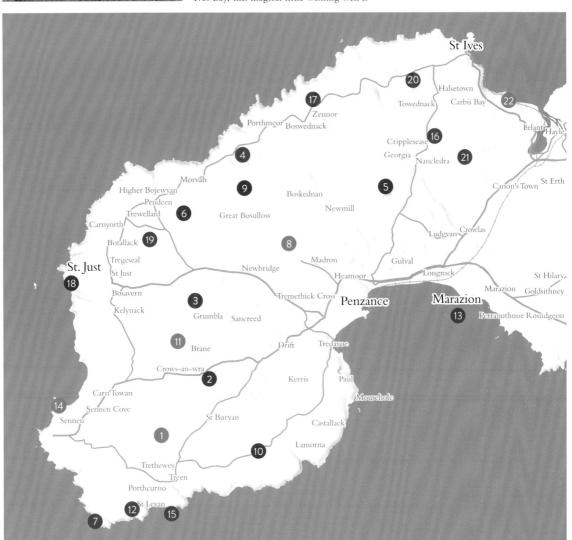

CENTRAL & EAST CORNWALL

Cornwall is a land of legends and its ancient Brythonic language, which is related to the other Celtic languages of Welsh and Breton, lends it a unique culture and character. Its extensive rocky shoreline is punctuated by sandy coves carrying legends of mermaids, while the cliffs contain magical caves with hidden secrets. Cornwall is also the legendary birthplace of King Arthur, said to have been conceived in Tintagel castle with the help of Merlin's trickery and then hidden beneath in the magical cavern now known as Merlin's Cave. Nearby is St Nectan's Glen, an enchanted wooded valley that ends in a narrow gorge with a tall waterfall – a place that exudes magic from every rock and stone. Just a little further along the coast is the old fishing village of Boscastle, with its tales of witches and a unique witchcraft museum that together make this stretch of coast the most visited part of Cornwall for seekers of magic and legends.

Just inland from Tintagel, mysterious Bodmin Moor features many Neolithic sites hidden among its rocky tors. Near the centre of the moor is the abode of the Lady of the Lake, Dozmary Pool, where Sir Bedivere is said to have cast the sword Excalibur after the disastrous battle of Camlann. On the southern flank of Bodmin are the three stone circles of the Hurlers and the impossibly top-heavy rock formation known the Cheesewring, which is linked to druidic rites.

In the 5th and 6th centuries Cornwall was visited by Celtic missionaries, mainly from Wales and Ireland, who later became canonised. Preaching and performing miracles, they established many small chapels and hermitages, often beside pagan sacred springs that had healing properties. These healing springs, of which there are many – often in ancient well-houses – were subsequently Christianised and dedicated in the saint's name.

The uplands of Cornwall were said to have been inhabited by a race of giants who hurled boulders around and fashioned the landscape we see today. However, the Celtic saints always seemed to get the better of these giants, fooling the dim-witted creatures who often paid with their lives or had to convert to Christianity.

Cornwall also has its fairy folk, but is more famous for the mischievous piskies (pixies) who often play tricks on people, leading them astray or visiting them in their slumber. Local people traditionally left offerings for the piskies to avoid offending them, and sometimes were even granted a wish or two!

FALMOUTH

1 Piskey's Hall Fogou, Constantine

The small, dark entrance to Piskey's Hall Fogou is almost concealed by bushes. Once inside, a short, stone-lined passage leads down to a dark and mysterious chamber that is capped by huge megalithic blocks. Strange noises have sometimes been heard emanating from this chamber which is said to be the home of The Piskey, a powerful supernatural being who presides over western Cornwall. He is a very different and altogether more powerful being than the small mischievous pixies or piskies who inhabit the rest of the West Country. Six kilometres south of Piskey's Hall Fogou on the Trelowarren estate is a larger and more easily accessible fogou known as **Halliggye Fogou** (50.0715, -5.1969; SW713239; closed in winter, bring a torch). Steps lead down to a long, dark passageway, with side passages, that extends deep underground.

50.1268, -5.1802; SW727300; Private Land; Secret/Secluded; No Paths; Bring a Torch

2 Poldhu Cove, Mullion

A fascinating mermaid legend is associated with this large sandy beach on the Lizard peninsula. An old smuggler named Lutey was checking the shoreline for flotsam near Poldhu Cove when he heard a strange wailing sound. It was a very low tide and the wailing seemed to be coming from some rocks that were not usually exposed. Lutey crept up and saw a mermaid had been stranded there on the rocks. They were both startled to see each other but after gaining her trust he agreed to carry the mermaid, whose name was Morwenna, back to the sea in return for three wishes. Lutey wished for the power to break evil spells, to charm away illness and to restore stolen goods. The mermaid then gave him her comb, and told him he had only to stroke the water with it and she would come to his aid. However just as Lutey was placing her back in the waves she gripped him tightly and tried to lure him down to her beautiful underwater caverns and gardens. Suddenly Lutey heard his dog bark and thought of home, so the charm was broken. Taking out his knife he threatened Morwenna and she let him go. The mermaid kept her promises and Lutey became a famous pellar (expeller of evil). However nine years later, while Lutey was out fishing, Morwenna came back to claim him and he disappeared into the waves. Lutey's comb and his magical abilities, however, were passed down through the generations of his family.

Parking £: 50.0343, -5.2591; SW667199; Popular

3 Carn Brea, Redruth

Overlooking the town of Redruth, the large hill topped by rocky outcrops known as Carn Brea was the home of legendary giants and the last of them was known in medieval times as John of Gaunt. The giants of Carn Brea are said to have buried their treasure in a system of tunnels under the mountain. Many old mining tunnels still exist but have been blocked up for safety reasons, which is probably just as well because the treasure is said to be protected by terrible and potent spells. Should it be disturbed, the wrath of the giants and the spriggans who guard the treasure would be unleashed, bringing forth storms, floods and lightning strikes. A large rocky outcrop on the eastern side of the hill is said to be the petrified head of a giant, although now it looks more like that of a dragon. Other rocks on the hill are known as the Giant's Hand, the Giant's Couch and the Giant's Cradle, and there is also a Giant's Well. Carn Brea was once crowned with a Neolithic tor enclosure and later by a chapel dedicated to Archangel Michael. Legend speaks of a heavenly host who fought and defeated Lucifer on top of the hill, which recalls the iconic Christian story of Archangel Michael subduing the Devil. The hilltop now boasts an 18th century castle-folly that was built as a hunting lodge and now serves as a restaurant.

50.2210, -5.2489; SW683407; Popular

4 Ralph's Cupboard, Portreath

This dramatic cleft in the towering cliffs west of Portreath was home to a giant named Ralph. Hiding in the natural inlet known as Ralph's Cupboard he would ambush passing ships by hurling rocks at them. The South West Coast Path passes right by the inlet providing stunning and vertigo-inducing views of Ralph's former home. In spring and summer the cliffs are alive with nesting sea birds and adorned with wild flowers.

50.2585, -5.3049; SW645450; Trailhead Parking: 50.2612, -5.2925; SW654453; 1km

5 Carne Beacon, Veryan

This huge Bronze Age burial mound stands on top of a hillside overlooking Gerrans

Bay. An ancient king called Gereint is said to be buried there in his golden boat with silver oars – a magical craft that conveyed his body across the bay before he was laid to rest. It has been suggested that Gereint could represent the ancient sun god, while the path his ship took across the bay could indicate the direction of the sun on the summer solstice. Looking out from **Pedn-vadan** (50.1859, -4.9682; SW882359) on the far side of the bay, the solstice sun rises directly behind Carne Beacon, creating a glistening path across the bay.

50.2109, -4.9269; SW912386; Trailhead: 50.2103, -4.9269; SW912385; 50m

6 Holywell Cave, Holywell *

A stunning natural sea cave with a magical secret, Holywell cave lies at the northern end of the broad sandy expanse of Holywell Beach and can only be reached when the tide is out. Venture inside this liminal place and you'll see the most amazing coloured rocks including stepped bowl formations that fill with crystal-clear spring water. The spring is located in a small chamber just above and can be reached by climbing up time-worn steps. From the Christian era, this magical natural spring was known as St Cuthbert's Well after Bishop Aldhun of Lindisfarne was shipwrecked near here in 995AD carrying the sacred remains of St Cuthbert. The saint's remains are said to have touched the side of the well, endowing it with miraculous healing properties. Children from the neighbourhood were subsequently immersed in the well water on Holy Thursday to cleanse their bodies of sickness and deformity. The disabled would also travel to the cave and, leaving their crutches behind, were said to crawl up to the spring to drink the water in the hope of a miraculous cure.

50.3976, -5.1440; SW766600; Low Tide Only; Trailhead Parking £: 50.3858, -5.1425; SW767587; 1.5km

7 St Agnes Beacon & Chapel Porth

The giant Bolster lived in a stronghold called *Carn Bury-anacht* on top of the prominent coastal hill known as St Agnes Beacon. Midsummer fires were traditionally lit on top of this landmark, which has excellent 360-degree views overlooking the Atlantic and the surrounding landscape. Its bare, heather-covered slopes are devoid of rocks because Bolster reputedly cast them all at his rival who dwelt on **Carn Brea.** Bolster was so huge that he could stride the 9km from St Agnes Beacon to Carn Brea in a single step! He was a terrible tyrant who bullied his wife and then fell in love with the virginal St Agnes, following her around everywhere and becoming quite a pest. Wily St Agnes eventually asked him to prove his love by filling a hole with his blood and Bolster readily agreed to what he considered a simple test. Unbeknown to him, the hole was a tidal cave so it never filled but drained into the sea and the towering giant bled to death. Every year around May Day, local people re-enact this event and a giant puppet accompanied by local performers is carried through the streets of St Agnes and across the cliffs to Chapel Porth.

The 'hole' where Bolster shed his blood is off the coast path at the end of a suspended valley overlooking **Chapel Porth** cove (50.3013, -5.2350; SW697496), while the cave below can be visited at low tide. At low tide you can walk further north along the beach where there are more caves and rocks that are said to be stained red from Bolster's blood.

The original name for the parish of St Agnes was *Breanek* which may mean the 'Hill of Anek'. This could refer to the pagan goddess Annis who over time was transformed into the Christian St Agnes.

50.3080, -5.2173; SW710502 (St Agnes Beacon); Trailhead Parking: 50.3114, -5.2231; SW706506; 600m

ST AUSTELL

8 Mawgan Porth, Newquay

The popular surfing cove of Mawgan Porth is bounded by low cliffs and has a huge expanse of flat golden sand. On three consecutive days in 1827 some very strange occurrences took place there. When the tide was extremely low, a cave filled with deep pools was exposed and a boy out fishing for pilchards late one evening heard some unusual noises coming from it and went to investigate. What he saw filled him with

terror and he fled, later describing a strange beast that was half-human and had hair hanging all about its body. The next day three men standing on the cliffs above near Bre Pen (50.4606, -5.0319; SW849667) looking for shoals of pilchards spotted three shapes on the rocks offshore and were convinced they'd seen a trio of mermaids. On the third day, there were five more mermaids and people watched them for over an hour, amazed by their long, trailing hair, pale skin, and fish-like lower body with a fin. All of this was reported in the local newspaper and caused a great stir at the time.

Parking: 50.4643, -5.0311; SW849671; Very Popular

9 Menacuddle Well, St Austell

Tucked away among ornamental gardens on the outskirts of St Austell, Menacuddle Well sits beside a gently flowing river and tranquil waterfall. The medieval stone well-house contains healing water in a deep stone trough and the water flows freely around the well through shallow stone channels. Sick children and those afflicted with ulcers came here to be cured, and bent pins were thrown into the waters for divination and to bring good fortune. Its name is derived from *maen-a-coedl* which means 'the hawk's stone'. The well still retains a magical atmosphere, enhanced by the ribbons and crystals hung all around by visitors and pilgrims.

50.3456, -4.7958; SX011532

10 Nine Maidens & St Breock Downs, St Columb Major

On the summit of St Breock Downs, in a landscape with other Bronze Age monuments, is Cornwall's largest and heaviest standing stone, the 3m tall grey-shale St Breock Monolith with white feldspar veins, also known as **Men Gurta** or the **Longstone** (50.4793, -4.8656; SW967683). When excavated it was found to lie on a bed of white quartz crystals, which may have been placed to amplify the powerful energies of the place. The stone sits in the centre of a late Neolithic to mid-Bronze Age cairn monument and was thought to be a meeting place in medieval times.

About 3km to the west lie a row of similar but smaller standing stones known as the Nine Maidens who, according to legend, were turned to stone for dancing on the Sabbath. The row is over 100m long and lies on the edge of a grassy field flanked by gorse bushes. Aligned with this row, 600m north, is another standing stone called the Fiddler (50.4771, -4.9058; SW939681) who was playing the dance music.

50.4717, -4.9093; SW936675 (Nine Maidens Stone Row); Trailhead: 50.4724, -4.9122; SW934676; 200m

11 Roche Rock *

Just south of the village of Roche the jagged outcrop of Roche Rock rises out of the flat heathlands, its grey pinnacles of granite infused with black tourmaline crystals. It is capped by a ruined medieval chapel that is wedged between the two highest pinnacles and seems to grow from the living rock. The 15th-century chapel is dedicated to Archangel Michael whose shrines often occupy high places of ancient pagan sanctity, where communion with gods and spirits or the heavenly powers was said to be possible.

The chapel was built on the site of an ancient hermit's cell and several legends grew up around the holy men who dwelt here. One was named Ogrin and in the medieval romance of Tristan and Iseult he provided the fleeing lovers with shelter, while another was a leper whose daughter Gundred used to fetch water for him from a local healing well that is now named

after her. **St Gundred's Well** (50.4207, -4.8378; SW985617. Trailhead: 50.4172, -4.8380; SW984613; 600m; no paths at end), 2km north of Roche Rock is hidden away in a small wooded valley behind a farm. The pointed medieval roof of the tiny well-chamber can be seen poking through thick undergrowth in boggy ground beside a stream. Through the tangle you can see the clear well water contained in a stone trough inside the well-chamber. The waters, which were said to ebb and flow with the tides and cure mental illness, were visited by young women who would throw pins and stones into the well and count the bubbles to predict when they would get married.

50.4020, -4.8282; SW991596; Popular

12 Doom Bar, Padstow

As the river Camel spills out across broad sand flats into Padstow Bay it flows over this wide sandbar that stretches out across the mouth of the estuary. The story of the Doom Bar concerns a local man who had fallen in love with a beautiful mermaid while he was out hunting seals. Unable to join him on land, the mermaid tried to drag him down to her underwater realm but he shot at her in order to make his escape. Suddenly a terrific storm arose and threw up the sand bar which for ever afterwards was a hazard to shipping and a curse on the people of Padstow who could no longer fish from its harbour.

50.5602, -4.9364; SW921775; Visible at Low Tide; Trailhead: 50.5432, -4.9365; SW920756; 2km; Or view from Trebetherick (50.5613, -4.9254; SW929776)

13 Fairies' Well, Tregenna, Blisland

This magical little fairy well is rarely visited. A broken-down gate leads into a narrow lane flanked by high stone walls with overgrown vegetation and tree branches making access very difficult but the adventurous will eventually make it to a small, dry-stone walled enclosure entirely hidden by trees. A small rivulet of water seeps across the ground from its source in the next enclosure, the magical Fairies' Well, which looks like a pile of mossy rocks out of which fresh clear water flows freely from the earth. It is easy to imagine the fairies dancing and singing in the twilight in this enchanted, hidden place.

50.5314, -4.6949; SX091736; Private Land; Secret/Secluded; Trailhead: 50.5326, -4.6947; SX091737; 200m; No Path

14 Helman Tor, Bokiddick *

Rocky outcrops cover the summit of Helman Tor, a prominent hill in an isolated location just south of Bodmin. The hilltop was modified in early Neolithic times to create a tor enclosure. On the summit of Helman Tor there is a huge logan stone weighing many tons. These rocking stones were once thought to have magical

properties and also believed to be the site of druidic rituals as well as witches' gatherings. Some believed that touching a logan stone nine times at midnight would turn you into a witch!

Helman Tor is located along the Saints' Way, an ancient trackway that links Padstow on the north coast of Cornwall with Fowey on the south, and originally used by ancient traders, transporting goods from Ireland to the continent. In the Dark Ages early Irish missionaries spreading the gospel in pagan Cornwall may have travelled along it as well as Welsh settlers who were fleeing to Brittany to escape the marauding Anglo-Saxons.

Parking: 50.4204, -4.7295; SX062613; Popular

15 Jesus Well, Rock

This lovingly restored well is hidden away on a golf course near the village of Rock, west of St Minver. It features an old stone well-house surrounded by a walled enclosure and despite the location, still retains a sacred atmosphere. Parents would dip their children into its waters to cure whooping cough, while bathing in the well on three separate occasions was also said to bring about healing. Coins were once placed in a niche by the well, or cast into its waters as an offering. Jesus Well was named after a nearby 'Jesus Chapel' which no longer exists. The well was reputedly created when a saint planted his staff in the ground where the spring now flows.

50.5509, -4.9126; SW937763; Trailhead: 50.5469, -4.9067; SW941759; 800m

CAMELFORD

16 Boscastle

Boscastle retains the atmosphere of an old-fashioned Cornish fishing village yet one with uncanny witchcraft associations, especially around the harbour. The houses that run down to this steep, narrow inlet are situated on either side of the Mill Leat stream, and it is here that you'll find Boscastle's famous **Museum of Witchcraft and Magic** (50.6906, -4.6949; SX097913; ££). According to legend, local witches would stand by the harbour 'selling the wind' to fishermen who would procure spells and lucky charms for good weather. Travelling upstream from the harbour, you pass through the village, which contains several pagan and New Age shops, before entering Minster Wood. Here, hidden in a side valley, **Minster Church** (50.6833, -4.6758; SX110904; 2.3km) stands in a beautiful woodland setting fronted by bubbling springs and wildflowers. Pagan rituals are said to take place at this 'White Church' on the Celtic Sabbats.

50.6907, -4.6955; SX097913 (Boscastle Harbour) Popular; Parking £: 50.6899, -4.6912; SX100912; 300m

17 St Clether's Well Chapel, St Clether *

Peacefully located in a shallow green valley, this ancient chapel was founded in the 6th century by Welsh Saint Cleder who chose to build his hermitage by this sacred spring. The well-chapel, the largest in Cornwall, was specifically constructed so that the water that collects in the upper well house runs through the chapel and underneath an ancient granite altar, re-emerging in a lower well in the chapel wall before flowing down to join the river Inny which runs through the valley bottom. A remarkable survival from the medieval period when the

chapel and well-house were constructed is the megalithic granite altar. The relics of St Clether were reputedly placed upon it so the spring water flowing beneath would be infused with their power. Pilgrims could then take the waters from the lower well in exchange for a small offering.

Upon entering this ancient place of sanctity, the sound of constantly flowing water behind the huge granite altar gives the chapel a strange otherworldly atmosphere that harks back to the days of the early Celtic church, and even further back, into our pagan past. The chapel is still venerated today and visited by pilgrims who hang ribbons beside the well house.

50.6333, -4.5436; SX202846; Trailhead: 50.6306, -4.5387; SX205842; 500m

18 St Julitta's Well, Camelford

Julitta or Juliot was a 5th-century Celtic saint whose tiny stone well-house is set into a grassy bank in a secluded location by a tributary of the river Allen. After walking through Juliots Well Holiday Park and descending into the secluded river valley, you leave the modern world behind and, as the small well-house comes into view you enter a more enchanted world. The well is surrounded by wildflowers in spring and adorned by clooties left as offerings on an overhanging tree. Ask at the holiday park for permission to visit.

50.6153, -4.6998; SX090829; Private Land; Secret/Secluded; Trailhead: 50.6133, -4.6972; SX092827; 350m

19 St Nectan's Glen *

One of Cornwall's most magical places, St Nectan's Glen is a liminal place where you feel magic really can happen. Walking through the fairy-haunted woodland by the banks of the river Trevillet you eventually

reach the enchanted waterfall at St Nectan's Kieve, hidden away in a rocky gorge at the head of the valley. The 18m waterfall drops down through a narrow fissure in the rock before filling a churning cauldron with white frothing water. This cauldron (known as a keeve) then overflows through a large circular hole that has been worn through the rock face. The water pours out into a shallow pool at the foot of the waterfall that can be accessed from the base of the gorge via stepping stones. A fine mist of water droplets fills the air with 'orbs', which add to the mystical atmosphere.

Flowing out from the pool, a shallow stream runs through the wide gorge, which is overlooked by mossy cliffs and bedecked with a myriad of pagan and New Age offerings left by the thousands of pilgrims who visit this site every year. Ribbons, rock stacks, incised stones, coins, crystals and figurines are just a few of the many magical tokens on display. The water eventually flows out over a broad waterfall into the wooded valley of St Nectan's Glen.

Above St Nectan's Kieve there is a café and pagan/New Age gift shop where you can purchase tickets to visit the kieve. To the side of the gift shop, there is a small room full of offerings and figurines that acts as a pagan shrine (ask for the key). The shop is said to have been built on the site of the cell, where the Celtic saint lived in the 6th century. He was said to have possessed a silver bell that he rang to warn

sailors of bad weather. Some say the bell can sometimes be heard ringing from the keeve, where it lies hidden.

Others believe that St Nectan never visited the area and that the name was a Victorian invention or that it is derived from the Irish Celtic water god Nechtan who had a spring at the Well of Wisdom at the source of the river Boyne.

On the other side of B3263, downstream from St Nectan's Glen, **Rocky Valley** (50.6728, -4.7293; SX072894. Trailhead: 50.6694, -4.7296; SX072890; 400m), where the river Trevillet eventually flows out into the sea is worth visiting. About two-thirds of the way down the valley, by a ruined chapel adorned with ribbons and offerings, are a pair of famous rock carvings of unknown origin depicting labyrinths.

50.6648, -4.7168; SX080885 (St Nectan's Kieve); £ Popular; Trailhead Parking £: 50.6708, -4.7251; SX075892; 1.4km

20 Tintagel **

At this legendary birthplace of King Arthur, Merlin cast a spell on Uther Pendragon, giving him the appearance of Gorlois of Cornwall so he could seduce Gorlois' wife Igraine. The deception is said to have occurred where the ruins of Tintagel Castle now stand – a dramatic headland sur-

rounded by 100m high cliffs of dark grey slate in contorted folds. When Arthur was born, there were many who wanted to kill him and so Merlin hid him in what is now known as **Merlin's Cave** (50.6682, -4.7593; SX051890; low tide only). This enchanted cave, which is flooded every day by the tide, extends all the way through the neck of the headland. At low tide it is possible to walk down to the sandy beach of Tintagel Haven, enter its huge black maw and scramble through to reach a small cove on the other side where the sea still laps against the rocks. It is said that the spirit of Merlin haunts this cave and many people have reported undergoing mystical experiences here that have transformed their lives and set them on magical quests.

Tintagel Castle ruins are medieval, but excavations have revealed that a Romano-British settlement existed here, trading with the Mediterranean and Roman world by exporting Cornish tin and other items in exchange for luxury goods. On the southern edge of the headland facing the mainland, you can find **King Arthur's Seat** and **King Arthur's Footprint** (50.6676, -4.7619; SX049889), a foot-shaped indentation in the rock that may once have been used for the inauguration of Cornish kings. King Arthur's Seat itself is a rock shelter beside a gully on the edge of the cliff. There is a small opening in the back called King Arthur's Window, and bowl-shaped depressions around the seat are known as King Arthur's Cups and Saucers. The small seaside town of Tintagel has a string of New Age and pagan shops as well as King Arthur's Great Halls £ (50.6629, -4.7496; SX057884), a 1930s stone recon-struction of a medieval great hall. The headland and castle ruins are accessible via a newly constructed footbridge, which saves the arduous climb down and then up to the castle. **St Nectan's Glen** and the traditional fishing village of **Boscastle** with its witchcraft museum are also within reach, making this the most enchanted area in East Cornwall.

50.6681, -4.7596; SX050890 (Tintagel Castle); £££ Very Popular; Trailhead: 50.6642, -4.7534; SX055885; 750m

LISKEARD

21 Hurlers & Cheesewring *

Just outside the village of Minions, on the edge of wild and mysterious Bodmin Moor, are three large stone circles known as the Hurlers. They are arranged in a row that is aligned in a roughly northerly direction towards a large grassy mound known as Ril-laton Barrow (50.5211, -4.4557; SX260719; 900m from car park). On a hill beyond this Bronze Age barrow, you'll see the unusual rock formation known as the **Cheesewring** (50.5254, -4.4593; SX257724; 1.4km from car park). These sites feature in folklore about druids, saints and giants.

The three incomplete circles of the Hurlers stand like broken teeth on the open moor-land. These stone circles were once linked by a processional way and the central circle is known to lie on a bed of white quartz crystals. Dowsing has revealed strange patterns of energy around these stones, and in recent times some have reported unusual experiences and seen visions of a white lady or goddess there. The stones lie on the Michael/Mary ley Line, which links directly to **St Michael's Mount** and **Glastonbury Tor** along the Beltane/Lugh-

nasa sunrise line. According to a Christian legend, the stones were people who St Cleer punished for playing hurling on the Sabbath. He also turned two others – the nearby Pipers – to stone for playing music. Like many other stone circles, the stones of the Hurlers are said to be uncountable.

The Cheesewring is a naturally formed outcrop of granite slabs that sits like a top-heavy stack of pancakes just outside a Neolithic tor enclosure on top of Stowe's Hill. The 9m high stack is composed of seven flat rocks that increase in size towards the top, and the topmost is said to turn around three times when the cock crows. Another legend states that the Cheesewring was the result of a rock-throwing contest between a saint and giant. With help from an angel, the saint won the contest and so the pagan giant was defeated.

Near the Cheesewring is a hollowed-out rock known as the Druid's Chair. Whenever a hunting party passed by, the Druid who sat there would offer them wine

from his golden goblet and no matter how many drank from it, it never ran dry. One day one of the hunters laid a wager that he could drink the cup dry, but try as he might he could not empty it. Enraged he threw the drink in the face of the Druid, who vanished, never to be seen again. According to folklore, whoever sits in the Druid's Chair will either go mad or become a poet, or even gain the ability to com-municate with the Devil. Strangely, when Rillaton Barrow was excavated, the mound was found to contain a golden cup!

50.5164, -4.4584; SX258714 (Hurlers Stone Circles); Popular; Trailhead Parking: 50.5158, -4.4522; SX262713; 300m

22 Piskies' Well, Pelynt *

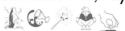

Just below a remote country lane northeast of Pelynt, the Piskies' Well is tucked away

into a hillside and has a magical atmosphere. Water trickles from an overgrown well-house set beneath the roots of a large tree and surrounded by verdant growth. Inside the dark, tiny well-chamber with its ancient stone basin, glowing green mosses and liverworts cover the various fairy statues and magical offerings deposited there. This is no ordinary holy well and it is said that anyone who enters without leaving an offering will offend the mischievous pisky inhabitants.

According to the earliest recorded stories, the well was the haunt of a beneficial elf who granted health and good fortune to all who entered reverently; those who were disrespectful would earn his enduring anger. By the end of the 19th century, local people would leave bent pins to obtain the goodwill of the piskies. A local farmer once tried to remove the stone basin for use in his pigsty using a rope attached to two oxen, but the basin broke free and returned to its original location. The oxen dropped dead and the farmer became lame and lost the power of speech. In a more recent anecdote, a local woman related how her son had helped to restore the well, but not believing in the pixies he had refused to leave an offering. That evening, the spirits of the well visited him and he had terrible nightmares so the next day he quickly returned to leave an offering! When the owner of the famous Joan the Wad pixie shop in Polperro (see **Willy Wilcox Hole**) visited the well, she blessed each of her lucky pixies by dipping it in the well water. The well is also known as St Nonna's well, St Non's Well, St Nun's Well and St Ninnie's Well, so it seems as though the piskies like to confuse!

50.3807, -4.4992; SX224564

23 St Keyne's Well, St Keyne

Hidden amid lush vegetation beside a country lane just outside the village of St Keyne, this ancient well-house is reached by stone steps that lead to a secluded and tranquil spot. According to local folklore, after a wedding the first partner to drink from its enchanted waters will always have the upper hand in the marriage. One unfortunate newly married Cornishman, raced directly to the well only to discover that his bride had secreted a bottle of the well water about her person and already drunk it! St. Keyne was a 6th-century Celtic missionary who was known for her great beauty, but she swore a vow of chastity. After her travels she settled in a valley near the well that now bears her name.

50.4157, -4.4669; SX248602; Secret/Secluded

the main chamber has a large square section cut out of it, perhaps enabling the passage of spirits. It is not known which giant lived here or how King Arthur came to be associated with this quoit, which stands in a green field by a country lane northeast of St Cleer. In the village itself, an elaborate stone well-house has been built around an ancient 'bowsenning' well known as **St Cleer Holy Well** (50.4883 -4.4691; SX249683). Bowsenning, a Cornish term, describes the practice of submerging people with mental illness in sacred wells to cure insanity or rid them of evil spirits. The well-house and adjacent stone cross are of medieval origin and it is said that any stones removed will mysteriously return overnight. Both are easily accessible but the pool can no longer be used for immersion as it is covered by an iron grille.

50.4932, -4.4554; SX259688
(Trethevy Quoit)

25 Willy Wilcox Hole, Polperro

Polperro is a traditional Cornish fishing village with small winding alleyways and old whitewashed cottages. Set into the cliffs beside the harbour and below a row of cottages, is a shallow cavern known as Willy Wilcox Hole. It is named after a local smuggler who once hid in this cave and somehow managed to make his way into a maze of tunnels where he got lost. Unable to escape, his ghost is still said to haunt the cave, wailing as he tries to find his way out. In Polperro, Joan the Wad's piskie shop (50.3312, -4.5188; SX208509) sells all kinds of charms and artwork relating to piskies. The shop is adorned with wooden carvings of Cornish Piskies, including Joan the Wad, Queen of the Piskies. The 'wad' she carries is a flaming torch, and images of her are said to light the way, bringing good luck and protection. Joan, however, may also be

24 Trethevy Quoit & St Cleer Holy Well

Also known as the Giant's House and Arthur's Quoit, this is one of the most impressive Neolithic dolmens in the country, formed of six massive granite slabs with a 20-tonne capstone. Uniquely the capstone has a large round hole in it, while the slab dividing the ante-chamber from

associated with Jack o' Lantern, a will o' the wisp who would lead people astray with his light. As a Cornish rhyme states:

Jack o' the lantern! Joan the wad,
Who tickled the maid and made her mad!
Light me home, the weather's bad.

Another piskie character depicted in the shop is Billy Bucca, Duke of the Buccas, who lived deep in the Cornish mines. Also known as 'knockers', these spirits would guide miners with their knocking sounds to rich seams of ore in exchange for small offerings.

50.3312, -4.5182; SX208509; Low Tide Only; Nearest Parking £: 50.3371, -4.5231; SX205516; 1km

ST GERMANS

26 Dupath Well, Callington

Located just behind a farm outside the small town of Callington, Dupath Well is an elaborate stone well-house with an ornate steeple and small turrets. Water flows into it along a stone channel, collects in a trough inside, and then flows out of the back into a stone basin. The impressive well house was built in the 16th century by monks from the nearby priory of St German's, but the origins of this sacred spring are much older. Legend says that two Saxon warriors once fought a duel near here over the hand of a lady and the victor created this well as an act of atonement for killing his opponent. Local people once visited the well, seeking cures for whooping cough and other ailments.

50.5004, -4.2925; SX375692; Trailhead: 50.4996, -4.2938; SX374691; 100m

LAUNCESTON

27 Dozmary Pool, Bolventor

Located high on Bodmin Moor, the small lake known as Dozmary Pool has existed since the end of the last Ice Age. The legendary abode of the Lady of the Lake, this is the place where Sir Bedivere cast the sword Excalibur as King Arthur lay dying after the Battle of Camlann. At this mysterious lake the ghost of the evil local magistrate Jan Tregeagle was doomed to carry out endless and impossible tasks – in this case to empty the pool with a leaky limpet shell. The many flint flakes and tools found around the lake are evidence of early Mesolithic hunter-gatherers. Today it is sur-

rounded by farmland and flows out into the much larger Colliford Lake reservoir.

50.5397, -4.5494; SX194742; Trailhead: 50.5370, -4.5521; SX192739; 400m

28 Warbstow Bury Hillfort

The large, sprawling Iron Age hillfort of Warbstow Bury lies on a low grassy hill just outside the village of the same name. Double ramparts lead to a large central enclosure and to a mound in the centre, known as the **Giant's Grave** (50.6887, -4.5478; SX201907).

According to legend, Warbstow Bury was once the home of a giant who was killed by the giant of Condolden Beacon (50.6532, -4.7030; SX090872) near Tintagel, though some say he was killed by the giant of Launceston Castle (50.6376, -4.3615; SX331846) who threw a hammer at him. He was then buried in the grassy mound known as the Giant's Grave. When

archeologists tried to excavate the mound around the end of the 19th century, it was reported that a great clamour of thunder and lightning forced them to flee and give up their work.

Parking: 50.6879, -4.5454; SX202906

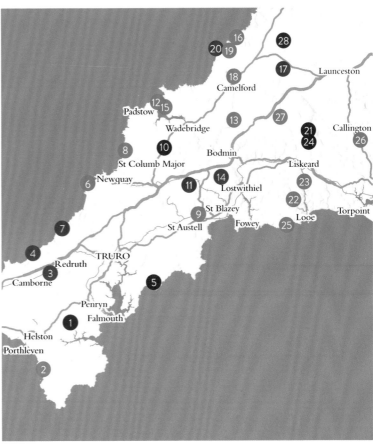

93

DEVON

Devon is rich in magical landscapes and legends, which are concentrated in and around Dartmoor's wild expanse of mysterious uplands and valleys. Characterised by large areas of windswept and isolated moorland, home to herds of wild ponies and sheep, Dartmoor abounds with ancient stone circles, hillforts and standing stones. Ancient stone clapper bridges cross meandering waterways and join trackways still in use after thousands of years. Towering granite outcrops overlook secret wooded valleys, where remnants of Britain's original wildwood still flourish, their twisted limbs and roots growing over mossy boulders.

Dartmoor contains a higher concentration of prehistoric sites than anywhere else in the British Isles and many of them are steeped in myth or have a magical significance. Some ancient stones were once said to have been living people, while other locations on Dartmoor are home to the old gods themselves. Old Crockern, a watchful spirit of the land, presides over Crockern Tor, while Dewer the Huntsman haunts the Dewerstone Rock. Leading the wild hunt across the bleak moor, Dewer rides with his fearsome pack of wisht hounds who reside in haunted and mysterious Wistman's Wood.

Devon also has many pixie legends. The Devonshire 'piskies' are small mischievous fairy beings, known for leading travellers astray and being easily offended. Their names are associated with caves, rocks and other natural features, notably on Dartmoor – especially the area around Dartmeet and in the remote Dart Valley. Pixies are also fond of partying and have been seen enjoying their midnight revels at Bellever Tor and gathering at the Pixies Trysting Place by the river Dart.

Just to the west of Dartmoor the iconic hilltop church of Brentor lies not far from an enchanted chasm of rushing water known as Lydford Gorge where the falls are haunted by a 'white lady'. While east of Dartmoor two hills on either side of the river Exe were on the flightpath of a dragon who guarded the hoards of treasure buried within each hill.

Early Celtic saints were also known to have visited Devon in the distant past. The Hartland peninsula was home to St Nectan while St Brannoc settled near Braunton and today you can still visit their healing wells.

1 Brent Tor, North Brentor *

The tiny church of St. Michael de Rupe, perched dramatically atop the crags of Brent Tor, dates back to the 12th century and it is said that this lofty location can be attributed to a tussle between the Devil and Archangel Michael. The villagers had started to build their church at the foot of the hill, however each night the Devil moved the foundation stones to the top. This continued until St Michael intervened and threw a boulder at the Devil who, enraged at being struck, abandoned his efforts. The villagers decided to keep building the church on top of the hill in dedication to St Michael.

Brent Tor is a power spot linked to other hilltop churches situated along the Michael/Mary ley line which have similar dedications to Archangel Michael (see **St Michael's Mount** and **Glastonbury Tor**). Visitors who make the climb up to the church will be rewarded with dramatic and far-reaching views on a clear day. Once inside the tiny hilltop church and gazing up at the stained-glass window of Archangel Michael behind the altar, you can feel a sense of deep peace and latent power.

50.6033, -4.1623; SX470804; Popular; Trailhead Parking: 50.6044, -4.1657; SX468805; 400m

2 Dewerstone Rock, Shaugh Prior *

Looming above the thickly wooded valley of the river Plym, the granite cliffs of the Dewerstone are associated with Dewer the Huntsman and the wild hunt. Dressed in black robes and with a pack of spectral black dogs known as wisht hounds which he collected each evening from **Wistman's Wood,** Dewer would lead travellers astray across the moors before luring them over cliffs of the Dewerstone to fall to their deaths. He was also known to hunt the souls of unbaptised babies. One unfortunate man encountered Dewer and his pack of black hounds while riding over Dartmoor, and foolishly called out:

"What sport, Mister? Give us some of your game!"
With a laugh, the huntsman threw a bag at his feet. Upon reaching home the man unwrapped the bundle and was horrified to find the dead body of his own child.
Today's visitors can explore leafy trails along the Plym where trees with contorted

boughs overhang the river, then walk up through Dewerstone Wood to the top of the cliff where there are spectacular views over the **River Plym** valley.

50.4551, -4.0598; SX538637; Trailhead Parking: 50.4540, -4.0673; SX533636; 1.5km

3 Piskies House, Sheepstor

Rising above Burrator Reservoir, the slopes of Sheepstor are liberally scattered with countless piles of granite boulders. Amidst this impossible jumble of rocks is the small entrance to a cave known as the Piskies House and locals used to leave pins and other offerings here to placate its pixie inhabitants. Although very small, the cave is still accessible if you are willing to spend time searching for it and can squeeze through its narrow entrance. Sheepstor is approached via a mossy, tree-lined lane, but once on the tor, scrambling over the boulders to find the cave requires some determination.

50.4946, -4.0230; SX566680; Secret/ Secluded; Trailhead: 50.4937, -4.0330; SX567678; 300m

4 White Lady Falls, Lydford Gorge *

The mossy green canyon of Lydford Gorge has enchanted visitors for centuries. It is the deepest river gorge in the southwest, created by the rushing waters of the river Lyd. White Lady Falls, the highest waterfall in Devon, lies at the southern end of the gorge and gets its name from a mysterious apparition. Some say the white lady is the ghost of a woman who drowned in the pool beneath the waterfall, while others have suggested her image is formed by the flow of water, which at times resembles a bride dressed in flowing white gown and veil. Whether a spirit of the dead or of the river itself, it has been claimed the white lady can either entice people to their doom or save them from drowning.

Further up the gorge the walls lean inwards and the water is forced through a narrow cleft in the rock called the **Devil's Cauldron** (50.6417, -4.1108; SX508845). Beneath it, the water whirls and bubbles in a deep bowl carved by the flow of the water into the living rock.

Close by, the Pixie Glen (50.6417, -4.1118; SX507845; no paths) is more tranquil, and a nearby woodland clearing is now a picturesque picnic area.

50.6320, -4.1212; SX500835 (White Lady Falls); ££; Trailhead Parking: 50.6291, -4.1208; SX501831; 400m

4

DARTMOOR NATIONAL PARK

5 Bellever Tor

Said to be located at the geographical centre of Dartmoor, Bellever Tor is topped by a granite outcrop that provides dramatic views over the landscape. Surrounding the tor are the remains of prehistoric settlements and ritual features and the hill has long been associated with pixies. Local legend tells of a young farm labourer who passed Bellever Tor on his way to court a pretty dairymaid who lived on the other side of the moor at Huccaby. Busy on the farm during the day, he could only go visiting late in the evening and coming home later than usual one night he was puzzled to hear faint singing and laughter as he approached Bellever Tor. Moving closer he realised that among the stones was a large gathering of pixies who drew him into their revelry. Trapped in a whirling ring of pixies, he was compelled to dance all night but as the first rays of the sun shone over the tor the spell was broken and the pixies vanished. Sadly for the pretty dairymaid her suitor was so shaken by his experience he vowed never to visit her again and ended their liaison. The pixies were also said to have lived at nearby Laughter Hole Farm (50.5672, -3.8966; SX657758; private. Trailhead Parking: 50.5789, -3.8997; SX655771; 1.4km) where the old couple spoke of their many children. Yet whenever visitors came to this lonely place, they saw no children but a gaggle of tiny figures who would scurry away into the bracken when approached. Word got around that these were not human children at all, but a troop of pixies somehow adopted by the couple. The old farm still exists and is situated on the side of Laughter Tor which, like Bellever Tor, is dotted with prehistoric remains.

50.5720, -3.9155; SX644764;
Trailhead Parking: 50.5789, -3.8997;
SX655771; 2km

6 Bowerman's Nose & Hound Tor, Manaton *

The imposing granite stack known as Bowerman's Nose has the air of an ancient megalithic idol as it gazes out over the landscape towards Hameldown Tor. So uncanny and unnatural is its appearance that it was believed by some to have been created by the Druids. Its base is almost perfectly square, while on top of the column is a grim face that appears to be wearing a cap.

Local legend offers an alternative origin for this monumental stone. A hunter named Bowerman offended a coven of witches by disrupting their ceremony while chasing a hare (who was actually a witch in disguise). In revenge they turned the hunter into stone, while his hounds became the rocks of **Hound Tor** (50.5970, -3.7786; SX742789; very popular), just over the valley to the south. Hound Tor is a popular destination for day trippers while Bowerman's Nose still retains a sense of dramatic isolation.

50.610241, -3.780738; SX741804
(Bowerman's Nose); Trailhead Parking 50.5989, -3.7817; SX740792 (Hound Tor); 1.6km

7 Crockern Tor, Two Bridges

Since time immemorial the rough granite outcrops of Crockern Tor have stood sentinel above an ancient trail crossing Dartmoor. Legend tells us that these rocks are home to Old Crockern, the spirit and protector of Dartmoor, who has been described as:
"The gurt old spirit of the moors, Old Crockern himself, grey as granite, and his eyebrows hanging down over his glimmering eyes like sedge, and his eyes as deep as peat water pools."
This ancient spirit does not take kindly to those who wish to exploit the moor as evidenced by the story of a rich man who bought up thousands of acres. Intending to reclaim the moorland for farming, he was approached by a local bearing a message from Old Crockern: *"If he scratches my back, I'll tear out his pocket."* The warning, however, went unheeded, the farming enterprise failed and the businessman went bankrupt soon after. On dark stormy nights Old Crockern was said to emerge from his rocky abode – a spectral figure atop a skeletal horse. Galloping over the moors to **Wistman's Wood** to release the wisht hounds, he would lead the pack in pursuit of any unwary travellers they encountered.
Today it is said that the features of Old Crockern can still be discerned in the craggy rocks of Crockern Tor. Whether an old pre-Christian god or a nature spirit, he is said to reside within, silently keeping watch over the land.
50.5657, -3.9559; SX615758

8 Dartmeet & The Dart Valley **

Lying at the confluence of the East and West Dart rivers, Dartmeet and the surrounding area is rich with pixie legends. The **Pixie's Holt** (private land; secret; 800m from

parking; no paths at end) is a secret cave hidden in the 'pixie woods' along the banks of the West Dart. Heavily overgrown with moss and vegetation, the tunnel-like cave is reputed to be home to pixies. It lies in **Huccaby Cleave** (50.5407, -3.8825; SX667729) where the modern world fades away amidst a mossy tangle of trees. At nearby **Huccaby Tor** (50.5501, -3.8974; SX656739. Trailhead: 50.5465, -3.8922; SX660735; 600m) the pixies liked to dance in circles and Huccaby also features in a terrifying encounter with the pixies at **Bellever Tor**.
Dartmeet is an attractive area to explore and very popular with tourists. The picturesque remains of an ancient clapper bridge adjacent to 18th-century East Dart bridge draw

the crowds, but the huge Stepping Stones (50.5427, -3.8767; SX671731) over the West Dart River are less visited. Visitors may also visit Pixieland (50.5463, -3.8825; SX667735), a unique garden and shop filled with pixie-related gifts and gnomes of the static variety. Beyond the confluence, the river Dart rushes along the wild and remote Dart Valley, twisting and turning over boulders and under fallen trees. The steep sides are shrouded with oak trees, while rocky tors overlook the secluded valley. After heavy rainfall the force of water can be fearsome, giving rise to the old rhyme:

"River Dart, River Dart! Every year thou claim'st a heart!"

The 'cry of the Dart' when the spirit of the river called to its victim and lured them to a watery death, was a common Dartmoor superstition. On occasion, the drownings were blamed on pixies, who had long been thought to haunt the valley. One was said to live by the river Dart at **Blackpool** (50.5328, -3.8567; SX685719) where, night after night, residents of nearby Rowbrook Farm heard a mysterious voice calling "Jan Coo", the name of one of the farmhands. Although others heard the voice, it was only ever Jan's name called out. Eventually he slipped out into the night, eager to find who – or what – was calling him. Jan

was never seen again, presumed by all to have been pixy-led and drowned in the Dart.

Just downstream the Dart runs over large granite ledges at a spot known as the **Broadstone** (50.5362, -3.8516; SX688723). Here too the 'cry of the Dart' has been heard as a loud, rushing sound. The cry is said to increase in volume at night, especially during winter, and is a harbinger of misfortune and bad weather. At such times the spirit of the river seems like a living being, calling out to its victims. Over the Dart Valley from Rowbrook Farm lies **Bench Tor** (50.5317, -3.8493; SX690718. Trailhead parking: 50.5262, -3.8561; SX685712; 900m), where the pixies were more mischievous than malevolent. One man who was pixy-led over the tor one dark night couldn't find his way home, even though he'd been walking that way all his life. Further downstream at New Bridge, is the **Pixie's Trysting Place** (50.5258, -3.8145; SX714711; popular. Trailhead parking: 50.5268, -3.8173; SX712712; 200m). On a stretch of the Dart considerably calmer and more tranquil than higher up the valley, this green riverside meadow was much favoured by pixies as a place to hold their midnight revels.

The Dart Valley is a nature reserve in the care of Devon Wildlife Trust and features a walking trail along the east bank of the river, starting in Dartmeet. The route, however, is long and strenuous, requiring stamina and a willingness to clamber over boulders and up steep inclines. Care must also be taken when the river is in full spate lest the Dart claims another 'heart'. Short cuts can be taken down into the Dart Valley by descending from Rowbrook Farm (50.5375, -3.8582; SX684725; private) or from the parking at Bench Tor, although there are no marked paths from either of these places.

Parking £: 50.5440, -3.8752; SX672732 (Dartmeet); Very Popular

9 Fice's Well, Princetown

Near the edge of a Dartmoor field, beside a small steam, lies Fice's well. This natural spring is surrounded by a circular granite enclosure and stone lintel bearing the initials I.F. and the date 1568. Now a listed ancient monument, the well was built by a man called John Fitz (or Fice) in gratitude after being pixy-led on the moor. Hopelessly lost and exhausted, Fitz and his wife wandered far from home. After many hours they came upon a spring rising from the ground. The water from the spring brought such refreshment that not only did it slake their thirst, but it also restored their strength and broke the pixie spell. Today, the water of Fice's Well is still said to have many miraculous and healing qualities.

50.5653, -4.0102; SX577758; Trailhead: 50.5574, -4.0082; SX578749; 1km

10 **Grey Wethers, Chagford** *

Lying east of Sittaford Tor, the pair of stone circles known as the Grey Wethers were so named because they were thought to resemble sheep that had been turned to stone. 'Wether' comes from an Old English term for a castrated ram, and the animals were said to have been turned to stone when their owner angered an ancient sun god. On Midsummer Eve the stones are said to turn back into sheep for one night and anyone who manages to shear one of the flock before dawn will become rich. The stones are also reputed to rotate slowly at sunrise, so each face is warmed by the sun in turn. The Grey Wethers were the final stop on a penitential journey for 'faithless wives and fickle maidens' which began at **Cranmere Pool**. The stones would fall and crush those women whose crimes were too heinous to be forgiven and this is said to account for the stones' recumbent state before they were restored to a standing position in 1909. The Grey Wethers are reached by walking around the Fernworthy Reservoir to Fernworthy farm before taking the trail though Fernworthy Forest and then across the moor to the stones. At **Fernworthy Farm** (50.6396, -3.8974; SX659839; 2km) a hapless farmer angered some local 'gnomes' by quarrying granite from their rocky home to extend his farmhouse. The gnomes took their revenge by stealing his firstborn child, who was never seen again. The gnomes also reputedly took exception to the reservoir, and delayed the building of the dam by flooding the site. The farm now lies abandoned and overgrown, since the building of the reservoir,

The trail through Fernworthy Forest passes by the evocative Fernworthy Stone Circle and Stone Row (50.6412, -3.9038; SX654841) which lie in a pixie-haunted clearing beside the path.

50.6321, -3.9263; SX638831; Trailhead Parking: 50.6394, -3.8832; SX669838; 5km

11 Grimspound, Postbridge

The Bronze Age builders of Grimspound sited their settlement on the northern slope of Hameldown Tor, circling the village with walls 3m thick. The evocative name 'Grim' links the site to Norse god Odin, or his Saxon counterpart Woden – a relative newcomer considering the great age of the settlement. Long after the original settlement had been abandoned, a connection to old gods, giants or legendary figures gave such ancient sites new meaning. The name Grimspound was first recorded in the 18th century by a Reverend Polwhele, who also claimed the site was one of the 'principal temples of the druids'. Hookney Tor (50.6163, -3.8412; SX698812) to the north and Hameldown Tor (50.6104, -3.8343; SX703805) to the south are both accessible by path and provide good vantage points to see the scale of the site.

50.6134, -3.8381; SX700809; Popular

12 Heltor & Blackingstone, Bridford *

The exposed and rounded summits of Heltor and **Blackingstone** (50.6573, -3.7182; SX786855) are clearly visible from each other, protruding above the surrounding pastures and woodland. The weathered, stacked pancake-shaped rocks on their summits were said to have been formed after an argument broke out between two giants who agreed that it should be settled by a game of quoits. These giants later became personified in folklore as King Arthur and the Devil. After Arthur positioned himself upon Blackingstone and the Devil took Heltor, the giants of legend proceeded to throw huge stones at each other until eventually King Arthur emerged victorious. The stone quoits remained, raising the height of each tor and creating the landmarks we see today.

50.6706, -3.7000; SX799870 (Heltor); Trailhead: 50.6687, -3.6996; SX799868; 200m

13 **Oakery Bridge, Princetown**

Picturesque Oakery Bridge crosses the Blackbrook River just outside Princetown. This traditional stone-built clapper bridge was also the setting for a strange pixie encounter. Late one night a woman coming home from market was surprised by the sudden appearance of a pixie, prancing and darting across the bridge. Unable to cross the bridge due to his antics, she reacted by scooping him up and shoving him into her basket! Immediately he began making a furious racket, screaming and gibbering and swearing in a strange language. The woman merely crossed the bridge and continued on her way, however after a short while the noise suddenly stopped. Curious, the woman peered into her basket – at which point the pixie leapt out and ran away.

50.5504, -3.9845; SX595741

14 **Sharpitor, Lustleigh Cleave**

The mysterious and thickly wooded hill known as Sharpitor is scattered with huge boulders that lie hidden in the trees and dense undergrowth. Many of them look as if they could have been put there by giants, forming all kinds of nooks, crannies and caverns. It was said that the pixies inhabited some of these caves, coming out of their 'pixy holes' at night.

The Nutcracker was a logan stone that used to sit on the top of the hill. Its rocking motion was so sensitive that nuts could allegedly be cracked under it. According to one story, the army was called in to try and reposition the stone after vandals knocked it out of place, but they only succeeded in shifting it further down the hill. However, others say that the Nutcracker is one of the boulders that still sits atop the summit of Sharpitor.

Below Sharpitor is an enchanted wooded valley known as Lustleigh Cleave (50.6166, -3.7442; SX767811; 1.2km) through which the river Bovey flows.

50.6203, -3.7358; SX773815; Trailhead: 50.6212, -3.7333; SX774816; 250m

15 Spinster's Rock, Whiddon Down

Once part of a larger complex of standing stones, the dolmen known as Spinster's

Rock is all that remains of a Neolithic burial chamber. According to legend the huge stones were erected by three spinsters - women who spun thread. This could be a reference to the three Wyrd Sisters of Anglo-Saxon legend who are said to spin and weave the fates of men. Another story relates how the stones were set up by a mysterious old man and his three sons who descended from the hills. The three sons can be seen as the three uprights, while the huge capstone is the old father. Spinster's Rock is located in a grassy field grazed by sheep.

50.7021, -3.8410; SX700907

16 Teign Tolmen, Chagford *

In the upper reaches of the river Teign a huge boulder has been pierced by a large, water-worn hole big enough for an adult to climb right through it. This is the Teign

Tolmen and passing through its hole is said to cure rheumatic illnesses, increase fertility and bring good luck.

The path to the Teign Tolmen passes by **Scorhill Stone Circle** (50.6706, -3.9053; SX654873; 700m). Remaining relatively intact, the ancient and jagged stones standing on the lonely moor retain a mystical atmosphere. Scorhill Stone Circle and the Teign Tolmen were stops on a penitential journey for women which also included **Cranmere Pool** and the **Grey Wethers**.

A little distance south at Shovel Down, stands the **Longstone** (50.6554, -3.8967; SX660856. Trailhead: 50.6688, -3.8808; SX671871; 2.4km), a standing stone that is said to slowly rotate at sunrise. The Longstone sits at the end of a prehistoric stone row, and the walk there passes by many Bronze Age ritual features including concentric stone circles and other stone rows.

50.6680, -3.9046; SX655871; Trailhead Parking: 50.6736, -3.8963; SX661877; 1km

17 Wind Tor, Widecombe in the Moor

Surmounting the gentle slopes of Dunstone Down, the rocky outcrop of Wind Tor was the scene of a strange pixie encounter. A washerwoman known as Nanny Norrish was crossing the moor one night from Dockwell Farm (50.5652, -3.8337; SX702755; private) to her home in Dunstone when she was startled by the sight of a whole 'tower' of gambolling pixies as she approached the summit. Not wanting to interrupt such acrobatics, she hurried on by as quickly as she could! The story is from the 18th century, but the farms of Dockwell and Dunstone still exist, and seem little changed by the passage of time. Interestingly, an ancient Bronze Age stone boundary known as a 'reave' can be seen passing down the side of Wind Tor in a straight line towards Dockwell Farm, as if marking out this ancient 'songline'.

In the hamlet of Lower Dunstone is the **Dun Stone** (50.5683, -3.8138; SX716758) itself – a large granite rock with a hollow on top. Manor courts were held here and rents were deposited in the hollow, a practice that continued well into the 20th century. Nearby is the Dun Stone Cross, a squat little cross carved from granite and perched on a stacked stone pedestal.

50.5677, -3.8255; SX708758; Trailhead: 50.5723, -3.8265; SX707763; 500m

18 Wistman's Wood, Two Bridges *

A tangle of stunted and twisted oak trees grow amidst a jumble of mossy boulders in this remote Dartmoor valley beside the West Dart river. This is the mystical Wistman's Wood, rightly famous for its unusual appearance, as well as its eerie folklore. The rocks around the trees are thought to be inhabited by poisonous adders, while the woods themselves were said to be kennels for the spectral wisht hounds, an otherworldly pack of coal-black dogs that hunt for the souls of the dead. They are called to join the wild hunt by their master Dewer the Huntsman (see **Dewerstone Rock**) or by Old Crockern from nearby **Crockern Tor.** These woods were also held to be an ancient grove, sacred to the Druids.

Wistman's Wood is a remnant of Dartmoor's ancient wildwood and the gnarled, mossy oaks give the impression of great antiquity. The local dialect word *wisht*, meaning eerie or uncanny, gives its name both to the hounds and the wood, and seems entirely suitable for such a strange and mysterious place.

50.5786, -3.9610; SX612772; Trailhead Parking: 50.5587, -3.9648; SX609750; 2.3km

OKEHAMPTON

19 Nine Stones Cairn Circle, Belstone

Many of the stone circles and standing stones around Britain were once said to be living people. The windswept stones of this circle at Belstone are commonly known as the Nine Maidens and commemorate a group of women who were turned to stone for dancing on the Sabbath. Legend has it that every day at noon they are compelled to dance once more. There are actually 16 stones, more if you include some smaller, toppled stones. Nine, however, is a magical number that appears linked to several other sites such the **Nine Maidens** stone row in Cornwall. Further south in the desolate heart of Dartmoor lies **Cranmere Pool** (50.6542, -3.9748; SX604856; 7km no paths at end). It was said to be a place of banishment,

where evil wrongdoers and unquiet spirits were sent to perform impossible tasks, such as emptying the pool with a leaky thimble. One man who was transformed into a black colt and forced into Cranmere Pool, was tasked to spin the sand at the bottom of the pool into ropes. 'Faithless wives and fickle maidens' were also compelled to make the long journey to Cranmere, which was the starting point for a cleansing ritual. After washing in the pool, they then had to tramp all the way back to **Scorhill Stone Circle** and run around it three times before passing through the **Teign Tolmen**. From there they made their way over to the **Grey Wethers** stone circles where they had to kneel before one of the stones and pray for forgiveness. If their crimes were too heinous to be forgiven then the stone would fall over and crush them!

Today, Cranmere Pool is little more than a small patch of boggy ground, but the bleak and treeless moorland surrounds lend it a strange, otherworldly atmosphere. Said to mark the geomantic centre of the dark and mysterious moors, its central location is significant because three of Dartmoor's greatest rivers have their source just near the pool. These are the East Dart, the Taw, and the West Okement, which flows directly from Cranmere Pool itself. One of the sources of the river Tavy also begins its journey nearby, so rivers from this one area lead to all four corners of the moor.

50.7186, -3.9671; SX612928; Trailhead: 50.7252, -3.9583; SX618935; 1.2km

HARTLAND

20 Hartland Point & Isle of Lundy

The high, rocky headland of Hartland Point thrusts out into the Atlantic at the northwestern edge of Devon. The point was known to the Romans as the 'Promontory of Hercules' and an old legend tells how the demi-god Hercules sailed from Gaul to Devon in a golden bowl. He fought and defeated Britain's native giants, led by Albion – a personification of the island of Britain.

The Isle of Lundy (51.1627, -4.6543; SS145437), 18km off the coast of Hartland Point, is well known for its unspoilt nature and tranquillity. In Welsh mythology Lundy was known as Ynys Wair, the island of Gwair. According to the Song of Taliesin, Gwair was held prisoner at Caer Sidi, a fairy fortress on Ynys Wair, but was freed from captivity by King Arthur.

51.0222, -4.5254; SS229277 (Hartland Point); Popular, Trailhead Parking: 51.0195, -4.5179; SS234274; 600m

21 St Nectan's Well, Stoke

Hidden away down a dark and watery, tree-lined alleyway in the village of Stoke, lies St Nectan's Well. Nectan was a 5th-century Celtic saint who left Wales intending to settle wherever his boat landed, eventually ending up on the Hartland peninsula. When two robbers stole his cows, he attempted to convert them to Christianity but they responded by cutting off his head. He then miraculously carried his severed head back to his hermitage in Stoke and wherever drops of his blood fell foxgloves grew. People were said to make an annual pilgrimage to the stone well-house on 17th June, the anniversary of his martyrdom, carrying foxgloves in his honour. The nearby church is said to mark the site of his hermitage and has been dedicated to St Nectan since at least Saxon times. The decapitation story could be a memory of the ancient Celtic 'cult of the head': severed heads were believed to possess magical powers and were venerated.

Welcombe is another village associated with St Nectan and the holy well there, enclosed within a medieval stone well-house beside a country lane, is also dedicated to him and known as **St Nectan's Well, Welcombe** (50.9376, -4.5226; SS228183). The saint is also said to have lived in a hermitage at **St Nectan's Glen** in Cornwall. The name Nectan is very similar to that of the Irish water god Nechtan, guardian of the well of wisdom.

Travelling south from Welcombe along ancient, narrow lanes you pass through the Marsland Valley Nature Reserve (50.9277, -4.5300; SS222172), which straddles the Cornish border. These lanes were said to be haunted by fairies and the vicar of Morwenstow recorded one of the tales. A man returning home one night saw lights and heard strange music coming from behind one of the roadside hedges. Peering through it, he saw an elf sitting on a toadstool carrying a lantern made from a harebell, from which poured forth a strange glow. Nearby, a group of fairies danced in a ring. He watched them for a while, and then out of malice or curiosity he picked up a large stone and threw it amongst them before mounting his horse and riding swiftly away. The next day he returned and found the stone lying exactly where he had thrown it, but the fairies had departed.

50.9944, -4.5147; SS236246

22 St Brannoc's Well, Braunton

St Brannoc originally hailed from Wales, but relocated to Braunton to found Braunton Church (51.1130, -4.1597; SS489370), which has been dedicated to St Brannoc since at least 854. St Brannoc originally tried to build his church on a hill overlooking Braunton, but the stones were moved by the Devil. Following this setback, the saint dreamed of a white sow and piglets and when he saw the animals at the foot of the hill he decided to build his church there. This story is commemorated in one of the stained-glass windows and also in a roof boss of the church, which features a sow feeding her litter.

St. Brannoc's Well is some distance from the church, tucked beside a small Catholic chapel in a little wooded dell. Constructed in the 20th century, this chapel occupies the site of a previous chapel dedicated to St Brannoc. The paved, circular pool is surrounded by lush vegetation and garden flowers, and is fed by a natural spring. Overlooking it is a small shrine dedicated to Our Lady of Lourdes.

51.1156, -4.1624; SS487373

23 Swincombe Rocks, Challacombe

Rising above Challacombe Common on Exmoor, the series of rocky outcrops called Swincombe Rocks have long been considered a pixie haunt and are known to locals as the Pixie Rocks, being long thought of as a haunt of pixies. From the moss and lichen-encrusted rocks there are views over the valley of the river Bray, while the moors above conceal numerous barrows.

51.1678, -3.8667; SS695426; Trailhead: 51.1586, -3.8714; SS692415; 1.3km; no paths at end

TIVERTON

24 Cadbury Castle & Dolbury Hill

Located either side of the River Exe, Cadbury Castle and Dolbury Hill are hillforts dating back to the Iron Age. They are reputed to be visited by a dragon who flies back and forth between the two, guarding the treasure buried in both hills. The hoards were so rich that:

"If Cadbury Castle and Dolbury Hill delven were All England might plough with a golden share"

Cadbury Castle sits in a beautiful elevated location reached by an ancient lane full of wild flowers. Like **Brent Tor** it is also a power spot on the Michael/Mary Ley Line. **Dolbury Hill** (50.7943, -3.4580; SS973004) is hidden within the woodlands of Killerton House (parking £: 50.7923, -3.4524; SS977001; £££ popular), a National Trust property open to the public.

50.8368, -3.5446; SS913052 (Cadbury Castle); Trailhead: 50.8319, -3.5427; SS914047; 700m

OTTERY ST MARY

25 Pixies' Parlour, Ottery St Mary

Around midsummer, the town of Ottery St Mary holds its annual Pixie Day festival. While this celebration only dates back to the mid-20th century, it commemorates the banishment of the town's troublesome pixies to a nearby cave known as the Pixies'

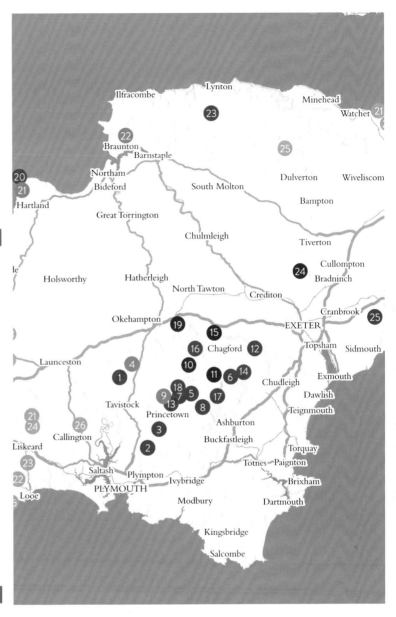

Parlour. Many hundreds of years ago a set of iron bells were to be installed in Ottery St Mary church. Hating both iron and the sound of church bells, the pixies knew this would spell the end of their presence in the area so they kidnapped the bell-ringers and imprisoned them within a sandstone cave. However, the men managed to escape and when the peal of bells at last rang out from the church the pixies were banished forever into the very same cave.

Pixie Day recreates this event with hordes of children in costume and a fake cave, but the real cave can be found south of town just above the river Otter. The entrance to the shallow cave features faces carved into the swirling rock, along with more modern carved graffiti.

50.7422, -3.2826; SY095944; Secret/ Secluded; Trailhead: 50.7490, -3.2852; SY094951; 900m

SOUTHWEST ENGLAND

There are certain magical places in the southwest of Britain that need no introduction. The enigmatic stone trilithons of Stonehenge were once thought to have been built by giants and transported by the wizard Merlin to their current site on Salisbury Plain, while Glastonbury Tor is forever entwined with Arthurian legend in its guise as the mystical Isle of Avalon. But there are many more places across the counties of Dorset, Somerset and Wiltshire which have their own lesser-known tales of magic. There are stories of otherworldly encounters with fairies, black dogs, dragons, pixies and mermaids; while holy wells and shrines speak of ancient rites that sometimes endure to this day.

The Southwest boasts both the largest and second largest stone circles in Britain (Avebury and Stanton Drew) and the highest artificial hill in Europe (Silbury Hill) which feature in the rich tapestry of folklore and legend from the region. Britain's largest chalk figure is also found here, the 'rude man' of Cerne Abbas in Dorset who is associated with fertility rites.

According to legend, the landscape of Somerset and Avon owes some of its distinctive features to the work of the giants Goram and Ghyston, including the vast Avon Gorge which was carved out in a contest to win the love of the river goddess. At Bath the goddess Sulis presided over the subterranean hot springs there for thousands of years. Cadbury Castle has long been heralded as the site of Camelot, and deep within the hill King Arthur and his court are said to lie sleeping. Glastonbury Tor is reputed to be a hollow hill ruled by the fairy king Gwyn ap Nudd and linked by the famous Michael/Mary ley line to other hilltop churches across southern England. Considered by many to be the spiritual heart of Britain, Glastonbury is home to a vibrant alternative community and attracts pilgrims from all over the world.

Dorset has a covering of Celtic hillforts including Britain's largest at Maiden Castle which is associated with fairies and giants, Badbury Rings with its links to King Arthur and Eggardon to the goddess Diana who leads the wild hunt.

Wiltshire is rightly famous for its complex prehistoric ritual landscapes that encompass the world heritage sites of Stonehenge and Avebury. Despite the abundance of tourists at these sites there is still a lingering sense of magic, particularly at the less-visited places such as Swallowhead Spring. Offerings of clootie ribbons adorn the trees here as well as at Avebury stone circle, a gesture repeated by countless people who have been drawn to explore these special places.

DORSET

1 Agglestone & Old Harry Rocks, Studland

Perched atop a heathery knoll on Studland Heath is an immense boulder known as the Agglestone, said to have been hurled there by a giant (or some say the Devil). Legend has it that the giant was sitting on the Needles, off the Isle of Wight, when he threw the boulder at Corfe Castle. However, his aim was poor and the boulder came to rest in its current hill-top position looking out towards Studland Bay. At Handfast Point on the eastern extremity of Studland Bay stand **Old Harry Rocks** (50.6426, -1.9230; SZ055825). These dramatic white structures are all that remains of an ancient chalk coastline that once joined Old Harry to the Needles. Here people once claimed to have seen a mermaid sunning herself on the rocks. Other geological marvels found along this stretch of coastline have given rise to fantastical tales of creation by larger-than-life supernatural forces.

50.6452, -1.9680; SZ023828 (Agglestone); Trailhead: 50.6455, -1.9548; SZ032828; 1.2km

2 Badbury Rings, Shapwick

The concentric circular earthworks of Badbury Rings are said to be haunted by a troop of ghostly warriors. The clashing of weapons has been heard on nights when King Arthur and his men ride in spectral cavalcade around the ramparts, while during the day Arthur may appear in the form of a raven as he watches over the hill. Tradition links this site to King Arthur's decisive battle against the invading Saxons at Mount Badon. Another legend claims a golden coffin is buried somewhere along the Roman road that connects this site to nearby Shapwick. Now crowned with a covering of mature trees, the hillfort was constructed during the Iron Age. By day Badbury Rings has the enchanted atmosphere of a woodland glade but by night it has a haunted feel.

Parking: 50.8272, -2.0582; ST959030

3 Blue Pool, Furzebrook

Surrounded by woodland and heath, the Blue Pool is a tranquil beauty spot with a sinister secret. Located on the Isle of Purbeck peninsula, the area is teeming with wildlife

including rare reptiles and amphibians, yet despite this it is said that nothing can live in the pool. Nothing that is, except for a tribe of dark fairies who, having promised eternal youth to those that bathe in the water, lure them into the murky depths to drown. The Blue Pool is now part of a private nature reserve which visitors can explore for a fee – but swimming is strictly forbidden.

50.6501, -2.0927; SY935833; £ Popular

4 Cerne Abbas Giant & St Augustine's Well *

Britain's largest chalk hill figure is found near the village of Cerne Abbas. Wielding a large club, the 'rude' man of Cerne Abbas is an archaic-looking naked man with a huge erect phallus. This imposing 55m giant is carved on a hillside, just below an ancient earth enclosure called the Trendle, where May Day celebrations traditionally took place. The giant was reputedly endowed with the power to grant fertility to child-less couples, providing they consummated their union upon his grassy erection. Young women wishing to be blessed with many children would spend a night sleeping within the giant's outline. Local legend also claims that a giant once terrorised the district until the villagers slew him as he slept on the hill then cut a chalk outline around his corpse. In the village of Cerne Abbas, **St Augustine's Well** (50.8110, -2.4752; ST666013) is tucked away in a leafy nook beside an old graveyard. The spring here is said to have appeared after the saint struck the ground with his staff and its waters have many magical properties including a reputation for curing infertility and to soothe sore eyes. Young women wishing to find a marriage partner would pray at the well while turning around three times while new born babies dipped in the water just as the sun's rays first touched their skin would be blessed with good luck. It was also said if you visited the well at dawn on Easter Day and gazed into the water, you would see images over your shoulder of all those fated to die that year. Today St Augustine's Well feels very peaceful and secluded, with many clootie ribbons and other offerings deposited by modern pilgrims. The water flows freely and the outflow from the well forms the local village pond, which is overgrown by reeds and home to many ducks. The Cerne Abbas giant is best viewed from a distance as walk-ing - and other activities - on the giant are discouraged in the interests of conservation.

50.8137, -2.4748; ST666016 (Cerne Abbas Giant); Parking: 50.8129, -2.4806, ST662015 (viewpoint)

5 Church Ope Cove, Portland

A mermaid was once washed up in Church Ope Cove, a small and secluded beach sheltered by verdant cliffs. She was found by parishioners who were heading to a service at St Andrew's, but she died shortly after being taken into the church. Today the scant ruins of St Andrew's church are hidden in woodland above the cove, while the pebbled beach and brightly coloured beach huts of Church Ope provide a tranquil respite from the bustling Isle of Portland.

50.5383, -2.4284; SY697710; Trailhead Parking: 50.5398, -2.4315; SY695712; 400m

6 Eggardon Hillfort, West Compton

The sound of baying hounds and the blast of a horn have been heard emanating from Eggardon Hillfort – a sure sign that the legendary wild hunt is close by. A farmer once saw a man running for his life through hedge and ditch, closely pursued by a pack of hounds. Following behind was a tall black figure striding with unnatural speed, sparks of fire flashing from his boots! Earlier legends say that it was Diana, the Roman goddess of the hunt, who led a host of fairies, demons and witches over the summit of the ancient hillfort. Standing on the bare hillside looking across the land, lashed by wind and rain, it's not hard to imagine a wild and elemental spirit world howling overhead.

50.7503, -2.6515; SY541947

7 Knowlton Henge

An abandoned medieval church sits in the centre of the ancient prehistoric earthwork known as Knowlton Henge, its well-preserved banks and ditches completely encircling the roofless building. Local legend states this is the seventh church on the site, the previous six having disappeared entirely. The presence of the church within the henge could be seen as an attempt to erase the ancient pagan power of the site. Yet with the church in ruins and yew trees at the edge of the henge covered in offerings of brightly coloured clootie ribbons, it would seem those efforts were none too successful.

50.8921, -1.9676; SU023102

8 Lewcombe Church & Castle Hill, East Chelborough

According to local legend, the old stone church at Lewcombe was originally to be sited at Castle Hill, but the fairies living there had other ideas. Building began at the foot of Castle Hill, however the next day the stones for the church were found a kilometre north at Lewcombe Manor. The villagers persevered, yet night after night the stones were relocated, until eventually they gave in and completed the building at Lewcombe. Today Lewcombe Church seems the more enchanted of the two locations, lying well off the beaten track in a peaceful glade surrounded by mature trees, alongside a babbling brook. **Castle Hill** (50.8464, -2.6384; ST551054) was named for the Norman motte and bailey which once stood there, although nothing but faint earthworks remain, so perhaps the fairy folk also objected to that intrusion into their territory.

50.8659, -2.6281; ST558075 (Lewcombe Church)

9 Maiden Castle, Dorchester

The massive fortifications at Maiden Castle are on such a huge scale that people once believed they were the work of giants. Covering 47 acres and surrounded by four massive banks and ditches, this is the largest hillfort in Britain. The Iron Age Celts constructed the huge earthworks, but aside from a later Romano-British temple, Maiden Castle has lain abandoned throughout subsequent centuries. However, strange lights have been reported hovering over the gateways and banks of the hillfort, and people say that fairies sometimes gather there for feasts. According to another tale, a secret tunnel leads from the southern flank of the hill to the centre of Dorchester, 3km away. Today the monumental size of Maiden Castle is still awe inspiring and it is a popular place to explore.

Parking: 50.6991, -2.4709; SY668889; Popular

10 Nine Stones, Winterbourne Abbas

Tucked away in a small enclosure yet located alongside the main road through Winterbourne Abbas, the Nine Stones manage to retain an air of otherworldly tranquillity. Folklore says that the stones were once children who were turned to stone for playing games on the Sabbath. Although the circle is small and not particularly showy, the sense of timelessness is palpable. These stones stood here long before the coming of the traffic which now rushes past, and perhaps they will endure long after the traffic has ceased to flow.

50.7122, -2.5527; SY610904; Trailhead: 50.7134, -2.5467; SY614905; 450m

11 Upwey Wishing Well

Located behind the Wishing Well Tearoom, the source of the river Wey gushes forth from underground aquifers to fill this magical, mossy, stone-lined well with attached water gardens. The water was reputed to have healing properties and it is said King George III came here looking for a cure. The traditional ritual for wish-making required visitors to take a few sips of well-water from a glass and then throw the remaining water back over their left shoulder. From here, the Wey flows strongly along the foot of a wooded hillside towards Weymouth.

50.6655, -2.4810; SY661852

AVON

12 Aquae Sulis, Bath *

Established in Roman times over an ancient Celtic shrine, the subterranean complex of sacred hot springs known as Aquae Sulis was dedicated to the goddess Sulis Minerva and the therapeutic qualities of the abundantly flowing, mineral-rich water have attracted bathers for over 2000 years. The original Roman foundations survive below 19th-century buildings that now house the Roman Bath Museum. The Romans equated the Celtic goddess Sulis with their goddess Minerva, building a temple and enclosing the

12

sacred spring at the heart of the bath-houses. The votive offerings to Sulis Minerva from within the sacred pool form the largest hoard ever found in Britain, and include numerous metal tablets inscribed with curses. The temple portico was carved with an enigmatic bearded male face with snakes in his hair. This Medusa-like figure continues to defy identification and adds mystery to this already sacred place. And before the Roman era, according to medieval legend, the fabled magician-king Bladud founded the baths after curing himself of leprosy by wallowing in the muddy spring with his pigs. Several statues of Bladud can be found today in Bath, the oldest of which stands in a niche overlooking the King's Bath within the museum complex. Although the Roman pools are considered unsafe for bathing, the sacred waters can still be experienced at the nearby Thermae Bath Spa (51.3804, -2.3616; ST749646; ££££££). The Roman Baths are one of the most visited heritage sites in the country, but walking through subterranean Roman tunnels filled with the sounds of the gushing, steaming water still creates a sense of awe and mystery.

51.3811, -2.3596; ST750647 (the Roman Baths); ££££ Very Popular

13 Avon Gorge, Bristol *

The river Avon flows towards the Bristol Channel through a vast gorge, said to have been carved out by a giant called Ghyston. At the point where the iconic Clifton suspension bridge passes overhead, the Avon Gorge is over 200m wide and sheer cliffs plunge 90m to the river below. According to legend, Ghyston undertook the immense task of creating the gorge to win the affections of Avona, goddess of the river Avon. He lived in a cave which emerges 30m below the cliff-top on the Clifton side of the gorge and for a small fee his dwelling place, the **Giant's Cave** £ (51.4567, -2.6266; ST565732), can be reached from inside the Clifton Observatory. Today the Avon Gorge is busy with traffic, but standing in Ghyston's Cave and gazing out over the gorge you can still imagine a time when titanic forces carved out this impressive landscape. At nearby Henbury a stream called the Hazel Brook runs through a heavily wooded gorge before joining the Avon. This smaller gorge was also said to be the work of a giant –

12

12

Ghyston's brother, Goram. He also wished to impress Avona but lacked the energetic fervour of his brother and fell asleep on his chair after digging only a narrow channel. The rock formation where he slept is known as **Goram's Chair** (51.5000, -2.6368; ST558780) and juts out over the valley, its two great ledges of stone resembling the arms of a great armchair. When Goram awoke and found his brother had won the contest, he stamped his foot with such force it left a huge footprint embedded in the ground and his **Giant's Footprint** (51.5024, -2.6344; ST560783) is still visible in an area of limestone pavement within the woods of the gorge. In his distress, Goram drowned himself in the Bristol Channel – his head and shoulder forming the islands of Steep Holm and Flat Holm.

Hazel Brook Gorge along with the Giant's Footprint, Goram's Chair and a pool called Giant's Soap Dish (51.5011, -2.6370; ST558782) all now form part of the Blaise Castle estate which is freely accessible to walkers.

51.4564, -2.6270; ST565732; Very Popular

SOMERSET

14 Cadbury Castle, South Cadbury *

The ancient hillfort known as Cadbury Castle is believed by many to be the site of King Arthur's legendary fortress of Camelot. Archaeology has confirmed that the Iron Age hillfort was reoccupied and the defences strengthened sometime during the 6th century when the historical Arthur was thought to have lived. All over the country, a traditional belief persists that Arthur never really died, but that he and his knights lie in a magical sleep only to awake and return at the hour of Britain's greatest need. Cadbury Castle is one such location, where the enchanted Arthur and his court are said to sleep in a hidden cavern beneath the hill. On midsummer, the gates to the cavern open briefly but only the pure of heart will be able to enter and

catch a glimpse of those within. On certain nights of the year Arthur and his warriors, mounted on silver-shod horses, are said to ride around the hill and down to the church at Sutton Montis (51.0214, -2.5370; ST624248) so the horses can drink from the nearby stream. There is also a belief locally that when the wild hunt rides, it is Arthur who leads it and on blustery winter nights Arthur and his hounds can be heard rushing along an invisible pathway known as Arthur's Hunting Track, which leads straight to **Glastonbury Tor**.

King Arthur's Well (51.0257, -2.5292; ST629252) is found among trees near the base of the hillfort. Here too, the horses belonging to Arthur and his knights were sometimes said to drink. The spring that fed the well has now run dry, but it was once an acclaimed wishing well. Often overlooked, the well can be identified by a semi-circular stone hood set into the bank. On the northwestern ramparts there is another wishing well known as Queen Anne's Well (51.0259, -2.5332; ST627253), its waters now flowing into a metal trough.

From here it was said you could hear activity at King Arthur's Well as the sound echoed through the hill's hidden chambers. Today the huge defensive banks and ditches of Cadbury Castle are shaded by trees and overlook acres of peaceful, rolling green fields. From the hilltop you can imagine a time when ancient warriors occupied this fort. People in South Cadbury have always believed their village was the location of Camelot and the legend of King Arthur and his court remain forever entwined with this land.

Parking: 51.0264, -2.5263; ST631253

15 Castle Neroche and the Blackdown Hills, Buckland St Mary

The Blackdown Hills were once described as one of the most fairy-haunted places in the country. Small in stature and wearing brightly coloured garb, the fairies would sometimes hold fairs, especially on the side of Blagdon Hill (50.9506, -3.1260; ST210174), where they had stalls selling shoes, trinkets, food and drink. When approached they would fade away, though it is said their presence could still be felt all around. One man who tried to push his way into the throng soon found himself in pain and was paralysed down one side. On the eastern edge of the Blackdown Hills, surrounded by enchanted woodland, lies an ancient fortress known as Castle Neroche featuring a Norman motte and an earlier Celtic hillfort. It stands on the summit of a hill said to be filled with fairy gold and although many have tried to dig for it, either the hole mysteriously fills in overnight or they die in unusual circumstances. The gold was also said to be guarded by a dragon who lived on the hill. Another legend claims that the Devil (or a giant) once stood on Castle Neroche and threw rocks at the builders of Staple Fitzpaine Church (50.9589, -3.0497; ST263182) but gave up once they had completed it. In another version of the tale the rocks were rolled down the hill from Castle Neroche, along the track now known as Green Lane. On seeing the finished church, however, the Devil abandoned the stones and one, which became known as the Devil's Stone (50.9561, -3.0462; ST266179), now lies completely hidden in a hedge. It was later said that it would bleed if pricked. Further west the linear alignment of round barrows known as **Robin Hood's Butts** (50.9087, -3.0882; ST235127) was said to have been created by giants, presumably standing at either end of the alignment of barrows, throwing huge clods of earth at each other that fell short. Three of the barrows are close together and sheltered by a copse of tall beech trees just east of the hamlet of Otterford, while the remainder are spread out in arable land to the south. The largest mound is said to hide a hoard of gold that cannot be retrieved as, like the treasure of Castle Neroche, anyone who digs will find the hole magically refilled overnight.

Parking: 50.9357, -3.0351; ST273156

he sat upon began to squirm. Taking up his axe, the woodcutter killed the dragon by cleaving it in half. A spring midway between Dowsborough and Shervage wood bears the curious name **Knacker's Hole** (51.1513, -3.2043; ST158398; 1km from Dowsborough; no paths at end). In Sussex 'knuckerholes' are deep pools of water where dragons live, 'knucker' being derived from an old English word which meant water monster. It is tempting to see a connection between Knacker's Hole and knuckerhole and speculate that this spring was the lair of the Gurt Wurm.

Below Dowsborough to the south, in a wooded valley known as Lady's Combe is another enchanted spot, the Lady's Fountain Spring (51.1405, -3.2035; ST159386).

51.1456, -3.2023; ST159391 (Dowsborough Hillfort); Trailhead: 51.1422, -3.1991; ST162388; 500m

16 Dowsborough Hillfort & Shervage Wood, Nether Stowey *

The whole area around Dowsborough feels enchanted and the crowds of gnarled oak trees stretching spindly branches towards the sky add greatly to the other-worldly atmosphere. These oaks shroud the earthworks of Dowsborough hillfort, constructed by Iron Age Celts on a large oval hill that now lies within an extensive area of woodland in the Quantock Hills. Locals call the hill Danesborough and claim a raiding party of invading Danes were slaughtered here centuries ago. However,

on wild autumn nights the sounds of these long-dead Viking warriors fighting, feasting and making merry can sometimes be heard around midnight, emanating from deep inside the hill. Dowsborough was once linked to the hillfort at Cannington Camp (51.1585, -3.0795; ST246404) via an ancient trackway and Odin with his wild hunt was said to ride through the sky on stormy nights between the two forts.

The woodland at Dowsborough continues north to become Shervage Wood, once home to a fearsome dragon known as the Gurt Wurm. This rotund dragon's girth was as wide as three great oak trees and it would eat half a dozen ponies and sheep in one sitting, before laying down to sleep. According to legend, a woodcutter stopping to rest was horrified when the huge 'log'

17 Glastonbury **

The small town of Glastonbury has long enticed seekers of spiritual enlighten-ment, religious pilgrims, and those simply looking for an alternative way of life. The distinctive hill of **Glastonbury Tor** (51.1448, -2.6987; ST512386; very popular) surmounted by its iconic church tower dominates the horizon for miles around, while the ruins of the once-powerful medieval abbey still stand in the heart of Glastonbury town. The whole area is extraordinarily rich in magic and myth and closely linked to Arthurian legend. There is

a widespread belief that Glastonbury is the magical Isle of Avalon where the wounded Arthur was taken after his final battle. When the mists of Avalon roll in to conceal the lowlands and the Tor rises above a blanket of white mist, Glastonbury does indeed resemble an island. In the past, the marshy Somerset levels were completely submerged by water, turning Glastonbury into a peninsula best accessed by boat. Standing proud on the summit of the Tor is the medieval tower – all that remains of a church once dedicated to Archangel Michael. Like **St Michael's Mount** in Cornwall and **Brent Tor** in Devon, Glastonbury Tor sits on the Michael ley line, which also passes through nearby **Burrow Mump** (51.0706, -2.9164; ST358305), a green hill remarkably similar to the Tor with its own ruined church dedicated to St Michael. It was the close proximity of the Tor and Burrow Mump that first alerted ley hunters to the existence of the now-famous Michael ley line. There is also a story that the river Parrett, which runs by Burrow Mump, was thought to separate the Land of the Pixies (to the west) from the Land of the Fairies (to the east). Legend tells us the Tor is a hollow hill, home to a magnificent fairy court ruled by Gywn ap Nudd, Lord of the Otherworld, who leads the wild hunt on wind-lashed nights. St Collen, who lived as a hermit at the foot of the Tor, denounced Gwyn and his people as demons, and twice refused an invitation to visit the fairy king. The third invitation he accepted, and although the palace of Gywn ap Nudd was indeed beautiful and splendid, the saint showered holy water over the assembled host. All at once the fairy palace disappeared and St Collen was left standing alone on the windswept hillside. An entrance to the fairy realm of

Gwyn Ap Nudd is said to be marked by the **Egg Stone** (51.1439, -2.6992; ST511385; secret/secluded). This smooth, vaguely ovoid boulder is often missed by visitors because it is located around the far side of the Tor away from any path. Local people and those in the know come here to hold ceremonies and attach offerings of brightly coloured clootie ribbons to nearby bushes. Other 'egg stones', which were thought to have magical significance, can be found dotted around the Tor, including one by the Abbot's Kitchen in the Abbey grounds. Rumours of secret tunnels that run from the Tor to the Abbey persist. The limestone cavern where the **White Spring** (51.1436, -2.7058; ST507384; popular) emerges at the foot of the Tor was once also thought to be an entrance to the underworld of Gwyn ap Nudd. It is concealed behind a Victorian water pumping station that has now been converted into a serene temple containing several pagan altars. The dark interior is lit by candles and the silence broken only by the sound of rushing water and murmurs of devotion. Pilgrims may bathe in the pools here and enjoy the space for quiet reflection. On the other side of Well House Lane, enclosed by high stone walls lie the tranquil **Chalice Well Gardens** (51.1436, -2.7064; ST506384; £ popular). The gardens are a living sanctuary, a designated World Peace Garden welcoming pilgrims of all faiths to experience the abundant waters of the Red Spring, its iron-rich waters venerated for their healing properties. Also called the Blood Spring on account of the water colour, the spot where the spring now emerges is said to be the place where Joseph of Arimathea buried the Holy Grail. The well-cover bears a design incorporating the Vesica Piscis –

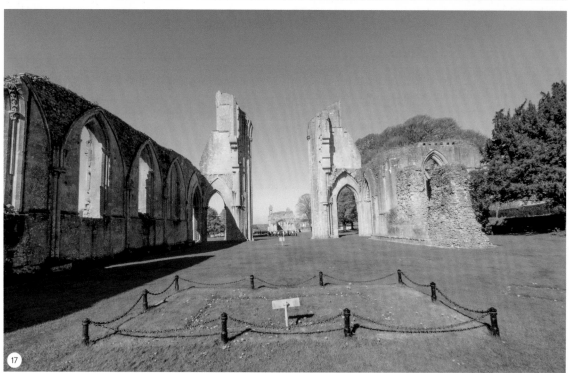

two interlocking circles bisected by a sword or spear and surrounded by foliage that represents the Holy Thorn. The waters of the Chalice Well and the White Spring both flow into Well House Lane where visitors bottle and drink them for their magical potency. The ruins of **Glastonbury Abbey** (51.1467, -2.7163; ST499388; $\mathcal{LL}$ popular) are set in peaceful parkland at the centre of town. Joseph of Arimathea is said to have founded his original 'wattle' church here, the first in Britain, making this a particularly holy destination for medieval pilgrims. Around the 12th century, the Glastonbury monks also claimed to have unearthed a hollowed oak-log coffin containing two skeletons. Alongside the bodies was a lead cross bearing an inscription in Latin declaring 'here lies buried the renowned King Arthur with Guinevere his second wife, in the Isle of Avalon.' The cross is long since lost, and it is likely the whole discovery was a hoax carried out by the monks who knew it would bring more pilgrims and therefore more money to the abbey. Nevertheless, it further cemented the link between Glastonbury and King Arthur. Even today the site of Arthur's tomb is marked out with stones in the grass within the abbey ruins.

Although Glastonbury is an important centre of early Christian history, it was a sacred place before Christianity and its modern pagan community continues to flourish. These beliefs manifest in many forms, but Glastonbury is a particular centre for the Goddess movement. Since 2002 there has been a permanent **Glastonbury Goddess Temple** (51.1473, -2.7174; ST499389) located just off the High Street, a dedicated space for prayer, meditation, celebration and worship. This lavishly decorated room changes with the seasons and is open to all who wish to pay their respects to the Goddess in all her myriad forms. Overlooking the abbey grounds a large Georgian house has been converted into a healing and educational venue called Goddess House (51.1461, -2.7180; ST498387) and the town is also host to the annual Goddess Conference. Followers of the Goddess movement believe that the sacred isle of Glastonbury is watched over by the Lady of Avalon.

Just to the southwest of Glastonbury town, Wearyall Hill (51.1418, -2.7256; ST493383) was once home to the Holy Thorn. This unusual hawthorn bloomed twice a year – once in spring and again at Christmas. Local legend claims the first tree took root and grew from a walking staff placed there by Joseph of Arimathea. Cuttings have been taken from this tree ever since, and although the Holy Thorn on Wearyall Hill has recently been destroyed many descendants of the original tree still grow elsewhere including in the abbey grounds, Chalice Well Gardens and St John's

churchyard. A sprig of the tree with flower buds has been sent to the reigning monarch at Christmas for the past 400 years.

Today Glastonbury is a vibrant melting pot where those with diverse spiritual, magical and continuously evolving religious beliefs converge. People from across the world are brought together at the numerous pagan and esoteric events, workshops, celebrations and rituals held throughout the year. The High Street is a bustling place of New Age crystal shops and pagan curiosities, yet peaceful places of contemplation and respite such as the Abbey or Chalice Well Gardens can still be found. By climbing the footpath up the Tor you are following in the footsteps of the countless pilgrims who have long been drawn to this most magical of places.

Parking: 51.1465, -2.7172; ST499388; Very Popular

18 Goblin Combe, Cleeve

Hidden in the wooded limestone gorge known as Goblin Combe, a secret rock acts as a portal to the land of Faerie. According to local legend, when a little girl got lost in the Combe while gathering primroses and accidentally dropped her posy of thirteen flowers onto the rock, she unwittingly opened the portal. The fairies emerged and seeing the little girl's tears, gave her a golden ball in return for the primroses and led her safely back home. Later a greedy man, thinking he too should have some fairy treasure, threw his own posy of flowers at the rock. However, this time the fairies were angered and spirited him away, and neither he nor the portal were ever seen again. Goblin Combe is now a nature reserve where wildflowers grow among

strangely twisted trees and ancient yews. The name 'Goblin Combe' seems to affirm the belief that this narrow, wooded valley is occupied by supernatural beings.

51.3836, -2.7586; ST473652; Trailhead: 51.3846, -2.7786; ST459653; 1.5km

19 St Agnes' Well 'The Pixie Well', Cothelstone

Once described as the most beautiful of the Holy wells in Somerset, St Agnes' Well was visited for healing and divination. Sitting at the edge of a field by Colthelstone Manor, the medieval stone well-house has a small gothic door under which the spring water flows. It is channelled through a cobbled area into a small oval pool then away through the trees and into the nearby stream. The pixies were said to live here, in the woods and in the well itself, which does indeed look like a little pixie house. Fear of the mischievous pixies kept many people away, but young women sometimes came to the well hoping to divine

the identity of their future husband. As patron saint of engaged couples, St Agnes was thought to look favourably on single girls who would visit the well on St Agnes' Eve (January 20th) and gaze into the water to catch a glimpse of their intended. The waters were also beneficial for healing sprains and sore eyes, and aiding fertility, in exchange for an offering of pins to placate the pixies. St Agnes' Well has undergone a dedicated restoration project and the thoughtful addition of a small cobbled pool and low stone seat make it even more appealing to modern-day romantics who still make their wishes in the magical flowing water.

51.0803, -3.1665; ST183318; Secret/Secluded

20 St Aldhelm's Well, Doulting

Emerging from a bank in a peaceful woodland copse, the water of St Aldhelm's Well, said never to stop flowing even in times of drought, is renowned for its healing properties. It flows out through two small arches set into a wall, along a wide stone channel, then through another wall and into a stone trough in the lane below. During the medieval period, the stone channel between the two walls may have had a roof, creating an enclosed bathing pool. The well and nearby church are dedicated to Aldhelm

who was canonised in the 8th century and it is said the saint himself took the healing waters and would sit there reciting psalms. The well, which is surrounded by ferns and ivy with wild garlic scenting the air in springtime, is still visited by local people who take the waters and sometimes leaving offerings of flowers and candles.

51.1873, -2.5099; ST644432

21 St Audrie's Bay, West Quantoxhead

Facing the Bristol Channel at the foot of the Quantock Hills, St Audrie's Bay was once a favourite haunt of mermaids as well as a terrible dragon. The wide bay features great swathes of rock interspersed with shingle and sand, while at the western side a natural waterfall plunges over the rocky cliffs. It was at the base of this waterfall, where the rocks are bright green with algae, that a fisherman once found a baby. This child of a Sea Morgan, the local name for a mermaid, had been left behind by accident when her mother swam out to sea. She looked like a human child and was raised as one after being adopted by the fisherman and his wife, yet her hair always remained slightly damp. Eventually, she returned to the sea after hearing the eerie call of her people from the waves.

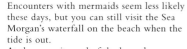

Encounters with mermaids seem less likely these days, but you can still visit the Sea Morgan's waterfall on the beach when the tide is out.

At the opposite end of the bay a long stretch of scaly-looking, cracked, blue-grey rock is said to be the petrified remains of Blue Ben, a ferocious fire-breathing dragon. The beast had gone to cool himself in the waters of the bay, but was so heavy after a feast that he was unable to rise again from the muddy shore and drowned as the tide came back in. **Blue Ben** (51.1874, -3.2634; ST118438; low tide only) marks an exposed layer of fossil-rich Jurassic Blue Lias stone, which viewed from above does appear dragon-like in shape – a clear case of landscape inspiring legend.

51.1805, -3.2802; ST106431 (waterfall); Low Tide Only Trailhead Parking £: 51.1785, -3.2817; ST105429; 200m

22 Stanton Drew Stone Circles & Maes Knoll *

The three stone circles at Stanton Drew form one of the largest complexes of standing stones in Britain. The Great Circle, second largest in Britain after **Avebury**, is flanked by a slightly smaller stone circle to the northeast, while a much smaller stone

circle (51.3653, -2.5772; ST599630) can be found in a secluded location in a field to the southwest. A long-standing local legend tells of a wedding held one Saturday when the guests danced long into the night to the frantic fiddling of a strange musician. Too late they realised this was actually the Devil in disguise, who kept them circling faster and faster into the early hours of Sunday morning until the sun rose and all were turned to stone. The stones of Stanton Drew were supposed to be uncountable, and anyone who tried to count or sketch them would be struck dead on the spot or sicken and die soon after. It was said on the sixth day after a full moon the stones moved down to the river to take a drink. Nearby, a trio of stones called T**he Cove** (51.3655, -2.5796; ST597630) stands in the garden of the Druid's Arms pub. Shaded by trees, these stones are said to be the bride, groom and parson from the unfortunate wedding party. Just on the other side of the river Chew, another stone is known as Hautville's Quoit (51.3720, -2.5736; ST601638). It was said to have been thrown from Maes Knoll by a giant called Hakewell, who possessed superhuman strength. Unfortunately, most of the stone has been chipped away and it is no longer visible.

North of Stanton Drew, **Maes Knoll** (51.3925, -2.5750; ST600660) is a roughly triangular, steep-sided hill with spectacular, far-reaching vistas from its flat-topped summit. The remains of an Iron Age hillfort

crown the hill, and a large mound on the summit known as the Tump was said to have been created by the giant Gorm (or perhaps Goram, see **Avon Gorge**). He was wandering around with a shovelful of dirt, but having forgotten what it was for he dumped it on the ground, thus forming Maes Knoll Tump. Extending from Maes Knoll are the visible remains of a long defensive earthwork called the Wansdyke, a great feat of Dark Age engineering that runs for many miles through Wiltshire and into Somerset. Named Woden's Dyke by the Anglo-Saxons, it was supposedly created by the devil in a single day.

The stones of Stanton Drew stand on the edge of the village in a grassy field, starred with buttercups in the summer and occasionally surrounded by grazing livestock. They remain somewhat mysterious – the site having never been properly excavated and often overlooked by visitors in favour of **Stonehenge** and **Avebury**. Yet the wealth of legends and close vicinity to Maes Knoll and other magical sites make for a fascinating day of exploration.

51.3675, -2.5754; ST600633 (Stanton Drew Stone Circles); Trailhead Parking at Druid's Arms Pub: 51.3653, -2.5795; ST597630; 600m

and two cairns on the summit. In the story, a thick mist rolled in from the sea causing the farmer to lose his way on the hill. While stumbling around he suddenly felt the furry back of a large dog beneath his hand. Thinking it was his own sheepdog come to lead him home, the farmer followed and was indeed guided safely back to his own cottage. However, just as he realised his own dog was still indoors, he witnessed a most terrifying sight – the strange black dog appeared to grow larger and larger, before suddenly fading away into the mist! The Quantocks were known for frequent encounters with a black dog who locals called the 'Gurt Dog'. Elsewhere a run-in with a spectral black dog often foretold death, but in this instance the dog was strangely helpful. Weacombe lies towards the northern end of the Quantocks, not far from **St Audrie's Bay**.

51.1531, -3.2481; ST128400; Trailhead: 51.1489, -3.2724; ST110396; 2km

25 **Winsford Hill Wambarrows, Withypool**

Found within the great expanse of Exmoor, Winsford Hill is topped with three Bronze Age barrows known as the Wambarrows. Legend says these barrows contain treasure that is guarded by a spectral black dog. Travellers on the hill must stand absolutely still if they encounter the apparition, and remain so while it gradually disappears and only its glowing, saucer-like eyes remain visible. If the witness moves during this unsettling display they will be struck down dead. The Wambarrows are also said to be home to a family of pixies who relocated to Winsford Hill after church bells were installed at Withypool Church. The pixie family, who originally lived in Brightworthy Barrows (51.1030, -3.6905; SS817351) to the west, were on friendly terms with the owner of Knighton Farm. The pixie father asked to borrow a cart and ponies so he could move his "good wife and littlings out of the noise of they ding-dongs". The farmer obliged and once the pixies had moved, the ponies were sent back looking as sleek and beautiful as animals half their age. It is perhaps these same pixies who liked to sit at **Comer's Gate** (51.1064, -3.6289; SS860353), the main access point to Winsford Hill and alarm passers-by. On the northeastern side of Winsford Hill a large hollow known as the Punchbowl (51.0987, -3.5975; SS882344) was created when a giant scooped up a great quantity of rock and soil. This was hurled some 7km north to form **Dunkery Beacon** (51.1627,

23 **Stoney Littleton Long Barrow**

Set amid remote farmland on a hill overlooking the Wellow Brook, Stoney Littleton long barrow has long been considered a fairy haunt. The stone-clad entrance to this impressive Neolithic barrow leads into a long passage that is flooded with light at the Winter Solstice sunrise. At the end of the passageway are several small chambers. In folklore, barrows and burial mounds were often associated with the fairy folk, and Stoney Littleton was one of Somerset's 'Fairy Toots', where they were said to live. Reaching the barrow involves traversing narrow

lanes and grassy fields, but once inside the dark interior the serene silence is all-enveloping. Before leaving, look for the impression of a fossil ammonite on the left-hand door jamb – a decorative flourish connecting us to the ancient barrow builder who placed this stone here thousands of years ago.

51.3134, -2.3817; ST734572; Trailhead Parking: 51.3103, -2.3828; ST734568; 600m

24 **Weacombe Hill, Bicknoller**

Patches of heather and windswept trees dot the slopes of Weacombe Hill, where a farmer once had an eerie encounter with a black dog. It has three small round barrows

-3.5864; SS891415. Trailhead parking: 51.1541, -3.5804; SS895406; 1.1km). This hill is the highest point on Exmoor, littered with prehistoric remains and topped with a large stone cairn. The heathland around Dunkery Beacon and Winsford Hill is blanketed with heather and home to an abundance of wildlife.

In an enchanted woodland valley just below Winsford Hill are the **Tarr Steps** (51.0772, -3.6177; SS867321), one of the most ancient clapper bridges in the country and still used to cross a wide shallow section of the river Barle. Constructed from rough megalithic blocks, the bridge was said to have been created in a single night by a giant (or the Devil) to win a wager against another giant in a show of power.

51.0970, -3.6064; SS876343; Trailhead Parking: 51.0958, -3.6031; SS878341; 200m

26 **Worlebury Hill, Weston-super-Mare**

The thick, wild woodland of Worlebury Hill contrasts sharply with the busy streets of Weston-super-Mare below. Stepping into the fairy-haunted woods is like stepping

into an enchanted world, with its mysterious heaps of stones and fairy dew ponds. An overgrown Iron Age hillfort surmounts the summit, with ramparts uniquely constructed of immense piles of stones. Many hollows in the earth are known locally as fairy dew ponds, though archaeologists claim they are simply ancient storage pits. A stone cairn near the middle of the summit was known as Pickwinna's Mound (51.3584 -2.9766; ST321626; no longer visible). Traditionally fishermen from the area would pass by the mound each day and add

another stone to the heap, saying as they did so, "Peek weena, send me a deesh of feesh for my deener." The identity of Pickwinna remains mysterious but he may have been a hob-like spirit (see **Obtrusch Roque**).
In a cave at the base of the hill, at Spring Cove (51.3573, -2.9943; ST308624), a 'dipping well' was revered for the healing powers of its waters. In return for the fresh, sweet water of the well the old fishermen would always throw back the first portion of their day's catch. A landslide has since cut off access to the cave, but a secret tunnel was said to run from the cave up through Worlebury Hill to the hillfort. Little remains of the cave at Spring Cove save a small opening just big enough to wriggle into, but the sweet spring water is said to still drip from the cliff walls. From Spring Cove, the islands of Steep Holm and Flat Holm are clearly visible in the Bristol Channel. They were said to have been formed from the body of the giant Goram (see **Avon Gorge**).

51.3577, -2.9843; ST315625 (Hillfort entrance); Trailhead: 51.3563, -2.9901; ST311623; 600M

27 Adam's Grave & The Wansdyke, Alton Priors

Sited on a prominent hilltop position overlooking the Vale of Pewsey, the large Neolithic long barrow known as Adam's Grave is said to be the resting place of a giant, and at 65m long, it is certainly large enough to contain one. The giant's ghost is said to be seen on occasion and can be raised if someone runs around the barrow seven times. The Anglo-Saxons called this place Woden's Barrow and it lies close to a section of the Wansdyke, 'Woden's Dyke' (51.3826, -1.8325; SU117648) a vast defensive earthwork said to have been dug by the god Woden in a single night, which runs all the way to **Maes Knoll** in Somerset.

51.3696, -1.8401; SU112634 (Adam's Grave); Trailhead Parking: 51.3732, -1.8350; SU115638; 900m

(28)

28 Avebury **

Situated at the centre of a complex ritual landscape, the village of Avebury contains the world's largest stone circle. The large, pale-grey standing stones form a vast outer ring surrounded by a ditch and this huge henge surrounds the entire circle of stones as well as two inner circles. Uniquely, a village complete with manor house, pub and church, has grown up within and around the stones of Avebury. Pious villagers in later centuries were uneasy about this close proximity to a pagan temple and toppled many stones into pits where they remain buried, while others were broken up and incorporated into the walls of cottages. Thankfully enough of the stones survive to give us an impression of the former grandeur of this site. The lichen-encrusted stones shine brightly in the sunlight, vast and ancient, yet surprisingly little folklore

exists about Avebury itself. The Diamond Stone (51.4299, -1.8552; SU101701) in the outer ring is said to cross the road when the clock strikes midnight, while the stone known as **Devil's Chair** (51.4272, -1.8533; SU102698) possibly served a ritual purpose as it features a hollow where you can sit under a natural funnel that traps rain. Witnesses have reported strange lights and heard music emanating from the stone circles, and small figures have been seen flitting about on moonlit nights. A stand of beech trees (51.4292, -1.8510; SU104700) on the outer bank of the henge has distinctive roots that form an entrancing criss-crossing pattern upon the ground. These trees have become something of a shrine and are hung with clootie ribbons and other offerings.
Heading southeast from Avebury, pairs of standing stones mark the West Kennet Avenue (51.4237, -1.8489; SU106694) which takes a slightly meandering course towards the Sanctuary (51.4111, -1.8314; SU118680), a stone circle at West Kennet that was destroyed in the 18th century. Although many of the West Kennet avenue stones

(28)

have been lost, enough remain to give an impression of the broad processional pathway snaking through the landscape. Locals claim the stones have grown in height over time, and it is thought that the cylindrical stones represent men while the triangular ones are women. The B4003 more or less follows the course of the avenue, sometimes one crosses the other, but the avenue is best appreciated by walking along it in the footsteps of the ancestors. A second avenue ran southwest from Avebury towards Beckhampton and has all but disappeared except for two remaining

stones known as the Adam and Eve Stones (51.4227, -1.8735; SU088693).

A most mysterious feature of the Avebury prehistoric landscape is **Silbury Hill** (51.4158, -1.8575; SU100685). Whatever purpose it originally served remains an enigma, but at 40m high it is the largest artificial mound in Europe and would have taken an immense effort to construct. The neat, conical hill was made largely from chalk and would have shone brightly against the surrounding grassland, visible for miles. There are tales of great thunderstorms that arise when any excavations are attempted, and although several have taken place over the centuries, Silbury Hill has held on to its secrets. Legend claims it is the resting place of King Sil, who was buried in the centre of the hill, wearing golden armour and sitting upright on his horse. On moonlit nights King Sil's phantom is said to emerge from the hill and ride around the mound. Other sources maintain the mound was formed when the Devil dropped a sackful of dirt. Until the 19th century, Silbury Hill was a gathering place for local families, who came every Palm Sunday to picnic on fig cakes and sugared water on the summit. Today the hill is surrounded by a fence to prevent erosion caused by excessive footfall.

On a hill opposite Silbury, a row of massive irregular monoliths marks the entrance to **West Kennet Long Barrow** (51.4086, -1.8508; SU104677. Trailhead parking: 51.4142, -1.8525; SU103683; 700m) behind which a dark passage leads to five stone-lined chambers. One of the largest Neolithic barrows in Britain, it is unusual in that you can enter standing upright, rather than having to crouch and crawl. From the top of the barrow the views encompass Silbury Hill and many other sacred sites in the surrounding landscape. Legend tells the barrow is home to an otherworldly white dog, whose blood-red ears attest to its fairy heritage. The dog is said to follow the figure of a man into the barrow at dawn on midsummer.

Halfway between Silbury Hill and West Kennet long barrow, in a hollow at the foot of the hill lies **Swallowhead Spring** (51.4115, -1.8563; SU100680; private land; secret/secluded; no paths). There are stepping stones across the river Kennet to reach it and willow trees bend low as if in supplication, creating portal-like archways. Country folk once regarded the herbs growing there to be particularly potent for healing, but today the spring is often overlooked by people visiting its more popular neighbours. Those who do make the small detour to Swallowhead Spring will see clootie ribbons adorning the tree branches, lending this magical place a sense of sanctity. Both the spring and the river run dry in high summer.

The Michael and Mary ley lines converge at Avebury, which lies at the centre-point of the line as it crosses southern England from Cornwall to the Norfolk coast. These lines of earth energy take a meandering, serpentine route that connects all of the magical places around Avebury including Windmill Hill (51.4416, -1.8763; SU086714) to the north. Along with West Kennet Long Barrow, Windmill Hill marks the earliest development at Avebury with a Neolithic settlement overlain with Bronze Age round barrows. Fairies were said to inhabit **Hackpen Hill** (51.4713, -1.8157; SU128747), which sits on a ridge of hills to the northeast of Avebury. The ancient Neolithic trackway known as the Ridgeway crosses the hill and its flank displays a white horse, cut into the chalk in the 19th century. Hackpen Hill overlooks the sacred landscape of Avebury, and mysterious crop circles are often seen etched into the fields around there. Fairies have been encountered upon the hill in the twilight or within the thick mists that sometimes envelop it. One man heard ethereal fairy music and was led to strange places within the fairy hill, while another, enticed into a fairy dance, went all the way to Devizes. The Avebury sacred landscape is a world heritage site and popular with visitors all year round. Yet despite the crowds within the central henge, Avebury retains a special atmosphere. The ancient stones, tracks and barrows embedded in the landscape together create a network of magic that co-exists but transcends the mundanity of the modern world.

Parking: 51.4254, -1.8579; SU099696; ££ no parking inside village. Very Popular

29 Cley Hill, Warminster

The distinctive outline of Cley Hill is topped by an enigmatic burial mound that has been the scene of many strange and magical happenings. According to local legend, Cley Hill was formed from earth dumped by a giant (or the Devil) who was on his way to Devizes. A stone up on the hill is said to display the Devil's face on its underside and will put a curse on anyone who looks upon it. On Palm Sunday locals would gather on the hill for a ritual burning of the grass to 'burn the Devil out' – an event with a fair-like atmosphere and featuring riotous games.

In recent decades the hill has become known as a UFO hotspot after reports of strange lights in the sky and the appearance of crop circles in the surrounding fields. It was previously said to be the home of the king of the Wiltshire fairies and also the guardian spirit

of Bugley, who lived in one of the barrows. This guardian directed the folk of Bugley to a spring that emerges at Hog's Well (51.2002, -2.2180; ST848445; private land) where the water could be used for eye ailments when mixed with ground ivy. However he also warned that the water was not for drinking, and an old woman died after disregarding his advice. The small car park at the base of Cley Hill gives access to a steep track leading up to the windswept summit with its strange, otherworldly atmosphere.

In the nearby village of Temple, which was reputedly founded by the Knight's Templar, can be found the Temple Yew (51.2023, -2.2504; ST826448; private land), a huge ancient tree growing in a garden just beside the road.

Trailhead Parking: 51.1976, -2.2337; ST837442

30 Stonehenge, Amesbury *

Standing isolated on Salisbury Plain, the huge megalithic blocks of Stonehenge have awed onlookers for millennia and are testament to human ingenuity as well as an enduring mystery. What we see today consists of a circular ditch and bank enclosing a circle of huge trilithons made from local sarsen stone and an inner circle of smaller bluestones. Within this is are five more

(30)

(30)

trilithons set out in a horseshoe shape and a further formation of bluestones set out in similar fashion. The open end of the horseshoe faces an outlying standing stone known as the Heel Stone, which aligns with the midsummer sunrise. The henge itself is set within a vast ritual landscape containing ceremonial avenues, a long enclosure known as the Cursus, Neolithic long barrows and hundreds of Bronze Age burial mounds. The reasons why, and indeed how, this fabled solar temple was built are lost in the mists of time, though there is no shortage of theories.

Early modern antiquarians attributed the construction of Stonehenge to the Druids, an association which has endured to this day. However, in medieval times Stonehenge was known as the Giant's Dance, and it was believed that in the distant past the stones were brought to Ireland from Africa by giants. Merlin then magically transported the stones from Ireland and placed them in their present location.

It has now been proved that the magically potent bluestones had originally been quarried and erected in the Preseli Hills of west Wales before being moved overland to Salisbury Plain (see **Pentre Ifan**). Each individual bluestone in the Stonehenge monument was said to cure a particular ailment. Water was poured over the required stone and herbs added, before the sufferer was bathed in the healing water. Even in the 18th century, scrapings from the stones, mixed with water, were believed to heal the sick and wounded.

Many ley lines are said to pass through Stonehenge with one connecting it to **Old Sarum** (51.0931, -1.8047; SU137326; £) and Salisbury Cathedral to the south. The huge earthworks of Old Sarum, an Iron Age hillfort and later a Norman castle, once housed the original Salisbury Cathedral. The cathedral was relocated and a new site chosen by means of an archer firing an arrow from the ramparts. The arrow's flight follows the ley line from Stonehenge and the place where it landed marked the spot where the new cathedral should be built. It was once possible to walk freely amongst the stones, but today the inner circles are opened up only for the solstices and equinoxes, and for private ceremonies when modern-day Druids and other spiritual seekers still perform rituals. From the path that circles the stones at a short distance, you peer up at the grey trilithons that tower overhead, impossibly ancient and timeless. A public footpath also passes near the stones from where they can be viewed for free.

51.1789, -1.8262, SU122421; ££££ Very Popular; Stonehenge Visitor Centre Parking: 51.1843, -1.8583; SU100427

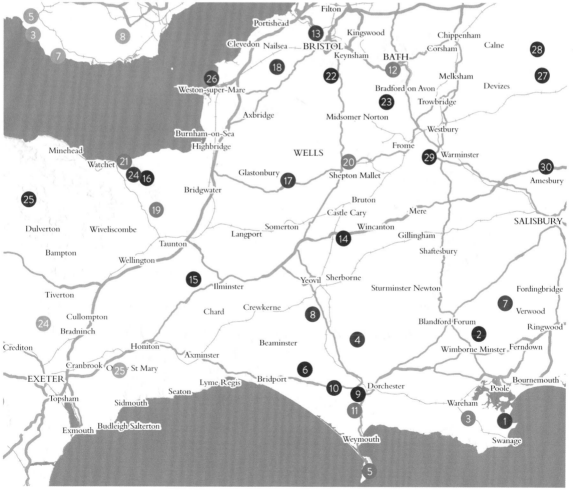

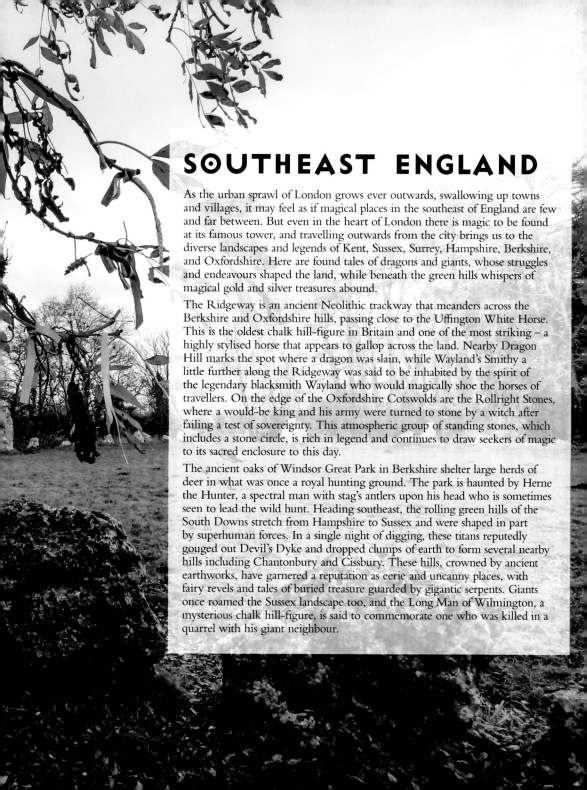

SOUTHEAST ENGLAND

As the urban sprawl of London grows ever outwards, swallowing up towns and villages, it may feel as if magical places in the southeast of England are few and far between. But even in the heart of London there is magic to be found at its famous tower, and travelling outwards from the city brings us to the diverse landscapes and legends of Kent, Sussex, Surrey, Hampshire, Berkshire, and Oxfordshire. Here are found tales of dragons and giants, whose struggles and endeavours shaped the land, while beneath the green hills whispers of magical gold and silver treasures abound.

The Ridgeway is an ancient Neolithic trackway that meanders across the Berkshire and Oxfordshire hills, passing close to the Uffington White Horse. This is the oldest chalk hill-figure in Britain and one of the most striking – a highly stylised horse that appears to gallop across the land. Nearby Dragon Hill marks the spot where a dragon was slain, while Wayland's Smithy a little further along the Ridgeway was said to be inhabited by the spirit of the legendary blacksmith Wayland who would magically shoe the horses of travellers. On the edge of the Oxfordshire Cotswolds are the Rollright Stones, where a would-be king and his army were turned to stone by a witch after failing a test of sovereignty. This atmospheric group of standing stones, which includes a stone circle, is rich in legend and continues to draw seekers of magic to its sacred enclosure to this day.

The ancient oaks of Windsor Great Park in Berkshire shelter large herds of deer in what was once a royal hunting ground. The park is haunted by Herne the Hunter, a spectral man with stag's antlers upon his head who is sometimes seen to lead the wild hunt. Heading southeast, the rolling green hills of the South Downs stretch from Hampshire to Sussex and were shaped in part by superhuman forces. In a single night of digging, these titans reputedly gouged out Devil's Dyke and dropped clumps of earth to form several nearby hills including Chantonbury and Cissbury. These hills, crowned by ancient earthworks, have garnered a reputation as eerie and uncanny places, with fairy revels and tales of buried treasure guarded by gigantic serpents. Giants once roamed the Sussex landscape too, and the Long Man of Wilmington, a mysterious chalk hill-figure, is said to commemorate one who was killed in a quarrel with his giant neighbour.

1

1

2

1 Cold Pixies Barrow & The New Forest, Beaulieu

At the edge of the New Forest lies Cold Pixies Barrow, an ancient burial mound associated with Puck, the fairy trickster made famous by Shakespeare. The round barrow, now overgrown with gorse and heather, is visible in heathland adjacent to the Beaulieu road. Also known as Cold Pixies Cave, the curious name is thought to be derived from 'Colt-Pixie', a type of fairy-horse which delighted in leading the New Forest ponies astray and was one of Puck's favourite disguises. Earlier writers record the numerous Puck and pixie names that appear in the area including Puck's Hill and Pixey Mead, while 'ragged as a colt-pixey' is a common local saying.

This ancient royal hunting ground was named 'New Forest' by the Normans almost a thousand years ago. It covers an extensive area of heath and ancient woodland that is particularly magical in late spring when bluebells flourish in an entrancing haze between the venerable old trees. In the northern reaches of the New Forest, modern-day fairies feature at **Furzey Gardens** ££ (50.9021, -1.6131; SU273114) where fairy doors are set into trees, while rustic wooden and thatched structures give the garden a whimsical, magical appearance. 50.8133, -1.5046; SU349016

2 Godshill

The medieval church at Godshill was reputedly constructed on its current hilltop position after the intervention of unseen forces. Its original site was a flat meadow in the village below, but overnight the foundation stones were relocated to the top of the hill. Some blamed the fairies, whose dancing grounds were in the meadow but guards set to watch over the building site were startled when a loud rumbling began deep underground and the stones bounced and rolled uphill, before rearranging themselves perfectly at the top. Declared a miracle by the local bishop, the church was completed on this new site and the area renamed Godshill. The church still stands on its grassy mound, overlooking the thatched cottages of the village. 50.6337, -1.2559; SZ527818 (church)

3 The Longstone, Mottistone

Found at the edge of Mottistone Common and standing over 4m tall and 2m wide, the Longstone is a remnant of a Neolithic long barrow. Legend, however, claims the Longstone and the smaller recumbent stone alongside it were hurled there in a contest between a giant (or some say the Devil) and a local saint. Indeed, the Isle of Wight itself was said to have been created by a large clod of earth that fell off the Devil's cloven hoof after he dug **Devil's Dyke**. The Longstone was also a reputed meeting place for ancient Druids and the name Mottistone could be a corruption of 'moot stone' – moot being the Saxon word for meeting place. There are very few prehistoric monuments surviving on the Isle of Wight but the Longstone is the most impressive, not only for its size, but for the presence it commands in the landscape.

50.6562, -1.4253; SZ407842; Popular;
Trailhead Parking: 50.6520, -1.4185;
SZ412837; 1km

WEST SUSSEX

4 Chanctonbury Ring, Washington

An eerie atmosphere pervades Chanctonbury Ring, an ancient hillfort in West Sussex now overgrown with beech trees. Numerous barrows and a Roman temple once occupied the hill, which is believed to have been a centre of ritual activity rather than a defensible settlement. The trees are said to be uncountable, growing together in a circular copse that obscures the earthworks and plunges the summit into a shadowy silence. The sound of horses' hoof beats can sometimes be heard there, although no horses are seen, while the ghost of an old man with a long white beard haunts the hilltop, endlessly searching for buried treasure. According to folklore if you run around the hill backwards seven times on Midsummer's Eve you will summon the Devil, who will offer you a bowl of soup. There are several variations on this tale but it could suggest a corrupted folk memory of ancient pagan rituals once performed on the hilltop. Another tradition claims Chanctonbury Hill was formed after a lump of earth dropped from the spade as the Devil dug **Devil's Dyke**. A prehistoric trackway traverses the hill that today forms part of the South Downs Way, making Chanctonbury Ring, a destination for walk-

cast-off clod of earth from the digging of **Devil's Dyke**. Today the well-preserved earthworks are grazed by horses, with only a few trees standing stark against the sky. North west of Cissbury Hill the earthworks of a small hillfort sit atop Harrow Hill (50.8793, -0.4640; TQ081099. Trailhead: 50.8641, -0.4629; TQ082083; 2km). Here too are depressions in the ground left behind by Neolithic flint mining. Locals believed Harrow Hill to be the last home of the fairy folk in England.

50.8603, -0.3833; TQ138079; Popular, Trailhead Parking: 50.8576, -0.3971; TQ129076; 1km

6 Devil's Dyke, Poynings

A steep-sided cleft running through the South Downs is known as Devil's Dyke, and was said to have been created by supernatural forces. The Devil, enraged that the local villagers were converting to Christianity and building churches, vowed to drown them all by digging a huge channel through the hills to the sea in a single night. As he worked, great clods of earth dropped from his spade to form the nearby hills of **Chanctonbury Ring**, **Cissbury Ring** and **Mount Caburn**, while a large boulder was hurled towards Hove. However, when an old woman reflected the light of a candle and made a cock crow, he was tricked into thinking it was dawn and abandoned his task. It is likely that in the original version of this story it was a giant, rather than the Devil, who created this landscape feature, as he is said to be buried in a mound at the foot of the dyke valley, alongside his giantess wife. Devil's Dyke has been a popular day-trip destination since Victorian times and walkers still like to explore the valley and rolling green hills. As for the boulder thrown by the Devil, it is now known as the Goldstone (50.8395, -0.1738; TQ286060) and stands in a fenced-off enclosure in Hove Park, where it has garnered a reputation as an ancient druidic relic.

Parking: 50.8846, -0.2124; TQ258109; Popular

7 Devil's Humps, Stoughton

According to legend, Kingley Vale in West Sussex is haunted by the ghosts of Norse warriors whose leaders were buried in four large round barrows that lie in a row along the ridge of Bow Hill. These barrows, thought to be Bronze Age, are known as

ers. Yet despite its popularity, its reputation as an uncanny, haunted place persists.

50.8969, -0.3813; TQ139120; Popular; Trailhead Parking: 50.8966, -0.4083; TQ120119; 2km

5 Cissbury Ring, Findon

The largest hillfort in Sussex, and second largest in England, Cissbury Ring is an Iron Age earthwork about which several curious legends are told. The hill marks the highest point in the Worthing area,

with views from the summit across the South Downs to the coast. Craters pockmark the western end of the hill where the shafts of Neolithic flint mines, some up to 12m deep, have long since been filled in. It is perhaps these mineshafts and interlinking underground tunnels that gave rise to the legend of a secret passage that connected Cissbury Ring to the now demolished Offington Hall. A great treasure hoard was said to be hidden in the tunnel that was guarded by huge serpents. Some also claimed to have seen fairies dancing in the ring on Midsummer's Eve. Like nearby **Chanctonbury Ring**, Cissbury hill was reputedly created by a

the Devil's Humps owing to a belief that spirits could be raised by running around them a number of times. Sometimes they are also called the King's Graves in reference to a local tradition that a party of Norse warriors were defeated in a fierce battle here by the men of Chichester. While the lords were buried within the barrows, the remaining dead were left where they fell on the slopes of the hill. A dense forest of yew trees grew up over the bodies and their ghosts are reputed to haunt the shadowy groves. The ancient yew trees that line the hilltop with their thick, twisting boughs are themselves said to come alive at night and move around the vale. The yew grove, a rare remnant of an ancient forest with some trees thought to be over 2,000 years old, was reputedly sacred to the Druids and somewhere amongst the yews was a single oak tree used in sacrificial rites.

The Devil's Humps are located in a large woodland clearing along the crest of the hill with extensive views all around. Along with the surrounding yew groves, they now form part of the Kingley Vale Nature Reserve but the area has retained a reputation as an eerie, haunted place.

50.8932, -0.8364; SU819110; Trailhead: 50.8959, -0.8623; SU801113; 2.2km

EAST SUSSEX

8 Alfriston Church

This pretty flint and greensand church sits atop a low mound that rises from an area of flat, open countryside beside the Cuckmere River. The circular mound is thought to be man-made and of ancient pagan origin. According to a legend accounting for the church's location, when builders tried to establish the structure in the village the stones would be mysteriously moved to the mound overnight. Unsure whether it was the Devil's work or the will of God, the builders consulted a wise man who had a vision of four oxen lying on the mound in the shape of a cross. This convinced them to build the church on the mound in an unusual equal-armed cross layout. Near Alfriston there is an earthwork known as Burlough Castle (50.8171, 0.1710; TQ530041) that was said to be a last refuge of the fairies in Sussex. So perhaps it was these fairies who moved the church stones? Today the church is famed for its beauty and sometimes referred to as the 'Cathedral of the South Downs'.

50.8065, 0.1581; TQ521029

9 Ditchling Beacon, Westmeston

One of the highest points on the South Downs, Ditchling Beacon is a reputed haunt of the wild hunt. Leaving the modern-day bustle of Brighton behind, a steep road winds its way north to the summit, where on a bright summer's day rare butterflies and wild flowers can be found. However, on stormy nights up on the beacon, the baying of dogs accompanied by the pounding of horses' hooves can sometimes be heard overhead as the spectral hunt races through the sky. Also, a lane that runs from Ditchling village towards Westmeston skirts the edge of Blackdog Hill (50.9120, -0.1016; TQ335142), which is said to be haunted by a solitary black dog. Encountering a black dog is often seen as an ill omen, but this apparition is all the more terrifying as the dog is headless.

Parking: 50.9010, -0.1052; TQ333129

10 Firle Beacon & the Long Man of Wilmington

The long barrow on the summit of Firle Beacon is said to be the burial place of a giant. He regularly quarrelled with another giant on Windover Hill and they would hurl boulders at each other until eventually the Windover giant was struck and killed. His outline was cut into the turf and the figure became known as the **Long Man of Wilmington** (50.8099, 0.1880; TQ542034). At around 70m tall he is the largest representation of a human in Britain, but unlike the embellishments on his **Cerne Abbas** cousin, the Long Man is utterly featureless – just an outline of a figure holding a long upright staff in each hand. In the ley line community some say these two staves identify the Long Man as a 'dodman', a prehistoric surveyor. Another curious link between the two hills comes from tales of a silver coffin said to be buried on Firle Beacon and a golden coffin buried beneath the Long Man on Windover Hill. The Long Man is best viewed at a distance, although the South Downs Way passes above his head and leads westwards to Firle Beacon where a steep climb to the summit is rewarded with far-reaching views over the Sussex countryside.

50.8338, 0.1048; TQ483059 (Firle Beacon); Trailhead Parking: 50.8257, 0.1199; TQ494050; 1.5km

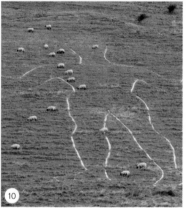

11 Mount Caburn, Glynde

The undulating remains of an Iron Age hillfort crown the summit of Mount Caburn, a distinctive hill overlooking the Sussex countryside that was said to have been home to a giant and conceals buried treasure. The steep hill is believed to have been a prehistoric ritual centre after excavations revealed numerous pits containing carefully deposited votive offerings. Local legend claims the hill was created by the Devil from a large clod of earth that flew from his spade as he furiously dug **Devil's Dyke**, which likewise formed the hills at **Chanctonbury Ring** and **Cissbury Ring**. A giant called Gil used Caburn as a base from which to throw his hammer, and was buried in a now-lost barrow in the nearby village of Glynde. It is also claimed that buried somewhere in the hill are a silver coffin and a knight in golden armour. Mount Caburn is now grazed by sheep and forms part of a nature reserve, but its sense of sacredness echoes across the centuries.

50.8619, 0.0509; TQ444089; Trailhead Parking: 50.8604, 0.0695; TQ457088; 1.8km

12

12 Coldrum Long Barrow, Trottiscliffe

Overlooking the peaceful Kentish countryside, Coldrum Long Barrow is a place of enchantment that still draws seekers of magic some 5,000 years after it was built. Located on a low ridge looking over the North Downs, the large slabs of stone that once formed a burial chamber now stand exposed on top of a high mound. Surrounding this is a roughly rectangular arrangement of sarsen kerbstones. Coldrum Long Barrow lies on a ley line around 7km long that aligns with several sacred sites including the nearby Trottiscliffe Church. An old local legend tells of a secret tunnel containing buried treasure that links Coldrum and Trottiscliffe Church, which could indicate a folk memory of the ley. Certainly, today the earth energies are thought to be particularly potent here, with several local neo-pagan groups regularly gathering and performing rituals on the site. In recent years a Morris troupe has come to dance here at dawn every May Day. The surrounding trees are laden with offerings of clootie ribbons left by reverent visitors.

51.3216, 0.3729; TQ654607; Trailhead Parking: 51.3218, 0.3666; TQ650607; 500m

SURREY

13 Devil's Jumps, Churt *

The trio of conical hills known as the Devil's Jumps watch over the flat, heathery expanse of Frensham Common. It was said that a giant (later personified as the Devil) liked to jump from one hilltop to the next but this playful act annoyed the god Thor who shouted at him to stop. The giant replied with mocking laughter saying that Thor was just too old to jump himself. The angry god retaliated by throwing a huge boulder which struck the giant who then fled howling in pain. Another legend tells of a devil who was being chased by a witch called Mother Ludham after stealing her cauldron. He jumped from hill to hill and finally into the Devil's Punch Bowl to escape her wrath. The Devil's Punch Bowl (51.1173, -0.7220; SU895361) is a a huge, deep, wooded basin in the hills above Hindhead Common to the southeast of the Devil's Jumps. The steep-sided hollow was originally said to have been created when the Devil landed there as he fled from digging **Devil's Dyke**.

Next to the River Wey, opposite Waverley Abbey and a few kilometres north of the Devil's Jumps is **Mother Ludham's Cave** (51.2043, -0.7549; SU870457. Trailhead:

13

51.2031, -0.7539; SU871456; 100m). A benevolent witch, Mother Ludham would lend out items for two days to anyone in need who stood on the rock outside her cave and turned around three times at midnight. One man who asked to borrow her cauldron failed to return it in the allotted time, so the enraged witch stopped the practice. The cave, which still bears her name, contains a natural spring that bubbles from the earth and flows out towards the river. The monks of Waverley Abbey (51.2002, -0.7592; SU867452) dedicated the spring to St Mary and the area was known as Ludewell in the medieval period. Later, the cave was turned into an enchanting grotto with a stone wall and an arched doorway was built across the front of the cave. Today an ornate, fixed metal gate keeps out curious visitors and protects the bats which now roost within. The interior is also partially blocked by landslides, although the spring water still flows. A more ancient version of the legend says that the cauldron once belonged to the fairies. To borrow it from them one had to climb Borough Hill, knock on a certain stone there and whisper a request through a hole in the stone. The fairies would then lend the cauldron, or whatever else was needed including oxen and money, providing it was returned at the agreed time. When one man forgot to return the cauldron, he was put under a curse and followed constantly by the enchanted cauldron. He took refuge from this unusual pursuer in the church where he collapsed and died from the shock, leaving the cauldron trapped inside. The large metal cauldron stands in **Frensham church** (51.1661, -0.7973; SU841414) to this day and wishes can be made by tossing coins into it. Known as the Witches' Cauldron or the Fairies' Cauldron it is still thought by some to have a supernatural origin. Borough Hill is thought to be the easternmost, and highest, of the Devil's Jumps and you can walk to its rocky, heather-clad peak via public footpaths. 51.1489, -0.7626; SU866395; Trailhead: 51.1453, -0.7618; SU867391; 600m

14 St Mary's Well, Dunsfold

The church of St Mary's and All Saints in Dunsfold, Surrey, has been described as one of the most beautiful country churches in all of England, yet this was a sacred place long before the church was built. Dominating the churchyard is an ancient yew tree, which

14

is thought to be over 1,500 years old. This tree pre-dates the medieval church building by centuries and would have been venerated in pagan times. Another sacred site is found down by the river, where the waters of the spring were once thought to be especially good for treating eye diseases. According to local tradition, the Virgin Mary appeared here in a vision and a roofed shrine with a carved wooden statue of St Mary now covers the well. The presence of the yew and holy well in this ancient and sacred place probably accounts for the church being built here, away from the village centre.

51.1167, -0.5741; SU999362

LONDON

15 St Blaise Well, Bromley

An ancient healing well dedicated to St Blaise lies hidden behind the Bromley Civic Centre car park in suburban South London. Hemmed in by busy roads and buildings, the well lies on the edge of a park where a small lake surrounded by trees provides a welcome green respite from the urban sprawl. The well was originally in the grounds of the medieval Bishop's Palace but had fallen into disuse and been lost after the Reformation. However, following its rediscovery in the 18th century, the spring water was acclaimed for its high mineral content and healing properties. Although the popularity of St Blaise Well has waned over the years, the rocky enclosure containing the spring water has been restored and the secluded well is once more an attractive and magical place, its trickling waters surrounded by lush vegetation.

51.4039, 0.0225; TQ407691;Secret/Secluded

16 White Mount, Tower of London

The head of the legendary Celtic hero Bran was said to have been buried under Bryn Gwyn, 'The White Hill', now the location of the famous Tower of London. The White Hill was a sacred mound, said to be the burial place of ancient kings, before evolving over time from a burial mound to a Norman keep and then a royal medieval castle at the heart of the city of London that has borne witness to many tumultuous scenes throughout Britain's history.

14

15

After Bran was mortally wounded in Ireland, he asked his followers to cut off his head and return it to Britain. The head could still talk and kept them entertained as they journeyed home. The company spent seven years on the **Rock of Harlech** in Wales, entranced by the birds of Rhiannon, and then another 80 years on an island called Gwales where they were unaware of the passing of time. Despite this, the head remained uncorrupted and was excellent company. Eventually they came to the White Hill in Lloegr (England) and as instructed they buried the head facing France, so that Britain would always be protected from its enemies. It was said that King Arthur later had Bran's head removed so that he himself might be the sole protector of Britain. The Tower is home to ravens, traditionally kept within the castle grounds, and they have effectively taken over Bran's role of protecting the kingdom from its enemies. It is said that if the ravens should ever leave the Tower, both it and the kingdom will fall. Curiously the name Bran means 'raven' in Old Welsh, the ancient British tongue, and so the ravens continue the tradition of guarding the realm. They still roam freely around the Tower and so it is possible to interact with these magical beings.

51.5081, -0.0761; TQ336805; ££££
Very Popular

17 Beedon Barrow, Stanmore

Found within open farmland on the Berkshire Downs and dating back to the Bronze Age or earlier, Beedon Barrow is said to be inhabited by fairies. These fairies were usually well-disposed towards respectful humans and a farmer who left his broken ploughshare on the mound found it fixed by the fairies on his return. The round barrow is also known as Burrow Hill and there are legends of a gold or silver coffin hidden within, however any attempt to dig into the mound is met with fierce thunderstorms that terrify any would-be treasure hunters. The barrow is said to be impossible to plough, and it does indeed still sit isolated amid heavily cultivated land, unploughed and overgrown with vegetation.

51.5044, -1.3276; SU467785

18 Grimsbury Castle, Cold Ash

Located within woodland in the western reaches of Berkshire, Grimsbury Castle is a

hillfort named after the Anglo-Saxon god Woden, whose alias was Grim. Woden, or his Norse equivalent Odin, is associated with numerous ancient earthworks around the country, although the hillfort at Grimsbury is of an earlier Iron Age Celtic construction. According to legend there is a pool in the woods nearby in which a golden calf is hidden. A small road now bisects the hill and the ramparts of the fort are overgrown with trees but it remains an atmospheric place to explore.

51.4468, -1.2669; SU510722

19 Windsor Great Park

The historic royal park at Windsor is said to be haunted by Herne the Hunter, the spectral figure of a man bearing the great ragged antlers of a stag upon his head. Windsor Great Park covers some 4,800 acres of forest and formal gardens linked to Windsor Castle, and was first established as a royal hunting ground over a thousand years ago. The park is home to a herd of red deer and they are frequently seen amongst the ancient oak trees. According to the tale, Herne was the king's forest keeper who was mortally wounded while hunting a rare white stag. A local wise man advised Herne's life could be saved if the stag's antlers were tied to his head. Herne recovered but was never the same again, and ultimately hanged himself on an oak tree. From then on, his spirit has appeared in the vicinity of the tree and elsewhere in the park, sometimes seen leading a pack of hounds in a wild hunt, while at other times only the baying of the hounds and the thunder of hooves can be heard. It has been suggested that Herne is reminiscent of the ancient Celtic god Cernunnos, who also wears stag's antlers, or that he could be some remnant of prehistoric shamanistic practices. Whatever his origin, Herne is inextricably linked to Britain's folklore and frequently appears as a character in literature and film to this day. Herne's Oak, where he died, stood in Home Park near Windsor Castle, which is off-limits to the public, but the remainder of Windsor Great Park contains many other venerable old oaks and woodlands to explore.

Parking: 51.4264, -0.5963; SU976706; £

OXFORDSHIRE

20 Rollright Stones *

Legend claims the trio of megalithic monuments that form the Rollright Stones were a king and his army turned to stone after encountering a witch. Lying on the border of Oxfordshire and Warwickshire, the Rollrights comprise a solitary standing stone known as the King's Stone, a 33m- diameter stone circle called the King's Men and a cluster of five stones named the Whispering Knights. A modern road now divides the King's Men from the **King's Stone** (51.9762, -1.5703; SP296309), while the stones known as the **Whispering Knights** (51.9752, -1.5657; SP299308) seem to huddle together conspiratorially some distance away. All these natural,

oolitic limestone boulders have deeply pitted, lichen-encrusted surfaces. Their forms are irregular and contorted, especially the top-heavy King's Stone whose curious shape is thought to be the result of visitors chipping off pieces as good luck charms over the years. According to legend a would-be king and his army met a witch while riding along the Ridgeway, and she challenged him with this rhyme:

"Seven long strides shalt thou take, If Long Compton thou canst see, King of England thou shalt be."
The leader then ascended the hill but on the seventh stride the ground mysteriously rose up in front of him forming a mound still visible today beyond the King's Stone, and so the village of Long Compton remained out of sight. Triumphantly the witch then turned the king and his men to stone, while she herself transformed into an elder tree. It has been suggested that the mound could have been an inauguration site for ancient kings and this one's failure to reach the top of the mound proved him unworthy.
The stones of the King's Men circle are said to be uncountable, and anyone who moves or damages one of the stones will have no rest until the stone is restored. It is also said on certain nights the stones move down the hill to drink from a stream. There are reports of fairies seen in the vicinity, especially dancing around the King Stone, where they are said to emerge from a small hole in the mound. Sleeping knights are also said to lie hidden there within the mound.
With such rich folklore, it is little wonder the Rollright Stones attract groups of neo-pagans who still perform rites there. Investigations into the site's earth energies concluded that a possible three ley lines run through the Rollrights, including one that links to the **Uffington White Horse**, and another to the church at Long Compton (51.9950, -1.5827; SP287330). The area around Long Compton was known to be home to many witches, one of whom is represented in an ancient stone effigy in the church porch.

51.9755, -1.5709; SP295308; Popular

21 St Margaret's Well, Binsey & Oxford

The parish church of St Margaret in the tiny village of Binsey, on the outskirts of Oxford, has a famous healing well in its churchyard. The miraculous waters of the spring are said to have arisen in response to the prayers of the Saxon St Frideswide, patron saint of Oxford, who used the water to perform acts of healing. The well was a popular place of pilgrimage during the medieval period and the curative powers of the water were so effective that the church was said to have displayed dozens of crutches cast off by those who had been healed there. In later centuries women would visit the well for protection and for help with conception and pregnancy. Today a low stone enclosure has steps leading down to the well, covered by a small arched vault, where the healing water still flows. Nearby Oxford features in a curious Welsh tale from The Mabinogion about the brothers Lludd and Llefelys. Plagued by a hideous and disturbing scream that echoed throughout the land each May Day, Lludd asked his brother Llefelys for advice and was told that the scream was caused by two dragons who must be captured in a pit at the exact centre of the kingdom, which turned out to be Oxford. After being lured into a vat of mead the sleeping dragons were sealed in a stone coffin and taken to the fortress of **Dinas Emrys** in Wales, where they were buried. Oxford has a long history as a sacred centre and the exact centre, or *omphalos*, of Oxford is marked by St Martin's/Carfax Tower (51.7519, -1.2581; SP513061). Could this be where the troublesome dragons were captured long ago?

51.7691, -1.2978; SP485080

22 Uffington White Horse & Dragon Hill *

This stylized chalk outline of a horse is thought to have been carved into the side of Uffington Hill by the ancient Celts. It appears to gallop across the landscape above Dragon Hill, a smaller hill where St George is said to have killed a dragon. Overlooking a vast expanse of Oxfordshire countryside, the horse lies just below Uffington Castle, an Iron Age hillfort on the Ridgeway escarpment. The White Horse has been tentatively dated to the Bronze Age, making it by far the oldest chalk hill-figure in Britain, and it has traditionally been renewed every seven years with accompanying festivities and games. There is very little folklore about the White Horse itself, but there is a belief that a wish made while standing on the horse's eye will come true. The ancient long barrow known as **Wayland's Smithy** is a little over 2km to the southwest and a golden coffin is said to be buried somewhere between these two places. The horse overlooks **Dragon Hill** (51.5798, -1.5674; SU300868), a small, naturally formed chalk hill with an artificially flattened top. According to legend, it was here that St George fought and defeated the dragon, whose blood seeped into the ground and poisoned the earth so nothing would grow there. There is indeed still a bare chalk patch on top of the hill where no grass grows, and some say the dragon itself is buried inside the hill. It has also been suggested the White Horse is not a horse at all, but a representation of the dragon. As it traverses Britain from north to south, the Belinus ley line crosses the Michael ley line near Uffington. As these are the longest north to south and east to west ley lines that can be drawn across Britain, their intersection marks Uffington out as a significant sacred centre.

51.5773, -1.5667; SU301865 (Uffington White Horse; Popular

23 Wayland's Smithy, Ashbury *

The Neolithic chambered longbarrow known as Wayland's Smithy was once thought to be home to an invisible blacksmith of legendary skill. Concealed in a small copse of trees just off the ancient Neolithic track known as the Ridgeway and close to the **Uffington White Horse**, the entrance to Wayland's Smithy is marked by a row of huge megaliths that conceal a small stone chamber and a long, low mound stretching away behind. It was widely believed that Wayland the Smith, an Anglo-Saxon demigod of unsurpassed skill in metalworking, had his smithy within the barrow. Any traveller whose horse lost a shoe on the road could leave his horse tethered at the entrance together with a coin in payment, and return the next morning to find the horse newly shod by the invisible blacksmith. Wayland's Smithy has a lonely atmosphere, feeling somewhat cut off from the Ridgeway and the land beyond, and yet it also has an air of great power. If you were to press an ear to the mound, you sense that the faint sounds of a hammer beating against an anvil might well be heard coming from deep within.

51.5667, -1.5961; SU280853; Popular; Wayland's Smithy: 51.5667, -1.5961; SU280853; Popular

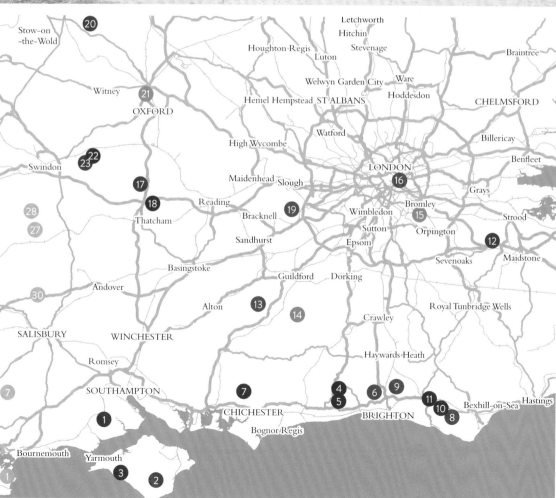

Stow-on-the-Wold

20

21 OXFORD

Witney

Swindon

22
23

17
18 Thatcham

28

27

30

SALISBURY

WINCHESTER

Romsey

SOUTHAMPTON

Bournemouth

Yarmouth

1

3

2

Letchworth
Hitchin
Houghton Regis   Stevenage
Luton
Welwyn Garden City   Ware
Hemel Hempstead   ST ALBANS   Hoddesdon
Watford

High Wycombe

Maidenhead   Slough
Reading
Bracknell
Sandhurst

Basingstoke

Andover

Alton

13

14

Guildford   Dorking

Crawley

Haywards Heath

7

CHICHESTER

Bognor Regis

4
5

6

9

BRIGHTON

11
10
8

Braintree

CHELMSFORD

Billericay

Benfleet

LONDON

16

Wimbledon   Bromley
15
Sutton   Orpington
Epsom

Grays

Strood

12

Maidstone

Sevenoaks

Royal Tunbridge Wells

Bexhill-on-Sea   Hastings

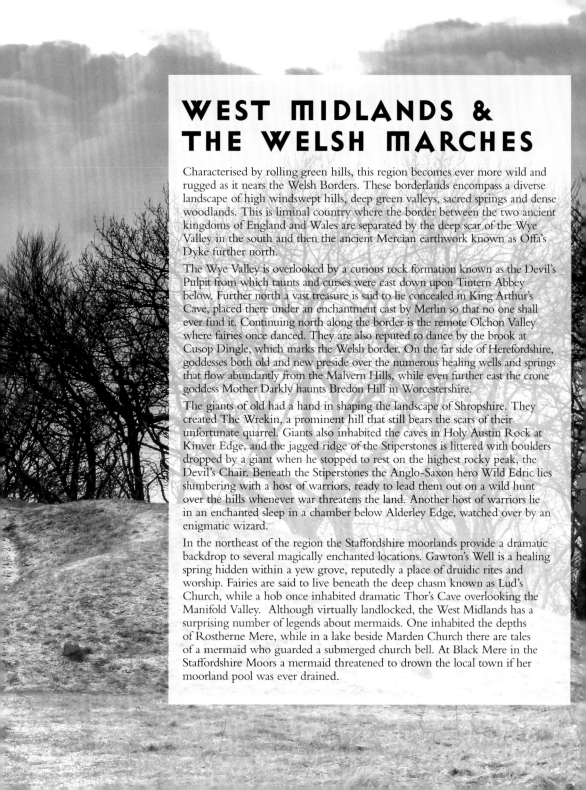

WEST MIDLANDS & THE WELSH MARCHES

Characterised by rolling green hills, this region becomes ever more wild and rugged as it nears the Welsh Borders. These borderlands encompass a diverse landscape of high windswept hills, deep green valleys, sacred springs and dense woodlands. This is liminal country where the border between the two ancient kingdoms of England and Wales are separated by the deep scar of the Wye Valley in the south and then the ancient Mercian earthwork known as Offa's Dyke further north.

The Wye Valley is overlooked by a curious rock formation known as the Devil's Pulpit from which taunts and curses were cast down upon Tintern Abbey below. Further north a vast treasure is said to lie concealed in King Arthur's Cave, placed there under an enchantment cast by Merlin so that no one shall ever find it. Continuing north along the border is the remote Olchon Valley where fairies once danced. They are also reputed to dance by the brook at Cusop Dingle, which marks the Welsh border. On the far side of Herefordshire, goddesses both old and new preside over the numerous healing wells and springs that flow abundantly from the Malvern Hills, while even further east the crone goddess Mother Darkly haunts Bredon Hill in Worcestershire.

The giants of old had a hand in shaping the landscape of Shropshire. They created The Wrekin, a prominent hill that still bears the scars of their unfortunate quarrel. Giants also inhabited the caves in Holy Austin Rock at Kinver Edge, and the jagged ridge of the Stiperstones is littered with boulders dropped by a giant when he stopped to rest on the highest rocky peak, the Devil's Chair. Beneath the Stiperstones the Anglo-Saxon hero Wild Edric lies slumbering with a host of warriors, ready to lead them out on a wild hunt over the hills whenever war threatens the land. Another host of warriors lie in an enchanted sleep in a chamber below Alderley Edge, watched over by an enigmatic wizard.

In the northeast of the region the Staffordshire moorlands provide a dramatic backdrop to several magically enchanted locations. Gawton's Well is a healing spring hidden within a yew grove, reputedly a place of druidic rites and worship. Fairies are said to live beneath the deep chasm known as Lud's Church, while a hob once inhabited dramatic Thor's Cave overlooking the Manifold Valley. Although virtually landlocked, the West Midlands has a surprising number of legends about mermaids. One inhabited the depths of Rostherne Mere, while in a lake beside Marden Church there are tales of a mermaid who guarded a submerged church bell. At Black Mere in the Staffordshire Moors a mermaid threatened to drown the local town if her moorland pool was ever drained.

1

GLOUCESTERSHIRE

1 Devil's Pulpit &
The Wye Valley

Perched on the edge of a thickly wooded slope, the contorted limestone column known as the Devil's Pulpit overlooks Tintern Abbey and the river Wye in the valley far below. The Wye Valley is a verdant, tree-clad cleft in the landscape that winds its way down from Monmouth all the way to the river Severn at Chepstow, forming the border between England and Wales. According to legend, the Devil would stand on his rocky 'pulpit' to tempt and berate the monks of Tintern Abbey below. Eventually the monks lured the Devil down and sprinkled him with holy water, causing him to flee to Llandogo where he re-crossed the river Wye, leaving behind his footprint in the rock. This story hints at a pagan past when the Devil's Pulpit was perhaps a former druidic altar whose pagan associations had to be neutralised by the pious monks.

Tintern Abbey £ (51.6969, -2.6770; SO533000) now lies in ruins and is a popular tourist destination, while the Devil's Pulpit sits on the Offa's Dyke path high above and is popular with walkers. A twisted yew tree grows in a secret hollow directly behind the stone pulpit, its roots entwined around a stone column, giving it the ancient and magical appearance of a secret shrine.

On the Gloucestershire side of the Wye Valley you can also find a fairy-enchanted forest of twisted trees and bizarre limestone galleries known as **Puzzlewood** (51.7800, -2.6102; SO580092; ££ popular). Through it, wooden walkways have been created from branches, giving the whole place an intensely magical atmosphere.

51.6926, -2.6633; ST542995; Trailhead: 51.6865, -2.6425; ST556988, 1.7km

1

1

2 Hetty Pegler's Tump, Uley

Uley Long Barrow, also known as Hetty Pegler's Tump, retains a strange, numinous atmosphere nearly 6,000 years after it was first constructed. Situated in a quiet corner of a field, the earth mound backs onto a peaceful area of woodland. The very low entrance requires visitors to crawl through, but once inside the long, spacious passage gives access to three chambers that would have once housed the bones of the dead. Some of the huge blocks of stone that line these chambers are punctuated with natural holes and cavities which some identify as 'vulva' stones – a memory of the ancient cult of the Goddess – where people sometimes leave offerings of flowers and crystals. Enclosed within the dark, womb-like interior, you can almost feel the immanent presence of the Goddess as well as dark ancestral spirits.

51.6987, -2.3060; SO789000; Trailhead:
51.6984, -2.3019; SO792000; 300m

3 Long Stone, Minchinhampton

The deeply weathered and pockmarked limestone monolith known as the Long Stone was thought to possess the power to heal childhood diseases. It stands over 2m tall, with a pitted, lichen-speckled surface, and several natural holes that pierce the body of the stone. Infants with rickets, measles or whooping cough would be passed through the largest of these holes in hope of a cure. The stone was said to move around the field at the stroke of midnight, but when a farmer yoked his oxen to the stone to drag it from the ground, some mysterious force kept it fixed firmly in place. There are also reports of a phantom black dog that haunts the vicinity. Today the Long Stone sits in a fenced-off corner of a field, yet still commands the attention of passers-by.

51.6979, -2.1700; ST883999

4 St Anthony's Well, Mitcheldean

Hidden just inside an extensive area of open woodland lies St Anthony's Well. The water of the spring, long reputed to have healing powers, is surrounded by a stone enclosure large enough to accommodate an adult bather. Steps lead down into the water,

which is over a metre deep and icy cold even on the warmest days. The water is said to heal skin diseases, although to receive the full effects of the cure the afflicted must bathe at sunrise on nine successive days within the month of May. Adjacent to the well, a stone supported by a low wall forms a sort of altar where offerings are often placed by visitors.

51.8394, -2.4802; SO670157; Trailhead:
51.8410, -2.4718; SO675159; 700m

HEREFORDSHIRE

5 Arthur's Stone, Dorstone

The Neolithic burial chamber known as Arthur's stone is said to mark the grave of a giant who was slain by King Arthur. The burial chamber with its large flat capstone supported by nine uprights sits right on the side of a quiet country lane. A boulder nearby was said to have borne the imprints of the giant's elbows as he struck the stone and was killed, although some say the hollows were made by King Arthur himself as he knelt there to pray. According to a curious legend, the stones have dwindled in

contain treasure that was concealed there for safekeeping when Arthur was being pursued by his enemies. The wizard Merlin cast a spell over the cave so that the treasure could never be found. This large limestone cave has two interconnected entrances leading to two main chambers called the Bear's Den and Lion's Cave after the ancient animal remains found there. One of numerous caves in this area of the Wye Valley, King Arthur's Cave was once inhabited by Neolithic people, but it was the Iron Age Celts who built **Little Doward Hillfort** (51.8408, -2.6707; SO538160) on the hill above, which became associated with Vortigern, the tyrannical warlord of Arthurian legend. A medieval legend tells of King Herla, an early Briton who once ruled these lands, possibly from this very hillfort. One day a strange little man arrived at his hall claiming that he too was a king, and that if he could attend King Herla's upcoming wedding then Herla would receive an invitation to his own wedding in return. King Herla agreed and the little king attended the wedding, returning a year later as promised to escort Herla and his men to his own wedding. The entrance to the little king's land was through a cave in a cliff that led deep into the hill, finally emerging into a magnificent chamber with magical lights. The wedding feast continued for three days and Herla and his entourage were bestowed with countless gifts, one of which was a bloodhound. As Herla prepared to leave, the little king warned that none of the men should dismount from their horses until the dog jumped down first. When they finally emerged from the cave, Herla and his men encountered a shepherd and asked how the kingdom had fared in their absence. The shepherd could barely understand them as he was not a Briton but a Saxon. The Saxons had taken over the king's lands two hundred years ago but the shepherd said he'd heard an old story of the last British king being led away into the lands of Faerie. Shocked at how much time had passed, some of the men forgot the little king's warning and jumped down from their horses, but as soon as their feet touched the ground they crumbled to dust. King Herla and his remaining men were forced to keep riding forever, their ghostly passage spurring on legends of the wild hunt throughout the land. They would perhaps still be riding now had they not encountered an armed band during Henry II's reign, who forced the cursed company off a cliff into the river Wye, where they disappeared in mid-air and were never seen again.

51.8374, -2.6594; SO546156; Trailhead Parking: 51.8390, -2.6573; SO548158; 250m

size over the years and were once so large that 100 sheep could lie in the shadow cast by the monument and a grown man could stand easily beneath the capstone.

52.0823, -2.9954; SO318431

6 Cusop Dingle, Hay-on-Wye

The small leafy glen known as Cusop Dingle lies directly on the border between Herefordshire in England and Powys in Wales, a liminal place where fairies have been seen dancing under the foxgloves. From time to time, strange glowing 'witch lights' or will o' the wisps have also been seen flitting amongst the trees. A quiet

country lane now runs through the glen but to appreciate the real magic of the place climb down to the enchanted stream known as Dulas Brook where the water rushes down waterfalls and over mossy boulders overhung with trees and vegetation. The brook is the liminal zone that marks the border between two nations and between this world and the magical Otherworld.

52.0572, -3.0997; SO246404

7 King Arthur's Cave, Great Doward *

Found in woodland close to the Welsh border, King Arthur's Cave is said to

8 Marden Church

The medieval church at Marden sits in a peaceful location on the banks of the river Lugg and, according to legend, was the scene of a dramatic encounter with a mermaid. The old church bell had fallen into the river where it was seized by the mermaid who refused to return it. A wise man advised the parishioners to use a team of white cows yoked with yew wood and driven by rowan switches to pull the bell from the depths – all to be done in absolute silence. The bell, with the mermaid asleep inside it, was successfully dragged as far as the river bank when one man forgot himself and exclaimed "In spite of all the Devils in hell, now we'll land Marden's great bell!" The mermaid awoke and plunged back into the river with the bell, which she hid away in a deep pool where it lies to this day. Some say it can still be heard ringing there. Curiously, an early Christian bell was recovered from the river here in 1848, and so over time its story has become entwined with that of the mermaid. The bell may be linked to St Ethelbert whose holy well is still housed within the church. The saint was murdered on this site in the 8th century and the spring miraculously arose at the spot where his body lay. St Ethelbert became a popular saint in medieval times, particularly after his remains were relocated to a shrine in Hereford cathedral.

52.1197, -2.7145; SO511470

9 Olchon Valley, Longtown

On the eastern edge of the Black Mountains, the remote and isolated Olchon Valley was said to be home to fairies who danced beside the Olchon Brook. One day a group of young people returning from the market in Longtown (51.9508, –2.9822; SO325284) spotted them dancing, but one man went too close and was drawn into the ring. He reappeared a year later, still carrying the oranges and gingerbread he'd bought at the market which were as fresh as the day they had been sold. Unfortunately, he did not live long after his return.
In the Olchon Valley you can find Cae Thomas Well, an ancient healing spring that bubbles up from under a tree in a hidden location. It flows out over bright mossy boulders and beneath holly trees into the Olchon Brook below. Time seems to move more slowly in this secluded valley, which feels a world away from the bustle of modern life.

51.9819, -3.0435; SO284320 (Cae Thomas Well); Secret/Secluded

WORCESTERSHIRE

10 Bredon Hill

Rising up from the surrounding plains of the Vale of Evesham, Bredon Hill is so large that a dozen villages back onto it, yet it is crossed by no roads. It is said to be haunted by a crone called Old Mother Darkly who would come down to steal children from the villages and then turn them into hounds to do her bidding. Their cries could be heard emanating from the mist that often wreathed the hill, but after a year they would be released and returned to their families. Thereafter, legend held that these children could never leave the hill and its surrounding villages, and in fact a tradition still exists that those born around the hill will never leave the area. The story of Old Mother Darkly could be a memory of the ancient Celtic crone goddess or even of the goddess Diana who leads the wild hunt. The mist that sometimes cloaks the hill is said to be a portent of bad weather, and an old rhyme states:

"When Bredon Hill puts on his hat
Ye men of the vale beware of that!"

Near the north-facing summit of the hill, on the edge of a Celtic hillfort known as Kemerton Camp, lies a strange rock formation called the Banbury Stone. It is said to hide buried treasure, and also to go down to the river Avon to drink when the bells of Pershore Abbey strike midnight. In former times people would ascend Bredon Hill on Good Friday and kiss the Banbury Stone for luck, and the stone itself was thought to have healing properties. There is also a legend that a tunnel links Pershore Abbey (52.1104, -2.0776; SO947457) to Bredon Hill, so these tales hint at some ancient spiritual connection between the two sites. Several of the villages around the hill also have their own tunnel legends, perhaps memories of lost ceremonial pathways. On the opposite side of the hill, hidden down a wooded slope, is another rock formation known as the **King and Queen Stones** (52.0461, -2.0807; SO945386; 600m along trail). These are also thought to have healing properties, the healing ritual possibly being performed by passing through the gap between the stones.

Given Bredon Hill's size and lack of roads, its upland areas can only be reached by hiking up one of the numerous trails, giving it a remote atmosphere. Even the surrounding villages feel like they come from another age, with old stone-built cottages, ancient churches and more than their fair share of creepy tales and hauntings.
52.0603, -2.0645; SO956402 (Banbury Stone); Trailhead: 52.0413, -2.0816; SO945381; 3km

11 Malvhina Spring, Great Malvern

A modern-day goddess presides over the waters that flow from a drinking fountain on Belle Vue Island in the centre of the town of Great Malvern. Sculpted in bronze and stone, Malvhina's design incorporates a triple theme inspired by the three springs which feed the spout and the triple aspect of the Celtic goddess. From a bronze disk held in the goddess's hands the water flows into a basin carved with spirals.

Many other springs can be found in the Malvern Hills, some of which have a reputation for healing. At **St Ann's Well** (52.1103, -2.3350; SO771458), up on the hillside above Great Malvern and reached via a steep wooded lane, the spring flows out into an ornamental pond. The waters have healing properties and the well's name suggests that it could originally have been sacred to the Celtic goddess Anu. For centuries, the sick and weary have also visited **Holy Well** (52.0788, -2.3366; SO770423), to the west of Malvern Wells village, seeking cures for their ailments. Just south of Holy Well, Bright's Spring (52.0761, -2.3340; SO772420), also known as Devil's Well, emerges from a wooded hillside. This area is called Puck's Wood after the fairy who is also known as Robin Goodfellow. Those who found themselves afflicted with the confusion, melancholy and even madness that Puck could invoke would bathe in the water of this spring to break the enchantment. Both Holy Well and St Ann's Well are housed in ornate Victorian buildings that have a sanitised feel whereas Bright's Spring is now totally overgrown and overlooked. A map showing all the springs around the Malvern Hills can be seen in the well-house of Holy Well and the most enchanted of these is Westminster Bank Spout (52.1132, -2.3449; SO764461). The water emerges from under the roots of a tree that is often covered in brightly coloured offerings, giving the place a fairy-like atmosphere.

52.1111, -2.3298; SO775459; Popular

12 Osebury Rock, Lulsley

A cave in Osebury Rock, a steep cliff overlooking the river Teme, was said to be inhabited by helpful fairies who would mend broken tools that had been left at the cave entrance by villagers. On one occasion, a man and boy ploughing a field nearby heard a cry coming from the trees growing on the rock. Following the sound, they found a distraught fairy who had lost his pickaxe. The two helped the fairy to find it and were rewarded with a feast of bread, cheese and cider, which the ploughman ate gratefully although the boy was too scared to try any of it. The exact location of the fairy cave is now unknown but the dense woodland and rocky escarpments overhung with ivy make this an interesting place to explore.

52.1975, -2.3855; SO737555; Secret/ Secluded; Trailhead: 51.1965, -2.3884; SO735554; 300m

WARWICKSHIRE

13 Guy's Cliffe, Warwick

A cave in the cliffs beside the river Avon, just outside Warwick, was said to be the dwelling place of Guy of Warwick, a celebrated Saxon folk hero who was popular in medieval times. His legendary exploits included slaying a dragon, hunting a giant boar, killing a giant Danish invader and ridding the countryside of a troublesome fairy cow known as the Dun Cow. The animal had been transformed into a monster after a greedy witch milked her dry. Guy's exploits were well known until at least the 17th century when a rib from the Dun Cow was on display in the Chapel of St Mary Magdalene. The chapel is partially carved into the rock of Guy's Cliffe and features a stone effigy of a knight in armour nearly 3m tall and said to represent Sir Guy himself. The chapel and Guy's Cliffe are privately owned but tours do take place on occasion and the cave can be viewed from a public footpath on the opposite side of the river. Sir Guy's sword and cooking pot can be seen on public display in Warwick Castle £££ (52.2797, -1.5852; SP283646).

52.2987, -1.5716; SP293668 (Chapel of St Mary Magdalene); Private

14 Southam Holy Well

With records dating back to Saxon times, Southam Holy Well is thought to be the oldest recorded holy well in the country. It was visited to cure sore eyes and, magically, it never froze over. Today it sits in green fields to the west of the village of Southam and has recently been restored.

155

1,000 years old and from domesticated herds. This would suggest the antlers – if no other aspects of the ritual – were imported from Scandinavia, as Britain no longer had reindeer at that time. The dance formerly took place around Christmas but it is now performed in early September, beginning at the village green and travelling around the village and to several outlying farmsteads. For the rest of the year the costumes can be seen hanging up in the local church, where the headdresses, looking eerily pagan and ancient in the dim light, peer down at you.

52.8185, -1.8837; SK079245 (church)

16 Black Mere, Morridge

A small lake lying in an isolated stretch of moorland between Buxton and Leek, Black or Blake Mere is a lonely spot with an eerie reputation. According to legend it was haunted by a mermaid, a female lake-spirit who was ill-disposed towards people. The pool was thought to be bottomless and it was said that no animals would drink the water, and that no birds would fly over it. Over the centuries many people have been found drowned in the lake, some reputedly lured to their deaths by the mermaid. In one tale, workmen came to dig a trench to drain the water, but the mermaid appeared to them and warned she would drown Leek town if her pool was disturbed. The terrified men abandoned their work but traces of the unfinished trench still survive to this day. The lake is now commonly called Blakemere Pond, but to some it will always be the Mermaid's Pool so it is best not to stray too close to the water's edge.

53.1489, -1.9419; SK039613

The well's semi-circular stone enclosure now has a wooden bench and sits within an artistic arrangement of wooden posts and gates, all carved with unusual designs in an 'elven' style.

Edged by older stonework, the well features two pools of clear, fresh spring water. Steps lead down to one of them for immersion in the healing waters and there are also mysterious stone heads embedded into the stonework. These heads are of unknown origin but are reminiscent of the Celtic cult of the severed head. The footpaths leading to the well are popular with local dog walkers and families who often visit the well, although few are aware of its significance.

52.2534, -1.4008; SP410618; Popular, Trailhead: 52.2529, -1.3886; SP418618; 1km

STAFFORDSHIRE

15 Abbots Bromley

In the Abbots Bromley horn dance, an ancient annual tradition, a team of six men perform dances with large reindeer antlers resting on their shoulders, while a further six enact the roles of other characters including the fool, a hobby horse and Maid Marian. The 'horns' are a set of antlers with a carved wooden head, mounted on a stick; three sets are painted white and the other three are black. Traditionally the dance was performed by generations of men from one particular family whose descendants still organise the event and dance today, drawing huge crowds every year. Although the origins of the horn dance have been lost to time it was first recorded in the 16th century and scientific analysis has shown the antlers are around

17 Gawton's Well, Knypersley *

Hidden away in dense woodland near the eastern shore of Knyspersley Reservoir, Gawton's Well is a healing spring with a magical atmosphere. A stone enclosure surrounds a series of basins and bathing pools through which the water passes before being channelled away down the slope. Many yew trees surround the well, some hung with clootie ribbons. The date of the well is uncertain but according to local legend a man called Gawton, afflicted with the plague, was driven from his village and came here to be cured by the spring water. He lived as a hermit at **Gawton's Stone** (53.0957, -2.1538; SJ897553), a large block supported by three stones, close to the well. The well was believed to be particularly

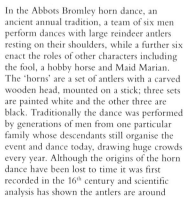

effective at treating the King's Evil, or scrofula – a disease that causes painful swelling of the lymph glands. The presence of the yew grove around the spring suggests this has long been a sacred place, with some claiming the Druids once worshipped here. The peaceful woodland setting of the well makes it one of the most magical places in Staffordshire.

53.0971, -2.1536; SJ898555; Trailhead Parking: 53.0927, -2.1597; SJ894550; 1.5km

18 Holy Austin Rock, Kinver Edge

A giant and his wife once lived on Holy Austin Rock, which is full of ancient caves carved into the soft red sandstone. One day while the giant was out collecting water from the Giant's Water Trough he caught his wife kissing another giant who lived in Sampson's Cave near Enville. Enraged, he threw a long stone shaped like a javelin at his rival, which became embedded in the earth and was later known as the Bolt Stone. Neither the Bolt Stone nor the Giant's Water Trough survive today and

the caves in Holy Austin Rock were long ago converted into cottages more suitable for human habitation. Inhabited until the 1950s, they have now been restored by the National Trust and are open to visitors. Further along Kinver Edge, the natural cave in **Nanny's Rock** (52.4409, -2.2527; SO829825) was said to be the home of Meg O'Foxholes, a wise woman who would mix herbal potions for the local people. To the north, **Sampson's Cave** (52.4665, -2.2521; SO829854; secret/secluded) is hidden within woodland on the edge of the Enville estate. A door and windows have been carved into the rock and the cave served as a dwelling until the 20th century when it was finally abandoned. Inside, a fireplace and other remnants of occupation still remain in situ. Six kilometres to the south of Kinver Edge in the beautifully wooded Habberley Valley, there is a pinnacle known as **Pekket Rock** (52.399651, -2.292433; SO802780). As with the Banbury Stone on **Bredon Hill**, local people ascended it on Good Friday, kissing the rock for luck as part of an ancient springtime ritual.

52.4500, -2.2420; SO836835; £ Popular

19 Lud's Church, Allgreave *

Steep stone steps lead down into the chasm known as Lud's Church, a deep and narrow cleft in the landscape that is imbued with legend. The cleft runs for over 100m through woodland known as the Black Forest bordering the river Dane. Direct sunlight rarely penetrates the depths of the chasm where verdant mosses cling to high walls that are peppered with little caverns and crevices. With such dramatic surroundings it is little wonder Lud's Church has become steeped in myth and folklore. Fairies living in caverns below ground are said to come out and dance at dawn, there have been

reports of strange lights seen floating in the air, and of numerous apparitions including that of a headless green man. This may be linked to the belief that Lud's Church was the 'Green Chapel' where Sir Gawain went to meet the Green Knight's challenge in the climax of the Arthurian romance. The anonymous author of *Sir Gawain and the Green Knight*, wrote the long poem in a local northwest Midland's dialect, which perhaps lends credence to the association of Lud's Church with the Green Chapel.

53.1878, -2.0206; SJ987656; Popular, Trailhead Parking: 53.1931, -2.0029; SJ999662; 2km

20 Thor's Cave, Wetton *

A large cavern in the rock face high above the river Manifold is known as Thor's Cave. It was originally called Hob Hurst's House as it was believed to be inhabited by a hob. These household spirits were usually helpful around the home and farm if properly treated, but this particular hob liked to play the fiddle and so was known as the Fiddling Hob. The sounds of his violin music, or some say 'screeching', could be heard drifting out of the depths of the cave. Viewed from the valley below the

large entrance to Thor's Cave is clearly visible in the dramatic limestone peak rising above the trees, and a steep path leads up to it. Once inside the cave, the walls are streaked with colours – greens and rusty browns – and curve high overhead as they twist away into the darkness, while a pillar called the Altar has rumours of ancient sacrifices attached to it. On account of its name, most people associate the cave with the Norse god, but it is more likely to be derived from 'thurse', a local dialect name for a hob or fairy.

53.0918, -1.8542; SK098549; Popular,
Trailhead Parking: 53.0856, -1.8522;
SK099542; 1.6km

21 Bury Ditches, Lydbury North

Dating back to the Iron Age, the well-preserved oval earthworks of Bury Ditches have established its reputation as one of the finest hillforts in Britain. Covering the lower slopes around the fort are pine plantations, but from the summit there are extensive views. Somewhere within the boundaries of Bury Ditches the fairies were said to have buried a pot of gold,

the site of which was marked with a fine golden thread. If you can find the thread and follow it, it will lead you to the gold. Wild Edric's Way, a long-distance footpath running through Shropshire, passes through Bury Ditches en route to nearby **Clun Forest** and north to the **Stiperstones**.

52.4471, -2.9913; SO327837; Trailhead
Parking: 52.4498, -2.9813; SO334839; 700m

22 Clun Forest

The Forest of Clun was the hunting ground of Wild Edric, an Anglo-Saxon noble who led a resistance against the Norman invaders towards the latter part of the 11th century. According to a popular medieval legend Edric met his wife Godda, a fairy, while out hunting in the forest. Edric was hunting alone when he heard sweet music and then saw light coming from a cottage nearby. He peered inside and saw a gathering of tall, exceptionally beautiful young women dancing around another who was more beautiful still. Overcome with love for her he burst in and seized the woman but her companions attacked him, scratching and clawing at him with their nails. Edric made his escape and carried the fairy woman away on his horse. All the while she remained quiet and calm, but after they reached the nobleman's home she did not speak or stir for three days. On the fourth day Godda decided that Edric's intentions were honest and true and agreed to marry him, saying that he would always have her love as long as he did not reproach her about her fairy sisters. After they were married, Godda was so famous for her beauty that even King William requested that the couple visit him in London. All went well for Edric until one day his wife arrived home late and he angrily accused her of spending time with

159

her sisters in the forest. She gazed at him sadly and then disappeared, never to be seen again. From then on Edric's fortunes waned and he spent many years searching for Godda in the forest, but all to no avail. After Edric died, his spirit was said to haunt Clun Forest, leading the wild hunt in a ghostly chase. Some say that his fairy wife Godda could be seen riding with him, and their appearance was a portent of war. Edric is also said to haunt the hills of **The Long Mynd** (52.5335, -2.8497; SO424931) near Church Stretton in the form of a huge black dog with spectral eyes. There is also a local tradition that Edric and his court were imprisoned within the ancient lead mines at the **Stiperstones**, waiting for the country to rid itself of the troubles brought on by the Norman conquest. Meanwhile, like the Cornish spirits known as knockers, they would lead miners to the richest lodes of ore and warn them of danger.

The royal hunting ground of Clun Forest no longer exists and has been replaced by green fields and hedgerows, but gaze out from the ruins of Clun Castle into the early morning mist and you may still imagine you can see a forest hiding a fairy cottage, hear Edric's solemn wailing or catch sight of the ghostly wild hunt.

52.4221, -3.0331; SO298809 (Clun Castle)

23 **Cole Mere, Ellesmere**

From below the secluded waters of Cole Mere, the bells of a drowned monastery are said to be heard tolling on windy, moonlit nights. In another version of the legend, the bells fell into the lake from a chapel that once stood on the thickly forested banks. Cole Mere is one of many lakes found in this part of Shropshire; the biggest, **Great Mere** (52.9065, -2.8853; SJ405347) just to the north, also has an inundation legend. Where the lake now lies there was once a meadow containing a well, but the owner was so mean that he used to charge local people for the water. One day they prayed for help and the well overflowed, flooding the meadow and providing free water for all. Great Mere is also said to be haunted by Jenny Greenteeth, an evil water hag draped with pond weed who would drag children under the water with her long arms. Today, Great Mere is popular with visitors and bounded by busy roads and a café, but Cole Mere retains a secluded, haunted feel, especially out of season when the attached boating club is closed.

52.8931, -2.8469; SJ431331

24 Hope Bagot Holy Well

Tucked away in a sleepy village churchyard, an ancient yew tree spreads its boughs over a holy well set into the bank below. The water emerges from a small stone grotto that is overhung with ivy and ferns. The yew predates Hope Bagot's quaint little Norman church by centuries, indicating this was a sacred site long before the coming of Christianity. Incorporated into the wall of the church is an archaic stone head, possibly of Celtic origin, which suggests this well may have been in use for at least two millennia. Modern-day pilgrims still visit here as evidenced by the colourful clootie ribbons and other offerings left hanging from the old yew's branches.

52.3633, -2.6058; SO588740

25 Mitchell's Fold, Priest Weston

The area now occupied by this stone circle was once said to be farmed by a giant who kept a pure-white fairy cow. The animal who would freely give up her milk to anyone who milked her, providing they took no more than one pailful at a time. This arrangement continued happily until one day a witch named Mitchell came and milked the cow into a sieve, not stopping until the poor cow ran dry and became crazed. The cow then ran away, never to be seen again – although there are some who say this fairy cow became the fearsome Dun Cow that was killed by Guy of Warwick (see **Guy's Cliffe**). As punishment for her wicked deed, the witch was turned to stone and stands there still as the tallest stone, while the circle of stones was said to have been placed around her to prevent her escaping. Mitchell's Fold is thought to date to the Bronze Age and stands high on an exposed hilltop, close to the Welsh border. A rock formation not far to the northeast is called the Giant's Cave (52.5859, -3.0102; SO316991; private land) and is perhaps where the fairy cow's giant owner once made his home.

52.5787, -3.0282; SO304983; Trailhead Parking: 52.5759, -3.0305; SO302980; 350m

26 Ogo Hole, Llanymynech

Llanymynech Hill straddles the border between England and Wales with the entrance to Ogo Hole, traditionally believed

to be an entrance to Fairyland, found on the English side. Although likely to be a remnant of an ancient Roman copper mine it was said that many more mysterious tunnels once stretched deep underground. One of these tunnels passed directly beneath the local village inn, where people could sometimes hear the faint strains of violin music emanating from the cellar floor below. The music was thought to be played by a blind fiddler who had once accidentally wandered into Ogo Hole. There he encountered the fairy folk under the hill, who kept him as their unwilling guest. Always fond of music, the Llanymynech fairies also liked to dance outside at midnight in the fields surrounding the cave entrance.

Found in an overgrown area of trees and scrub on the edge of a golf course where public footpaths pass close by, the mouth of the cave is framed by jagged rock overhung with trees and bushes. Today the cave does

not extend more than a few metres into the hill and the entrance is now too low for anyone to accidentally wander inside and become lost in Fairyland.

52.7923, -3.0944; SJ2622221; Trailhead: 52.7881, -3.1007; SJ258217; 700m

27 St Cuthbert's Well, Albrighton

Tucked away in a little roadside nature reserve in the village of Albrighton, the historic St Cuthbert's healing spring flows out into a landscaped pond in a garden-like enclosure surrounded by trees. The waters of the well were said to be beneficial for eye problems and to even cure blindness. Although the well in its present form is probably 19th century, the presence of old yew trees nearby suggests the area has a long history as a sacred site.

52.6385, -2.2845; SJ808045

28 St Milburga's Well, Stoke St Milborough

Flowing out from under a stone basin the gushing waters of St Milburga's Well form a fast-flowing rivulet that cascades down a wooded gully. The spring was said to have been formed by the hoof of St Milburga's white horse striking the ground to provide healing waters to bathe her wounds when she was fleeing from her enemies. She then performed another miracle by causing a field newly sown with barley to become fully grown. When St Milburga's pursuers reached the spot they were baffled when told by the local people that she had passed by just after the barley had been sown! In another version of the story, she caused a stream to swell to block her pursuer's path. She later became the protectress of the river Corve, which she miraculously caused to flow. All these stories hint at memories of an ancient fertility and nature goddess who could make crops grow and water flow. In one final twist, the original name of Stoke St Milborough was Godestoch (Godda's Stoke) – Godda being the fairy woman who married Wild Edric of **Clun**. Like the fairy queen of folklore, Godestoch rode around on a white horse, so the story of St Milburga may be linked to the fairies as well as to goddess worship.

To the north of Stoke St Milborough at Holdgate you can find another 'goddess' in the form of a stone carving of a Sheela-na-Gig protruding from the outside wall of **Holy Trinity Church** (52.5025, -2.6473; SO561895). Like other female figures of this type, this one is also clearly displaying her genitalia which she is spreading apart with her hands. Newlyweds would visit the statue because it was believed she had the power to help them conceive.

52.4371, -2.6374; SO567823

30

29 St Winifred's Well, Woolston

Hidden away down a small lane on the edge of the village, the waters of St Winifred's Well emerge from beneath a tiny, half-timbered building that once served as the local courthouse. According to legend, monks who were carrying the relics of the saint stopped to rest here on their journey to Shrewsbury Abbey and the well became a place of pilgrimage during the medieval period. The waters were reputed to have miraculous healing powers, being particularly effective for healing broken bones, bruises and wounds. Stones found in the water bearing red spots were said to have been stained by the blood of the saint. Today the building is a secluded holiday cottage but the well water still flows from an arched chamber beneath it into a stone plunge pool and from there into a pond.

52.8132, -3.0070; SJ322244; Private Land

30 Stiperstones, Pennerley *

Rising above a windswept expanse of moorland, the Stiperstones form a long,

29

jagged ridge of rocks, the highest of which is called the Devil's Chair. It is here that a giant, or some say the Devil, sat down to rest while carrying an apron-load of stone from Ireland. As he stood up again the apron strings broke and scattered the boulders which still lie all over the hill. Another pile of stones forming a cairn was said to have been dropped by a giantess who later tried to carry some of the stones away.

The Devil was reputed to sit on his chair at every available opportunity in the hope that his weight might hasten the prophecy that England shall be ruined when the Stiperstones have sunk back into the earth. One day while sitting there he pulled a pebble from his shoe and threw it towards Bishop's Castle where it became known as the Lea Stone. Deep within the hill are the shafts and tunnels of ancient lead mines, where Wild Edric of **Clun** and his court are said to lie sleeping, only venturing out at times of war to lead the spectral wild hunt across the land.

Today the Stiperstones still feel wild and remote and the grey, craggy rocks silhouetted against the skyline look like the splintered backbone of some huge and ancient beast. The area is a designated nature reserve and the Shropshire Way footpath now follows the entire length of the ridge.

52.5866, -2.9336; SO368991 (Devil's Chair); Trailhead Parking: 52.5734, -2.9320; SO369976; 1.6km

31 The Wrekin, Little Wenlock *

The prominent hill known as The Wrekin has been a landmark for travellers entering Shropshire for centuries. It rises steeply over the surrounding flat farmland and is crowned with an Iron Age hillfort that once provided refuge for the local tribes. According to legend, the hill was built by two giants who intended to create a secure home for themselves, but during the work they began to quarrel. The first giant took a swing at the second with his spade, but missed and hit the hillside, leaving a cleft in the rocks now called the Needle's Eye. He was then attacked by a raven belonging to the second giant, which plucked out both his eyes. As his tears ran, they filled a rock basin called the Raven's Bowl (52.6683, -2.5510; SJ628079) which is said will never be emptied. The blinded giant was then imprisoned within Ercall Hill (52.6840, -2.5278; SJ644097) and the victor took the Wrekin for himself. Bare patches of earth on the hill are said to mark the giant's footsteps.

Another creation story concerns a giant who came over the border from Wales intending to bury the town of Shrewsbury with the huge spadeful of earth he carried. While trying to find the town he encountered a wily cobbler who claimed the sack he carried was full of shoes that had been completely worn out during the long, hard walk from Shrewsbury. The giant decided he was weary enough already and dumped the mound of earth, forming the Wrekin. He then scraped the mud off his shoes and created Ercall Hill.

A May Day celebration known as the Wrekin Wake used to take place on top of the main hill. There, people would ritually drink from the Raven's Bowl, which was also known as the Cuckoo's Cup as it was

31

thought by some to have been miraculously created for those birds. Today the Wrekin is a popular place to walk and has a number of footpaths leading over and around its flanks. There is a local tradition that a young woman who walks through the Needle's Eye will receive a vision of her future true love. If she looks back, however, she will always remain unmarried. According to another saying, a person could never be a true native of Shropshire unless they had walked through the Needle's Eye.

52.6680, -2.5534; SJ626079 (Needle's Eye); Trailhead Parking: 52.6799, -2.5363; SJ638092; 1.8km

CHESHIRE

32 Alderley Edge *

The wooded, rocky ridge of Alderley Edge is an area steeped in history and legend. Bearing the scars of many ancient mines and quarries, it is overgrown with trees and criss-crossed by footpaths. It was in this woodland that a farmer taking a white mare to sell at market met an old man with a long beard. The old man asked to buy the horse but the farmer rudely refused, believing he would get a better price at the market. The old man retorted that although many would admire the horse, no-one would buy her that day. This indeed proved true, so the disappointed farmer set off home. Once more he met the old man at the same spot, who now asked the farmer to follow him to a rock face in the hillside. As the old man touched the rock it split with a thunderous crack to reveal a magical iron gate that led to a cavern beyond. Within the cavern a host of warriors lay sleeping, all with a white horse beside them except for one. The terrified farmer now gladly accepted the gold coins offered as the old man explained the warriors lay sleeping until the hour of a mighty battle when the fate of England would be decided. As the farmer hastily left, the rock face sealed itself once more and no one has seen the enchanted cavern since. The wizard-like old man is popularly identified as Merlin, while the sleeping knights are thought to be King Arthur and his court.

At the side of one of the paths that leads along the Edge lies the Wizard's Well. Springwater said to have healing properties drips into a small basin at the foot of the rock face, while above it, carved into the living rock, is a bearded face representing the wizard himself, along with the rhyming couplet:

Drink of this and take thy fill,
For the water falls by the wizard's will.

Further along the Edge another well has long been a popular place to make wishes, traditionally by dropping a bent pin into the water or tying a clootie ribbon onto one of the nearby trees. The **Wishing Well** (53.2970, -2.2145; SJ858778) has a stone trough placed to catch the water that spouts from the rock above. It is found at the entrance to the Hermit's Cave, a small hollow in the rock carved out by human hands long ago.

Alderley Edge has breathtaking views and many more mysteries to explore including a holy well, Druid's Circle, Castle Rock, Stormy Point, the Beacon and the Golden

32

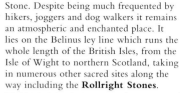

Stone. Despite being much frequented by hikers, joggers and dog walkers it remains an atmospheric and enchanted place. It lies on the Belinus ley line which runs the whole length of the British Isles, from the Isle of Wight to northern Scotland, taking in numerous other sacred sites along the way including the **Rollright Stones**.

53.2990, -2.2183; SJ855780 (Wizard's Well) Popular, Trailhead Parking: 53.2920, -2.2119; SJ859772; 1.6km

33 Rostherne Mere

Close to the southern shore of Rostherne Mere, the largest natural lake in Cheshire, sits a church. According to local legend workmen were transporting a large new bell to be installed there, an exhausting task that caused one man to curse the bell in frustration when he cried out, "I wish the Devil would take you!" At this the ropes tethering the bell snapped and it rolled out of the cart, crushing the workman who swore, then kept rolling right into the mere. It sank beneath the waters and was never seen again. However, the bell could be heard ringing every Easter Sunday when a mermaid visited the mere by swimming along a submerged tunnel linking the mere to the Irish Sea. Although she was seldom seen her songs could be heard drifting up from the depths as she sat atop the bell, deep below the surface of the water. Today the mere is a nature reserve, and although the church still stands the mermaid's song is seldom heard.

53.3496, -2.3880; SJ742837 (Church)

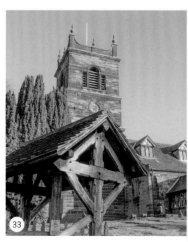

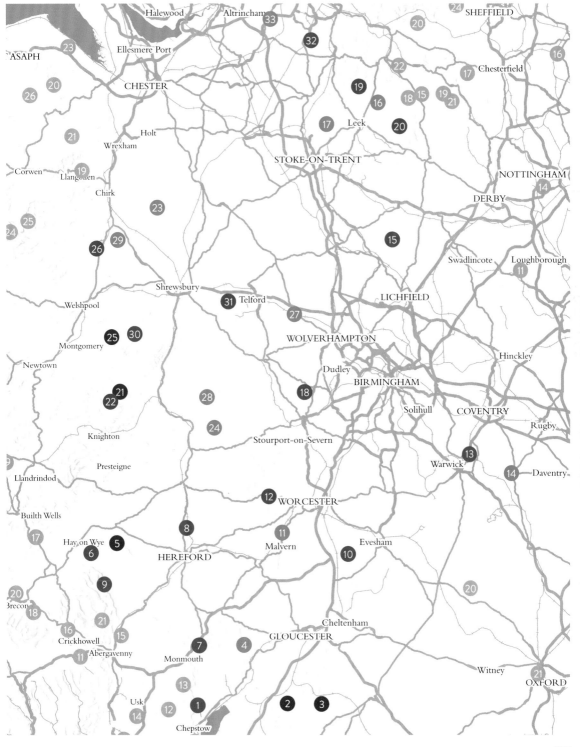

EASTERN ENGLAND

Eastern England covers a broad area from the wild hills of the Derbyshire Peak District in the west, to the low-lying areas of former marshland in Norfolk and Lincolnshire to the east. Hundreds of years of industrial-scale farming and modern development have obliterated so much of the ancient past in this area, that it is only in the Pennine region that many ancient traditions and sites still survive. Although most of eastern England lacks the rich and ancient magical folklore of the Celtic west, it retains some fascinating medieval and later folk traditions that echo more ancient stories.

Tales of spectral black dogs haunting the country lanes around villages like Blyborough in Lincolnshire are a memory of the ancient wild hunt that once traversed the land seeking lost souls. Unwary travellers walking near Norfolk's Cromer Cliffs were met with the horrifying sight of a black dog with huge glowing red eyes. To encounter the beast, known in this region as Black Shuck, was a terrifying experience, and just like an encounter with the wild hunt, it was a portent of doom. Medieval tales of giants and dragons are also to be found in this region. The legend of a destructive dragon survives at Ludham in Norfolk, while the Dragon of Wantley from Wharncliffe Crags in South Yorkshire was dispatched by a brave night in a novel way. The landscape of eastern England was transformed by primeval giants who reputedly created the hill on which Wandlebury Ring in Cambridgeshire sits, as well as the hills and islands near the Norfolk Broads alongside the river Ant. In Norfolk, too, the grave of a medieval giant called Tom Hickathrift can be found at Tilney-All-Saints church. Memories of the Celtic druids and their pagan rites remain at the eerily twisted Hemlock Stone in Nottinghamshire and at the Druid's Stone in Bungay churchyard in Suffolk. In Derbyshire the carvings at Rowtor Rocks owe their creation to the 18th-century Druid revival, but are no less magical for their lack of a more ancient history.

Only in the Peak District do we encounter the magic of standing stones and the land-protecting spirits known as hobs and boggarts. The Grey Ladies of Nine Stones Close in Derbyshire are said to come alive at night while Arbor Low stone circle is haunted by malevolent boggarts. Thirst House Cave in Deepdale was home to a hob who endowed a nearby spring with healing powers, while the extensive caves of Peak Cavern – once known rather evocatively as the Devil's Arse – were thought to lead straight to the Underworld. Eastern England, however, contains very few holy wells that can still be visited today. A couple of rare survivals are Stevington Well in Bedfordshire, where healing waters flow freely from a secluded alcove below the church mound, and ancient St Botolph's Well in Hadstock, Essex.

1 St Botolph's Well, Hadstock

Beside the graveyard of Hadstock's small village church, which dates back to Saxon times, there is an ancient healing well that flows out into a small roadside pond, overhung with vegetation. A path runs beside the pond, and then past the well into the churchyard. The waters of the well, which never run dry, were said to be a cure for scrofula, a glandular disease characterised by swellings. According to another tradition, young women could be assured of meeting their true love if they offered up a ring to the sacred waters of the well.

52.0796, 0.2732; TL558448

2 Bungay and Blythburgh

In St Mary's churchyard, in the centre of the quiet market town of Bungay, sits a small lichen-covered rock known as the Druid's Stone. Its presence is not obvious as it barely exceeds the height of the surrounding gravestones, but it is said that if you run round it 12 times or tap on it 12 times and place your ear to the stone, you can hear answers to your questions or make wishes. A story that the Devil can be summoned there on certain days of the year is likely to be a memory of an old pagan ritual that was performed at the stone in times gone by.

St Mary's Church is also known for a curious event that took place during a violent storm in 1577 when the congregation was visited by a manifestation of a huge spectral dog that rampaged through the church, attacking people and seriously injuring several. **Blythburgh church (52.3213, 1.5944; TM450753)** had a similar visitation on the very same evening, and the burn marks caused by the dog's claws can still be seen on the church door there. One theory suggests that the rare phenomena of ball lightening may account for these apparitions, but why the congregations should have perceived them as a spectral hound remains a mystery.

52.4556, 1.4377; TM336897 (Druid's Stone, Bungay Church)

3 Lady's Well, Woolpit

A medieval chronicle first recounts the tale of the 'green children' of Woolpit – two children, a brother and sister, who were found in a dazed and fearful state. Both the children had green-tinged skin and later claimed to have come from 'St Martin's Land', which they described as a place of perpetual twilight. From there, they had followed the sound of bells through a cavern and emerged into the bright sunlight of this world, then remained almost senseless until they were found and brought to a local landowner's house. At first, they spoke in an unintelligible babble and would eat only raw beans. The boy sickened and died soon after but the girl eventually lost her green pallor, learned to speak English, grew into a young woman and married a Norfolk man. The origins of the children have been the cause of much speculation, with many believing their green skin and twilight home indicate they had come from the land of Faerie. It has also been suggested that the tale could be a remnant of a pre-Christian pagan tradition attached to an ancient healing well in Woolpit known as the Lady's Well. A partial moat encloses this spring, which emerges in a small area of

woodland near Woolpit church (52.2250, 0.8895; TL974426). The waters were said to cure eye diseases and the spring remains an enchanted spot with clootie ribbons in the trees. The tale of the green children is commemorated within the church and at various locations around the village.

52.2265, 0.8922; TL976626

NORFOLK

4 Cromer Cliffs

Just to the east of the busy seaside town of Cromer, the flat coastline rises steeply and the cliffs are covered in lush vegetation. The clifftop paths in this area were said to be haunted at night by Black Shuck, a celebrated spectral black dog the size of a calf with huge, red glowing eyes. Anyone who encountered Black Shuck and met his gaze was believed to die within the day. Another spectral hound was said to haunt the beaches around Cromer, luring people into the water to drown, but the dog would vanish into a mist if approached.

Parking: 52.9199, 1.3409; TG246410

5 Little Walsingham Shrine & Wishing Wells

The shrine to Our Lady of Walsingham with its small chapel-house was established in the 11th century following a devout noblewoman's visions. When Walsingham's priory was built, it soon developed into a major pilgrimage centre but, along with the other religious buildings, it was destroyed during the Reformation. The shrine was rebuilt nearer the priory ruins in the 1930s and the holy well was discovered there. Two further wells and a large pool are also in the grounds of the priory (52.8936, 0.8765; TF935367). Originally thought to be healing wells, they now have a reputation as wishing wells. It is said the wells must be approached in silence and the wish made while kneeling at first one and then the other, and that the wish will come true so long as it is never spoken aloud. While they lack the sanctity and modern infrastructure that has built up around the well within the shrine, these wells – framed by medieval ruins – have a more authentic appeal.

52.8946, 0.8759; TF935368 (shrine)

6 Ludham & St Benet's Abbey*

Legend has it that a dragon used to live in a tunnel near the church under the quiet rural village of Ludham. All attempts to block up the tunnel failed and the dragon would emerge each night to terrorise the villagers. Then one day, to their horror, the dragon emerged into the sunlight, at which point a quick-thinking villager ran to block the tunnel with a single, huge round boulder. Unable to return to its lair the angry dragon howled and flew into a rage. He fled to nearby **St Benet's Abbey** (52.6874, 1.5206; TG380157) where he thrashed around, destroying the masonry, before flying through an archway and disappearing under the gatehouse, never to be seen again. Little remains of St Benet's Abbey today except for some foundations lying in a green field beside the river Ant, but the gatehouse that marked the entrance to the dragon's lair still stands.

The landscape around the river Ant further to the west was said to have been created by a giant (often personified as the Devil) who scooped out gravel from the Norfolk Broads and then dropped it to form the nearby hills and islands including Readham Hill (52.7220, 1.5048; TG367195) and How Hill (52.7175, 1.5123; TG373191).

52.7093, 1.5338; TG388182 (Ludham Church)

7 Tilney-All-Saints

In the graveyard of Tilney-All-Saints church, a long slab of stone is reputed to mark the grave of a local giant known as Tom Hickathrift. He was said to have fought the Ogre of Smeeth, who was blocking the road to King's Lynn market. Tom defeated him using only a cart axle as a sword and a cartwheel as a shield. Indentations in a stone plinth in the churchyard are thought to have been made by Tom's fingers.

52.7366, 0.3212; TF568179 (Church)

CAMBRIDGESHIRE

8 Wandlebury Ring, Cambridge

An early medieval legend tells of a ghostly black knight who could be encountered at Wandlebury Ring hillfort on moonlit nights. If you entered the fort alone and called out, "Knight, knight, come forth and fight", his ghostly form would appear and challenge you to a duel! This huge Iron Age ringfort just outside Cambridge is now a country park and a popular destination for day-trippers. The southern edge of the interior is now occupied by 17th-century and later buildings but the overgrown, forested ramparts still retain an air of magic and mystery.

Wandlebury Ring lies in the Gogmagog Hills, whose three peaks were said to have been created when the giant Gog, who lived in a cave nearby, had an argument with his wife Magog. He threw three huge clods of earth at her, which formed the three hills: Telegraph Clump (52.1623, 0.1845; TL495538), Little Trees Hill (52.1547, 0.1744; TL488529) and Wandlebury Hill where Wandlebury Ring is now found. There was once thought to have been a giant chalk hill figure carved onto Wandlebury Hill who perhaps represented the giant Gog. He may have been similar in style to the one at **Cerne Abbas**, Dorset.

Parking £: 52.1575, 0.1806; TL492532; Popular

BEDFORDSHIRE

9 Stevington Holy Well

A rare example of a surviving holy well in eastern England, Stevington Holy Well lies under a small hill topped with a medieval church – probably built to Christianise this ancient site of pagan veneration. The water emerges from a stone arch set into a wall in the side of the hill and flows out into marshy ground dotted with purple butterbur flowers in early spring. The cold, clear water was thought to have healing properties and nuns from a local convent were said to have used it to treat sick patients.

52.1723, -0.5529; SP990536

in poverty. It is said to be aligned to other nearby standing stones and a secret tunnel was thought to link it to the site of the former Leicester Abbey. The stone now sits incongruously by a busy roundabout on the Leicester bypass, but roads built nearby avoided the stone as superstition persisted that ill-fortune would follow anyone who tried to disturb it.

52.6580, -1.0787; SK624070

11 Whitwick Holy Well

Whitwick church sits in a natural amphitheatre near to the confluence of two streams and the spring of fresh water that emerges from under the chancel of Whitwick church is reputed to have healing properties. The water is channelled out from beneath the church to emerge through a stone wall into a wooded recess in the churchyard before flowing out into the stream. It is thought the presence of the spring accounts for the siting of the church, indicating that this was a pre-Christian sacred site.

52.7418, -1.3569; SK435162

RUTLAND

12 Braunston-in-Rutland Goddess

A curious, carved-stone statue depicting a bare-breasted female figure with protruding tongue and eyes stands by the wall of All Saints Church in Braunston-in-Rutland. The stone was in use as the church doorstep until the 1920s and the carving on the downward-facing side was only discovered when it was removed for repairs. Many people believe it to be a rare survival of an ancient Celtic goddess figure and although the church itself dates back to Norman times no one knows for sure how old the statue is, or how it came to be hidden at the threshold of the church.

52.6506, -0.7709; SK832065 (church)

LINCOLNSHIRE

13 Blyborough

The quiet rural village of Blyborough with its quaint parish church was once said to have been haunted by a huge phan-

LEICESTERSHIRE

10 Humberstone, Leicester

Also known as the Hellstone or Holystone, the Humberstone is a large boulder made of pink granite that was probably deposited in the last Ice Age and has subsequently become submerged in the earth. Attempts have been made to completely bury it in the past but it is said to always rise to the surface of its own volition. Only the top of the stone is currently exposed, but at various times it has been both completely covered and entirely exposed in a man-made hollow.

According to local legend, it was dropped by a god or a giant and is haunted by the fairy folk who protect it from harm. Deep groaning sounds have sometimes been heard coming from the stone and sleeping nearby was not advised for fear of abduction by the fairies who live either in or under the stone. The Humberstone is also said to be cursed and anyone who harms it will suffer misfortune. A local farmer who tried to remove the stone suffered nothing but bad luck for years afterwards and ended his life

(13)

tom black dog with spectral eyes. He was encountered at night in the lane heading north to Grayingham, especially in the area around the fish ponds.

53.4464, -0.5944; SK934953 (Blyborough to Grayingham lane)

14 Hemlock Stone, Stapleford

This huge and strangely twisted sandstone column was said to have been thrown by the Devil from Castleton in Derbyshire. He was aiming at Lenton Priory (52.9436, -1.1786; SK552387) but missed his target. The tale could also be linked to the memory of a prehistoric trackway known as the Portway that once ran from Mam Tor near **Peak Cavern**, all the way to the Hemlock Stone. The trackway could have had ritual significance as it passes by several other sacred sites, such as **Rowtor Rocks** and **Nine Stones Close**. The Druids were once believed to have gathered at the Hemlock Stone to perform rituals and until the beginning of the 19th century fires were kindled there on Beltane Eve. The stone itself is now surrounded by iron railings and overlooks a busy road into Nottingham.

52.9431, -1.2581; SK499386

15 Arbor Low, Youlgreave *

Arbor Low is the Peak District's most impressive prehistoric site. Sitting high on a wild plateau this large, well-preserved Neolithic henge monument has wide grass-covered banks and deep ditches enclosing a circle of huge recumbent stones that were thought to have once stood upright. It is considered a major centre of earth energies, with a number of ley lines that pass through and intersect at the henge. In the past, the circle was avoided at night as it was reputedly the haunt of malevolent spirits known as boggarts who prowled around the stones. No records remain of what the boggarts looked like but their appearance was said to induce terror in all who encountered them.

53.1690, -1.7617; SK160635 (access to Arbor Low); £ Trailhead Parking: 53.1709, -1.7643; SK158637; 400m

16 Creswell Crags

The wide limestone gorge known as Creswell Crags is lined with numerous caves that have been the focus for folk-magic practices throughout the centuries. Celebrated for its cave art, Creswell Crags' Ice Age prehistoric inhabitants carved images and symbols onto the cave walls and on fragments of bone over 12,000 years ago, including a woolly rhinoceros' bone featuring a man with a beast-like head that was found at Pin Hole Cave. This cave, at the western end of the gorge, owes its name to the custom of making wishes while leaving offerings of pins within. There is also Robin Hood Cave, where the legendary outlaw was said to hide from the authorities, and Mother Grundy's Parlour, named for a witch some say once lived there, and first excavated in the 19th century after a local woman dreamed there was treasure hidden in the cave.

It has recently been discovered that the caves also contain the largest concentration of apotropaic 'witch marks' found in Britain. These marks, usually found in old buildings, were supposed to ward off witches and malign

influences and were in use from the 16th century onwards. Over a thousand of these symbols have been found at Creswell Crags, although most of them are carved in a deep recess of Robin Hood Cave usually inaccessible to the public. The marks have been made by different people over a long period of time, but what dark forces prompted such an undertaking is unknown. The cave might have been regarded as an entrance to the Underworld whose inhabitants had to be prevented from entering the human world. Verdant ivy now clings to the sides of Creswell Crags, framing the many caves that overlook a small lake running the length of the gorge. With such picturesque surroundings where families enjoy a fun day out, it is hard to imagine any lurking horrors within the shadowy depths of the caves, but these fears were all too real, even to our recent ancestors.

Parking £: 53.2640, -1.1929; SK539744; Popular; Free but Cave Tours ££

17 Hob Hurst's House, Beeley

Lying in an isolated location high on Beeley Moor, Hob Hurst's House is a Bronze Age mound containing a stone cist (burial coffin). The mound was once said to be inhabited by a helpful hob, known locally as Hob Hurst. One day the hob followed a local cobbler home and offered to make shoes for him. Hob Hurst turned out the shoes very quickly but unfortunately also very shoddily, so the cobbler threw them all out of the window as fast as the hob could make them. Hence the Derbyshire expression about something made too quickly: "It's bin done faster than Hob Hurst can chuck shoes out o' t' winder." On another occasion a woman who sheltered the hob in her house for the night was able to give a description of him. She said that he was small and dark-skinned with gleaming eyes; his singing sounded like wind through the moorland cotton grass, while his laughter was like a bubbling stream. The mound is said to have a supernatural aura and if you listen carefully, you may still catch the sound of the hob's voice echoing from within.

53.2194, -1.5711; SK287692; Trailhead: 53.2088, -1.5720; SK286680; 1.8km

18 Lud Well, Pilsbury

Flowing around moss-covered boulders and twisted trees directly into the river Dove, Lud Well is a natural spring that gushes forth from a tunnel-like cave. The dark,

flooded cave mouth is almost high enough to stand up in and feels like an entrance to the mysterious Celtic Otherworld. The well is sometimes associated with the Celtic god Lludd or the ancient Celtic king Lud who is remembered at Ludgate in London.
53.1596, -1.8169; SK123625

19 Nine Stones Close, Elton

These four standing stones, also known as the Grey Ladies, are part of an ancient stone circle that now sits on the edge of a grassy field by an old dry-stone wall. According to folklore the stones are said to come alive at midnight and dance around the moor. Viewed through the mist they can appear like ancient sentinels, patiently awaiting the time when they can once more spring back to life and dance. The fairies also like to dance within the circle here when the moon is full and at special times of the year. Witnesses have heard the sound of fairy pipes and seen hundreds of fairies dancing and sitting on and around the stones. One man found a little fairy pipe near the stones and used it to smoke his tobacco, which subsequently induced a vision of Fairyland.
Visible nearby is **Robin Hood's Stride** (53.1571, -1.6659; SK224622) where the

legendary hero is said to have leapt between the two rocky pinnacles that surmount this castle-like rock formation. Another stone circle lies 2.5km away, the atmospheric **Nine Ladies Stone Circle** (53.1680, -1.6288; SK249634) who were turned to stone for dancing on the Sabbath. The out-lying King Stone was said to be the fiddler.

53.1605, -1.6643; SK225626; Private Land; Trailhead: 53.1605, -1.6678; SK223626; 250m

20 Peak Cavern, Castleton

The entrance to Peak Cavern lies at the end of a short but dramatic gorge, its towering cliffs hung with mosses and ferns. Known alternatively as The Devil's Arse, the cavern was once seen as an entrance to the Underworld. At the base of the cliffs, beneath the cave entrance, a stream emerges directly from this underworld and flows along the length of the gorge. Following the excavation of a nearby spring, which flows into this stream, hundreds of offerings from Celtic times were found, including a complete stone head that can be seen in the local museum.

According to a curious 12th-century tale, one winter a man searching for his pregnant sow near the entrance to Peak Cavern stepped inside the cave. He suddenly found himself in a strange but beautiful land where the harvest was just being gathered. There he found his sow, which had just given birth to piglets, so he guided her out of the cave, only to find himself back in winter's chill at the cave entrance. Today, Peak Cavern is a popular show cave but it was said that in medieval times prisoners from Peveril Castle, which sits directly above it, would sometimes be incarcerated in the cave, further adding to its sinister reputation.

Towering over the valley opposite is **Mam Tor** (53.3492, -1.8097; SK127836) the 'Mother Mountain' which provides dramatic 360-degree views of the sur-rounding landscape. Once topped by a Celtic hillfort, it was the start of an ancient trackway called the Portway that ran south all the way past **Nine Stones Close** and **Rowtor Rocks**.

53.3403, -1.7784; SK148826; £££ Very Popular

21 Rowtor Rocks, Birchover

At the rocky outcrop overlooking the vil-lage of Birchover, the form of the natural gritstone has been enhanced by human

hands to create a magical druidic landscape. The mossy green boulders of Rowtor Rocks form numerous caves and passages, with trees growing up and around the rocks. Steps wind their way through these rocks leading to caverns that have been enlarged to create atmospheric meeting places for rituals, while large stone altars have been carved from the living rock. On top of some large boulders a row of seats, complete with ornate arms, has been carved. Most of this work is attributed to a local 18th-century landowner who had a keen interest in the Druid revival at that time. However, there are also some genuine and unique prehistoric rock carvings which, in addition to cup and ring marks, also include a serpent and a flower-like design. Despite its more dramatic but less-ancient

features, Rowtor Rocks has a timeless, magical atmosphere that has only been heightened by the alterations that people have been called to create there.

53.1561, -1.6490; SK235621

22 Thirst House Cave, Chelmorton

The deep, wooded cleft of Deepdale was once thought to be a favourite haunt of the Derbyshire fairy folk. One cave in particular, known as Thirst House Cave, was home to a hob who would assist with the farm chores or cause havoc if offended in some way. Hob Hurst, as he was known, was guardian of the spring that emerged into the valley there. Each Good Friday it was said the hob would enchant the waters so those who came to quench their thirst would be cured of any afflictions. The mouth of Thirst House Cave is visible from the path through the valley below and can be reached by a short steep path. The cave soon descends into mysterious, dark depths, while the entrance presents a perfectly framed view across the wooded Deepdale valley.

53.2380, -1.8561; SK097712; Trailhead Parking £: 53.2491, -1.8469; SK103724; 1.8km

SOUTH YORKSHIRE

23 Bailey Hill, High Bradfield

Said to be of ancient pagan origin, Bailey Hill was a defensive motte in Norman times.

It was thought by local people to contain treasure buried in underground passages that connected to other sites nearby. Trees now swathe the summit of the distinctive conical hill, found to the west of the village. The nearby High Bradfield Church (53.429028, -1.599331; SK267925) was originally meant to be built in Low Bradfield, just under a kilometre away, but the building materials were mysteriously transported to High Bradfield every night by unseen hands. Such legends usually arise to account for the siting of churches on old pagan sites.

53.4302, -1.6008; SK266926

24 The Head Stone, Hallam Moors

A landmark visible for miles around, the Head Stone stands proud on a rocky outcrop amongst the heather of Hallam Moors, and from certain angles the craggy grit stone stack resembles a crude head gazing out over the land. The large and eerily weathered stone forms an imposing column of primeval rock that was once thought to have been man-made and a site of Druid worship. It was also known as the Cock Crowing Stone because at certain times of the year, when the cock crowed (presumably at sunrise) it would magically turn around.

53.3826, -1.6170; SK255873; Trailhead: 53.3859, -1.6123; SK258877; 700m

25 Wharncliffe Crags

Hidden in a dense woodland of twisted trees with craggy outcrops, the range of imposing grey cliffs known as Wharncliffe Crags lies on the western edge of Wharncliffe Chase – a medieval royal hunting park set on a plateau above the cliffs. The crags were once said to have been inhabited by a troublesome dragon known as the Dragon of Wantley who lived in a cave still known as the Dragon's Den. Legend tells that the dragon was eventually dispatched by a knight wearing spiked armour who landed the mortal blow by kicking the dragon up the backside! Today the area is popular with hikers and rock climbers and the northern stretch of Wharncliffe Crags is a nature reserve, while the Dragon's Den (53.4593, -1.5409; SK305959) can be seen at the southern end of the crags near Wharncliffe Lodge.

53.4716, -1.5506; SK299973; Trailhead Parking: 53.4504, -1.5119; SK325949; 5km, passing by Dragon's Den

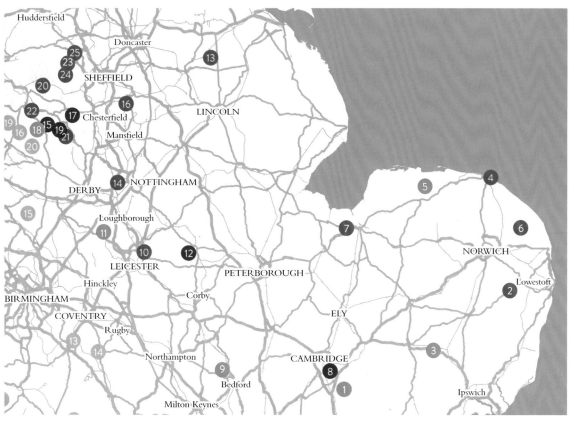

LANCASHIRE & YORKSHIRE

Away from the heavily populated south of this region is an idyllic rural landscape of high moors interspersed with lush green valleys, their ancient fields enclosed by old drystone walls. The Yorkshire Dales and the North York Moors, in particular, have retained an authentic old-world feel and are both designated national parks. The traditional farming communities retained a wealth of old folklore about the otherworldly beings that once inhabited these windswept moors and hidden valleys. Although secure in their stone-built cottages, they were fearful of the moorland spirits populating the wild uplands beyond their thresholds and kept them at bay with crosses of rowan wood or witch marks carved on the house beams. Yorkshire in particular is known for its abundance of hobs. These hairy and unpredictable household spirits sometimes helped out on remote farms, churning butter and threshing corn at night. On the Yorkshire coast mischievous hobs and boggles also inhabited sea caves and some could help heal sick children.

The whole region abounds in folklore, from the fairy queen of the Yorkshire Dales who dwells in a cave behind Janet's Foss waterfall to an altogether more malevolent fairy, Jeanie o' Biggersdale of Mulgrave Woods in the North York Moors. A cave in the side of Elbolton Hill in the Yorkshire Dales is reputed to be a portal to the land of Faerie and fairies are said to inhabit the Forest of Bowland in Lancashire. Pendle Hill and the surrounding Lancashire villages will forever be associated with witchcraft owing to the infamous witch trials of the 17th century. While the Pendle witches were accused of being malevolent, Mother Shipton of Knaresborough foretold the future and warned of danger to come. You can visit the cave where she lived, alongside the famous Dropping Well where objects left hanging seem to be turned to stone.

East Yorkshire boasts the tallest standing stone in the country, Rudston Monolith. According to local tradition, the Devil deliberately threw the stone but just missed the church. In North Yorkshire are three more huge monoliths, the Devil's Arrows – more projectiles that missed their mark. Also not to be missed are dramatic White Mare Crag and Roulston Scar that stand fortress-like at the entrance to the North York Moors. The whole area around the White Mare Crags is rich in folklore, with druidic altars, a fairy cave, a drowned village and legends about a white horse.

1

LANCASHIRE

1 Fairy Holes, Forest of Bowland

In the woods above the river Hodder near Whitewell, the limestone caves are known as the Fairy Holes and only one is large enough to enter without crawling. A Clitheroe midwife was reputedly brought to the caves to attend a fairy birth and when the father told her to use a special ointment, she stole a small amount for herself. Following the successful birth, she was paid handsomely in fairy gold and returned home. After smearing the ointment on her eye, she had the power to see the fairies and one market day she noticed the fairy father stealing apples from a stall. When she reproached him, the fairy demanded to know which eye she had seen him with and touched it. The spell was instantly broken and the midwife never saw the fairies again. Whitewell is located in the Forest of Bowland, a rural farming area with clusters of tiny stone-built settlements overlooked by windswept fells and wooded valleys

called 'cloughs' with tumbling rivers and streams. Many fairy traditions are associated with the area, including at Dinkling Green (53.9162, -2.5516; SD638468) near White-well where fairies were seen dancing on the 'White Stone', only to disappear down holes in the ground. The exact location of this stone is unknown but the limestone landscape provides plenty of hiding places for the little folk. According to local legend a fairy oak tree once stood nearby that was a focus for midsummer revelry. Meanwhile a couple of kilometres to the south, fairy washerwomen were seen at work in the waters of Leagram Brook, which runs through Buckbanks Wood (53.8958, -2.5547; SD636445. Trailhead: 53.8915, -2.5489; SD640440; 1.3km). Near Bashall Eaves an ancient stone bridge with magical associations crosses Bashall Brook (53.8869, -2.4536; SD702435. Trailhead: 53.8879, -2.4575; SD700436; 300m). Saddle Bridge was created by fairies in a single night to save an old woodcutter who was being chased by witches, hence its alternative name the Fairy Bridge.

53.9153, -2.5267; SD655467; Private Land; No paths at end; Trailhead: 53.9166, -2.5208; SD658468; 900m; crosses river via stepping stones

2 Peggy's Well, Clitheroe

Situated in the grounds of Waddow Hall on the northern bank of the river Ribble, Peggy's Well is named after a malevolent female water spirit said to haunt this stretch of water. Every seven years Peg would take the life of any unfortunate soul who crossed the ford where **Brungerley Bridge** (53.8810, -2.3988; SD738428) now stands and the fearful locals would regularly drown a bird, cat or dog in the river to appease her. Standing by the well, a time-worn, headless stone statue is said to represent Peg, who some say was a servant at the hall who slipped and drowned when she was sent to fetch water on a wintry night. Drownings and accidents in the immediate area were subsequently blamed on this restless spirit and her story may have superseded that of an ancient pagan river deity who also required appeasement.

53.8787, -2.4038; SD735425; Private Land; Trailhead: 53.8825, -2.4001; SD737429; 900m

3 Pendle Hill, Newchurch-in-Pendle

Home of the 17th-century witches executed outside Lancaster, dark, flat-topped Pendle Hill dominates the local landscape. The witches were said to meet in the Forest of Pendle on the southern side of the hill to cast spells and utter curses. When put on trial, the details of their lurid confessions – probably obtained under torture – included meetings with the Devil and the use of witches' familiars to inflict harm. Pendle's somewhat sinister reputation lingers and visitors are drawn to the churchyard at Newchurch-in-Pendle (53.8503, -2.2706; SD822393), where there is a grave said to contain the body of one of the accused, Alice Nutter. High on the church tower a curious eye-shaped inset, known as the 'Eye of God' was reputedly created to protect the church from witchcraft.

The Devil himself is said to have left his footprint on Pendle Hill. When he jumped from Hameldon Hill (53.7551, -2.2892; SD810287) over 10km south of Pendle, the Devil landed on a rock at Deerstones that bears his imprint.

53.8499, -2.3259; SD786393 (Deerstones); Trailhead: 53.8356, -2.3347; SD780377; 2.2km

4 The Written Stone, Longridge

Set into a bank on a quiet country lane, this huge sandstone slab bears the curious inscription: 'RAVFFE RADCLIFFE LAID THIS STONE TO LYE FOR EVER AD 1655'. According to local legend, the 2.7m Written Stone was set down to confine a boggart that plagued the Radcliffes, a farming family, after a dreadful murder. Some said the restless spirit of the victim manifested as a boggart and caused several

members of the family to die in mysterious circumstances. Yet even after the stone was laid, strange happenings continued and locals said the slab was cursed. Years later a new tenant farmer decided the stone would be useful in his dairy. Using a whole team of horses, he finally moved the stone but a strange sound emanated from inside

it. That night the farmer and his family were subjected to a terrifying supernatural attack and he decided to return the stone, although curiously only one horse was needed to move it back. In another incident a doctor was knocked from his horse and nearly squeezed to death by a shapeless mass that had materialised from the stone.

6 Brimham Rocks, Summerbridge

Brimham Rocks, which cover a large swathe of Brimham Moor, have been naturally weathered into all kinds of fantastical shapes. This magical landscape has been a popular destination since the 18th century and there are numerous footpaths. Fairies and Druids were said to haunt this rocky landscape and once used their powers to save a couple who, having made a suicide pact, jumped off a rock now known as **Lover's Leap** (54.0801, -1.6873; SE205649). When the pair survived, the woman's father relented and consented to their marriage. Another stone is called the **Druid's Writing Desk** (54.0818, -1.6873; SE205651) after its lectern-like appearance, while the most awe-inspiring structure of all is the **Idol** (54.0821, -1.6865; SE206651) whose huge bulk is supported by the slimmest of rock bases. These names recall ancient druidic rituals which some say took place at the site.

Other strange features include the **Rocking Stones** (54.0813, -1.6849; SE207650) which will only respond to the touch of an honest person and a **Wishing Rock** (54.0821, -1.6862; SE206651) whose power is evoked by sticking the middle finger of your right hand into a hole in the stone.

Parking £: 54.0767, -1.6829; SE208645

7 Diana's Well, East Witton

Also known as Cast Away Well, this natural spring and grotto in private woodland on Witton Fell is said to have an ancient association with the roman goddess Diana. The water flows from the mouth of an evocative stone-carved head, known affectionately as 'Slavering Sal' and the attached grotto is of 19th century construction, with mosses and ferns growing on the walls and a small stone table and basin of pure spring water. Traditionally, small items would be cast into the water while making a wish, while a local rhyme states:
Whoever eats Hammer nuts and drinks Diana's water,
Will never leave Witton town while he's a rag or tatter.
54.2613, -1.7906; SE137850; Private Land; Trailhead: 54.2676, -1.7788; SE145857; 1.8km

Perhaps the Written Stone was once a pagan altar or part of a stone circle. Whatever its origins, the stone's eerie reputation persists and its location, once known as Boggart Lane, has now been renamed Written Stone Lane.
53.8360, -2.5695; SD626379

5 Cottingley Beck

While Britain was dealing with the trauma of World War I, two young girls brought some welcome magic by publishing photos of fairies they'd seen playing in the woods around Cottingley Beck, not far from their home. The photographs caused a sensation and experts from Kodak couldn't see how they had been faked, especially by two youngsters, and declared them genuine. Controversy, however, dogged the story and the two photographers,

now elderly women, admitted they'd faked them using drawings stuck on hat pins. However, Frances Griffiths (the younger of the two) maintained until the end of her life that the fifth and final photo taken in 1920 was not a fake. In this image, titled *Fairies and Their Sun-Bath*, ethereal fairy women are seen in a nest-like enclosure of grasses and flowers. In addition to fairies and wood elves, the girls also saw little men dressed in green around the waterfall at the beck.

Cottingley Beck now flows behind a modern housing estate to the south of the village and this little patch of wilderness amid the development can only be reached by scrambling down beside a bridge that provides access to the estate. In recognition of the story, some of the estate's roads were named after the fairies in Shakespeare's *A Midsummer Night's Dream*. The original photographic prints and cameras used by the girls are on display in Bradford's National Science and Media Museum (53.7908, -1.7561; SE161327).
53.8256, -1.8250; SE116366; Private Land

8 Ebbing and Flowing Well, Giggleswick

At the foot of Giggleswick Scar is the Ebbing and Flowing Well, whose water exhibits a curious phenomenon. As you watch, the water level in the stone basin of the well falls imperceptibly slowly and then rises again, all of its own accord. According to a legend reminiscent of classical mythology, a nymph being pursued by an amorous satyr beseeched the gods to help so they transformed her into a spring emerging from the earth. It is the nymph's inward and outward breaths that cause the water level to rise and fall.

The well later became known as a place of healing, but on at least one occasion its waters have bestowed magical powers. In the 17th century a famous Yorkshire highwayman, 'Swift Nick' Nevison, stopped to water his horse at the well while on the run from the militia. After drinking, his horse reputedly acquired supernatural speed and agility, allowing Nevison to leap over vast distances and escape his pursuers. In other versions, the spirit of the well supercharged the horse by means of a magic bridle. Today the waters' ebb and flow is less noticeable but the well remains a magical place, despite the busy main road which runs alongside.

54.0840, -2.3011; SD804653

9 Elbolton Hill, Threshfield

Near the summit of Elbolton Hill is a near-vertical shaft known as Navvy Noodle Hole that leads down to deep underground caverns. It is said to be an entrance to the land of Faerie, whose inhabitants have been seen dancing at night on the grassy flanks of the hill. One man who tried to join the dancing was pushed and jostled. Forced to leave, he grabbed one of the fairies and stashed it in his pocket but when he looked inside, the fairy had escaped. Another encountered a band of fairies and their queen, describing her voice as like the sound of a silver trumpet. He felt compelled to follow and the fairies enjoyed leading him astray until he became lost, but later released him from their spell.

In the nearby village of Threshfield, the spring-fed pond known as **Our Lady's Well** (54.0701, -2.0046; SD997637; private land) is said to offer a refuge from supernatural beings. One night, a man chased by 'Pam the Fiddler and a host of imps' leapt into the pool to save himself. The well,

which is also said to have healing properties, now lies in a private garden but can be visited (with permission). The immersion pool is surrounded by a low stone wall and an old tankard still hangs there on a chain. **Calf Holes** (54.0773, -2.0559; SD964645; private land), a limestone cave on the far side of Threshfield near Skirethorns is another magical site where fairy pipes have reputedly been found.

54.0494, -1.9897; SE007614 (Navvy Noodle Hole); Trailhead: 54.0502, -1.9830; SE012615; 500m

10 Fairies' Hole, Crackpot

Concealed behind a waterfall that cascades into a small pool, the Fairies' Hole is a crevice in the rock said to give access to the land of Faerie. The opening leads down to extensive caverns that are popular with cavers, although with names like Knee-Wrecker Passage these are not places for the inexperienced to explore. Fairies' Hole is now more commonly known as Crackpot Cavern but its old name hints at tales and legends now lost.

54.3541, -2.0569; SD964953; Trailhead: 54.3566, -2.0564; SD964956; 350m

11 Harmby Fairy Well

Emerging from beneath the boughs of twin hawthorns and an elder, the fresh spring water of Harmby Fairy Well cascades down over a jumble of stones and boulders into a field close to the village. The presence of hawthorns can indicate a fairy haunt in Celtic folklore, while elder is often associated with witches as well as fairies. The name Fairy Well goes back more than two centuries and people have reported seeing strange lights around the well in the twilight.

54.3027, -1.8106; SE124896; Trailhead: 54.3021, -1.8057; SE127896; 350m

12 Janet's Foss, Malham *

As the water of this enchanted waterfall in the Yorkshire Dales deposited limestone-rich tufa, hidden chambers were created and it is in these caverns that the fairy queen Janet is said to dwell. Janet, Jeanie or Jenny is a common name for a fairy in the north of England and she is often associated with water (see **Mulgrave Woods** and **Wharton Tarn**). The entrance to Janet's tiny cave lies

partially hidden behind the curtain of water on the upper right side of the fall.
The waterfall drops down into a wide shallow pool bordered by lush vegetation. You can cross it via stepping stones that lead to another, much larger cave (not to be confused with the fairy queen's cave). Janet's Foss can be a popular destination in summer, but visit it out of season or at dawn and dusk and you cannot fail to be enchanted by this most magical of places.

54.0657, -2.1370; SD911633; Popular

13 Trollers Gill, Skyreholme *

This deep gorge with towering grey crags and trees clinging to the sides may have been named after the legendary troll inhabitants who threw rocks at anyone navigating the treacherous terrain below. The bottom of Troller's Gill is indeed strewn with boulders over which the Skyreholme Beck flows but only during the wettest periods; at other times the gorge is dry.
Troller's Gill was also the scene of a terrifying encounter with a 'barghest', a fearsome spectral black dog said to be a death omen. A local man, determined to enter the gorge and slay the barghest, succeeded in raising the

awful spirit, but was found dead the next day. In the tale, his mauled body is said to have borne wounds to the chest that could only have been made by the gigantic dog. In the daytime, Troller's Gill is popular with hikers, but tread warily if you enter there at night. The Skyreholme Beck eventually emerges further downstream and flows into the river Wharfe. A little further down the river, in a narrow gorge called **The Strid** (54.0044, -1.9049; SE063564. Trailhead parking: 54.0032, -1.9119; SE058563; 600m), the Wharfe gushes through the enclosing rocks. According to local folklore, each year on Beltane morning the river goddess appears in the gorge, taking the form of a white horse. Her appearance is a sign that a sacrifice is due and a drowning in the river will soon follow.

54.0521, -1.8967; SE068617; Trailhead: 54.0445, -1.8976; SE068609; 1km

NORTH YORKSHIRE

14 Devil's Arrows, Boroughbridge

Three immense monoliths, survivors from the distant past, stand on arable land not far from the A1 motorway. Arranged in a straight line, two stand in a field while the third is tucked away in trees by the field boundary. The massive stones are weathered and furrowed towards the top, almost as if deliberately sharpened, and this gave rise to the belief they were bolts (or arrows) thrown at the town of Aldborough either by the Devil, or by an ill-tempered giant standing on How Hill (54.0985, -1.5795; SE275670) near Fountains Abbey, over 11km to the west. The hill, now topped by an old chapel, may have been a site of ancient pagan significance. The Devil's Arrows fell short of their target but their position gives them the air of sentinels, watching over the land since ancient times and no doubt for centuries to come.

54.0932, -1.4037; SE390665. Trailhead 54.0928, -1.4025; SE391664 100m

15 Mother Shipton's Cave & Dropping Well, Knaresborough

The prophesies of Mother Shipton have long been celebrated for their apparent veracity. She is said to have predicted many events including the arrival of the Spanish Armada,

the English Civil War, and the Great Fire of London. Her birthplace, towards the end of the 15th century, and where she spent her days was this dank cave on the banks of the river Nidd. In later stories, her appearance was that of a stereotypical witch with a humped back and hooked nose that nearly reached her chin. A statue of Mother Shipton now stands inside her cave. Next to Mother Shipton's Cave is the famous Dropping Well, where mineral-rich water flows over a small cliff to form a curtain of smooth flowstone deposits. Dangling from it are a selection of modern objects that in a matter of weeks appear to turn to stone. Behind this curtain of flowstone there is a cave and at one end of it, clear water flows into a natural basin where people make wishes. On the opposite bank of the river are two of the oldest medieval cave shrines in the country. The first, St Robert's Cave (53.9996, -1.4508; SE360560) is now dark, empty and abandoned but served as his hermitage and the layout of a small chapel in the rock outside the cave is still visible. The second is the shrine of **Our Lady of the Crag** (54.0029, -1.4655; SE351564) which features a life-size effigy of a knight carved into the exterior rock next to an ornate window and doorway. The cave was said to have been hewn out of the rock by a stone

mason in recognition and thanks for the divine intervention that resulted in his son surviving a huge rock fall. Unfortunately, the chapel is seldom open but the exterior can be admired from the peaceful garden.

54.0038, -1.4717; SE347565 (Mother Shipton's Cave); ££ Very Popular

EAST YORKSHIRE

16 Rudston Monolith

Towering over the surrounding gravestones in the village churchyard, the Rudston Monolith is the tallest standing stone in Britain at 7.6m. Local legend says the Devil threw the monolith at the church but it fell short and embedded itself in the ground. In fact, the stone stands in its original position and pre-dates the church by centuries. Rudston, the village's name may be derived from the Old English *rood-stane* meaning cross-stone, which suggests a crucifix may have been attached to the top of the monolith to Christianise this site of ancient pagan sanctity. Beneath the trees in a quiet corner of the churchyard lies a prehistoric stone-lined cist grave and a small standing

stone, while the remains of several ancient earthworks lead towards the monolith, indicating its ancient significance. A number of ley lines are said to pass through or end at Rudston Monolith, connecting the site to other ancient and sacred places such as **Willy Howe**. The stone remains an impressive and ancient presence in the landscape.

54.0939, -0.3226; TA098677

17 **Willy Howe, Wold Newton**

Fairies are said to inhabit Willy Howe, a large prehistoric round barrow in the Yorkshire Wolds not far from Wold Newton village. A 12th-century chronicle tells of a man passing the barrow late one night who heard singing and the sounds of revelry coming from within. Moving closer, he saw a door in the side revealing a brightly lit room where a magnificent banquet was taking place. A fairy servant saw him peering in and passed him a goblet full of drink, but the man poured away the contents, aware that drinking it would have put him under the fairies spell. Pocketing the goblet, he fled from the banquet with the fairies in pursuit and escaped by leaping over the Gypsey Race stream (54.1379,

17

18

18

19

-0.3746; TA062725), which the fairies could not cross. The goblet, curiously shaped and made of an unknown material in an unusual colour, was later presented to King Henry I. It passed into the hands of a number of English and Scottish kings before being lost. A chest of gold was reputedly buried within the mound, but any attempt to remove it would make it sink deeper – a legend that perhaps echoes the story of the treasure a fairy maiden once gave to a young man she had fallen in love with. He was permitted to take one gold coin from the barrow each day, so long as he never revealed its source. Inevitably he let slip his secret, was punished by the Willy Howe fairies and the gold disappeared forever. People said that if you ran around the barrow nine times and then pressed your ear to the mound, the sounds of fairy merriment could still be heard. The mound itself is now covered with trees and surrounded by private farmland but a public access lane passes right by the base.

54.1361, -0.3767; TA061723; Private Land, Trailhead: 54.1378, -0.3738; TA063725; 300m

NORTH YORK MOORS

18 Boggle Hole, Robin Hood's Bay

A small sea cave in the cliffs at Boggle Hole was once home to a boggle, a spirit of place much like a hob only more mischievous. When angered they are liable to harm people or damage their property. Boggle Hole is reached by a steep path leading down to a tiny inlet and beach. The cave itself is accessible from the beach only at low tide and once provided a convenient place for smugglers to stash their loot. Nearby, the Boggle Hole youth hostel has pictures and information boards about the boggle and his legendary cave.

54.4225, -0.5291; NZ955040; Low Tide Only

19 Fairy Cross Plain, Fryupdale, Danby *

Bounded by the river Esk to the north and the high moors to the south, the twin valleys of Great Fryup Dale and Little Fryup Dale are separated by a long ridge known as Danby Heads. At the southern tip of Danby Heads, where the two valleys merge, is a place steeped legend – Fairy Cross Plain, where the little folk would emerge from their underground tunnels to dance and

where fairy rings were a common sight. These circles of wild fungi expand outwards over time, creating a dark ring of grass and also a ring of toadstools once the fruiting bodies emerge. Running around a fairy ring nine times in the light of the full moon would enable you to hear the fairies laughing and dancing in their halls below, but local children in Fryupdale were strongly advised against this or the fairies would gain power over them or even whisk them away to fairyland! Local people tended to avoid the rings altogether and it was even said that sheep and cattle would not graze near them. Sometimes, people saw the fairies, dressed in green and wearing a strange cap, disappearing into the earth of the Plain. One woman even found a fairy baby hidden in some hay but, separated from its fairy family, it soon sickened and died. At night people reported hearing the sound of fairies making their fairy 'butter', which they would enjoy flinging at houses and farm buildings. Households around the **Butter Beck** (54.4264, -0.7776; NZ794041. Trailhead: 54.4304, -0.7802; NZ792045; 550m) near Egton Grange to the east, were frequently targeted and woke to find the 'butter' – a type of fungus that grows overnight – stuck on fence-posts and other wooden structures.

Fairy Cross Plain is located in an area of green pastures bounded by drystone walls. In the centre, where the two dales meet, a small rounded hill sometimes known as **Fairy Hill** (54.4341, -0.8981; NZ715048; private land) lies halfway between the uplands of Danby Heads and Danby Rigg. The latter is crossed by an ancient path known as the Old Hellway (54.4405, -0.9084; NZ708055) that was used to transport corpses over Danby Rigg for burial in the churchyard at Danby. People report sensing the spirits of the dead on this old corpse road. The neighbouring valley of Glaisdale to the east is also the site of magical occurrences. The first concerns the Hob of Hart Hall (54.4340, -0.8079; NZ774049; private) a little fellow, covered in shaggy hair and wearing nothing more than a threadbare tunic, who helped out around the farm at night. When some boys spied on him and, taking pity made him a new tunic the hob was insulted and left, never to return. In the second story a hare was seen by a local farmer nibbling his saplings. Realising it was a witch in disguise, he loaded his gun with silver pellets then shot and wounded the hare which took refuge in the cottage of a witch, Awd Maggie. She was found the next day with unexplained wounds. The slopes at the head of Glaisdale became known as Witch Hill (54.4110, -0.8587; NZ741023; private, but can be viewed from the open-access moors above or the road below).

54.4358, -0.8981; NZ715050

20 Hob Holes, Runswick Bay

A hob who lived in a sea cave in Runswick Bay was reputed to have healing powers. Children who were afflicted with whooping cough would be brought to the cave by their concerned mothers (their fishermen husbands were far too superstitious) who would chant:
"Hob hole Hob!
My bairn's gettin't kink-cough,
Tak't off, tak't off."
This hob would sometimes lead travellers off the moor into deep pot holes, or offer them the shelter of his cave on stormy nights, only for them to drown when the tide swept back in. The exact location of the hob's cave is unknown but several small caves pepper the cliffs of Runswick Bay. The reputed lair of another type of cave-dwelling hob is further down the Yorkshire coast at **Boggle Hole**.

Just inland from the bay, fairies were said to visit Claymore Well (54.5219, -0.7362; NZ819148; private land), a deep borehole in the grounds of a farmstead, to do their laundry by night. The sounds of them beating their clothes with wooden sticks could be heard in Runswick Bay over a kilometre away. Not far from Claymore Well is Wade's Stone (see **Wade's Causeway**), while in the opposite direction, Hinderwell village churchyard is the location of **St Hilda's Well** (54.5426, -0.7786; NZ791170), a water source that was summoned up by the saint during a drought and said to cure eye diseases.

54.5277, -0.7425; NZ814154; Trailhead Parking: 54.5325, -0.7505; NZ809159; 800m

21 Hobthrush Hall, Over Silton

Hidden away in a thickly wooded hillside bordering the North York Moors, Hobthrush Hall is an almost forgotten cave that was once home to a helpful household spirit. Hob, or Hobthrush as he was known, used to visit a local innkeeper to churn his cream at night in return for a slice of bread and butter. He was reputed to be a very athletic fellow, able to leap from his cave to the top of Carlow Hill (54.3332, -1.3127; SE447932; private land) over 300m away. Following a scramble up through the trees and undergrowth, natural stone steps provide access to the dark cave entrance.

Another hole appears to act as a window, allowing light to penetrate the small chamber. There are various nooks and crannies to explore, some too small for a human that seem to disappear into a mysterious underworld. It's easy to imagine the hob still dwells in one of these tunnels, keeping himself hidden from the world outside. Strange fossils in the rocks add a further air of mystery to this cave that, though a natural phenomenon, still resembles an ancient dwelling. Graffiti from the 18th and 19th centuries that was carved on the rock face near the entrance is still visible – evidence of the cave's former popularity.

54.3342, -1.3095; SE449934; Secret/ Secluded; Trailhead: 54.3333, -1.3075; SE451933; 200m; No paths at end

22 Hole of Horcum & Blakey Topping

The vast bowl-shaped valley known as the Hole of Horcum was said to have been dug out by the giant Wade (see **Wade's Causeway**). He deposited the earth a couple of kilometres to the east forming a hill known as **Blakey Topping** (54.3323, -0.6593; SE872937; 2.6km). This unusual flat-topped

hill appears to be an ancient ritual site with the remains of a stone circle (54.3286, -0.6608; SE871933) at its foot. The trail to Blakey Topping from the Hole of Horcum car park passes along an ancient trackway known as Old Wife's Way. In this version of the story the 'Old Wife' could be Wade's wife, the giantess Bel.

In a different version, the Hole of Horcum and Blakey Topping were created when the Devil dug up a clod of earth and threw it after a witch who was fleeing when he came to claim her soul. In both stories the two sites are connected and the Old Wife's Way may provide the link, perhaps recalling an ancient goddess. The nearby **Bridestones** (54.3110, -0.6598; SE872914. Trailhead parking £: 54.3025, -0.6527; SE877904; 1.2km. Or walk overland from Blakey Topping) may retain an association with the Celtic goddess Bride (Bridget). These weirdly shaped and weathered sandstone rocks are rumoured to be a pagan ritual site.

The Hole of Horcum itself is just off the A169, with a large car park opposite. There are footpaths down into it or you can walk from the car park around its rim. The 2km trail to Blakey Topping also starts here and passes through a hidden valley with a traditional moorland farm.

Parking £: 54.3318, -0.6903; SE852937 (Hole of Horcum)

23 Mulgrave Woods, Sandsend *

Stretching several kilometres inland from the coast at Sandsend, Mulgrave Woods was said to be home to a malevolent fairy known as Jeanie o' Biggersdale. This mysterious spirit was ill-disposed towards humans and blamed for any misfortune that occurred in the area. One farmer, emboldened by drink, thought he would rid Mulgrave of her malevolent presence once and for all. He approached her cave where she lived and called out her name but was so horrified when she appeared that he turned and fled with the enraged Jeanie in pursuit. The terrified man remembered that she could not cross running water and urged his horse to leap over the nearest stream. However, as the animal's front legs left the ground Jeanie reached out and struck its hind legs, instantly severing the horse in two. Fortunately for the farmer he was on the front half which continued its leap over the stream before falling dead on the other side.

The exact location of Jeanie's abode is uncertain, but some say she lived in a cave called Hob's Hole which was also home to a boggle that liked to jump out and scare people. Passers-by would call:

"Hob-thrust Hob! Where is thou?"

To which the boggle would reply:

"Ah's tying on mah left-fuit shoe;
An' Ah'll be wiv thee … NOO!"

Hob's Hole cave lies somewhere near the ruins of an old overgrown mill house in a gully below Foss Castle (see below). The Old Mill House (54.4938, -0.7185; NZ831117) features in a Victorian novel called *Jeanie o'Biggersdale* and is the site of a suicide brought about by Jeanie.

A large earthen mound known as **Foss Castle** (54.4943, -0.7174; NZ831117. Trailhead: 54.4968, -0.7217; NZ828120; 400m) was reused as an early Norman motte fortification but later abandoned and the more extensive Mulgrave Castle built 700m away. Foss Castle and Mulgrave Castle were reputedly constructed by the giant Wade while his wife Bel built a castle at Pickering. They had only one hammer between them and would throw it between the two sites (see **Wade's Causeway**). The eerie stone ruins of medieval **Mulgrave Castle** (54.4935, -0.7056; NZ839116; 2.5km from entrance) stand isolated in the centre of the woods, while the remains of a summer house and overgrown paths recall their use as a pleasure garden by the gentry of the Mulgrave estate. More overgrown still is the area around **Biggersdale Hole** (54.4897 -0.7056; NZ839112; secret/

Were big wi' deeds o' kindness, drink to him
one and all.
Him at fails to drain dry, be it mug or glass,
Binnot worth a pescod*, nor a buss* frae
onny lass."
* pescod = peapod, buss = kiss

A stone shrine to Elphi can be found
at Rydale Folk Museum (54.3010,
-0.9178; SE705900) in Hutton-le-Hole,
along with several other examples of local
folk-magic artefacts including a carved
medieval 'witch post' in the Stang End
cruck house. Said to act as a talisman
against witches, these posts are virtually
unique to North Yorkshire.

54.3410, -0.9842; SE661944; Trailhead:
54.3448, -0.9716; SE669948; 1.9km; No
paths at end

25 Roseberry Topping

Lying just beyond the edge of the North
York Moors, this prominent conical hill
has a magical spring, now known as
Roseberry Well, right on its summit. The
water was reputed to cure rheumatism and
eye diseases and the well also appears as
Odinsburg Spring in a folk tale. Odinsburg (or Othenesburg) was an old name
for Roseberry Topping and it's likely
that the hill was once associated with
the Norse god Odin. In the tale, Oswy,
the son of the Saxon king Osmund, was
fated to die by drowning on his second
birthday so just before the appointed date
his mother took him to the summit of
Odinsburg, away from any possible floods.
However, when she fell asleep in the
hermit's cave young Oswy crawled out and
drowned in the spring. The cave no longer
exists as it was destroyed by quarrying
but the spring still trickles out just below
the summit. Stunning views are to be had
from the hill's conical peak and there are
several footpaths crossing it.

54.5053, -1.1074; NZ578125; Trailhead
Parking £: 54.5075, -1.1208; NZ570128; 1km

26 Wade's Causeway, Stape *

Paved with flints and running for over a
kilometre across Wheeldale Moor, Wade's
Causeway is one of the best-preserved
stretches of ancient road in Britain. According to legend it was laid down by the giant
Wade and his wife Bel, who carried the
stones in her apron. The causeway allowed
Bel to cross the moor easily and tend her
equally gigantic cow, as well as connect-

secluded; no paths at end) where a waterfall tumbles over a rocky ledge into the
evocatively named Wizard's Glen below.
This hidden waterfall is seldom visited and
has a real air of magic and mystery.
Mulgrave Woods, part of the Mulgrave
estate, are open to the public on certain
days of the week. Numerous footpaths lead
through the wooded gullies and to the
abandoned castle but expect to go off-trail
to uncover the rest of Mulgrave's secrets.

54.5005, -0.6704; NZ862125 (entrance);
access on Wednesdays, Saturdays & Sundays
only; closed during May

24 Obtrusch Roque, Low Mill, Farndale

A prehistoric stone cairn with the curious
name of Obtrusch Roque sits high on a
lonely, windswept moor above Farndale and
was once home to a mischievous hob-
goblin known as Hobthrush. While most
hobs are helpful, Hobthrush's antics on his
farm caused one local farmer to pack up
his home in order to be rid of him. As he
trundled off, his cart piled high with all the
family's belongings, the farmer's neighbour
called out and asked where he was going.
"We're flitting", he replied. "Aye," came a
small voice from the butter churn in the
back of the cart, "We're flitting!" Realising
he would never be rid of the hob the farmer
sighed and turned the cart around, back
towards home.
The valley of Farndale was also home to
another hob, called Elphi, who was celebrated for his kind deeds and big heart. A
cookbook dated 1699 records the following
ode to Elphi:
"Elphi bandy-legs, bent, an' wide apart,
No one in the dale owns a kinder heart.
Elphi, great-head, greatest ever seen,
No one in this dale owns a brighter een.
Elphi, little chap, thof he were so small,

ing her stronghold at Pickering (54.2503, -0.7757, SE798845) with the castle Wade built at **Mulgrave Woods**.

Just north of the moors, near the coast, a solitary standing stone in a field near Goldsborough is known as **Wade's Stone** (54.5182, -0.7201; NZ829144). It is said to mark the head of Wade's grave, while a recumbent stone in a field over a kilometre away (54.5056, -0.7189; NZ830130; private land) near East Barnby marks its foot – a testament to Wade's immense size. Supernatural phenomena in the vicinity of Wade's Stone have been reported and the stone itself is said to release a mysterious energy. According to one theory, Wade existed and was a tall Saxon nobleman, but he also appears in Nordic mythology as a mighty demigod and father of Wayland the Smith (see **Wayland's Smithy**).

South of Wade's Causeway a road passes **Old Wives' Well** (54.3360, -0.7799; SE794940), a natural spring located on the edge of a forestry plantation at Stape. This roofed, stone chamber displays a rough inscription, 'Nattie Fontein', on the front. Some have suggested this is a corruption of *Fontana Natalis*, Latin for 'birth spring' and could refer to the birth of the sun at the winter solstice, or to some ancient association with fertility. The 'Old Wife' of the well may have been the giantess Bel, but whatever its origins, it is likely this well has been a focus of female ritual activity since ancient times, and the clootie ribbons hanging in the surrounding trees show that people still recognise its magic.

54.3706, -0.7591; SE807979; Trailhead Parking: 54.3641, -0.7656; SE803972; 1km

27 White Mare Crag & Roulston Scar, Sutton-Under-Whitestonecliffe **

The imposing limestone cliffs that run from Roulston Scar to White Mare Crag stand at the entrance to the North York Moors in a truly a legendary landscape. Rich in folklore, with magical atmospheric settings and stunning views from clifftop footpaths, this area is a must for lovers of myth and mystery. Standing proud of Roulston Scar across the valley lies dramatic, conical **Hood Hill** (54.2262, -1.2291; SE503814. Trailhead: 54.2188, -1.2127; SE514806; 2km), thought to be a place where Druids performed sacrificial rites on a stone altar. Christian priests reputedly drove out the Druids, and also the Devil who left his footprint on a rock. An ancient earthwork on the summit, which resembles a fairy fort, has a magical atmosphere and there are views across a thickly wooded valley – sometimes referred to as the Devil's Leap – to the cliffs of Roulston Scar. Hidden away at the foot of these cliffs is a cave known as the **Devil's Parlour** (54.2276, -1.2161; SE512816; no paths), indicating a connection and a sacred alignment between the two. It's also possible that the original inhabitant of the Devil's Parlour was a hob or similar spirit (see **Hobthrush Hall**). On the northern side of Sutton Bank, White Mare Crag appears in several local legends featuring a white horse. In one story the Devil, disguised as an abbot, tricked a knight called Sir Harry into mounting his white horse and riding to his death. When the beast rode over the cliff, the Devil laughed at him mockingly. In another story, the Devil rode his white horse over the cliff and the impact of the landing created what later became Lake Gormire. Lying beneath the waters of **Lake Gormire** (54.2422, -1.2272; SE504832; 1.3km from National Park Centre) itself, is a legendary drowned village with associated stories of people hearing the eerie ringing of church bells emanating from far below, or seeing spires and rooftops while passing over the surface. Lake Gormire, its surface completely still, is also reputed to have been created by a great earthquake. Some say it is bottomless while others believe there is a secret underground spring which caused a goose that was sucked under its surface to reappear in a well faraway, devoid of feathers! At one point, huge chunks of stone fell from White Mare Crags creating a massive jumble of megalithic blocks and hidden among them is the tiny entrance to a large

underground chamber known locally as the Fairies' Parlour (54.2454, –1.2229; SE507835; secret/secluded).

Legends of the White Mare are further recalled in the huge outline of the Kilburn White Horse (54.2248, –1.2128; SE514812) carved into the chalk hillside on the southern flank of Roulston Scar in the 19th century, and also in an old prophesy which states:

'*When Gormire riggs are covered in hay,*
The White Mare of Whitestonecliff shall bear
it away.'

54.246221, -1.226003; SE505836 (White Mare Crag); Trailhead Parking: 54.2409, -1.2091; SE516830 (Sutton Bank National Park Centre) £; 1.7km

28 Whorl Hill, Whorlton

Long ago, the village of Sexhow was terrorised by a fearsome worm (dragon) that demanded the milk of nine cows daily. If this was not delivered it would uncoil itself from Whorl Hill and blow its poisonous breath across the fields to ruin the crops. Eventually a passing knight confronted the dragon and killed it. For many years afterwards its scaly hide was preserved in the local church. This is one of a number of dragon legends associated with North Yorkshire featuring large serpent-like beasts, known locally as worms, that usually had a taste for livestock and pretty young women. At Nunnington, a fire-breathing worm ruined a midsummer festival by carrying off a maiden who was later devoured in its lair at Loschy Hill (54.2056, -1.0094; SE647793). The knight Sir Peter Loschy vowed to destroy the worm, clad in spiked armour. Although the spikes and the knight's sword slashes did indeed maim the worm, its wounds healed almost instantly so it fell to his faithful hound to snatch up pieces of the worm and bear them away to prevent them joining together again. The worm was destroyed but unfortunately for Sir Peter its poison had transferred to his dog, who licked the knight's face. Both man and hound fell down dead and Sir Peter was buried in the church at Nunnington (54.2031, -0.9807; SE665790) where a carved effigy of a knight with an animal at his feet was believed to represent him. At Slingsby the church (54.1659, -0.9344; SE696749) contains the tomb of another dragon-slayer, Sir William Wyvill who was said to have been killed in battle, along with his dog, by a worm with a taste for young women. Meanwhile at Filey a much larger worm reputedly drowned in the bay while trying to wash its teeth. Its bones formed the stony reef of Filey Brigg (54.2169, -0.2680; TA130815; low tide only), which extends many hundreds of metres out to sea.

54.4155, -1.2408; NZ493024

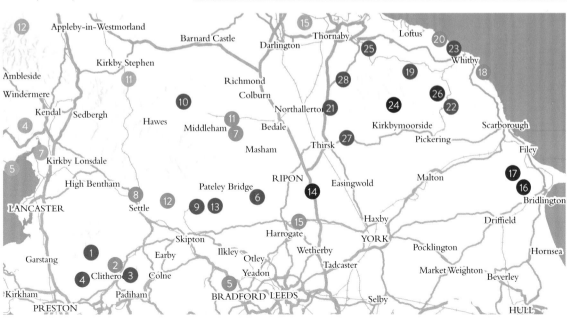

NORTHERN ENGLAND

Cumbria and Northumberland form a wild and sparsely populated border country where windswept fells provide a dramatic backdrop to dense forests and deep lakes. Ancient stone circles mark sacred points in the landscape and the ruins of Hadrian's Roman wall still snake across fields and over crags from coast to coast. Here folklore tells of King Arthur and his warriors who lie sleeping under Sewingshields Crags. They are also said to lie in a secret chamber within the mountain of Blencathra in Cumbria where a ritual must be enacted in the correct sequence to awake them from their enchanted slumber. High in the mountains by Hardknott Pass in Cumbria, a Roman fort was said to have been built by the fairy king Eveling, a shadowy figure who may be the ruler of Avalon from Arthurian legend. The castle of King Arthur's father, Uther Pendragon, can be found at Outhgill in Cumbria, while Sir Lancelot's Castle of Joyous Guard was said to be where Bamburgh Castle now stands on the Northumbrian coast.

There are many tales of the fairy folk who inhabit this region. In the idyllic Lake District valley of Borrowdale there is a magical fairy glen where in gullies with hidden waterfalls fairies hide among the foxgloves. Also in Cumbria the fairies are said to dwell at Castle Howe and in the mountains near Coniston, where one unfortunate copper miner learned why the fairies' secrets should never be betrayed. In the wooded escarpment near Beetham the fairies will grant a wish to anyone who can climb or descend the narrow Fairy Steps without touching the sides.

Northumberland is home to dragons, notably the two legendary beasts at Spindlestone Heughs near Bamburgh and Longwitton near Hartburn, while lone travellers in the Simonside Hills should be wary of the malevolent fairy folk that inhabit its crags and bogs. Attached to the Northumbrian coast by a tidal causeway, the island of Lindisfarne, or Holy Island, has been one of Britain's most significant spiritual destinations for centuries. The original monastery was founded by the Celtic missionary St Aidan in the 7th century and the ruined priory is now haunted by a spectral white dog as well as the spirit of St Cuthbert who is said to make his presence known on stormy nights. Further south near Stockton-on-Tees the haunting music coming from a fairy hill in the village of Bishopton was said to have inspired the creation of the Northumbrian pipes.

CUMBRIA

1 Blencathra, Threlkeld *

Hidden deep within the mountain of Blencathra there is a cavern where King Arthur and his knights lie sleeping, awaiting the hour of Britain's greatest need when they will ride forth to defend the land. This legend of sleeping warriors awaiting the final battle is attached to other prominent hills around the country such as **Cadbury Castle** and **Alderley Edge**, but Blencathra is surely one of the most dramatic sites. Situated on the northern edge of the Lake District, its saddleback profile lends it the appearance of a sacred twin-peaked mountain. On a clear day, there are extensive views from the summit across Northern England and over to Scotland and the Isle of Man.

Blencathra and its neighbouring fells provide a dramatic backdrop to **Castlerigg Stone Circle** (54.6028, -3.0984; NY291236) which sits on a plateau to the southwest. One of the best-known stone circles in Britain, Castlerigg is popular with visitors yet remains an atmospheric and magical place. The circle of stones seems to echo the

shape of the mountains that almost encircle the plateau, emphasising this sacred point in the landscape. Surprisingly there is little folklore about Castlerigg, although early in the 20th century two men encountered mysterious white lights that moved rapidly from the direction of the stones and flew over their heads.

To the east of Blencathra, Souther Fell (54.6533, -3.0017; NY354291) is the site of 18th-century apparitions. On no less than three occasions, a phantom army was seen crossing the northern end of the fell, always on Midsummer's Eve when witnesses described vast ranks of footsoldiers led by men on horseback. So convincing was this spectacle that after the third sighting people went up the fell to look for hoof prints on the ground, but not a trace was found.

54.6400, -3.0499; NY323277; Trailhead Parking: 54.6211, -3.0817; NY302256; 3.6km

3

2 Castle Howe & Bassenthwaite Lake

There are two fairy hills near Bassenth-waite Lake, which still retains a remote and enchanted feel, despite the main road to Kes-wick running alongside it. The closest hill, Castle Howe, lies on its northwestern shore. Originally an Iron Age hillfort, trees now cover the rocky hillock which is a known locally as a fairy haunt. A man walking up Castle Howe once accidentally knocked a stone out of place. When he looked back, he saw a little man dressed in green sitting on top of the same stone, although on second glance, the figure was gone. On another occasion two children were digging in the hill and uncovered what looked like a little hut with a slate roof, but on returning from lunch they could find no trace of the struc-ture. Their father later saw two little men, again dressed in green, on top of the hill and set his dog on them. However, the dog remained motionless, as if paralysed, while they disappeared back into the ground.
A few kilometres northwest of Castle Howe, Elva Hill (54.6758, -3.2818; NY174319; pri-vate land) is said to feature a concealed portal

to the Otherworld, which can be opened at certain times of the year. Where this portal might be found is unclear, but there is an ancient stone circle on the southern slope of the hill that would have been a focal point in the landscape. The association with elves goes back over 1000 years to Norse settlers who named the hill Elfhaugr (Elf Mound). On the eastern shore of Bassenthwaite Lake, ancient St Bega's Church (54.6479, -3.2002; NY226287) is dedicated to the Celtic saint who is said to have fled her Irish home-land to escape marriage, bringing only her golden bracelet with her. St Bega's cult may have grown up around this special bracelet (*beag* in Old English) which was kept as a relic at St Bees Priory (54.4939, -3.5934; NX968121) on the Cumbrian coast.
54.6661, -3.2393; NY201308 (Castle Howe)

3 Eveling's Rath, Hardknott Pass

A mysterious and shadowy figure, the fairy king Eveling or Afallach was said to hold court in this Roman fortress, which guards the Hardknott Pass in one of the wildest parts of the Cumbrian mountains. From this dramatic setting, Eveling protected a realm that

2

some equate to the mysterious Otherworld of Avalon. His main fortress was located at the Roman ruins of Ravenglass over by the coast of which only the ruins of the Roman Bath House (54.3507, -3.4042; SD088959) now sur-vive. The route over the pass follows the course of an old Roman road and is notoriously steep and narrow, but those who undertake the chal-lenge are rewarded by this well-preserved and atmospheric stone fortress that may guard the entrance to an enchanted realm.
54.4029, -3.2054; NY218014

4

5

Humphrey Head, a rugged limestone outcrop that juts out into the saltmarsh of Morecambe Bay. Within the 'church', prehistoric flints have been found in a small cave known as the Fairy Chapel, which may have been considered a fairy gathering place or even a portal to the Otherworld, although specific folklore has been lost. At the base of the cliff below the arch there was once a holy well. It proved so popular that a small building was constructed close by where visitors could stay for a few days while they took the waters to effect a cure. A second well was found a few hundred metres to the north where people would leave offerings of pins. Today little remains of the wells except trickles of water leaching out from the base of the cliff but the Fairy Church still stands and can be viewed from paths above and below. The adventurous may want to scramble to the arch itself but the Fairy Chapel cave is only accessible with climbing gear.

54.1573, -2.9356; SD390739; Trailhead Parking: 54.1584, -2.9353; SD390740; 100m

6 Fairy Glen, Borrowdale *

In the heart of the Lake District lies an idyllic valley where the crystal-clear waters of Stonethwaite Beck flow between rocky boulders overhung with mossy trees. This is the Fairy Glen, dominated by Galleny Force waterfall with a clear, cool pool at its foot, and where numerous streams rush down small side gullies to join the beck. In summer the tall pink foxglove spires dominate these enchanted gullies. Also called fairy bells, foxgloves are beloved flowers of the fairy folk who were said to dwell close to where they grew in abundance.

The massive **Bowder Stone** (54.5373 -3.1545; NY254163), reputedly thrown there by a giant, lies nearby in Borrowdale. The stone balances at a seemingly impossible angle and is estimated to weigh over 2000 tonnes. Local legend tells that the name is derived from Baldur, the Norse god who was slain by Loki using a dart of mistletoe. Although its surface is now deeply weathered, older images of the Bowder Stone show a face on one side which was said to represent Baldur, complete with a hole in the forehead from the fatal dart. The stone became a 'druidical' tourist attraction in the late 18th century when a standing stone and hermitage were also erected nearby. Over the centuries visitors have been able to climb up a ladder to enjoy the views from the top of the stone, a tradition that continues today after the recent installation of a sturdy metal staircase. Borrowdale is also home to the Borrowdale

4 Fairies Cave, Whitbarrow Scar, Witherslack

At the western edge of Whitbarrow Scar, the Fairies Cave is hidden away at the end of a narrow wooded gully, its rocky walls bedecked by moss and ferns. The tiny entrance stands like a portal to the Otherworld and is reached by a short scramble over moss-encrusted limestone rocks. Once inside, undulating white flowstone formations line the walls of the narrow cave, while deeper within a natural fairy 'wishing well', into which water constantly drips, has formed from the flowstone deposits. At the back of the dark cave, the sound of rushing water can be heard and torchlight reveals a narrow chute leading down to a deep pool that only the truly adventurous might be tempted to explore.

54.2818, -2.8708; SD434877; Private Land; Secret/Secluded; Trailhead: 54.2771, -2.8765; SD430871; 800m

5 Fairy Church, Grange-over-Sands

A natural stone arch known as the Fairy Church stands high on the cliff at

Yews (54.5020, -3.1828; NY235124) a grove of ancient yew trees thought to be up to two thousand years old.

54.5083, -3.1247; NY272131 (Galleny Force); Trailhead: 54.5139, -3.1407; NY262137; 1.4km

7 Fairy Steps, Beetham *

Cut into the rocks on the edge of Whin Scar plateau, a set of small, steep stone steps ascends a narrow cleft. These are the Fairy Steps and said to be haunted by the fairies who have occasionally been seen running up and down them. They will grant a wish to anyone who manages to walk up or down this narrowest of staircases without touching the sides – a task that is near impossible for all but the 'little people'! The Fairy Steps are reached by an ancient trackway that passes through the twisted trees and limestone pavement formations of Whin Scar before descending into Beetham village. Along this path, which is an old corpse road, coffins were transported from outlying settlements to Beetham church – a classic example of a corpse road also serving as a fairy path.

54.2036, -2.7875; SD487789; Trailhead: 54.2020, -2.8031; SD477787; 1km

7

6

8 Herding Neb, Seascale

A legendary giantess once intended to build a causeway linking England to the Isle of Man and its starting point was on the coast at Seascale. However, while carrying large boulders to begin construction her apron strings broke and the boulders tumbled to the ground at a point called Herding Neb. They can still be seen today, green with seaweed and strewn across the beach at low tide.

54.3939, -3.4863; NY035008; Low Tide Only

9 Howk, Caldbeck

The deep river-worn ravine known as the Howk has many fairy associations. At the foot of the waterfall is a cauldron of churning water known as the Fairy Kettle, while in the rock just above there is a mysterious cave called the Fairy Kirk (church). A natural stone arch called the Fairy Bridge also stood here but was removed during road development. The Howk is west of Caldwell village and is reached by a short walk along the river to the sound of rushing water cascading through the fairy-haunted gorge. It is also possible to hike along the floor of the gorge itself, right up to the waterfall.

54.7482, -3.0600; NY318397; Trailhead Parking: 54.7493, -3.0533; NY323398; 500m

10 Long Meg and Her Daughters, Little Salkeld *

One of the largest and best-preserved stone circles in Britain, Long Meg and Her Daughters were said to have been a coven of witches who were turned to stone. The stones stand in a grassy field with Long Meg herself, a 3.6m high sandstone monolith, a short distance outside the circle displaying faint carvings of a cup and ring mark and a spiral. The stones are said to be uncountable, but anyone who calculates the correct number and presses their ear against Long Meg will hear her whispering. If the correct number is counted twice then the spell keeping the witches petrified will be undone. There is also a tradition that Long Meg will bleed if damaged, and that a great storm will blow up if anyone attempts to move the stones. A small country lane now passes through part of the stone circle and sheep graze all around but Long Meg and her Daughters remain timeless and enigmatic.

Nearby, in St Andrew's churchyard, in the centre of the busy market town of Penrith, you'll find the **Giant's Grave** (54.6643, -2.7513; NY516301) which is marked by a collection of intricately carved stones including some Norse hogsback grave markers. While just outside the town near Eamont Bridge is the **Giant's Cave** (54.6656, -2.6823; NY560302) where he used to live (private land).

54.7281, -2.6677; NY570372

11 Pendragon Castle, Outhgill

Medieval Pendragon Castle lies on the site of a fortress that was reputedly built by Uther Pendragon, father of King Arthur. One of a number of Cumbrian sites with Arthurian associations, Pendragon Castle even has it's own rhyming couplet:

"Let Uther Pendragon do what he can,
The river Eden will run as it ran."
This commemorates Uther's failed attempt to divert the river Eden to make a moat around the castle. Local legend claims Uther and his men died here after the well was poisoned by invading Saxons laying siege to the castle. The present picturesque castle ruins are of 12th century origin, but despite a lack of any historical basis the Arthurian connection remains strong. Close to the castle there is a flooded pot hole known as Sandpot (54.4178, -2.3435; NY778025) which was said to have been inhabited by benevolent fairies. They wore green dresses and helped local people with baking bread, churning butter and milking cattle.
54.4187, -2.3378; NY781026

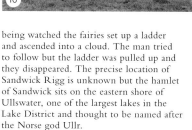

12 Sandwick Rigg, Ullswater

One curious encounter with some of Cumbria's fairy folk occurred at Sandwick in the 1850s when a local man was returning home one moonlit night. He saw a number of fairies dancing on a grassy mound called Sandwick Rigg, but on realising they were

being watched the fairies set up a ladder and ascended into a cloud. The man tried to follow but the ladder was pulled up and they disappeared. The precise location of Sandwick Rigg is unknown but the hamlet of Sandwick sits on the eastern shore of Ullswater, one of the largest lakes in the Lake District and thought to be named after the Norse god Ullr.
54.5691, -2.8926; NY423196 (Sandwick)

13 Simon's Nick, Coniston

A distinctive cleft in the crags of Coniston Fells is known as Simon's Nick in remembrance of a local miner who had dealings with fairies. Simon was poor but his luck seemed to change and he began extracting huge amounts of copper ore from a seam

above Levers Water beck. When pressed by his neighbours he refused to tell them why he had chosen that spot, but eventually he got drunk and let slip that the fairies had shown him exactly where to dig. Unfortunately for Simon, by betraying the fairies' secret his luck ran out and he died soon after, trapped in his mine after a mysterious rockfall. Coniston Fells is an area of bare peaks, hidden tarns and swift-moving becks that cascade down steep rocky valleys. It is also a post-industrial landscape where the remnants of centuries of copper and slate mining are slowly being reclaimed by nature. Dominating the western horizon, the Old Man of Coniston (54.3707, -3.1217; SD272978; 3.8km) is said to be haunted by the spirit of the 'Old Man' himself, the guardian of these mountains. Tucked away on its western flank is a small lake known as **Goat's Water** (54.3691, -3.1304; SD266976; 5.3km). At this remote lake, fairies who guard hidden treasure, have been sighted. The Old Man of Coniston is one of Britain's most climbed peaks, yet its remote fells retain a bleak, haunting beauty.

54.3805, -3.1067; SD282988; Trailhead Parking: 54.3777, -3.0951; SD289985; 900m

14 Wharton Tarn, Hawkshead Hill

A terrifying water hag known as Jennie Greenteeth was said to haunt the inky waters of Wharton Tarn, attempting to drown and devour anyone who ventured too close to the edge. Described as having green skin, long lank hair like pondweed and sharp, pointed teeth her appearance would certainly give you a fright. Jennie Greenteeth and others of her ilk are associated with numerous treacherous rivers and lonely pools in the north of England. Wharton Tarn is a small lake, only 2m deep, with marshy banks where the water hag is said to lurk. Wisely, the footpath around the lake is set back from it.

54.3809, -3.0321; SD330988

DURHAM

15 Bishopton Fairy Hill

At this large mound on the outskirts of Bishopton village, people have reported seeing fairy lights and the music drifting from it was said to have been the inspiration for the Northumbrian bagpipes. The fairies disliked being disturbed and when workmen

were digging near the mound a disembodied voice called out "All is well?" to which they replied "Yes". The voice then cried, "Then keep well when you are well and leave the fairy hill alone!" Ignoring the warning, the workmen kept digging and uncovered a large heavy chest which they hauled out of the ground and broke open, only to discover that the 'fairy treasure' was just a box of old nails. The mound is also known as Castle Hill since it was once a Norman motte, but the strong fairy associations remain.

54.5819, -1.4343; NZ366208

NORTHUMBERLAND

16 Drake Stone, Harbottle

Dominating the hilltop to the west of Harbottle is the Drake Stone, a vast boulder that was once the focus of a healing ritual to cure sick children. They would be carried up the steep hill from the village and passed over the top of the stone – no easy feat given the stone is over 9m high! You can still see the finger and toe holds and carrying a child up the stone must have been a terrifying experience. The Drake Stone is also said to be associated with ancient druidic rites.

A few kilometres down the lane, a rectangular pond known as the **Lady's Well** (55.3203, -2.0759; NT952029. Trailhead: 55.3185, -2.0732; NT954027; 300m) sits in a small enclosure surrounded by trees on the edge of the village of Holystone. This sacred spring dates back to at least the Roman era and is said to be the place where St Paulinus baptised over 3,000 converts in the 7th century. The pool has a stone cross

at its centre and a medieval statue of St Paulinus stands on top of a mossy stone at one end of the pool. Some say this mossy stone is the 'holy stone' which gave the village its name and this was probably a sacred site long before the coming of Christianity.

55.3337, -2.1267; NT920044; Trailhead Parking: 55.3370, -2.1122; NT929047; 1km

17 Druid's Lapful, Yeavering

This 2m high standing stone was said to have been dropped by a Druidess when her apron string broke. Such stories are usually associated with giants, not Druids, to explain the placement of large, random boulders, so this legend is unusual. The Druid's Lapful monolith stands at the foot

of a hill known as Yeavering Bell (55.5575, -2.1156; NT928293), its summit crowned by Northumbria's largest hillfort. Although a seemingly remote spot, the wealth of archaeological sites in the area suggest it was once a much more heavily populated and important location.

55.5670, -2.1127; NT929303

18 Lindisfarne **

The holy island of Lindisfarne is one of Britain's most sacred islands and has been an important destination for pilgrims for many centuries. Once an important centre of Celtic Christianity, the earliest monastery was established here in the 7th century by St Aidan who came from **Iona** off the west coast of Scotland and the ruins of the 12th century **Lindisfarne Priory** (55.6692, -1.8010; NU126417; ££) can still be seen. They are said to be haunted by a spectral white dog and the ghost of St Cuthbert, an early bishop at Lindisfarne whose cult arose when his body, after death, was found to be incorruptible – a sure sign of his exceptional holiness. Reputedly, the spirit of St Cuthbert can be heard on stormy nights hammering out beads on an anvil. These 'beads' are small marine fossils (crinoids) that were once collected by islanders and sold as rosary beads and charms.

Also in the priory is the **Petting Stone** (55.6693, -1.8014; NU125417), the focus of an age-old ritual in which a newly-wed bride would jump over the stone to ensure a successful marriage. The stone still serves the same purpose but the best man now passes the bride over it to the groom. The Petting Stone has a square socket carved into the top that once supported the base of a large cross and it is thought to date back to the earliest days of the monastery. Just off the southwestern shore of Lindisfarne lies **Hobthrush Island** (55.6679, -1.8061; NU122416) a small rocky islet accessible only at low tide. It was named after a hob who was said to dwell there. Later the island was renamed St Cuthbert's Island after the saint built a hermitage and chapel there.

Lindisfarne is cut off from the mainland at high tide but accessible via a causeway by car or on foot (check tide times). The whole island echoes with the sounds of the sea and abundant coastal wildlife, heightening the sense that this is a liminal location, poised between land and sea, and between the physical world and the realm of spirit. It remains a spiritual centre to this day, and is often referred to simply as Holy Island.

Parking £: 55.6751, -1.8013; NU125424; Low Tide Only

19 Longwitton Dragon's Den, Hartburn

Hidden away in woodland above the river Hart are three wells once guarded by a fierce dragon that could make itself invisible and prevented local people from accessing the healing waters. A wandering knight called Sir Guy of Warwick (see **Guy's Cliff**) decided to rid the district of this nuisance and after putting magical ointment on his eyes that enabled him to see the dragon, he went to confront it. The battle raged on for three days but every time he wounded the dragon it healed itself by dipping its tail into one of the wells. Guy eventually succeeded in enticing the dragon away from the wells and was finally able to despatch it. Today the wells are completely silted up and covered in leaf litter but the spring water still bubbles out of the ground, trickling through the enchanted tree-lined gullies down to the river.

55.1781, -1.8648; NZ087870; Private Land; Trailhead Parking: 55.1743, -1.8693; NZ084866; 1km

20 Pin Well, Wooler

Edged with a tumbledown assortment of stones, this fairy wishing well is found in a small green valley below Hordson Hill. Dropping bent pins in the water to gain the favour of the fairy who dwelt there, people

traditionally visited this pin well on May Day to make their wishes – a practice that continued well into the last century. Pins can sometimes still be seen at the bottom of the well, dropped by more recent wish-makers who may not have forgotten the old ways. On the hillside just above the well is the King's Chair, a rock outcrop where, according to local legend, an unnamed king sat while directing a battle in the valley below.

55.5375, -2.0228; NT986270; Trailhead: 55.5345, -2.0187; NT989267; 450m

21 Sewingshields Crags, Haydon Bridge *

As Hadrian's Wall snakes across the landscape it passes along the top of a rocky escarpment called Sewingshields Crags where tales of King Arthur abound. In a secret chamber deep below nearby Sewingshields castle King Arthur, Queen Guinevere and the knights of the Round Table are said to lie sleeping until Britain once more needs their help. A table placed beside their slumbering forms holds a horn, a sheathed sword and a garter and to awaken them one must draw the sword, cut the garter and blow the horn. One story tells of a farmer who was sitting in the castle ruins knitting when his ball of wool fell and rolled away down a crack in the stone that was hidden behind vegetation. The farmer squeezed in after it and found himself within the legendary chamber. There he saw the table laid out and so he unsheathed the sword and cut the garter – but neglected to blow the horn. King Arthur stirred from sleep long enough to lament:

"O Woe betide that evil day
On which this witless wight was born,
Who drew the sword, the garter cut,
But never blew the bugle horn…"

Today, not a single stone of the castle, thought to be a medieval tower built from the Roman wall's stone, remains so the exact location of the secret chamber remains a mystery.

Legends of King Arthur and ancient heroes sit well with this bleak and beautiful landscape. The king had a rocky chair on Sewingshields Crags, and another, to the north on King's Crags (55.0342, -2.3195; NY796711). While atop the latter, a giant-sized Arthur had an argument with the giantess Guinevere who was sitting on Queen's Crags (55.0295, -2.3217; NY795706). He threw a stone which broke her comb and the stone indented with comb marks is still said to be visible between the two outcrops.

The nearby lake of Broomlee Lough is one of many places said to be the final resting place of King Arthur's sword Excalibur. It is also said to

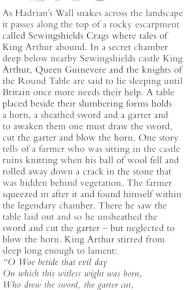

hold a secret treasure taken from Sewingshields Castle. A few kilometres east down the Roman wall at Carrawburgh are the remains of an ancient Roman temple to Mithras (55.0339, -2.2226; NY858710) and also close by is the site of Coventina's Well (55.0346, -2.2242; NY857711). In pre-Christian times this was one of the most important and revered goddess shrines in the country, but is now little more than a patch of swampy ground.

55.0259, -2.3068; NY804701; Trailhead Parking: 55.0099, -2.3236; NY794684; 3km

22 Simonside Hills, Great Tosson

The heathery slopes and craggy tops of the Simonside Hills are features of an ancient landscape that is said to be haunted by fairies who would lead unwary travellers into the peaty bogs. Usually seen only as lights called Will o' the Wisps, these fairies were described by one traveller as 'demonic-looking little men' carrying lanterns.

Confronted by a group of them upon the hillside, he had to fight his way through with a stick. Overcome by shock he fainted and did not recover until dawn.

These hills are also home to malevolent duergar (the dwarves of Norse mythology). One night a lone traveller crossing the hills encountered one of the duergar who invited him to sit by his fire. He kept beckoning for the man to move closer but the man wisely stayed at a distance. As the sky began to lighten the dwarf and

his fire vanished and the man realised he was sitting atop a rock outcrop. Had he moved closer he would have plunged to his death. The Simonside Hills are part of a nature conservation area yet retain an eerie atmosphere, especially when visited after dark.

55.2825, -1.9633; NZ024987; Trailhead Parking: 55.2913, -1.9431; NZ037996; 2.5km

23 Spindlestone & Bamburgh Castle *

A terrifying dragon known as the Laidley Worm had its lair in a cave on the rocky escarpment at Spindlestone Heughs and liked to curl itself around a stone pillar known as the Spindlestone. In the tale, which may date back to Anglo-Saxon times, King Ida remarried and his daughter, Princess Margaret of Bamburgh Castle, was turned into the loathsome worm by her jealous step-mother with the following curse:

"I weird ye to be a laidley worm,
and borrowed shall ye never be,
until Childe Wynd, the king's own son,
do come and thrice kiss thee"

(borrowed = disenchanted)

Margaret's brother, Childe Wynd, was overseas and returned to find the worm terrorising the local district, devouring sheep and poisoning the land with its venomous breath. The locals had to leave the milk from seven cows in a large stone trough near Spindlestone Heughs in order to placate it. Childe Wynd went to slay the worm but before he struck with his sword it shed a tear and revealed that it was his own sister under an enchantment. He broke the spell with three kisses and prince and princess returned to Bamburgh Castle, whereupon Childe Wynd confronted the wicked stepmother. He struck her with a rowan staff, turning her into a hideous toad that he threw into the castle well, where she still lurks awaiting three kisses to break the spell. **Bamburgh Castle** (55.6089, -1.7095; NU183350; ££), guarding the coast from its rocky plateau, is open to the public and you can still visit the well inside the castle. According to legend the castle was also the 'Joyous Gard', home to Sir Lancelot of Arthurian myth. Spindlestone Heughs lies a few kilometres inland, where the rocky escarpment stands above the Spindlestone on a hillside that is still named the Laidley Worm's Trough.

55.5986, -1.7584; NU153339 (Spindlestone); Trailhead: 55.5994, -1.7537; NU156340; 300m

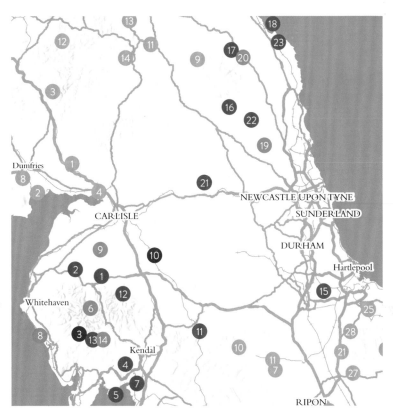

NORTH WALES

The Northern region of Wales has long been considered a land of legends, a mythical landscape where the giants of old dwelt on mountaintops and enchanted fairy courts lay hidden just below the surface. The mountains of Snowdonia and the Berwyns to the east were home to the Tylwyth Teg, the Welsh fairy folk, who lived there in a mysterious Otherworld realm. Tales of King Arthur and Merlin abound in this region and Celtic Christianity also played its part in shaping this landscape with countless healing wells and shrines dedicated to the saints.

Anglesey has been considered a sacred island since ancient times. It was the last stronghold of the Druids until the coming of the Romans, and then later when Celtic saints including St Seiriol and St Cybi established monastic settlements there it once more became a holy island.

The area around Mount Snowdon, the highest peak in Wales, is particularly rich with folklore and legend. King Arthur himself was said to have died there after being ambushed on the mountainside and his sword Excalibur was returned to the Lady of the Lake in Llyn Llydaw. The fairies are also thought to inhabit several places in these remote and sometimes eerie mountains.

On the southern flank of Snowdon, the overgrown and atmospheric hillfort of Dinas Emrys was named after Myrddin Emrys, the Welsh Merlin. It was here that young Merlin revealed to Vortigern that two dragons trapped in a cave beneath were to blame for his fortress repeatedly falling down. The red dragon has symbolised Wales ever since. On Bardsey Island, off the tip of the Lleyn Peninsula, Merlin is now said to lie sleeping in a cave alongside the 'thirteen treasures of Britain'.

Further south another fairy-haunted mountain was Cadair Idris, home to a giant whose stone seat on the summit could inspire poetic genius or cause insanity and death. Fairies are also said to dwell in the Conwy Valley in Clwyd and especially like to frolic in the Fairy Glen, a dramatic rocky ravine near Betws y Coed.

In Llangollen the ruins of the medieval Castell Dinas Bran sit atop a fairy hill said to conceal the palace of fairy king Gwyn ap Nudd. He would lead a wild hunt with a pack of white hounds across the Berwyn Mountains, which are the source of the water that cascades over the magical Pistyll Rhaeadr falls. One of the highest waterfalls in Wales and haunted by dragons, fairies and spirits, it serves as the gateway to a remote and enchanted mountain landscape.

GWYNEDD

1 Bwlch y Groes, Llanymawddwy

This rocky mountain pass is traversed by the highest road in North Wales and was the scene of a legendary battle between King Arthur and a giant. Arthur was travelling through the pass on his way to meet Merlin when he encountered the giant, Rhitta Gawr, who wore a cloak made from the beards of all the men he had slaughtered. Thinking Arthur's beard would make a fine addition to his gruesome cloak, Rhitta attacked but Arthur slew him with one mighty blow from his sword and threw the giant's body down the mountainside. The corpse of Rhitta was eventually buried under a cairn on the summit of **Mount Snowdon**. To the west of Bwlch y Goes is the mountain of Aran Fawddwy (52.7871, -3.6879; SH862223) with the lake of Creiglyn Dyfi (52.7882, -3.6824; SH866225) just below the summit. The whole area between the mountain and pass was a favourite haunt of the fairies who liked to play and dance on the green hillsides. A boy once encountered two fairy women whilst walking along the pass

and they tried to entice him into a dance. Knowing he would be lost forever if he joined them, he ran away as fast as he could! A small car park at Bwlch y Groes gives travellers a chance to stop to admire the breathtaking views and to explore the mountainous terrain around this legendary pass.
Parking: 52.7962, -3.6133; SH913232

2 Cadair Idris, Dolgellau *

The stark peaks of Cadair Idris mountain were once home to a giant known as Idris – a poet, astronomer and prince amongst giants. Idris liked to sit near the summit upon his stone 'seat' (cadair), a wide, shallow depression on top of a rock. Three huge rocks at the foot of the mountain are said to be 'pebbles' shaken from the giant's shoe as he sat on the chair. Possibly harking back to an ancient Bardic tradition, it was believed that anyone who spent a night sleeping upon the chair would be found the next morning either a poetic genius, insane or dead. There is a story that Idris and

his brother who lived on Cadair Bronwen in the Berwyn Mountains (see **Pistyll Rhaeadr**) would share a hammer which they threw back and forth.

Cadair Idris was also a meeting ground for witches who gathered there to dance on the Sabbats. There is said to be a rock on the mountain where the Devil left his hoof print as he danced, presumably while attending one of these Sabbats. The fairy king Gwyn ap Nudd also leads the wild hunt across the slopes of the mountain with his pack of Cwn Annwn – white fairy dogs with blood red ears. The fairy folk who lived on the mountain would come down and visit people's homes in disguise, rewarding those who provided them with good hospitality. One man, Morgan Rhys, was especially favoured by the fairies who gave him an enchanted harp. He could play any tune he wished simply by touching a finger to the strings. The lakes on Cadair Idris are said to be connected by underground caverns and a stick thrown into one lake could eventually surface in one of the others. Anyone who attempts to divert water from the lakes, however, will incur the wrath of the mountain spirits who will drive them away with thunder and lightning. A particularly sinister spirit haunts the waters of **Llyn Gwernan** (52.7267, -3.9206; SH703160; 1km) would watch people

2

climbing the highest tracks of Cadair Idris before sending forth storms and dense fog to disorientate them, hoping that they would stumble and fall down the mountainside. Another lake, **Llyn Cau** (52.6950, -3.9029; SH714125; 5.6km. Or trailhead parking: 52.6869, -3.8776; SH731115; 2.6km), is said to be the lair of an afanc, a fearsome water monster that King Arthur dragged from **Llyn Barfog** far to the south.

52.7008, -3.9068; SH712131; Popular, Trailhead Parking: 52.7194, -3.9293; SH697152; 4.5km

3 Coetan Arthur & Moelfre Hill, Dyffryn Ardudwy

At the foot of Moelfre Hill, near the town of Dyffryn Ardudwy, lies a Neolithic burial cairn with two intact dolmens known as Coetan Arthur. They were said to have been quoits thrown from Moelfre Hill by a giant, or by King Arthur himself who left his fingerprints indented into the stones. There is also said to be treasure buried there, the location of which will be revealed when the end of a rainbow touches the cairn. **Moelfre Hill** (52.8013, -4.0392; SH626245. Trailhead: 52.7872,

2

4 Dinas Emrys, Beddgelert *

Nestled amongst the mountains of Snowdonia, this densely wooded hill crowned by ancient overgrown fortifications was the scene of a legendary confrontation between Myrddin Emrys (Merlin) and the fatally flawed King Vortigern who was trying to build his fortress there. Work began on building a tower but each morning the structure was found in ruins. After consulting his magicians, Vortigern was advised to find a child with no human father who could be sacrificed and his blood mixed with the mortar to cement the stones together. Eventually young Myrddyn Emrys from Carmarthen was brought to Dinas Emrys to be sacrificed, but through his magical powers he saw that Vortigern's problems were caused by the presence of two dragons, one red and one white, asleep in a hidden pool beneath the foundations. So Vortigern's men dug down and uncovered the pool, waking the dragons who began to fight ferociously. The white dragon was defeated and fled, and ever since the red dragon has been the symbol of Wales. The fortress was built and named Dinas Emrys in honour of the young wizard, who later had his own fortress there. The tale of Lludd and Llefelys in *The Mabinogion* explains how the dragons were first captured near Oxford and came to be imprisoned at Dinas Emrys (see **St Margaret's Well**). Curiously, archaeological excavations have revealed traces of an artificial pool built during the 5th-century reoccupation of the fortress.

In a Welsh Arthurian legend, King Arthur

-4.0739; SH602230; 3km; no paths to summit) is the location of a story concerning three women who were turned to stone for winnowing corn up there on a Sunday. The three standing stones near the hill's summit are no longer there, but the story has led to speculation that they represented an ancient triple goddess who was 'defeated' by Christianity. By a small country lane that passes over the northwestern slope of Moelfre Hill lies **Ffynnon Enddwyn** (52.8095, -4.0582; SH613255), a holy well dedicated to the female St Enddwyn. It is enclosed by a rough stone wall and enjoys extensive views from the mountainside down

to the coast. When St Enddwyn was healed by bathing in the waters many others came to be cured of all kinds of diseases. As well as drinking the water they would also apply poultices made from the moss that grew around the well. The disabled would leave their crutches behind as a sign of their miraculous cures, while others would throw pins into the well to ward off evil spirits. It's likely that people have been venerating this well since pagan times, and that the story of St Enddwyn was attached to Christianise this sacred feminine site.

52.7846, -4.0942; SH588228 (Coetan Arthur)

began his final journey at Dinas Emrys, from where he and his men marched to **Mount Snowdon** and Arthur was slain in battle. Myrddin also reputedly buried his treasure in a cavern hidden within the hill and sealed the entrance. When its rightful owner, a youth with golden hair and blue eyes appears, a bell will ring and the stone boulder will magically roll to one side as soon as the chosen one touches it with his foot. One local man thought to uncover the treasure for himself but when he began to dig the ground shook violently and unearthly noises echoed from beneath his feet. The sun was swallowed by black clouds and a terrible storm blew up as the terrified man ran for home.

Little remains visible of the fortifications nowadays but the summit has the feel of an enchanted Otherworld with twisted trees and ancient earthworks. The associations with Myrddin and Vortigern give this place an air of myth and mystery that still hangs over this magical location.

53.0222, -4.0789; SH606492; Trailhead Parking £: 53.0195, -4.0891; SH599489; 1.2km

5 Llyn Barfog, Aberdovey

Lying in a remote spot in the hills above the Dyfi estuary, Llyn Barfog was once home to an afanc, a water monster that rampaged through the area killing livestock until it was eventually dispatched by King Arthur. He dragged it from the lake using magical chains and some say he killed it, while others claim he took the afanc to **Cadair Idris** and released it into the waters of Llyn Cau. A stone beside a footpath leading to Llyn Barfog bears a hoof print made by King Arthur's horse during his fierce battle with the afanc and is known as Carn March Arthur (52.5644 -3.9925; SN650981; 700m from Llyn Barfog).

Another legend tells of fairies living near the lake who were often seen in the evenings walking with their white dogs and grazing beautiful white cows on its shores. A farmer managed to steal one of these miraculous cows which became renowned for its rich and plentiful milk and equally bountiful progeny. In time the cow grew old so the farmer took it to be slaughtered but when the butcher raised his knife a cry sounded from the lake above. There stood a fairy woman clad in green who summoned the cow and all its offspring, and the farmer could only watch in dismay as each one slipped beneath the surface of the lake and back to the Otherworld.

52.5691, -3.9887; SN653986; Trailhead Parking: 52.5683, -4.0079; SN640986; 1.5km

6 Llyn Cynwch, Llanelltyd

According to legend a whole fairy kingdom lies hidden below the surface of Llyn Cynwch, a lake on the southern edge of Snowdonia National Park. A servant from the Nannau estate was on his way to visit his sweetheart at Dol-y-clochydd on the opposite side of the lake when he accidentally fell into the water. He sank down and down but instead of drowning he suddenly found himself on dry land where, welcomed by a little man, he attended a great feast where he stayed for hours until he remembered his sweetheart had been expecting him. The little man led him along a tunnel, then up a staircase that climbed higher and higher until it emerged from behind the hearth in the very house where his sweetheart worked. Amazed by this experience, his shock increased when he learned he had been missing for many months.

A serpent-like dragon known as a wiber was also said to terrorise the area around Llyn Cynwch, devouring its victims after paralysing them with a malevolent stare. However, a quick-thinking shepherd chanced upon the wiber as it slept on the hillside below the ancient hillfort of Foel Faner and, driving a stake through its eye, he killed it. A cairn was raised over the wiber's body and became known as **Carnedd y Wiber** (52.7664, -3.8778; SH734204).

Llyn Cynwch is in a beautiful location surrounded by mountains and woodland, and a footpath, the 'Precipice Walk,' passes over the hills on the western side of the lake and gives dramatic views across the landscape.

52.7724, -3.8711; SH738210; Trailhead Parking: 52.7737, -3.8609; SH745211; 1.3km

7 Llyn Tegid, Bala

A magical island in the largest natural lake in Wales, Llyn Tegid (Bala Lake), was once the legendary home of the goddess Ceridwen and her giant husband Tegid Foel. There, for a year and a day, she brewed a potion in a huge cauldron that would bestow ultimate wisdom (awen) upon her ugly and stupid son Afagddu. While a boy, Gwion, was tending the cauldron on the last day, the first three drops of the hot potion spattered on his thumb, which he accidentally sucked and thereby took all the wisdom for himself. Gwion fled and Ceridwen followed him in a rage but the boy shape-shifted three times turning into a hare, a salmon, and then a bird. Gwion eventually transformed himself into a grain of wheat and hid in a granary but Ceridwen, having spotted him, turned into a hen and ate him. Nine months later Ceridwen gave birth to the transformed Gwion who eventually became known as the famous bard Taliesin (see **Bedd Taliesin**).

In another story, the lake formed when some careless person forgot to put the lid back on the well at Llangower, which overflowed and drowned the valley and old Bala town in just one night. Some say the lake is rising still and will one day submerge the new town of Bala on the northeastern shore, and that on certain nights the lights from a palace can still be seen shining from the depths.

Llyn Tegid was also thought to be bottomless and when an attempt was made to ascertain its depth, a disembodied voice echoed over the water: "Line cannot fathom me. Go, or I will swallow you up!" In more recent years, there have been occasional sightings of a water monster described as having a long, humpbacked body and big eyes. Nicknamed 'Teggie', the monster was the subject of a Japanese TV documentary in 1995 and visitors still hope to catch a glimpse of this elusive creature who may be the embodiment of Ceridwen's husband Tegid Foel, the spirit of Llyn Tegid.

Parking: 52.9059, -3.6045; SH921354

8 Llyn y Dywarchen, Rhyd-Ddu

There was once a mysterious floating island on Llyn y Dywarchen, a small grassy knoll that the wind blew back and forth across the surface of the lake. It was here that a fairy bride met with her mortal husband after she had been forbidden to walk the earth with any human being. The couple had first met on the slopes of nearby Moel Eilio (53.0974, -4.1582; SH555577) while he was tending his sheep and he was allowed to marry the fairy woman on the condition that her skin was never touched by iron. They lived happily together with their two children for many years, until one day the fairy's leg accidentally brushed against her horse's stirrups and she left that night. From that time, the husband could only see his wife when she appeared on the mysterious floating island, a liminal place, belonging to neither this world nor the Otherworld, and they would talk when the island drifted close to the shore. Today the only island on Llyn y Dywarchen is fixed and motionless though it is still a liminal place with a magical otherworldly atmosphere. The lake with its backdrop of mountains is in a spectacular setting.

Views of the slopes of Moel Eilio can be enoyed from the campsite (53.0663, -4.1430; SH565542) on the shores of **Llyn Cwellyn** (parking: 53.0733, -4.1445; SH564550). Fairies were said to dance in the meadows around the lake's shores where the enticing strains of fairy music could be heard on moonlit nights. One man was drawn into

the dance but when he stepped into the ring he was transported to a beautiful country. He had arranged to meet his sweetheart and after a few hours of dancing decided to go on his way. The fairies allowed him to leave but on returning he found his parents dead and his sweetheart married to another man. He had been gone for seven years and he died of a broken heart within a week.

53.0580, -4.1508; SH559533

9 Merlin's Cave, Bardsey Island*

Pilgrims once flocked to Ynys Enlli, the holy island of Bardsey, where it is said the bodies of 20,000 saints lie buried, but according to some tales it is also the final resting place of the wizard Merlin. Barsdey Island sits a few kilometres off the tip of the Lleyn Peninsula and the island is dominated by a steep hill called Mynydd Enlli where Merlin is said to be sleeping in a cave there with the Thirteen Treasures of Britain. These treasures comprised the following items, each with unique magical properties:

Dyrnwyn, the Sword of Rhydderch Hael
The Hamper of Gwyddno Garanhir
The Horn of Bran
The Chariot of Morgan Mwynfawr

The Halter of Clydno Eiddyn
The Knife of Llawfrodedd the Horseman
The Cauldron of Dyrnwch the Giant
The Whetstone of Tudwal Tudglyd
The Coat of Padarn Beisrudd
The Crock, and also the Dish of Rhygenydd Ysgolhaig
The Chessboard of Gwenddoleu
The Mantle of Arthur in Cornwall

Many of the characters referred to are actual historical figures who come from the Scottish Borders region of the 6-7th centuries, an area referred to in Welsh history as Yr Hen Ogledd, 'The Old North', and in particular the kings of **Alcluid, the Rock of Dumbarton**.

The entrance to Merlin's cave on the western slope of Mynydd Enlli is marked by three white quartz boulders. It is also known as the Hermit's Cave after a more recent inhabitant. The cave entrance is small and can only be entered by crawling, but once inside it opens into a cramped cell blocked off by a low wall. Expect to find animal bones inside and big spiders! At the foot of Mynydd Enlli sits the farmhouse Plas-bach (52.7604, -4.7887; SH119217) where a remarkable apple tree grew against the wall, producing a variety of apple unique to the island. Only the roots of the original tree survive but propagation has

ensured that 'Merlin's Apple' is still cultivated and for some, Bardsey's association with Avalon, the Isle of Apples of Arthurian legend, continues.

Little remains of the medieval St Mary's Abbey (52.7643, -4.7876; SH120221) built on the site of the original 6th century Celtic monastery but it is said the spirits of monks can sometimes be seen there before a storm lashes the island. A number of ancient pilgrimage routes once led here from across Wales, including one from **St Beuno's Chapel** and another from Lllandanwg. The last stop for pilgrims before crossing to Bardsey Island was Ffynnon Fair, St Mary's Well (52.7921, -4.7612; SH139251), a freshwater spring that flows into a natural basin at the edge of the rocky shoreline on the mainland. The well is submerged when the tide is in but when the sea recedes fresh water fills the well. It was customary to make a wish by holding a mouthful of spring water while walking three times around ruined St Mary's chapel nearby.

52.7626, -4.7859; SH121219; Trailhead: 52.7605, -4.7884; SH119217; 400m; Boat Trip from Porth Meudwy £££££: 52.7960, -4.7262; SH162255

10 Mount Snowdon **

The highest mountain in Wales Snowdon and its lakes and valleys are fairy-haunted places that also feature strongly in local Arthurian legend. The Welsh name for Snowdon is Yr Wyddfa, meaning 'the tumulus' – a reference to a legend that a mound on the summit was the burial place of the giant Rhitta Gawr after King Arthur killed him (see **Bwlch y Groes**). Arthur himself was said to have set out from **Dinas Emrys** to face his enemies in battle but was killed in a hail of arrows during an ambush at Bwlch y Saethau (53.0665, -4.0690; SH614541; 850m from summit) close to Snowdon's summit. A cairn was raised over his body but this no longer exists. After his death, Sir Bedivere (Bedwyr) took the sword Excalibur and returned it to the Lady of the Lake at **Llyn Llydaw** (53.0691, -4.0488; SH628543; 3km from summit). Arthur's army is said to lie sleeping in a hidden cave called Ogof Llanciau Eryri high in the cliffs overlooking the lake, awaiting the day when the king returns to defend Britain. A shepherd once found his

way into the cave and accidentally brushed against a bell, at which sound the warriors woke briefly but were angered at being roused too early. Snowdon was also said to be inhabited by eagles that could foretell the outcome of a battle depending on how high they flew over the peaks.

A smaller lake, **Glasyln** (53.0713, -4.0639; SH618546; 1.7km from summit) lies above Llyn Llydaw just below Snowdon's summit. It was in this lake that a fearsome afanc (water monster) was deposited after being dragged by two oxen from the river Conwy near **Betws y Coed**. Reputed to be bottomless, Glaslyn had a somewhat sinister

reputation in the past: its waters were said to be teeming with monstrous fish and no birds would fly over the lake. However, a shepherd who helped a fairy woman he encountered near the lake was richly rewarded. He found the young fairy with her baby, shivering and dressed only in rags, in a dilapidated hut. After the kindly shepherd gave the fairy his shirt to wrap the baby in he found a silver coin in his old clog every evening and over time became a prosperous landowner.

Fairies and other strange creatures are said to dance on the shores of **Llyn du'r Arddu** (53.0803, -4.0892; SH601557; 1.7km from summit) on Snowdon's northern flank. This small lake has a remote and eerie feel with a fairy-bride legend very similar to those of other Welsh lakes, namely that a mortal man married one of the lake fairies but lost his bride after touching her with iron. There is also a large boulder by the lake Maen du'r Arddu (53.0823, -4.0981; SH595559) with a smaller rock on top of it. If two people were to spend the night here it is said one will awake a poet but the other will be mad.

Fairies are also said to inhabit **Cwm y Llan** (53.0498, -4.0669; SH615522. Trailhead parking: 53.0359, -4.0477; SH627506; 2.8km), a valley on the southern side of Snowdon. A shepherd once heard a loud wailing coming from beneath a large

boulder in the valley, which he moved and set free the fairy who had been trapped beneath. In gratitude the shepherd was given a magical walking stick and from that time all the ewes in his flock gave birth to twins until years later, when a flood swept away his stick, taking with it all his luck.

To the north of Snowdon is Nant Peris village where the waters of St Peris's holy well **Ffynnon Beris** (53.1043, -4.0799; SH608583; private land) were reputed to heal conditions such as rickets, scrofula and rheumatism. There were two fish in the well and if they emerged during bathing the cure would be successful; if they remained hidden the visit would have been in vain. Needless to say, those seeking a cure tried to tempt the fish out with pieces of bread sprinkled on the water before bathing. Prior to this, an eel living in the well would coil itself around bathers who were going to be cured. All went well until once day it coiled itself around a little girl who died of fright! The well now lies in a private garden and permission must be sought before visiting.

Lying at the heart of Snowdonia National Park, Mount Snowdon is one of the most visited places in Wales with thousands of people climbing the summit and exploring the lakes and surrounding countryside every year. Numerous walking paths wind their way up the mountainside and the Snowdon Mountain Railway has carried passengers to the summit from Llanberis since 1896. The giant Rhitta's burial mound no longer exists and the summit has been flattened to make way for a café and gift shop, but the views alone make the ascent worthwhile. On a clear day you can take in the whole of Anglesey and the Lleyn Peninsula before hiking downhill through a magically enchanted landscape.

Summit: 53.0684, -4.0762; SH609543; Very Popular; Snowdon Mountain Railway, Llanberis ££££ (One Way): 53.1159, -4.1194; SH582597; Advance Booking Essential

11 Rock of Harlech

Medieval Harlech Castle is built upon the ancient Rock of Harlech, a massive outcrop which, according to traditional folklore, is where Welsh hero Bran the Blessed's fortress was located. From Harlech, Bran and his men set out to Ireland to rescue his sister Branwen from her disastrous marriage to the Irish king Matholwch. A huge fleet of ships set sail but Bran was so gigantic he could wade across the Irish Sea on foot! During the ensuing battle Bran was mortally wounded and requested that his companions cut off his head and bury it at the **White Mount**, where the Tower of London now stands. The decapitated head could still speak and kept them company with his good humour. They returned to Harlech for seven years, and then spent a further 80 years on Gwales, a magical island (possibly Grassholm off the Pembrokeshire coast) before finally taking Bran's head to the White Mount. Now a World Heritage Site, Harlech Castle is an impressive ruin where you can look out to sea and conjure up visions of legendary expeditions.

52.8599, -4.1092; SH580312; Popular ££

12 St Beuno's Well & Chapel, Clynnog-Fawr

Pilgrims walking to **Bardsey Island** could stop off at St Beuno's Well and Chapel to partake in a healing ritual. After bathing in the well, the sick would spend the night spread out on St Beuno's cold stone tomb. If they could sleep, the cure would be effective. At the present-day church at Clynnog-Fawr, a narrow passageway leads to **St Beuno's Chapel** (53.0208, -4.3655; SH414496), thought to have been built on the site of the original 7th century chapel where St Beuno is buried. An ancient chest carved from a single ash log and once used

to collect alms from the pilgrims can still be found in the church, along with a stone where St Beuno inscribed a cross with his thumb. The well, surrounded by a rectangular stone enclosure, lies a short distance from the church alongside the road.

St Beuno's Well: 53.0187, -4.3670; SH413494

13 St Cybi's Well, Llangybi

The picturesque ruins of St Cybi's Well lie

in a secluded spot on the outskirts of Llangybi. The healing spring waters collect in two well chambers before flowing out along stone-lined channels across a grassy meadow. At one time a sacred eel lived in the well and when it coiled itself around a sufferer's legs, healing would be successful. Young women also performed a divination ritual at the well to determine a lover's faithfulness. If a rag thrown into the water floated south he would be loyal, but if the rag went north then only disappointment awaited. The ruinous state of the well and attached building only enhances the romantic and magical

11

12

13

atmosphere of this place through which the healing waters still flow strongly.
52.9457, -4.3421; SH427412; Trailhead: 52.9448, -4.3398; SH428411; 200m

ANGLESEY

14 Bryn Celli Ddu, Llanddaniel Fab

The reconstructed Neolithic burial mound of Bryn Celli Ddu, 'The Mound in the Dark Grove', is one of Wales' most iconic prehistoric landmarks. The entrance to the round grassy mound, flanked by large stone slabs, leads to a narrow interior passage that opens out into an octagonal chamber. As the sun rises on the summer solstice, a ray of light

aligns with the passageway and illuminates this internal chamber. Inside it is an unusual stone pillar, its phallic shape suggesting past associations with fertility, where people often leave offerings. Another standing stone outside the mound is incised with sinuous carvings and known as the Pattern Stone.
53.2077, -4.2362; SH507701

15 Holyhead Mountain

Off the western side of Anglesey, Holy Island was once Anglesey's most sacred place, both to the ancient Druids and in later Celtic Christianity. Its highest point is Holyhead Mountain and a hillfort, standing stones and traces of other ancient constructions are all found in the vicinity of the mountain, which has been a significant landmark for millennia.

In the 6th century St Cybi founded a monastic settlement in Holyhead within the old Roman fort, where the medieval St Cybi's Church (53.3116, -4.6325; SH247826) still stands. St Cybi was said to meet up regularly with St Seiriol from Penmon on the other side of Anglesey (see **St Seiriol's Well**). Walking eastwards in the morning and returning westwards in the evening, St Cybi always faced the sun and so was known as St Cybi the Tawny. St Seiriol, who travelled in the opposite direction and didn't catch the sun, became known as St Seiriol the Fair. They met at St Cybi's Well (53.3184, -4.4025; SH400828) in the centre of Anglesey. This curious tale linking the three sites with the passage of the sun possibly has some astrological significance. Towards the southern end of Holy Island at **St Gwenfaen's Well** (53.2473, -4.6100; SH259754. Trailhead parking: 53.2454, -4.5907; SH272751; 1.8km) a traditional

offering of two white quartz pebbles dropped into the water was said to cure mental illness. The spring is surrounded by the remains of a drystone well-house standing in an exposed location at the top of a cliff.

53.3134, -4.6755; SH218829; Trailhead: 53.3121, -4.6658; SH225827; 1km

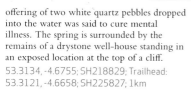

16 Llanddwyn Island, Newborough

On the southwestern tip of Anglesey, this island is actually a narrow peninsula connected to the mainland by a slender neck of dunes. Llanddwyn is sacred to St Dwynwen, patron saint of lovers (see also **Reynard's Cave**), who founded an abbey there in the 5th century and you can still see the remains of 16th-century St Dwynwen's Church (53.1375, -4.4129; SH386627). Immediately west of the church is a small sandy cove and just north of this, hidden in the grassy banks just above the rocks, is St Dwynwen's Well. Local people were said to visit the well to test the faithfulness of their potential marriage partners by sprinkling crumbs of fresh bread upon the surface of the water and then placing a handkerchief over them. If the well's magic eel dragged the handkerchief under as it ate the crumbs then the lover was unfaithful. Between the ruined church and the well is a curious rock with a deep gash in the top that miraculously appeared when St Dwynwen was dying and requested one last view of the sea. St Dwynwen also had a magical ability, granted to her by an angel: any true lover who came to seek her help would either achieve the object of their desire or be cured of their passion. She had chosen the latter for herself. Access to this 'Island of Lovers' is from the large car park by the popular sandy beach then a 1.5km walk along the shore. The island itself is fringed by hidden sandy coves and ends with a lighthouse at its southernmost extremity.

St Dwynwen's Well: 53.1386, -4.4132; SH386628; Secret/Secluded; Trailhead Parking £: 53.1443, -4.3852; SH405634; 1.5km

17 St Seiriol's Well, Penmon

A rare survival of early Celtic Christianity, 6th-century St Seiriol's Well and the foundations of his circular hermit's cell stand by a rocky crag just outside medieval Penmon Priory. St Seiriol founded his monastery at Penmon next to this well, now within a stone well-house. The well had a reputation for healing and was visited by many pilgrims seeking a cure after visiting the saint's

(18)

shrine. He was a great friend of St Cybi (see **Holyhead Mountain**) and the two would regularly meet near Llanerchymedd at the centre of the island – an indication of a possible ancient connection between these two sites at opposite ends of Anglesey. The well and the priory overlook Conwy Bay and Puffin Island, which is also known as Ynys Seiriol since the saint once also lived there and founded a monastery on the island.
53.3063, -4.0567; SH630807

18 Betws y Coed Fairy Glen & the River Conwy *

Flowing northwards towards the village of Betws y Coed, the river Conwy passes through the Fairy Glen, a narrow, wooded ravine strewn with boulders and rocks where the fairies are said to dwell. Narrow uneven steps lead down the side of the rocky gorge which is covered in mosses and ferns then the gorge widens into a more open area where you can sit on the rocks and contemplate the swirling waters and fairy-haunted

crevices. Numerous sightings of the fairies have been reported here over the years. Further north up the Conwy valley the fairies were said to dance on the flat ground between Trefriw (53.1509, -3.8245; SH780630) and Llanrwst (53.1400, -3.7936; SH801618). One young man who entered the fairy ring to dance was rescued a year later by his friends. At first, he refused to believe he had been dancing for so long but they pointed to his shoes, which had been new when he entered the fairy ring but were now tattered and worn. It was believed locally that the fairies of the river Conwy dwelt seven years on earth, seven in the air and seven underground.

A fearsome afanc (water monster) was also said to inhabit a pool in the Conwy just north of Betws y Coed. It was enticed out of the pool by a beautiful young woman who lulled the beast to sleep so it could be bound in chains and dragged away overland by the two famous long-horned oxen known as Dau Ychain Banawg. They hauled the afanc westwards, through the mountain pass at Bwlch Rhiw'r Ychen (53.0677, -3.9745; SH677540) the 'Ox Gap' and an area of moorland that became a pool, the Pool of the Oxen's Eye, was also named after them. Eventually the afanc was deposited in Glaslyn (see **Mount Snowdon**). Here we have a

classic example of a British 'songline' incorporating several named landscape features.
Fairy Glen: 53.0722, -3.7919; SH800542; Popular £; Trailhead Parking £: 53.0751, -3.7945; SH798546; 600m

19 Castell Dinas Bran, Llangollen *

Towering over the town of Llangollen, the atmospheric ruins of Castell Dinas Bran stand atop its dramatic fairy-haunted hill. The medieval castle was built on the site of an earlier Iron Age fort that some believe was a stronghold of the legendary hero Bran the Blessed although in Arthurian lore, this location is a strong contender for the Fisher King's Grail Castle. One early version of the Grail legend names the Fisher King as Bron and the castle *corbin*, an old French term for raven, which is also the meaning of the name Bran.

The town of Llangollen takes its name from St Collen. He was said to have confronted the fairy king Gwyn ap Nudd whose enchanted palace was concealed within the hill. Gwyn welcomed St Collen, inviting

him to join the feast but the saint threw holy water over the assembled fairy court which instantly disappeared leaving St Collen alone on the hillside. The same story is also told of **Glastonbury Tor** but given the saint's long association with Llangollen it would seem likely that the tale originated here.

One summer evening Tudur, a shepherd boy, encountered fairies dancing on the hillside. A tiny man with a fiddle was joined by a host of equally tiny dancers and the fantastic scene proved too tempting so Tudur was compelled to join them. The shepherd danced all night until his master came looking for him the next morning and broke the enchantment. The location of the encounter became known as Nant yr Ellyl-lon, 'Hollow of the Elves', which is likely to be the hollow on the far side of Castell Dinas Bran, away from the town.

In nearby Llandyn Hall Woods (52.9770, -3.1527; SJ226428) on the eastern edge of Dinas Bran a vast and ancient walnut tree grew and the fairies celebrated their marriages beneath its boughs. It was cut down over 200 years ago but in the process a branch fell and killed a man – reputedly an act of revenge by the fairies at the loss of their wedding tree. Fairies were also encountered at Eglwseg Rocks (52.9948, -3.1665; SJ218448) a rocky escarpment running north of Dinas Bran. A man walking there one summer night saw a group of fairies accompanied by a dog. The entrance to their subterranean home was said to be a hole hidden below a stone.

52.9793, -3.1589; SJ222430; Popular, Trailhead: 52.9813, -3.1524; SJ227432; 500m

20 Moel Arthur, Nannerch

This steep hill, crowned with an Iron Age fort, is said to be the site of a battle between King Arthur and Saxon invaders. The fight did not go in Arthur's favour and he escaped on his horse, a magical beast able to leap over large distances. As the pair rode south, they leapt over a cliff near Loggerheads and landed on a stone which still bears the imprint of the horse's hoof. Now named Carreg Carn March Arthur (53.1551, -3.1942; SJ202626), this ancient boundary stone lies next to the A494 road.

Moel Arthur is also reputed to contain treasure watched over by a mysterious woman in grey and buried in an iron chest. Sometimes the chest emits a supernatural light to reveal its location but whenever an attempt is made to uncover the treasure a fierce storm blows in and drives the diggers away. One man who went up the hill with his pickaxe encountered the grey lady who gave him a pea pod and told him to go home. He did as he was told and on returning home found golden peas inside the pod. The grey lady could be seen as a fairy guardian or an embodiment of the hill's spirit of place.

53.1845, -3.2805; SJ145660; Trailhead Parking: 53.1823, -3.2779; SJ146657; 800m

21 St Tecla's Well, Llandegla

The waters of St Tecla's well were reputed to cure epilepsy, known locally as clwyf Tegla, 'Tecla's disease'. In a bizarre ritual said to cure the condition and first recorded in the 17th century, the afflicted person washed their limbs in the well at dusk before walking around it three times while carrying a chicken. They then had to walk around the church three times before spending the night under the altar with the chicken. An offering of money was dropped in the well and the chicken was left in the church. If the chicken died, the ritual had been successful, leaving the patient cured. This practice was said to have continued for many years, with subsequent writers adding more elaborate steps to the ritual including pricking the chicken with a pin. An excavation at the well uncovered layers of pins and coins, suggesting that at least some aspects of the story are true. The well now sits in the dappled shade of overhanging trees and the spring water fills a shallow, stone-lined pool overgrown with vegetation.

53.0616, -3.2029; SJ194522; Trailhead: 53.0627, -3.2029, SJ194523; 100m

22 St Trillo's Chapel, Rhos on Sea

Laying claim to the title of smallest church in Britain, St Trillo's Chapel was founded by the saint in the 6th century on the site of an ancient sacred spring. St Trillo was guided to

the spot by a glowing column of light that emanated from the natural spring which he found to have healing properties. The well lies beneath the altar inside the tiny stone chapel close to the seafront with seating for only six people. It is opened daily for visitors.

53.3144, -3.7406; SH841811

23 St Winefride's Well, Holywell

The only holy well and religious shrine in the country to survive the Reformation intact, St Winefride's is one of the most famous holy wells in Britain. Founded in the

7th century it is still a major place of pilgrimage visited by thousands each year, and many miraculous acts of healing have been known to occur there. The spring is said to have emerged at the place where St Winefride's severed head struck the ground following her decapitation by Caradog, a local chieftain whose advances she spurned. Her uncle St Beuno miraculously restored the saint to life, although she bore a fine white scar around her neck as a reminder of her ordeal. Cast-off crutches and other memorabilia are displayed around the well – testament to the many who have been cured. The current elaborate stone chapel was built over the spring in the Tudor period and features a star-shaped pool where the crystal-clear waters emerge, and a large bathing pool where pilgrims immerse themselves before kneeling to pray on Beuno's Stone in the water. The red staining on this and smaller stones in the well are said to be from St Winefride's blood. To the side is St Winefride's shrine where pilgrims leave lighted candles, rosaries and other offerings. St Winefride's Well has been called one of the seven wonders of Wales and still retains the feel of a venerated Catholic shrine and pilgrimage site although its origins are far older and rooted in Celtic Christianity.

53.2771, -3.2235; SJ185762; Popular £

NORTHERN POWYS

24 Pennant Melangell Church

Within the remote little church at Pennant Melangell is the 12th-century shrine to St Melangell, the patron saint of hares, which are known locally as 'Melangell's lambs'. According to legend, Brochwel Prince of Powys and his hounds were pursuing a hare when they came across a strange young woman at prayer in the forest. The terrified hare hid beneath her cloak and despite being urged on by the prince the hounds refused to go near her. When Brochwel demanded her name she identified herself as Melangell, adding she had escaped an arranged marriage in Ireland so that she might worship God in peace. Realising he was in the presence of a saint, Brochwel granted her the land in the valley where the church still stands. The story of St Melangell, the hare and Prince Brochwel is carved into the 15th-century wooden rood screen in the church, while offerings are frequently left at her restored shrine which incorporates a natural rock outcrop. The church itself stands in a circular churchyard, thought to be a Bronze Age burial site and ringed by ancient yew trees – a sure sign that this sacred place is very ancient indeed. St Melangell may be a pre-Christian goddess whose story has been amended to incorporate changing beliefs over the centuries.

52.8276, -3.4497; SJ024265

25 Pistyll Rhaeadr & the Berwyn Mountains *

Described as one of the seven wonders of Wales, Pistyll Rhaeadr claims to be Wales'

highest waterfall where water from the Berwyn Mountains drops 80m over three stages. The middle fall passes beneath the 'Fairy Bridge', a natural stone arch that the fairies who live in the mossy cliffs are said to cross. Two spirits haunt the waterfall: at the upper falls a white lady with long skirts, her face concealed behind her hair, has appeared, while a monk has been seen by the pool at the bottom of the lower fall. On occasion the water would flow with a reddish tinge which gave rise to the belief that it was blood from the victims of a monstrous winged serpent that made its lair in the rocks at the top of the waterfall. The gwiber, a Welsh dragon, had lairs at Craig Sychtyn (52.8240, -3.1414; SJ231257), now just over the border in Shropshire, and at Penygarnedd. It would fly between them, wreaking havoc and killing people and livestock. It was eventually killed after a wise woman advised the locals to drape a red cloth over a pillar with sharp spikes attached. The gwiber, enraged by the red cloth, coiled itself around the post but as it squeezed tighter the spikes killed it. Known as **Post y Wiber** (52.8140, -3.2820; SJ136248; private land), this prehistoric stone pillar still stands at the edge of a field. The magical Pistyll Rhaeadr waterfall acts as a gateway to an otherworldly kingdom in the Berwyn Mountains and the entrance, guarded by a magical fish, lies in the waters of **Llyn Lluncaws** (52.8738, -3.3799; SJ072315; 2.8km). The trail past the lake leads along a high ridge and eventually reaches the summit of **Cadair Bronwen** (52.9014, -3.3729; SJ077346; 6.5km). Near the summit lies Bwrdd Arthur, 'King Arthur's Table' (52.9013, -3.3731; SJ077346), a large flat rock that conceals buried treasure although a terrible storm will blow up whenever anyone tries to uncover it. An alternative location for this treasure is a hidden chamber with a great sword hanging over the entrance that will fall on anyone trying to enter. Cadair Bronwen was once home to a giant whose brother lived on **Cadair Idris** and the two shared a hammer which they would throw back and forth between their mountaintops. One day Idris, angry at how often his brother used the hammer, threw it so hard that it sailed right over the mountain and landed some kilometres away near Llanarmon Dyffryn Ceiriog where it left a deep hollow in the ground. There is also a belief that the spirit of Welsh hero Owain Glyndwr, who led an uprising against the English in the early 15th century, resides in the Berwyn Mountains, waiting for the day when he will lead the Welsh to victory. South of the Berwyns, overlooking the village of Llanfyllin, **St Myllin's Well** (52.7661, -3.2788; SJ138194) was a popular healing site and visited by the villagers on Trinity Sunday. It is situated below a large sycamore tree and the water flows down through a series of stone basins.

Hikers and day trippers often spurn the remote and mystical Berwyn mountains in favour of the more popular Snowdonia The Pistyll Rhaeadr waterfall itself is often busy and has a small café with images of the dragon, but with such a wealth of folklore in the surrounding area it is well worth exploring farther afield.

Waterfall Parking £: 52.8550, -3.3768; SJ073295; Popular

26 St Dyfnog's Well, Llanrhaeadr

In the medieval era, St Dyfnog's was considered one of Wales' major holy wells and celebrated in poems that praised its healing waters. Being close to **St Winefride's Well** pilgrims often visited both places, doubling their chances of a cure. The waters of St Dyfnog's were noted for their particularly strong flow and were considered especially good for healing skin injuries and smallpox. Older accounts talk of a marble-lined pool surrounded by statues and ancillary buildings that housed a chapel and changing rooms. Today, hidden away in a clearing behind the church at Llanrheadr, all that survives is a large rectangular stone immersion pool with steps leading down into the water. Even though its glory days are long past, modern day pilgrims are rediscovering this ancient healing well in its enchanted woodland setting.

53.1592, -3.3779; SJ079633

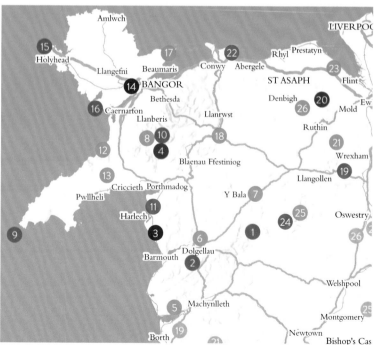

SOUTH WALES

The landscape of South Wales is as varied as its folklore with remote moors, rolling green pastures and wooded valleys where you'll find dramatic waterfalls and mysterious caves. This region is bordered by the Bristol Channel to the south while in the north, in the Brecon Beacons National Park, lies the picturesque village of Ystradfellte in a fairy-haunted valley famous for its waterfalls and the Porth yr Ogof cave. This was believed to be so deep it led directly to the Underworld. The fortress-like eminence of Craig y Ddinas nearby is said to be the last stronghold of the Welsh fairies and to conceal a hidden chamber where a host of sleeping warriors lie alongside a fabulous treasure.

Separated from the urban areas of the south, the Gower Peninsula stretches out into the sea, its rugged coastline ending in the distinctive Worm's Head promontory that looks uncannily like a huge dragon basking in the water. Inland is Arthur's Stone, a prehistoric dolmen that sits high on a hillside overlooking the Llanrhidian marshes. Said to have been flung there by a giant-sized King Arthur, it was also visited in the past by young women hoping to gain a glimpse of their future husband. There is another Arthur's Stone at Ogmore Castle, said to mark Arthur's burial place, while goblins would appear to anyone who slept by the Goblin Stone, a carved stone cross in the ruins of a nearby chapel.

Further along the Glamorgan coast the waves have carved out caves in the limestone cliffs, the largest of which is Reynard's Cave in Tresilian Bay. Unmarried men and women could determine how many years it would be until they wed by throwing stones over Dwynwen's Bow, a natural stone arch in the roof.

Numerous castles stand testament to this area's tumultuous past, their ruins haunted by ethereal ladies and other supernatural guardians, although none so fearsome as the bat-winged Gwrach-y-Rhibyn which lurks in the moat of Caerphilly castle. A little to the east of Caerphilly is the town of Caerleon in Gwent, where medieval chronicles placed King Arthur's court. The remains of a Roman amphitheatre there is still called King Arthur's Round Table. Also in Gwent, St Anne's Well at Trellech had such potent healing waters that it was known as the Virtuous Well and people came to make wishes by dropping a stone into the water. It was also beloved by the local fairies who would dance around the well on certain nights of the year, leaving behind their harebell-flower drinking cups.

1 Arthur's Stone, Reynoldston*

Located high on a hillside overlooking the Llanrhidian marshes, this striking prehistoric dolmen is capped by a vast stone which, according to folklore, was a 'pebble' plucked from his shoe by a giant King Arthur and then flung across the 11km wide Loughor estuary to its present location. The stones of the burial chamber are said to go down to the sea to drink on auspicious nights of the year such as Midsummer's Eve and New Year's Eve. In past times young women would visit Arthur's Stone in the hopes of gaining a vision of their future sweetheart or to test the faithfulness of their lovers. The ritual involved crawling around the stones several times before leaving an offering of cake and was best performed at midnight under a full moon. Also on nights of the full moon a ghostly warrior, dressed in glowing armour, is sometimes seen walking down to the sea. Some say that this is King Arthur himself. Also known as Maen Ceti, Arthur's stone was once even larger. The broken portion can still be seen lying alongside it, struck off by the sword Excalibur, or by a right-eous St David. There is often a puddle in the hollow beneath the dolmen, which is believed to be a spring governed by the tide, and a holy well lies a short distance to the southeast. The water in this well (51.5879, -4.1709; SS497899) is also supposed to ebb and flow with the tide and people used to make wishes here as they cupped their hands and drank from it. From its lofty position, Arthur's Stone commands breathtaking views across the Loughor estuary to Llanelli and the Carmarthenshire mountains beyond.

51.5935, -4.1793; SS491905; Trailhead Parking: 51.5888, -4.1800; SS490900; 500m

2 Caerphilly Castle

In the heart of Caerphilly town, this impres-sive medieval castle with its myriad towers and battlements surrounded by a large moat dominates the landscape. The castle is the largest is Wales, second in size only to Windsor in the whole of Britain. Legend tells of a lady dressed all in green who was sometimes seen gliding along the ramparts. Green is the colour of the fairies and in particular the Scottish house-fairy known as a glaistig who often haunts castles. The castle moat was haunted by another supernatural being known as the Gwrach-y-Rhibyn, an

unearthly hag with bat-like wings, long black hair and talons for fingers who could be heard wailing and groaning like a ban-shee. Today, visitors easily outnumber ghosts but the forbidding battlements and haunted moats can still evoke a sense of mystery. To the northeast of Caerphilly is Mynydd Eglwysilan (51.6256, -3.2683; ST123926. Trailhead: 51.6220, -3.2826; ST113922; 1.1km) where a woodsman and his wife lived in a cottage on the hillside. The woodsman often saw the fairies while out cutting wood, and would even talk to them. One day a branch fell and killed one of the fairies who then imprisoned the woodsman and only released him a year later. There is barely any woodland to be seen today but the hill can be explored via a number of footpaths that traverse the summit.

51.576065, -3.220298; ST155870; ££ Popular

3 Dunraven, Southerndown

The ancient fortress of Dunraven that once stood on the headland known as Witches Point, was the home of the mythical Welsh king Bran whose head was eventually buried in the **White Mount** at the Tower of London. According to local tradition, the famous Tower of London ravens that protect Britain were originally said to have come from Dunraven. A number of fortifications and a later mansion have also occupied the site but all that survives today are some indistinct earthworks and the walled garden known as Dunraven Park with mock castellated towers. Pictur-esque Dunraven Bay (51.4462, -3.6096; SS882731) below is peppered with unusual disk-shaped rock formations known as the Dancing Stones, while up the coast towards

Ogmore-by-Sea the waves have carved out curious indentations in the limestone cliffs including the Fairy Caves (51.4525, -3.6202; SS875738), as they are known locally and which are only briefly accessible via a long walk along the shore at low tide.

51.4425, -3.6026; SS887727; Trailhead Parking: 51.4461, -3.6054; SS885731; 500m

4 Llyn Fawr, Blaenrhodda

The steep cliff of Craig y Llyn towers above the lake of Llyn Fawr which was said to be frequented by a mysterious green lady. Every seven years she would materialise on one of the rocks on the lake shore, making necklaces of rowan berries that she gathered from the trees growing nearby and one year a man happened upon her. The green lady beckoned him closer and passed over a handful of rowan berries which later turned to gold. Some have seen a mermaid who combs her long golden hair while basking on the rocks, but whenever anyone approaches she dives into the water and disappears. It is also said that a stone thrown from the top of the cliff will never hit the water below as it will be caught by the unseen hands of the fairies who live on

Craig y Llyn. When the lake was turned into a reservoir in the early 1900s a hoard of ancient offerings including a sword, bronze axes and cauldrons were recovered, suggesting the spirit of the lake has been honoured here for a very long time.
51.7205, -3.5662; SN919035; Trailhead: 51.7182, -3.5591; SN923033; 600m

5 Ogmore Castle & Arthur's Stone

The landscape around Ogmore Castle, where the Ogmore and Ewenny rivers meet, is full of legends. The castle itself sits on the banks of the Ewenny and contains an ancient carved stone set upon a plinth – Arthur's Stone, which is said to mark the burial place of the legendary king. The castle is also haunted by the ghost of a white lady who guards hidden treasure. She once gave a man a portion of the treasure but when he returned for the rest she scratched him with her talons and he wasted away and died. Another carved stone can be found 2km up the Ogmore river hidden within the ruined St Roque's pilgrimage chapel on a private woodland estate. This is the **Goblin Stone** (51.4909, -3.6016; SS889781; private land; secret/secluded) and the goblins were said to appear if anyone slept by the stone. The stone is no longer in its original position as it was relocated from a nearby field. Local legend says the Ogmore river is haunted by the spirits of men who hoarded a golden treasure. These spirits will not be released until this hidden gold has been found and cast into the river. Upstream on the Ewenny river, **Ogmore Spring** (51.4741, -3.5823; SS902762; private land; secret/secluded) is hidden away in the woods. It is also called the Shee Well and was said to be guarded by river spirits described as 'water ogres'. When some men offended these river spirits the spring dried up, causing the Ewenny and Ogmore rivers to run dry and be filled with snakes and toads. The water spirits retreated up to a cave in the hills but when the terrified men arrived and repented the waters flowed freely once again. Trees then grew around the spring turning it into the magically enchanted spot that it is today.
51.4806, -3.6115; SS881769

6 Pennard Castle

From their dramatic perch, the ruins of Pennard Castle overlook the steep valley of the Pennard Pill as it flows out through a sandy

bay to the sea. As early as the 17th century the castle was described as looking desolate and ruinous, having been abandoned a couple of centuries earlier owing to encroaching sand dunes. The castle's sad fate was sealed when the local fairies were insulted and driven away for dancing outside the castle during a wedding feast. As they departed an ominous voice rang out from the darkness warning that the castle would perish, then a fierce sandstorm blew in and buried the castle. Today the gatehouse and part of the curtain wall still remain, the window openings providing stunning views of the fairy-haunted valley below. The castle is accessed by a footpath leading through a golf course.

51.5765, -4.1020; SS544884; Trailhead: 51.5731, -4.0943; SS549881; 800m

7 Reynard's Cave, Tresilian Bay

Located in Tresilian Bay near St Donat's this large and impressive sea cave is linked to the 5th-century Celtic St Dwynwen, patron saint of lovers (see **Llanddwyn Island**). According to a local tradition, unmarried men and women would try to throw a pebble over St Dwynwen's Bow, a natural rock arch that spans the roof of the cave. The number of attempts correlated to the number of years until their wedding day. There was also said to be a secret passage linking the cave to St Donat's Castle. Reynard's Cave is the largest of the caves in the bay's limestone cliffs, facing out towards the sea from the end of a headland only accessible at low tide.

51.3985, -3.5150; SS947676; Low Tide Only; Trailhead Parking: 51.3968, -3.5007; SS956674; 1.1km

8 St Lythans Dolmen

This 6,000-year-old burial chamber stands stark and exposed, having long since lost the mound of earth that once covered it. An old Welsh name for the dolmen was Gwâl y Filiast, the kennel of the greyhound bitch, which has possible links to the hunting dogs of Welsh mythology. On Midsummer's Eve the capstone is said to spin around three times and the stones go down to the Waycock river to bathe. A natural hole through one of the uprights was said to offer passage for the spirits of the dead and wishes spoken into the dolmen on Samhain would be granted if made in good faith. However, the field that the dolmen sits in has an evil

reputation and is known as the 'accursed field' where nothing will grow.

A little over a kilometre northwest is **Tinkinswood Burial Chamber** (51.4514, -3.3083; ST091733. Trailhead: 51.4399, -3.3048; ST094720; 1.3km), another huge dolmen with the largest capstone in Britain, weighing over 40 tonnes. It is said that anyone spending the night there on the eve of Beltane, Midsummer or Midwinter will either die, go insane or become a poet. The stones around the burial chamber are said to be witches turned to stone for dancing on the Sabbath.
51.4426, -3.2949; ST101723

9 Worm's Head, Rhosslli

Perched at the very tip of the Gower Peninsula like a vast serpent stretched out into the sea, the Worm's Head promontory resembles a living being cast in stone. Sometimes a loud hissing and booming can even be heard echoing from a blowhole at its farthest end. At high tide the Worm becomes an island and is divided into three sections, the Inner, Middle and Outer Head, these last two linked by the natural arch known as the Devil's Bridge. At the

far end of the Head a mysterious cave leads deep into the rock, which some say goes far inland, but the cave entrance is inaccessible to all but the most experienced climbers. Today the Worm's Head is a nature reserve which can be explored on foot after a long walk over slippery stones, but beware the incoming tide that has left more than one visitor stranded on the dragon's back!
51.5650, -4.3330; SS383877; Low Tide Only; Trailhead Parking: 51.5692, -4.2892; SS414880; 3.6km

GWENT

10 Caerleon

Geoffrey of Monmouth, the medieval chronicler who was the first to write extensively about King Arthur and the life of Merlin, places Arthur's court at Caerleon. The town lies beside the river Usk and has several Roman ruins including a circular amphitheatre known locally as King Arthur's Round Table. Caerleon was founded by the legendary Celtic king Belinus who called it Kaerusk, then during

Roman times it was known as the 'City of the Legions' owing to the huge garrison there. Sections of later medieval wall can still be seen and a mound in a private garden is said to be the location of Arthur's fortress (51.6099, -2.9509; ST342905; no access). Arthur and his men are said to lie in an enchanted sleep in a cave somewhere nearby. Today a sculpture trail, beginning outside the National Roman Legion Museum (51.6101, -2.9553; ST339905) in the centre of Caerleon, celebrates the town's Celtic and Roman heritage with carved wooden figures inspired by mythology. The town is also home to Spirit of Awen (51.6089, -2.9530; ST341904), a shop selling pagan and spiritual accoutrements and gifts, tucked away in a courtyard where further sculptures depicting tales from *The Mabinogion* and others in Welsh mythology can be seen.

51.6081, -2.9568; ST338903 (King Arthur's Round Table)

11 Cwm Pwca, Clydach Gorge

Adjoining the steeply wooded Clydach Gorge, this narrow gully known as Cwm Pwca (Puck's Valley) got its name after a local man had a close encounter with a 'pwca', a shape-shifting fairy spirit from Welsh folklore. Coming home late at night, he saw the glow of a lantern ahead and thinking it was a workmate he hurried to catch up. Yet however fast he walked the little man carrying the light always managed to stay ahead. Intent on pursuing the light, the man had not been paying attention and suddenly realised he was close to the edge of the gorge. With a nimble hop and a mischievous chuckle, the lantern-bearer jumped over the gorge and then disappeared and the man realised he'd been led astray by a pwca. Some have claimed that a visit to Cwm Pwca inspired Shakespeare's creation of Puck. Clydach Gorge is located in a former industrial area that has now been returned to nature with a number of trails leading through the wooded valley along the river Clydach and passing by Cwm Pwca.

Standing on a windswept ridge overlooking Clydach Gorge is the **Lonely Shepherd** (51.8226, -3.1344; SO219143. Trailhead: 51.8266, -3.1350; SO218148; 500m). According to folklore this limestone pillar was once a man, turned to stone as punishment for his cruel treatment of his wife. She drowned herself in the river Usk and now each Midsummer Eve the Lonely Shepherd must go down to the river to search for her, returning to his solitary position before dawn.

51.8055, -3.1370; SO217124; Trailhead: 51.8035, -3.1392; SO215122; 400m

12 Kilgwrrwg Church, Newchurch

Standing isolated on a hillside, high above the village of Newchurch, this unusual little church sits within a circular enclosure. Local legend tells that this curious location was chosen when two white heifers lay down on the mound where the church now stands. An ancient stone cross stands in the churchyard and built into the wall of Kilgwrrwg church is a stone head that some believe represents a female fertility figure. The current church has Norman origins but the circular enclosure and the siting legend suggest that this place has probably been a sacred site since pre-Christian times.

51.6822, -2.7792; ST462984; Secret/Secluded; Trailhead: 51.6799, -2.7705; ST468981; 900m

13 St Anne's Well, Trellech *

Also known as the Virtuous Well on account of its healing properties, St Anne's Well is fed by a number of springs, each of which once cured a different ailment. The name is thought to be a Christianised version of Annis, a Celtic goddess who presided over rivers, wells and wisdom. The water rises in a small arched hollow at the back of a semi-circular stone enclosure with seats around the edge for weary pilgrims to rest. There was a tradition of making wishes here by casting a stone into the water. Many bubbles rising to the surface indicated the wish would be granted quickly, a few bubbles meant there would be a delay, but no bubbles meant the wish would be unfulfilled.

The well was also beloved by the local fairies who would dance around it on Midsummer Eve and All Hallows Eve. Their blue harebell drinking cups would be found scattered about the next morning and were gathered by locals to use in magical cures. One farmer found he could no longer draw water after digging up a fairy ring growing around the well and it remained dry until a wizened old man appeared by the well, telling him once the turf from the ring had been replaced the water would flow again. Today St Anne's Well is a haven for wildlife with frogs and newts living around it. The overhanging trees are often adorned with colourful clootie ribbons from visitors who hope their wishes will be granted.

The water from St Anne's Well is said to flow directly beneath **Harold's Stones** (51.7428, -2.7266; SO499051) located on the opposite side of the village. This alignment of three standing stones gave the village its name – Trellech meaning 'Three Stones'. In folklore they are said to commemorate a battle won by Saxon King Harold but they predate his reign by over 2,000 years. In an alternative version they were thrown here by the legendary giant Jack o'Kent from **Skirrid Fawr** near Abergavenny during a hurling competition with the Devil.

51.7424, -2.7212; SO503051

14 St Cybi's Well & Stone, Llangybi

On the eastern edge of Llangybi village, across the road from the church dedicated to the saint, a rough stone well-house encloses St Cybi's healing well. The structure is thought to be medieval but St Cybi himself was said to have briefly settled here with his followers during the 6th century. At that time the land was owned by King Edelig who threatened to evict the saint, but as he approached his horse dropped dead and the king and his men were struck blind. Edelig then prayed for mercy and promised to dedicate himself to God, at which he and his men were immediately cured and his horse sprang back to life. In thanks for this miracle, Edelig granted St Cybi the land to found a church.

In a nearby field stands a 2m high wedge-shaped monolith known as **St Cybi's Stone** (51.6628, -2.8971; ST380963; 650m; private land). The reddish stone is believed to be Bronze Age but nothing is known of its connection to St Cybi.

51.6652, -2.9058; ST374966 (well)

15 Skirrid Fawr, Abergavenny

The holy mountain of Skirrid Fawr once had a chapel dedicated to St Michael on its summit and the soil there was believed to be especially sacred. Handfuls were collected and sprinkled on fields to bestow fertility and around farmhouses for luck and protection. Little now remains of the chapel except for a hollow and two

upright stones. From the summit a great cleft visible in the hillside was said to have been caused by the giant Jack o'Kent when he leapt there from Sugarloaf Mountain (51.8628, -3.0579; SO272187) to the west and his foot slipped as he landed. Jack o'Kent is a larger-than-life figure from local legend who was said to be responsible for several features in the landscape including Harold's Stones (see **St Anne's Well**).

51.8590, -2.9728; SO331182; Trailhead Parking: 51.8423, -2.9757; SO328164; 2km

16 Fish Stone, Tretower

At 5.5m high and probably the tallest standing stones in Wales, the Fish Stone was said to jump into the river Usk each Midsummer Eve for a swim. The Fish Stone is tucked away and hidden by trees at the top of a steep bank not far from the river Usk and sits on the private Glanusk Estate so is seldom visited. Permission must be sought first. The early Welsh epic of Culhwch and Olwen tells of the hunt for the Twrch Trwyth (an Irish king transformed into a boar) led by King Arthur, which passes many places across the south of Wales (see **Cerrig Meibion Arthur**). At Ystrad Yw, thought to be in the vicinity of the Fish Stone, the last of the fearsome boar's piglets was killed in a battle which also claimed the lives of the king of Brittany and Arthur's uncles.

51.8713, -3.1882; SO182198; Private Land

17 Llandeilo Graban Church

High above the Wye valley, the medieval church of Llandeilo Graban has a sturdy

stone tower which, according to legend, was once occupied by a dragon. The dragon terrorised the local community by day but returned to sleep at the tower each night. Eventually a ploughboy and a blacksmith got together and managed to kill the dragon by creating a dummy covered in red cloth and blades which they attached to the tower. The dragon attacked it and cut itself to shreds. It is possible the dragon represented the powerful pagan earth energies of the site, which was later Christianised and may explain why such a fine church was built in this tiny remote hamlet. The ancient yew trees in the churchyard lend further credence to this theory.

52.0931, -3.3243; SO093446

18 Llanfeugan Church, Pencelli *

Twelve ancient and twisted yew trees form a sacred enclosure encircling the remote little church of Llanfeugan, dedicated to the obscure Saint Meugan. Some of the trees may be more than 3,000 years old – far older than the current 13th-century church. Many believe the church sits on the site of an earlier church established in the 7th

century and deliberately placed within the grove of yews to Christianise this ancient pagan sacred site. A stream runs through a dell behind the church while a small rivulet cascades in front, adding to the magically charged atmosphere. Llanfeugan gives a unique insight into how being immersed in an original Druid's grove might have felt.

51.9119, -3.3292; SO086245

19 Llyn Gwyn, Nant Glas

Amidst fields and forests to the west of Nant Glas village lies Llyn Gwyn, a lake that has become associated with the fairy king Gwyn ap Nudd and is thought by some to be an entrance to his Otherworld realm. More traditional folklore says that St Patrick once rested by the lake and while there became embroiled in a quarrel over religious matters with a fellow saint. When a group of villagers overheard the conversation and rudely questioned him, he turned them into fish, except for one woman who became a white lady. She is sometimes seen by the lake accompanied by flashes of light. To make matters worse, St Patrick also cursed the lake so that the sun would never shine upon it except for one week a year.

The small natural lake is well stocked with trout descended from the original stock introduced by medieval monks. According to folklore, after their abbey was destroyed the monks cursed the fish, which croaked horribly so people would not eat them. The presence of fishing platforms around the lake, however, suggests that anglers pay no heed to either curses or croaking fish.

52.2719, -3.4488; SO012647; Trailhead
52.2786, -3.4411; SO017654; 1km

20 Maen-du Well, Brecon

Lying in a small wooded area on the edge of a modern housing estate just outside Brecon, Maen-du Well has a romantic reputation. The vaulted stone well-house encloses a pool of clear water that bubbles up through the sandy bottom. In times past young women would throw pins into the well and count the bubbles to see how many years it would be before they were married. Lovers also visited the well to cast pins while making a wish for a long and happy union. Today lovers rarely visit the well but it retains a peaceful atmosphere despite the encroachment of the modern world.

51.9568, -3.4000; SO038296; Trailhead:
51.9561, -3.3997; SO039295; 100m

19

21 St Issui's Well, Partrishow *

Housed within a stone chamber set into the riverbank, St Issui's healing well is hidden away in a dip in the road where a quiet lane crosses a small woodland stream. During the 6th century St Issui, or Ishow, lived in a hermitage on the site of the nearby church (51.8958, -3.0494; SO278224) a small, ancient-looking building a short distance uphill from the well. After his murder at the hands of a traveller, the place became a site of pilgrimage but today it feels very remote and secluded. People still visit the well to make wishes and prayers, often leaving

20

brightly coloured offerings hanging from the branches of trees or on the stone slab in front of the well. This is a tranquil place of ancient veneration where you can contemplate the spirits of nature as the stream gently trickles by and the birds sing in the trees all around.

51.8954, -3.0510; SO277223; Secret/Secluded

22 Ystradfellte and the Vale of Neath **

The Vale of Neath and its tributary rivers were once considered the most fairy-haunted area in the whole of Wales. The valley of

21

the Afon Mellte in particular, which runs south from the high mountains of the Brecon Beacons down to the Vale of Neath, contains many magically enchanted locations. The small road into this valley from the north first passes by **Maen Llia** (51.8609, –3.5637; SN924191), a large prehistoric standing stone that guards the entrance to the valley. It is said to travel over to the river Nedd to drink when the cock crows. Further along the valley the little village of Ystradfellte on the edge of the Brecon Beacons is the starting point for many scenic walks that pass through fairy woodland to dramatic waterfalls and atmospheric caves, the most popular being the Four Waterfalls walk. Travelling south from Ystradfellte, the Afon Mellte disappears into the gaping maw of **Porth yr Ogof** (51.8008, –3.5556; SN928124), a cave said to be so extensive that it led directly to the Underworld. Inside it is possible to walk beside the flowing river where side passages branch off into the immeasurable darkness. The river emerges back into the light some 300m downstream. The endless tunnels are very popular with parties of cavers who are often seen preparing for their expeditions.

The Afon Mellte then passes through a deep wooded valley where it is joined by the Afon Hepste. It is here that the magical Ystradfellte waterfalls can be found, including **Sgwd yr**

Eira, the 'Falls of Snow' (51.7783, –3.5544; SN928099) where the footpath passes behind the curtain of water. You can reach the waterfall by walking from Ystradfellte (3.9km), Porth yr Ogof (2.7km) or Craig y Ddinas (3.1km). Beyond the waterfalls lies the prominent wooded hill of **Craig y Ddinas** (parking: 51.759468, –3.578782; SN911079), wedged between the Afon Mellte and a tributary stream. This Iron Age hillfort was said to be the last stronghold of the Welsh fairies who could be seen dancing there on moonlit nights and tumbling head over heels down the hill. Local legend claims there is a hidden chamber within filled with treasure beside which is a host of sleeping warriors who some claim to be King Arthur and his knights. A local cattle drover once unknowingly cut a hazel staff from beside the rock that hides the entrance to the cave. Later, after selling his cattle in London, a wizened old man spotted the staff and told the drover that it could lead him to a great treasure. In return for his help in uncovering he treasure, all the old man wanted was to see the place where the snow fell in summer (Sgwd yr Eira, the Falls of Snow!) Eventually the two enteried the cave, the drover helped himself to handfuls of treasure and then he took the old man to Sgwd yr Eira where he disappeared behind the falls, never to be seen again. The drover went back

many times to the cave and became very rich but one day he accidentally rang the bell that hangs near the entrance. This the drover knew would wake the warriors but he forgot the magic words necessary to send them back to sleep and so they beat him and left him crippled. The entrance has remained hidden ever since. Craig y Ddinas is now a popular spot with a dedicated car park. Rock climbers are often seen ascending its face but scramble up the steep path to the top and you will find yourself in a different and altogether more enchanted world as the two mountain streams roar below and the entrance to the fabulous cave remains just out of reach. Further downstream in the Vale of Neath another secret doorway is said to lead to the land of the fairies. A boy named Elidor ran away from home and was found by the fairies who took him to their subterranean world where all was 'playtime and pleasure', yet the sun never shone on their twilight meadows. He was no captive and was allowed to return often to his own world to visit his mother. When one day she requested proof of his visits to Fairyland, Elidor tried to steal a golden ball belonging to the fairy prince but was caught and banished immediately. Never again could he find the entrance to that marvellous world.

Ystradfellte Parking: 51.8094, –3.5541; SN929134; Popular

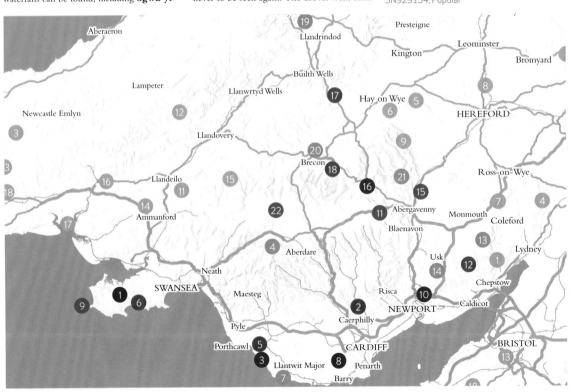

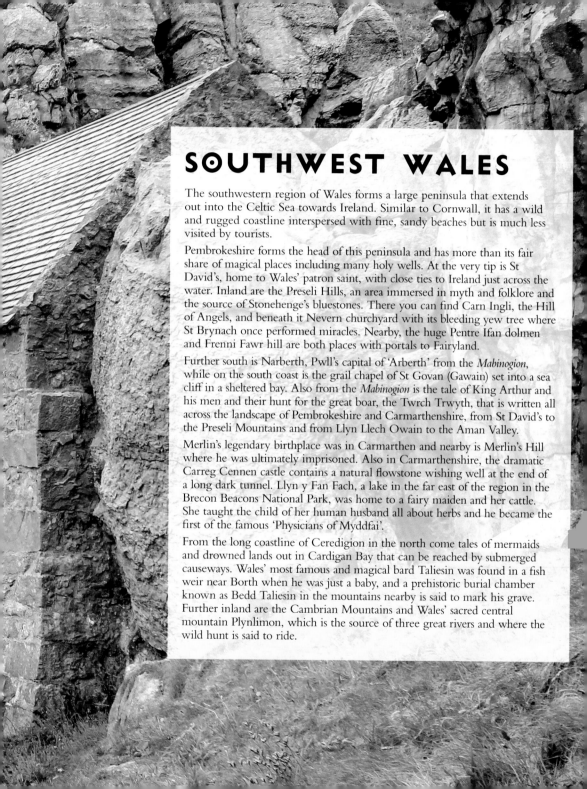

SOUTHWEST WALES

The southwestern region of Wales forms a large peninsula that extends out into the Celtic Sea towards Ireland. Similar to Cornwall, it has a wild and rugged coastline interspersed with fine, sandy beaches but is much less visited by tourists.

Pembrokeshire forms the head of this peninsula and has more than its fair share of magical places including many holy wells. At the very tip is St David's, home to Wales' patron saint, with close ties to Ireland just across the water. Inland are the Preseli Hills, an area immersed in myth and folklore and the source of Stonehenge's bluestones. There you can find Carn Ingli, the Hill of Angels, and beneath it Nevern churchyard with its bleeding yew tree where St Brynach once performed miracles. Nearby, the huge Pentre Ifan dolmen and Frenni Fawr hill are both places with portals to Fairyland.

Further south is Narberth, Pwll's capital of 'Arberth' from the *Mabinogion*, while on the south coast is the grail chapel of St Govan (Gawain) set into a sea cliff in a sheltered bay. Also from the *Mabinogion* is the tale of King Arthur and his men and their hunt for the great boar, the Twrch Trwyth, that is written all across the landscape of Pembrokeshire and Carmarthenshire, from St David's to the Preseli Mountains and from Llyn Llech Owain to the Aman Valley.

Merlin's legendary birthplace was in Carmarthen and nearby is Merlin's Hill where he was ultimately imprisoned. Also in Carmarthenshire, the dramatic Carreg Cennen castle contains a natural flowstone wishing well at the end of a long dark tunnel. Llyn y Fan Fach, a lake in the far east of the region in the Brecon Beacons National Park, was home to a fairy maiden and her cattle. She taught the child of her human husband all about herbs and he became the first of the famous 'Physicians of Myddfai'.

From the long coastline of Ceredigion in the north come tales of mermaids and drowned lands out in Cardigan Bay that can be reached by submerged causeways. Wales' most famous and magical bard Taliesin was found in a fish weir near Borth when he was just a baby, and a prehistoric burial chamber known as Bedd Taliesin in the mountains nearby is said to mark his grave. Further inland are the Cambrian Mountains and Wales' sacred central mountain Plynlimon, which is the source of three great rivers and where the wild hunt is said to ride.

PEMBROKESHIRE

1 Cemaes Head, St Dogmaels

The rugged cliffs of Cemaes Head are the site of one of Wales' most famous mermaid encounters. A fisherman from St Dogmaels known as Peregrine was sailing his small boat past the headland when he chanced upon the mermaid sitting on a rock. Catching her completely unawares, he dragged her onto his boat and marvelled at making such a rare catch. The mermaid wailed miserably and begged to be released so after a while Peregrine took pity on her and let her go. In exchange she promised to give him three shouts of warning if ever he was in danger. Peregrine went back to his life of fishing and started to wonder if he'd dreamt the whole thing, until one day out at sea he heard the mermaid's warning cry: "Peregrine, Peregrine, Peregrine! Take up your nets" she shouted. He immediately did so and sailed for home, just before a fierce storm blew up. Many fishermen lost their lives that day but not Peregrine who was saved thanks to his encounter with the mermaid.
St Dogmaels itself is an old fishing village on the estuary of the river Teifi with a ruined abbey and an ancient church containing some ogham stones (52.0811, -4.6807; SN164459). A wooden mermaid statue (52.0886, -4.6819; SN163467) by the riverside north of St Dogmaels commemorates Peregrine's encounter with the mermaid and a footpath passes over Cemaes Head but the rocks below, where the mermaid encounter took place, are not visible or accessible without a boat.
Further north at **Llanina Point** (52.2159, -4.3348; SN405600) near New Quay, a similar story is told of a mermaid who was sometimes seen sitting on a rock called Carreg Ina. She, too, was caught in a fisherman's net and warned him of a coming storm. The parishioners of St Dogmaels have reported many fairy sightings, and also some abductions. Even the local clergy were not safe as an elderly priest was once compelled to dance with the fairies all night.

52.1159, -4.7282; SN133499; Trailhead Parking: 52.1106, -4.7258; SN134493; 800m

2 Cerrig Meibion Arthur, Mynachlog-ddu

Known as the 'Stones of the Sons of Arthur' this pair of monoliths stand on a heather-covered hillside on the southern edge of the Preseli Hills. They are said to mark the spot near 'Cwm Cerwyn' which is mentioned in the tale, where one of King Arthur's sons was killed by the fierce boar

known as the Twrch Trwyth. The boar, an ancient king magically transformed, had been chased over from Ireland along with his equally fearsome piglets by Arthur and his men. They were on a mission to retrieve the scissors, comb and razor that were lodged between the Twrch Trwyth's ears. These magical items were needed in order to complete a quest to cut the beard of the fearsome giant Ysbaddaden – a seemingly impossible task among many that the hero Culhwch had to complete in order to win the hand of the giant's daughter Olwen.

Enlisting the help of King Arthur and his band of warriors Culhwch chased the boar and its piglets from where they made land at Porth Clais (51.8705, -5.2833; SM740242) just south of **St David's**. From there they pursued them all over South Wales passing **Nevern**, Cwm Cerwyn, **Llyn Llech Owain**, the Annan Valley and Llyn y Fan Fawr (51.8822, -3.6980; SN832217). All the piglets were eventually dispatched but many of Arthur's heroes and best hunting dogs were killed along the way before the Twrch Trwyth finally fled from Wales into the Bristol Channel. There they surrounded it in a tidal pool and snatched the scissors and razor from between its ears before it broke free and headed for Cornwall. By the Cornish coast the beast was cornered again and Culhwch himself managed to wrest the comb from the Twrch Twryth before it fled into the ocean, never to be seen again. Although traces of the story of the hunt for the Twrch Trwyth are imprinted all over the landscape of South Wales, the stones of Cerrig Meibion Arthur are the only standing monuments still associated with the tale. The mountain that towers above the stones to the north is often referred to as 'Cairn Mountain' due to the large numbers of prehistoric cairns situated upon its flanks. Amongst these are more sites associated with King Arthur such as Beddarthur 'Arthur's Grave' (51.9595, -4.7216; SN131325; 2.7km from trailhead

parking) and Carn Arthur 'Arthur's Cairn' (51.9573, -4.7170; SN134322; 400m from Beddarthur). Further into the mountains is Carn Goedog (51.9656, -4.7248; SN129331; 1.9km from Beddarthur) which is one of the source quarries of the Preseli bluestones of **Stonehenge**.

51.9458, -4.7394; SN118310; Trailhead Parking: 51.9439, -4.7261; SN127307; 1km

3 Frenni Fawr, Crymych

The green mountain of Frenni Fawr, an outlier of the Preseli Hills, was the site of a magical fairy encounter and journey into their Otherworld realm. A shepherd boy out on the neighbouring hill of Freni Fach looked over at Frenni Fawr to check the weather one day, as it was known that if fog fell on the Cardiganshire side of the mountain the weather would turn foul. Surprised to see small figures moving on Frenni Fawr, he at first thought they were soldiers but soon realised they must be the Tylwyth Teg, the fairy folk.
Curious, he made his way over the mountain towards them and saw that they wore bright red and white garments and little hats. Some were dancing in a perfect circle while others ran around chasing each other, laughing merrily. There were

also fairy women prancing by on beautiful white horses and everyone seemed to be having a carefree time. As he crept closer the fairies noticed him and invited him into their circle. He edged forward nervously then suddenly found himself transported to a magical land where all his wishes were fulfilled and beautiful fairy women tended to his every need. He was allowed to roam free there on just one condition: that he never touched or drank from the pond containing golden fishes. Inevitably, after a couple of years, even the delights of Fairyland started to wane and so his curiosity about the magic pool intensified. Cautiously dipping his hand into the water, he heard a loud scream and Fairyland instantly disappeared. He was back on the hillside of Frenni Fawr all alone, and he soon discovered that although he had spent two years in Fairyland only a couple of minutes had passed back home!
Frenni Fawr was previously known locally as Cadair Macsen, 'The Seat of Macsen', a male figure who features in the *Mabinogion* as Macsen Wledig and has been identified as the Roman emperor Magnus Maximus. There is also a story that legendary giant St Samson once threw a huge boulder from the summit of Frenni Fawr that landed near Llanfyrnach.

51.9835, -4.6182; SN203349; Trailhead: 51.9799, -4.6078; SN209344; 900m

local men on the coast nearby. They kept her captive for a while but eventually let her go in exchange for three pieces of the mermaid's advice, which included a seemingly trivial tip on how to sweeten pottage! Llanwnda's varied folk tales and secluded location lend a magical atmosphere to this small and much overlooked hamlet where a modern pilgrimage route now starts, winding its way overland to St David's cathedral. On the opposite side of the port town of Fishguard, near the village of Llanychaer, lies the site of another ancient Celtic church and holy well. Llanllawer Church (51.9857, -4.9332; SM986359) incorporates 6th-century incised crosses into its gateway and inside can be found the 'weeping stone', a hollow stone always reputedly filled with water. **Llanllawer Well** (51.9860, -4.9326; SM987360) lies in an adjacent field and flows from a large, arched stone structure, big enough to step inside. The well water is said to be good for sore eyes.

52.0161, -5.0149; SM932395

5 Nevern & Carn Ingli *

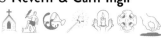

The churchyard at Nevern is doubly famous, both for its ancient carved stones and for its marvellous, bleeding yew tree. Beside the church stands a 3.6m high Celtic cross entirely covered in intricate knotwork designs in a Scandinavian style. It dates from the 10th or 11th century and is sometimes known as St Brynach's Stone. There is a legend that on St Brynach's day (April 7th) the first cuckoo of spring would land on top of the stone and sing, and mass could not be held on the saint's day until this had occurred. St Brynach was an Irish saint who is said to have floated over to Wales on a stone. He founded his monastery near where Nevern church now stands after he was guided by an angel to follow a white sow and her piglets to the spot. Nevern churchyard also contains an ancient phallic standing stone, while inside the church is the 5th-century Maglocunus Stone with inscriptions in Latin and ogham. The bleeding yew tree in Nevern churchyard, a modern-day miracle, has oozed a red sap that looks just like blood ever since a monk who was hung from the tree cursed it to bleed for him. The tree is one of an avenue of yews that forms a green tunnel leading to the church door. On the opposite side of Nevern village is a unique Wayside Shrine (52.0252, -4.7986, SN080400) featuring an ancient pilgrim's cross carved into the cliff face, with more crosses beneath cut by pilgrims while kneeling there. It stands on an ancient pilgrimage route from **Holywell** to **St David's**.

4 Llanwnda Church

At the end of a small country lane lies the tiny hamlet of Llanwnda with its little stone church. It was founded by the early Celtic saint Gwyndaf who established his hermitage there and six intricately carved Celtic stones from the 7th–9th centuries incorporated into the walls of the Medieval church are still visible. **St Gwyndaf's Holy Well** (52.0156, -5.0154; SM931395; secret/ secluded) is constructed of stone slabs and concealed in a clump of trees just opposite the church. Like many holy wells it was said to have healing properties.

An unusual ancient burial chamber known as Carreg Samson (52.0126, -5.0149; SM931392) is on the side of Garnwnda hill just south of the village. It incorporates two natural rock outcrops as well as a large capstone said to have been thrown from **Garn Fawr** hill (parking: 52.0081, -5.0627; SM898388) by the prodigious St Samson. Garn Fawr, a few kilometres west of Llanwnda, overlooks the coast and it is said you can sometimes see fairy islands out in the sea from its summit.

One final story relating to Llanwnda is that of a mermaid who was caught by some

From Nevern churchyard it is possible to see the sacred mountain of **Carn Ingli** (52.0001, -4.8218; SN063373. Trailhead parking: 52.0006, -4.8131; SN069373; 700m), the 'Hill of Angels', where St Brynach is said to have communed with shining beings. However, according to another tale, Ingli was a giant who lived on the mountain and created most of its ancient cairns. Many spirit paths are said to converge on Carn Ingli and it was believed that any man who spent the night up there would become a poet, a lover or a madman. At the foot of the path that leads up the mountain from the north is **Carn Cwn Well** (52.0096, -4.8237; SN063383. Trailhead: 52.0113, -4.8271; SN060385; 350m), a pin well where people came to cure warts and make wishes. Its shallow rock basin filled with water lies hidden under a crag of rock known as Carn Cwn, 'The Cairn of the Dog'.

Nevern Churchyard: 52.0256, -4.7955; SN083400

6 Pentre Ifan, Brynberian

The largest and most impressive dolmen in Wales, Pentre Ifan has close associations with the Tylwyth Teg, the Welsh fairy folk. The dolmen's massive 5m-long capstone, which almost seems suspended in the air, rests at a height of over 2m on three huge uprights. The structure dwarfs the diminutive fairy folk who have reputedly been seen near it. No bigger than children, they were said to be dressed like old-fashioned soldiers with red caps. A local story tells of Einion, a shepherd boy who was walking in the mountains near Pentre Ifan when he became lost in the fog. He wandered for hours until he came across a merry old man with gleaming blue eyes who led him to a secret fairy portal under a standing stone. Einion entered and then emerged into a beautiful land of green meadows and meandering rivers. He then approached a white and gold fairy palace where ethereal music filled every room and all kinds of luxuries were served to him by invisible hands. Seeing no one except the old man, he was starting to think that the fairy palace was deserted when suddenly an old woman appeared accompanied by three beautiful fairy sisters. It was then that he discovered he was unable to speak, but by kissing him on the lips one of the sisters, named Olwen, gave him back his voice. Although he was completely enchanted by the fairy palace, eventually he started to miss his home and was allowed to leave, vowing to the fairy Olwen that he would return. Back home people were shocked to see him, having given him up for dead long

ago as several years had passed. Nevertheless, a month later he returned to Fairyland and married Olwen, before bringing her back to his world with rich gifts from the fairies. Soon they had a child together and named him Taliesin. It is perhaps for this reason that an alternative name for Pentre Ifan is Ceridwen's Womb (see **Llyn Tegid**). People marvelled at Einion's new-found luck and prosperity, and when he told of his adventure and described the beautiful fairy sisters he called them the *Tylwyth Teg*, the 'Fair Folk', which is how the Welsh fairies acquired that name.

In the nearby village of Brynberian an afanc (water monster) once lived in the Afanc's Pool (51.9815, -4.7610; SN104350) in the river by the bridge. One day it was dragged from there and buried up on the side of the Preseli Hills in a prehistoric chambered tomb now known as Beddyrafanc, the 'Afanc's Grave' (51.9775, -4.7563; SN107345; no paths). Further downstream the Brynberian river passes by a dramatic outcrop of Preseli bluestone called Craig Rhosyfelin (51.9919, -4.7445; SN116361). It has recently been proved that some of the Preseli bluestones that make up the **Stonehenge** monument were originally quarried there, and traces of the Stone Age quarrying can still be seen. Remarkably, archeologists have also established that the stone circle was originally set up near the Preseli Hills before subsequently being moved overland to Stonehenge. According to the medieval historian Geoffrey of Monmouth, the wizard Merlin transported the stones.

51.9990, -4.7700; SN099370

7 St David's *

The tiny cathedral city of St David's (Tyddewi) was originally founded by Wales' patron saint in the 6th century. He was born just 1km to the south near the coast where the ruined St Non's Chapel (51.8722, -5.2688; SM750243) now stands. **St Non's Well** (51.8725, -5.2684; SM751243) is situated nearby and reached by a short flight of stone steps down to a stone arch. The water is said to have emerged during a thunderstorm when St Non gave birth to St David (Dewi Sant in Welsh). The well was subsequently often visited for healing, especially on St David's day (March 1st) and St Non's day (March 2nd) when ghostly hymn singing was said to emanate from St Non's chapel. Small offerings were left in and around the waters of the well and it was said that any wish made there in silence would be granted. Children would also be dipped in the water for protection against disease and misfortune.

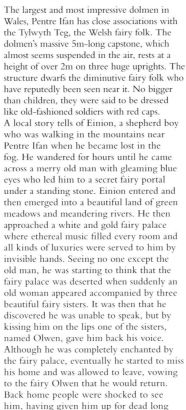

islands would soon lose sight of them, until one man took a clod of St David's turf in his boat and was able to land there. Unfortunately, he was never seen again. Others have landed on the islands by chance, only to see them disappear once they boarded their boat again.

St David's Cathedral: 51.8820, -5.2684; SM751254; Very Popular

8 St Govan's Chapel, Bosherston *

Wedged inside a cleft of the South Pembrokeshire coastal cliffs lies the mysterious grail chapel of St Govan. It is reached by stone steps that pass down from the clifftop and through the chapel itself before continuing past a holy well to the shore. It is said that the steps are uncountable and that anyone who breathes their hopes and dreams into the wind as they pass up or down them will have those hopes fulfilled.

According to local lore, Govan was none other than Sir Gawain of Arthurian legend. He fled to the chapel to escape his enemies, hiding in a narrow fissure in the rock face which then magically closed up and completely concealed him. The fissure is still there beside the altar and anyone who squeezes in and speaks their wishes into it without turning around will have them granted. The marks from Govan's ribs can still be seen imprinted into the cleft and it is said that strange ethereal noises can sometimes be heard within.

The small chapel itself is of 13th century construction but it's not hard to imagine a

St David's has been a major pilgrimage site for over 800 years and it was said that two trips to St David's was equivalent to one to Rome. The small river Alun passes right by the cathedral and was crossed by a stone slab called the Llechllafar, the 'Speaking Stone'. Legend says that when a corpse was carried across it, the stone protested loudly and cracked, and according to one of Merlin's prophesies, a king who conquered Ireland would also die after crossing it. The stone has since been replaced by a modern concrete slab that you can now walk over. The river Alun flows down to the sea at Porth Clais (51.8705, -5.2833; SM740242) just 2km to the southwest. This is the spot where the great boar the Twrch Trwyth is said to have landed from Ireland while

being chased by King Arthur and his men (see **Cerrig Meibion Arthur**). St David is reputed to be closely related to King Arthur through his mother St Non. At the western extremity of Wales, this whole area had close connections to Ireland with many Celtic monks passing back and forth including St Patrick himself who sailed to Ireland from Whitesands Bay (51.8944, -5.2958; SM733268).

Another legend says that if you take a piece of turf from St David's churchyard and then stand upon it near the coast you will be able to see the fairy islands out in the ocean. These were inhabited by fairy folk known as the 'Children of Rhys the Deep' and kept invisible by the magical herbs that grew there. Most who sailed out to find the

9

9

much earlier hermitage here in this secluded location that feels lost in time. The holy well was much visited for healing right up until the 19th century but is now unfortunately dry. There was once a bell inside the chapel that would ring by itself to warn of impending disaster at sea but it was said to have been stolen by pirates. Interestingly, some of the stones near the chapel will now ring if struck so perhaps there is some truth in the story that sea nymphs rescued the bell from the pirates and hid it within the living rock for safekeeping.

Just 400m west of the chapel a dramatic gash in the cliffs is known as Huntsman's Leap (51.5985, -4.9444; SR961929). Here, to save his soul from the Devil, a hunter had to leap across the chasm on his horse – a seemingly impossible task achieved by calling upon the blessing of St Govan. Heading north along the small country lane through the idyllic village of Bosherston, with its enchanting lily ponds, you eventually pass isolated standing stones strung out in a loose alignment. Known as the Devil's Quoits or the Dancing Stones of Stackpole, these consist of the Harold Stone (51.6247, -4.9374; SR967958), the Devil's Quoit, Sampson (51.6293, -4.9456; SR962963) and, on the other side of the ponds, the Devil's Quoit, Stackpole (51.6179, -4.9177; SR981950). These three stones, spread out over a distance of 2.5km, are said to get together to dance at Sais Ford 'The Saxon's Ford' (location unknown) once a year. To see the dance is said to be extremely lucky.

51.5987, -4.9368; SR967929; Trailhead Parking: 51.5996, -4.9369; SR966930; 150m. Access only when military range is open to public, ring to check: Castlemartin Range 01646 662367

9 St Teilo's Well, Maenclochog

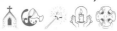

Just over a kilometre from Maenclochog lies a healing well dedicated to St Teilo. It was said that cures from this well would only be effective if drunk from a cup made from St Teilo's skull! Luckily, just such a cup was kept near the well until recent times and was known as Penglog Teilo. This combination was thought to be especially potent and people even used the cup and well to pray for an end to the First World War and the safe return of their loved ones. The water from St Teilo's Well now issues from a rocky wall overhung with hawthorn trees, some decorated with clootie ribbons. It then flows out into a series of unusual, overgrown, stone-lined pools surrounded by marsh grass and enigmatic standing stones. The nearby ruined church of Llandeilo Llwydarth (51.9082, -4.7645; SN099269) in its circular enclosure incorporates an early Celtic Christian site associated with St Teilo who, in his day, was almost as famous as St David. However, it's unlikely that the fragment of skull used as a cup was actually St Teilo's and may instead represent a tradition dating back to pagan times.

On the opposite side of the village of Maenclochog, by the roadside, lies another healing well, **Ffynnon Fair** 'St Mary's Well' (51.9087, -4.7996; SN05270), which is associated with a stone that once stood outside Maenclochog Church (51.9120, -4.7884; SN083273). This was a magical standing stone that rang when struck and would stop ringing only when dowsed with water from St Mary's Well. This stone gave the village its name – Maenclochog means

'Bell Stone' – but one day the curious villagers broke up the stone to see what was inside it! Luckily the well still exists and delivers a good flow of clear fresh water. Inside Maenclochog Church there are some ancient ogham stones.

51.9092, -4.7619; SN101270; Trailhead: 51.9104, -4.7627; SN100271; 150m

10 Tenby & Caldey Island

Castle Hill (51.6725, -4.6945; SN137005) overlooking the entrance to Tenby harbour was once an ancient royal fortress. It is mentioned in the 10th-century *Book of Taliesin* as the stronghold of Bleiddudd, the 'Wolf Lord'. A short ferry ride from

10

10

Tenby, Caldey Island was one of Wales'
most important early monastic settlements.
It was founded by St Pyr then taken over
by St Samson and later by St Illtyd. The
monastery was prone to flooding so St
Illtyd is said to have miraculously raised
the whole island higher above the sea. A
reminder of those early times can be found
in the ancient-looking **St Illtyd's Church**
(51.6345, -4.6879; SS140962; 1km from
Caldey Island jetty), which contains an old
carved ogham stone.

Just outside Tenby are the three **Gumfreston Holy Wells** (51.6766, -4.7360;
SN109010). They emerge side by side in
Gumfreston churchyard and bubble up
through the earth into stone troughs surrounded by lush greenery. Each spring
has a different source and its own unique
properties. The topmost spring was used for
healing leg complaints, the middle for arms
and hands, and the lower for eyes. Pins
were also cast into the wells, especially on
Easter Sunday, and pilgrims would sometimes stop at the wells on their way to the
port at Tenby or to St David's.

Ferry from Tenby: 51.6731, -4.6973;
SN135005; £££; Foot Passengers Only;
Easter – October

10

11 Carreg Cennen, Trapp

The medieval castle of Carreg Cennen hides
a long dark tunnel that leads to a magical
wishing well where the white flowstone has
naturally created a miraculous bowl shape
into which water constantly drips. Wishes
have long been made in this dark and
enchanted place by casting pins into the well.
The castle occupies a dramatic site, perched
atop a green hill with craggy cliffs. At the
bottom of one of these cliffs is reputed to
be another cave called Ogof Dinas where
the Welsh hero Owain Llawgoch (see **Llyn
Llech Owain**) lies sleeping with 51 com-
rades. It is said that when he awakens an
age of peace will begin.

51.8544, -3.9356; SN667190; £ Bring a Torch

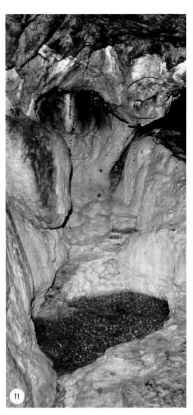

11

11

12 Carreg Pumsaint

The stone known as Carreg Pumsaint, the 'Stone of Five Saints', sits atop a grassy mound and its deep indentations are said to have been created by the heads of five saints. These saints, who were quintuplets, were lying in the nearby **Dolaucothi Gold Mines** ££ (52.0449, -3.9524; SN662403; popular) using the stone as a pillow. They kept turning it over, which explains why there are indentations on all sides, but they couldn't get comfortable so they threw it out. Presumably they got to sleep eventually because they are said to lie there still, awaiting a truly virtuous bishop at St David's or the return of King Arthur. A local woman was once led into the mines to see the saints and became trapped there. Her spirit now haunts the mine entrances on stormy nights when her wailing can sometimes be heard. The whole mining complex, which dates back to Roman times, is now a popular visitor attraction with tours of some of the mines. Before they entered the mines the saints used to bathe in five pools in the river

12

near Llanpumsaint at a place called Cwm Cerwyni (51.9334, -4.3033; SN417286). The pools subsequently became a popular pilgrimage site and the water in each was said to have unique healing properties when bathed in.

52.0454, -3.9505; SN663403

13 Gwâl y Filiast (Arthur's Table), Llanglydwen

In a magical woodland clearing just above the river Taf lies a dolmen known as Gwâl y Filiast, 'The Greyhound Bitch's Lair'. Its alternative name is Bwrdd Arthur, 'Arthurs Table', and King Arthur is also remembered at Crochan Arthur, 'Arthur's Cauldron' a natural hollow in the river below where the calm waters become a raging torrent. A footbridge (51.9018, -4.6610; SN170259) crosses the Taf and paths lead through the wooded valley.

51.8992, -4.6605; SN170256; Trailhead: 51.9021, -4.6469; SN180259; 1.1km

14 Llyn Llech Owain, Gorslas

The lake now known as Llyn Llech Owain was created by a magically overflowing well. Local shepherds had discovered the well, taking just enough for their needs and replacing the flagstone that covered the well each day to stop it overflowing. A warrior named Owain came across the well one day and in a state of exhaustion watered his horse and then fell asleep. He awoke to find the land flooded and was only able to stem the flow by galloping his horse around the perimeter of the lake as, magically, the water was unable to cross his horse's tracks. Thereafter this newly-formed lake was known as Llyn Llech Owain, the Lake of Owain's Flagstone. Some say that Owain was one of Arthur's knights, Sir Owain, while others say he was the Welsh hero Owain Llawgoch. Llyn Llech Owain also features in the story of the hunt for the great boar, the Twrch Trwyth, by King Arthur and his men (see **Cerrig Meibion Arthur**). Two of Arthur's warriors were killed there by the boar, before he broke free and headed for Llyn y Fan Fawr.

The magically created Llyn Llech Owain still exists but is now part of a country park and is popular with visitors.

Parking £: 51.8135, -4.0830; SN565148; Popular

15 Llyn y Fan Fach, Llanddeusant *

Lying within a sweep of green mountain-side in the Brecon Beacons National Park the enchanted lake of Llyn y Fan Fach is the location for one of Wales' most fascinating fairy legends. A widow's son from the nearby farm of Blaensawdde (51.9003, -3.7688; SN783238) was tending his sheep near Llyn y Fan Fach one day when he saw a beautiful fairy walking over the surface of the lake. Instantly falling in love with her, he tried to win her heart by baking her some bread, but it took three attempts before she was satisfied and agreed to marry him. The fairy made one condition: if he struck her three times without cause or touched her with iron she would leave. When they set up house at Esgair-Ilaethdy (51.9516, -3.7679; SN786296) near Myddfai, the fairy woman brought her fairy cattle with her and so the farm prospered and they had three sons together. All went well until he struck her twice and then accidentally touched her with an iron bridle bit and she left, taking her fairy cattle back to the lake. The cows were dragging a plough behind them and it's said that the furrow made could still be seen by the edge of the lake before it was later turned into a reservoir. The farmer never saw his fairy wife again but she appeared to her sons, teaching one all about medicinal herbs. He and his descendants became known as the Physicians

15

16

of Myddfai, and their skills were passed
down to many subsequent generations.
Local people used to gather at the lake's
edge on the first Sunday in August when
the water 'boiled' and they hoped to catch
a glimpse of the 'Lady of the Lake' and her
fairy cattle. It was also said that those who
bathed in the lake's waters would always be
beautiful. The lake also had another supernatural guardian in the form of a hairy water
monster who would come out and threaten
anyone who attempted to drain the lake. It is
said to be bottomless, which marks the lake
out as a portal to the Otherworld.

51.8837, -3.7395; SN803220; Trailhead
Parking: 51.8998, -3.7457; SN799238; 2km

16 Merlin's Hill, Carmarthen *

Known by its Welsh name, Bryn Myrddin, this
green hill just east of the town of Carmarthen
is said to be the final resting place of the
wizard Merlin (Myrddin) who was imprisoned
in a cave at the foot of the hill by the priestess
Vivien after teaching her his magic. The location of the cave is now unknown but it is said
that Merlin's groaning can sometimes be heard
emanating from the hill at dusk.

Halfway up the wooded path to the summit at magical **Merlin's Well** (51.8696, -4.2469; SN454214) fresh spring water flows into a stone basin, while in a field on the opposite site of the A40 is a standing stone known as **Merlin's Stone** (51.8671, -4.2395; SN459211; private land). Carmarthen, with its impressive castle, is reputed to be Merlin's birthplace and may even be named after him (Carmarthen possibly meaning Merlin's Castle). Until recently an ancient oak tree known as Merlin's Oak stood near the centre of the town and according to a prophecy if the tree were ever removed the town would sink and be inundated. By the 1970s, however, the rotting stump had become a traffic hazard and so was finally taken down but you can see fragments of it in Carmarthen museum.

51.8712, -4.2459; SN454215; Trailhead: 51.8707, -4.2521; SN450215; 600m

17 St Anthony's Well, Llansteffan

Near a sandy shell-covered beach where the estuary of the Taf meets the estuary of the Towy lies the healing well of St Anthony.

The enclosure contains a niche with an image of the saint and in the corner is the rectangular well chamber filled with offerings of shells and other items that pilgrims have deposited there to pray for healing or to make wishes. At one time, lovesick people would drop a white stone into the well while wishing for their heart's desire.
To visit the well, park in Llansteffan and then walk past Llansteffan Castle, which has stunning views of the estuaries leading out to sea. Take either the coast path or the inland path to reach the well, which is hidden in a stone-lined enclosure behind a gate, just beside the footpath that leads past St Anthony's Cottage down to the beach at Scott's Bay.

51.7636, -4.3983; SN345099; Trailhead; Parking: 51.7688, -4.3884; SN352104; 1.6km Secret/Secluded

18 St Canna's Chair, Llangan, Whitland

Beside a quiet country lane that few travel down lies the tiny church of Llangan, once a shrine to the Celtic saint, Canna. People visited to perform a healing ritual that involved throwing a bent pin into her holy

well, then drinking or bathing in the well water before going to sit on a rock called St Canna's Chair where the healing would take effect. The cure would be most effective if the afflicted person fell asleep on the 'chair' –an uneven rock with a hollow top. Reports from the 19th century indicate the well was full of pins but today it is no longer visible, having become overgrown and neglected. The stone seat, however is still there, located in the corner of a field just left of the entrance to this almost-forgotten churchyard.

51.8375, -4.6473; SN177187; Secret/Secluded

CEREDIGION

19 Bedd Taliesin, Tal-y-bont *

This collapsed Neolithic burial chamber is said to contain the grave of the legendary bard Taliesin. Cast adrift in a coracle by the goddess Ceridwen (see **Llyn Tegid**), the baby Taliesin drifted downstream until he reached the sea, but luckily he was caught in a salmon weir near Borth. This weir belonged to Prince Elphin, the son of Gwyddno Garanhair, lord of the sunken lands of the Cantre'r Gwaelod (see **Sarn Cynfelyn**), who raised the baby Taliesin as

19

20

his own and he grew to become the most famous bard in British history. His music and poetry were so inspired that they had the power to enchant all who listened. Many of Taliesin's 6th-century works were eventually transcribed and still survive in ancient manuscripts. The burial chamber has now lost some of its capstones leaving just a small stone-lined cist and anyone who sleeps there will either go mad or become a poet. Digging into the mound will also disturb the spirits of the place who have been known to raise a thunderstorm to halt the desecration. The views from Bedd Taliesin are dramatic, taking in the whole of the Dovey Estuary

and the hills beyond where the magical **Llyn Barfog** of Arthurian legend can be found. The coastline down to Borth is also clearly visible, and you can imagine baby Taliesin's coracle floating down the river and out to sea to be caught in Elphin's salmon weir. Beyond lies Cardigan Bay where the sea hides the sunken lands of Cantre'r Gwaelod.

52.5026, -3.9587; SN671912

20 Cwm Mabws, Llanrhystud

A cave known as Craig Rhydderch in this small wooded coombe was said to be inhabited by fairies who travelled around in horse-drawn carriages. A quiet country lane now runs the length of the combe while beneath it a trickling brook flows under the dappled shade of overhanging trees.

52.2955, -4.1169; SN557684

21 Plynlimon, Ponterwyd

Located in a wild and remote area of the Cambrian Mountains, Plynlimon is Wales'

central sacred mountain where several major rivers have their source, including the Severn (52.4940, -3.7351; SN822898), the Wye (52.4681, -3.7656; SN801870) and the Rheidol at **Llyn Llygad Rheidol** (52.4753, -3.7814; SN791878). The three goddesses who personified the rivers once had a race to reach the sea. The Rheidol won, finding a much shorter route, while her bigger sisters became the longest and the fifth longest rivers in Britain respectively. The mighty Severn was known to the Welsh as the goddess *Hafren* and to the Romans as Sabrina. Plynlimon mountain (Pumlumon in Welsh) has five peaks, each once surmounted by a beacon. It is covered in prehistoric burial cairns, one of which was reputed to be occupied by a sleeping giant. The hill is also haunted by the Cwn Annwn, a pack of spectral hounds that are taken out on the wild hunt by the lord of the Otherworld. Plynlimon is also the place were Cai and Bedwyr (Sir Kay and Sir Bedevere) plucked out the beard of the mighty hero Dillas Farfog using wooden tongs in the Arthurian tale of Culhwch and Olwen from the *Mabinogion* (see **Cerrig Meibion Arthur**).

Summit: 52.4671, -3.7831; SN789869;
Trailhead Parking: 52.4415, -3.7699;
SN797840; 3.5km

22 Sarn Cynfelyn, Borth

The stone causeway known as Sarn Cynfelyn disappears into the waters of Cardigan Bay and is said to lead to a sunken land under the waves. From the air it can be seen to stretch into the sea for kilometres while from the shore only the portion above the tideline is clearly visible, so it is best visited at low tide. There are three of these 'sarnau' reaching out into Cardigan Bay; the other two are Sarn Badraig (52.7402, -4.2441; SH485182) running under the sea southwestwards from Mochras Point, and Sarn-y-Bwch (52.6080, -4.1370; SH553032) near Tonfanau. Sarn Cynfelyn is the most visible and easily accessible from the shore. Geologists say that they are natural formations but according to folklore these causeways once protected a land known as Maes Gwyddneu, 'The Plain of Gwyddno' or the

Cantre'r Gwaelod, the 'Lowland Hundred', from inundation by the sea. This was a fabulous land of rich pastures with 16 great fortified cities ruled over by Gwyddno Garanhair (see **Bedd Taliesin** and **Alcluid, Rock of Dumbarton**), but one day the drunkard Seithenhin accidentally left the sluice gates open during a feast, causing the whole land to be submerged beneath the waves:

"Stand forth, Seithenhin,
and look upon the fury of the sea;
it has covered Maes Gwyddneu."

For this he is known in the Welsh triads as 'one of the three great drunkards of Britain'. Some believe that the survivors fled to Snowdonia, while others claim they became the merfolk. Many sightings of mermaids have been reported on this coast over the years, the nearest to Sarn Cynfelyn by the inhabitants of the farm at Llanychaearn who spotted a mermaid near the **Mouth of the River Ystwyth** (52.3958, -4.0942; SN576796). They followed her along the cliffs for some considerable time as she swam about, describing her as an attractive young woman with short, dark hair, unnaturally white skin and what appeared to be a black tail. She kept cupping her hand to her face as if drinking and made loud noises like sneezes.

The fairy folk known as the Children of Rhys the Deep are also thought to live in Cardigan Bay on invisible fairy islands (see **St David's**), and said to visit markets on the mainland using underground tunnels. Just north of Borth (once known as Porth Wyndo, 'Gwyddno's Harbour') the stumps of ancient forests have been revealed at low tide, lending some credence to the tales of sunken lands. Sarn Cynfelyn is the ideal location to contemplate the fabulous undersea realms and denizens of the deep ocean.

52.4515, -4.0812; SN586857; Trailhead: 52.4488, -4.0626; SN599854; 1.4km

23 Ysbyty Cynfyn Churchyard

Tucked away in the Cambrian Mountains, the small churchyard of Ysbyty Cynfyn has perimeter walls into which ancient megaliths have been incorporated. These stones, which probably formed part of a prehistoric stone circle, were integrated into the Christian stonework and look slightly incongruous. The church was once a hospice for pilgrims travelling to Strata Florida Abbey. The route passed over the treacherous river Mynach gorge but constructing a bridge there seemed impossible so, according to local legend, the bridge builder made a bargain with the Devil. In return for

allowing the construction, the Devil could claim the first living soul to cross it, but in the event a dog was sent to chase a loaf of bread over the newly built bridge and the Devil was outwitted. The original bridge, known as the **Devil's Bridge** (52.3771, -3.8497; SN741770), was probably commissioned by the abbey's monks, but two later bridges from the 18th and 19th centuries now stand above it, forming a 'triple' bridge. The ruined **Strata Florida Abbey** (52.2754, -3.8385; SN746657) is itself a magical place with ancient yew trees betraying its pre-Christian history. In one legend, the Holy Grail was carried there for safekeeping from **Glastonbury**, while another speaks of a secret tunnel linking the abbey to the sea at Monk's Cave (52.3486, -4.1228; SN555744).

52.3957, -3.8347; SN752791

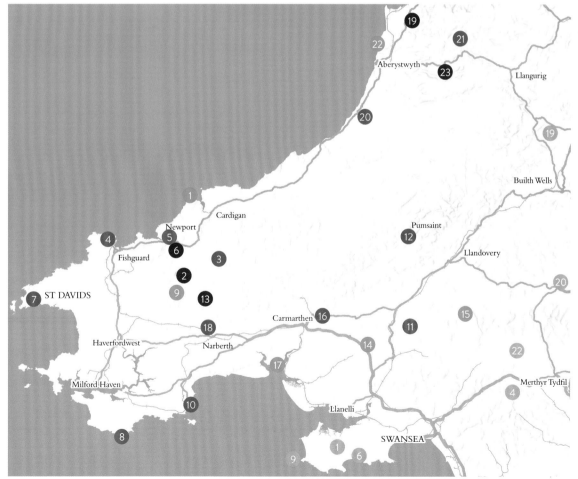

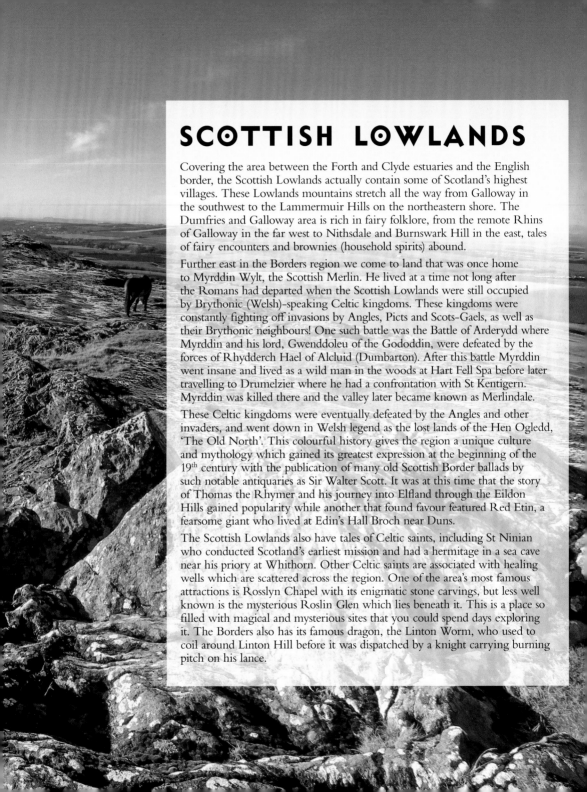

SCOTTISH LOWLANDS

Covering the area between the Forth and Clyde estuaries and the English border, the Scottish Lowlands actually contain some of Scotland's highest villages. These Lowlands mountains stretch all the way from Galloway in the southwest to the Lammermuir Hills on the northeastern shore. The Dumfries and Galloway area is rich in fairy folklore, from the remote Rhins of Galloway in the far west to Nithsdale and Burnswark Hill in the east, tales of fairy encounters and brownies (household spirits) abound.

Further east in the Borders region we come to land that was once home to Myrddin Wylt, the Scottish Merlin. He lived at a time not long after the Romans had departed when the Scottish Lowlands were still occupied by Brythonic (Welsh)-speaking Celtic kingdoms. These kingdoms were constantly fighting off invasions by Angles, Picts and Scots-Gaels, as well as their Brythonic neighbours! One such battle was the Battle of Arderydd where Myrddin and his lord, Gwenddoleu of the Gododdin, were defeated by the forces of Rhydderch Hael of Alcluid (Dumbarton). After this battle Myrddin went insane and lived as a wild man in the woods at Hart Fell Spa before later travelling to Drumelzier where he had a confrontation with St Kentigern. Myrddin was killed there and the valley later became known as Merlindale.

These Celtic kingdoms were eventually defeated by the Angles and other invaders, and went down in Welsh legend as the lost lands of the Hen Ogledd, 'The Old North'. This colourful history gives the region a unique culture and mythology which gained its greatest expression at the beginning of the 19th century with the publication of many old Scottish Border ballads by such notable antiquaries as Sir Walter Scott. It was at this time that the story of Thomas the Rhymer and his journey into Elfland through the Eildon Hills gained popularity while another that found favour featured Red Etin, a fearsome giant who lived at Edin's Hall Broch near Duns.

The Scottish Lowlands also have tales of Celtic saints, including St Ninian who conducted Scotland's earliest mission and had a hermitage in a sea cave near his priory at Whithorn. Other Celtic saints are associated with healing wells which are scattered across the region. One of the area's most famous attractions is Rosslyn Chapel with its enigmatic stone carvings, but less well known is the mysterious Roslin Glen which lies beneath it. This is a place so filled with magical and mysterious sites that you could spend days exploring it. The Borders also has its famous dragon, the Linton Worm, who used to coil around Linton Hill before it was dispatched by a knight carrying burning pitch on his lance.

DUMFRIES & GALLOWAY

1 Burnswark Hill, Ecclefechan

The fairies of Annandale who lived within
Burnswark Hill had a sinister reputation.
They were thought to abduct humans and
leave a lifeless simulacrum in their place,
fooling people into thinking their loved
ones had died. The 'deceased' person may
then be seen later, riding with the fairies as
they passed through the woods on auspicious nights of the year such as Hallowe'en.
One woman who was abducted from the
Corrie area appeared to her brother in a
vision, telling him that she was not really
dead and that he could rescue her if he
came to the barn at midnight. Three forms
would pass by and she would be the last
one. He just had to seize hold of her and
repeat a phrase she gave him; but when the
time came he lost his nerve and forgot the
words, so he never managed to rescue her.
A similar tale concerned a noble youth
called Elphin Irving who lived with his
twin sister Phemie. He disappeared one

stormy night while out tending his sheep near the Corrie Water (55.1412, -3.2837; NY182837) and his beloved sister had a terrifying vision of him being carried away by the fairies. "They have ta'en him away!" she cried, and disappeared into the woods to look for him. Phemie was found days later under an oak tree in a delirious state, saying that she had seen her brother riding with the fairies and had tried to hold onto him. He had transformed into a wild bull, a roaring river and a raging fire but at the last she was forced to let go. Meanwhile Elphin's lifeless corpse had been found by some locals washed up by the Corrie Water. The troublesome fairies of Burnswark Hill were eventually banished by a famous preacher called Donald Cargill who cast them into the Solway Firth. The summit of the hill is crowned by the grassy remains of an Iron Age Celtic hillfort, while craggy cliffs on the east side of the hill are still known as the **Fairy Craig** (55.0980, -3.2731; NY188789).

55.0966, -3.2761; NY186787; Trailhead: 55.0913, -3.2736; NY188781; 800m

2 Caerlaverock Castle, Shearington

Looking like a classic fairytale castle with its water-filled moat and drawbridge, 13th-century Caerlaverock Castle now stands as a dramatic ruin. The area around Caerlaverock was known to be a favourite fairy haunt and the fairies of this region had a nasty habit of exchanging human babies for one of their own changelings. One lady of Caerlaverock had her beautiful newborn baby exchanged for an 'antiquated elf of hideous aspect' who bit his mother's breasts and kept the house awake all night with his terrible wailing. Once, when the lady of the house was out, the changeling asked a servant girl to untie him. He then went about doing all her chores like a household brownie. Upon hearing this the lady despaired of ever getting her own baby back and so they boarded up the doors and windows and threw the changeling into a hot fire. He howled hideously but the ploy worked and the fairies, rattling at the windows and doors, returned her real baby while the changeling shot up the chimney with a loud laugh!

54.9757, -3.5239; NY025656; £

3 Hart Fell Spa, Moffat *

According to legend this lonely cleft in a bleak hillside was home to Merlin (Myrd-

din in the Brythonic tongue) when he was on the run from his enemies. He had been on the losing side in the disastrous Battle of Arderydd (near Arthuret, Cumbria) where his pagan lord, Gwenddoleu of the Gododdin (see **Traprain Law**) and many of Myrddin's kinsmen were routed and killed by their Christian enemy Rhydderch Hael of **Alcluid**. Their fortress of Liddel Strength was also stormed and taken. The huge ramparts of the fortress of Liddel Strength (55.0584, -2.9379; NY401741; private land) are still clearly visible, although now overgrown with trees. It sits perched atop a cliff overlooking the deep valley of the river Esk which marks the present-day border between England and Scotland. Driven to madness by the defeat, Myrddin fled from Arderydd into the Caledonian pine forest, ranting and raving. He eventually ended up at Hart Fell Spa where he slept in a crude cave and drank from the spring there. It was in this state of madness that Myrddin is said to have uttered his famous prophesies. His only companions were wild beasts and he is said to have become a lord of animals, and rode around on a stag. Myrddin eventually recovered his wits and left Hart Fell, travelling to Drumelzier in **Merlindale** where he went on to have an encounter with St Kentigern. In later times Hart Fell Spa became known as a healing spring and was often visited for cures. Its old stone well-house is big enough to walk into although it is now in a muddy and neglected state with rust-red deposits of iron-rich water staining the ground. Merlin's 'cave' (actually a cavity under a large slab of stone) looks equally damp and unwelcoming. The ancient Caledonian pine

forest that once covered the area now exists only in memory; in its place are bare hillsides grazed by sheep and some regimented plantations of spruce.

55.3897, -3.4274; NT096115; Trailhead: 55.3788, -3.4614; NT074103; 2.6km

4 Lochmaben Stone, Gretna

Also called the Clochmabenstane, 'The Stone of Maben', this megalith is associated with rituals to the Celtic god Mabon. The stout 2m high stone stands by the edge of a field not far from the shore of the Solway Firth. It once formed part of a stone circle that was subsequently destroyed by farming, although one other smaller stone does still remain, hidden in a hedge. Although its location now seems out of the way and difficult to access, bounded as it is by hedgerows, it was once an important gathering place and ritual centre.

Mabon was a youthful god of fertility and virility who in Roman times was adopted as a kind of Celtic Apollo. His cult probably survived until the adoption of Christianity and it is even speculated that Myrddin Wylt, the Scottish Merlin, may have performed rituals here. The site is associated with fertility rites and many important people came here including Urien of Rheged and also St Samson's parents who were unable to conceive until they were guided by a Druid to perform a ritual at this spot. The Clochmabenstane's associations with romantic liaisons and fertility continue in the nearby village of Gretna where, until fairly recent times, couples who had eloped could be married over an anvil by the local blacksmith. The Old Blacksmith's Shop £ (55.0052, -3.0628; NY321683) can still be visited.

54.9837, -3.0761; NY312659; Trailhead: 54.9849, -3.0710; NY315661; 360m; No Paths at End

5 Mull of Galloway & The Rhins

The southern end of the large peninsula known as the Rhins is an area abounding with fairy folklore. This most remote point of Galloway juts out into the Irish Sea towards the Isle of Man and at its tip is another, smaller peninsular, the Mull of Galloway. Travelling south down the Rhins we first come to the Compass Stone (54.7205, -4.9640; NX092402), a boulder hidden in long grass that was a fairy gathering-place perched on the top of the cliffs overlooking Port Logan Bay. On the opposite side of the peninsula is an uncanny place known as the **Loup of Grennan** (54.7164, -4.9094; NX126395) where twisted trees overhang the coastal road. It was here one Hallowe'en that a man saw fairy lights approaching from the coast, which resolved into a coach and horses filled with elfin figures. They were riding to his home in Auchneight

(54.6602 -4.9317; NX110334; private) to steal his newborn baby from his wife's bed and replace it with one of their changelings. When the fairies arrived, the house was surrounded by an eerie light and the door burst open of its own accord. Chattering little fairy folk dressed in green surrounded the wife's bed and in terror she cried out in the name of God and then fainted. When she came round she was relieved to find that her baby was still there in her arms.

Near the southern tip of the Rhins are the earthworks of Dunnan Fort (54.6514, -4.8819; NX141322) where a man once encountered a little fairy woman dressed in green who was carrying a sickly child. She appealed to him to help her fetch water from a spring, but he was too afraid and fled. Soon afterwards he sickened and died. At the very tip of the peninsula, on the Mull of Galloway, a path leads up to a lighthouse perched on the high cliffs. From there, its mountains clearly visible in good weather, is the Isle of Man, home of the Celtic god Manannan Mac Lir, the Rider of the Crested Waves, who was carried over the surface of the sea on his magical white horse. The Isle of Man is a deeply fairy-enchanted place that sits midway between Britain and Ireland yet is distinct from both, a liminal place out in the waves.

54.6350, -4.8571; NX156304 (Mull of Galloway lighthouse)

6 Nithsdale, Sanquhar

The valley of the river Nith was a favourite haunt of the fairy folk who were said to travel there from the districts all around and meet on Bail Hill (55.4065, -3.9593; NS760142) at Beltane. They would first gather on the Braes (slopes) of Polveoch not far from Polveoch Burn. From there they would travel up towards the source of Polveoch Burn and continue on to Bail Hill where a fairy door would open on the south side of the hill and they would enter two by two until they were all inside. The green sward would then close tightly shut behind them, making the door invisible. The Braes of Polveoch are now traversed by the A76 and a railway line, however it is still possible to find a quiet spot beside one of the springs that emerge there. The Polveoch Burn is a peaceful woodland stream with high waterfalls, and Bail Hill itself is now covered in upland pastures and located beside a minor road heading uphill from Crawick.

At the nearby town of Sanquhar, the fairies used to dance upon a green knoll known as the Fairy Knowe (55.3670, -3.9280; NS779098) that sits beside the Waird, a small lake near the centre of town. Not only fairies

6   Witches' Craig

6

but witches would gather just north of the town where the Crawick Water runs through a dark and mysterious woodland and is joined by the Conrick Burn. Here, on a stepped outcrop of rock known as the **Witches' Craig** (55.3817, -3.9206; NS784114. Trailhead: 55.3790, -3.9203; NS784111; 400m) witches from far and wide used to congregate and plot their mischief. They were much feared by the local people who blamed all kinds of misfortune upon them.

Travelling further south down the river Nith we come to **Drumlanrig Castle £** (55.2739, -3.8089; NX851992), an atmospheric 17th-century stately home where the fairies used to dance in the ornamental gardens in a favoured spot by a fountain. The castle is overlooked by forests with footpaths offering dramatic views of the building and the valley of the Nith beyond.

55.3881, -3.9931; NS738122 (Polveoch Burn)

6

7 St Medana's Well, Monreith

On the rocky shoreline at the southern end of Monreith Bay, St Medana's healing well consists of a number of natural rock pools where spring water collects before flowing on to the beach. The well was said to be especially effective at curing whooping cough. Medana was an Irish saint who had a chapel in a cave on the Rhins of Galloway (54.6452, -4.8784; NX143315). Pursued by a lustful suitor, she fled across Luce Bay by miraculously using a rock as a boat. When he eventually caught up with her and praised her beautiful eyes, she plucked them out and threw them at his feet. Where they landed her holy spring arose, and bathing her face in the water her sight was restored. Further down the coast is **St Ninian's Cave** (54.6938, -4.4497; NX422359), a natural sea cave that was the hermitage of Scotland's first saint. Ancient carved crosses have been found buried here and etched into the walls of the cave, a deeply spiritual place for quiet contemplation and meditation. St Ninian's Priory at Whithorn (54.7336, -4.4169; NX444403) was founded in the 4th century during the Roman occupation, many early Celtic crosses can be found displayed in the museum there.

St Ninian also has a chapel on the Isle of Whithorn (54.6980, -4.3608; NX479362). Heading northwest up the coast and overlooking Luce Bay is another early Celtic chapel, this time dedicated to St Finian. **Chapel Finian** (54.8056, -4.6802; NX278489) was a stopping place for pilgrims making their way on foot to see the shrine of St Ninian in Whithorn and there is a holy well in the chapel wall, right next to the road. These locations, although accessible by road, all feel very remote and retain a sense of those earliest of Celtic Christian missions from Ireland.

54.7288, -4.5418; NX364400; Trailhead Parking: 54.7238, -4.5408; NX364394; 650m

8 St Queran's Well, Islesteps

The healing well of St Queran lies over-shadowed by trees in a small patch of ground between two fields. Its circular arrangement of stones encloses the stone well-head out of which the face of the Celtic saint gazes upwards from a metal grille that lies just beneath the surface of the water. Queran himself lived in the 9th century and may have occupied a hermit's cell which has been discovered nearby. The well water was especially famed for curing sick women and children and the hundreds of bent pins and old coins discovered there, some dating back to the 16th century, are testament to its long use as a healing well. The bent pins could also indicate an appeal to the fairy folk to grant wishes. People still visit this isolated spot to tie colourful clootie ribbons and make their prayers and offerings to the well.

South of St Queran's Well, the village of New Abbey (54.9799, -3.6221; NX962662) is associated with the story of Alexander Harg who had just married a woman so lovely he believed the fairies would try and steal her away. Out fishing one day by the Nith estuary, he heard voices coming from one of the old wrecks that were beached in the sands. "What are you doing?" asked one of them. "I'm making a wife for Sandy Harg!" replied the other. Sandy rushed home in a panic and that night he gripped tightly onto his wife and told her to keep silent. Suddenly the doors banged loudly, the cows lowed and the horses whinnied, but the fairies could not gain entry while he held her and they both kept quiet. In the morning he found a mossy wooden tree trunk by his door, which the fairies had intended to leave in place of his wife. This he burned and was never bothered by the fairies again.

Excellent views of the fairy-haunted Nith estuary towards Carsethorn can be seen from the roadside parking near Drumburn (54.9410, -3.5935; NX980618).

55.0335, -3.6351; NX955722; Trailhead: 55.0304, -3.6386; NX953718; 400m

BORDERS

9 Dragon of Linton

The Somerville's of Linton are said to have won their land by defeating a dragon that once lived there. According to folklore this event is depicted in a carved stone tympanum above the church door which shows a warrior (said to be John Somerville) battling a dragon. The dragon was invulnerable to weapons and so he killed it by attaching a wheel of peat soaked in burning pitch to the end of his lance which he then thrust down the dragon's throat. The dragon, which was known as the Linton Worm (after the Old English *wyrm*, serpent) lived in a tree-lined dingle on the side of Linton Hill that is still called Worm's Hole (55.5561, -2.3297; NT793292). The hill itself was once known as Wormiston and it's said that the indentations from the worm's thrashing coils can still be seen on the side of the hill facing Linton church.

The church itself sits at the foot of Linton Hill on a grassy mound composed entirely of fine sand said to have been dug from a hole nearby and sifted, according to local tales, as a penance for murder. The church lies within an ancient circular churchyard, which along with its associations with dragons, hints at a former pagan significance to this site.

In the remote and desolate Cheviot Hills near the village of Hownam can be found a long row of standing stones known as the **Hownam Shearers** (55.4669, -2.3320; NT791192. Trailhead: 55.4659, -2.3493; NT780191; 1.6km), said to be people who were turned to stone while reaping a crop on the Sabbath.

55.5291, -2.3607; NT773262 (Linton Church)

10 Edin's Hall Broch, Duns *

One of the largest and most impressive stone brochs in Scotland, Edin's Hall Broch was once thought to be occupied by a giant. The word Etin (Eotan) is Old English for giant and the giant who lived here was known to raid the countryside for sheep and cattle. One day he returned with his plunder and picked a huge boulder from his shoe, which can still be seen. He then somehow ended up drowning in Whiteadder Water below. The broch is also associated with a giant known as Red Etin who features in one of Scotland's oldest fairy tales. This vicious three-headed giant kept young women as prisoners until one day a widower's son outwitted him and cut off his heads.

To come across this ancient fortress while walking along the flank of Cockburn Law above Whiteadder Water is like stepping into a fairytale. The romantic ruin does

look like the work of a giant and seems to belong in a museum rather than on this lonely and isolated hillside. Only its remoteness protects it from misuse. Cockburn Law is associated with the Cockburn family who were once in a land dispute with the legendary inhabitants of another ancient fortress, the fairies of **Duns Law** (55.7849, -2.3443; NT785546) to the south. The fairies loosened the foundations of the Cockburn mansion in an attempt to get them to move away.

Further north, living at Cranshaws Farm (55.8484, -2.5094; NT682618; private land) was a brownie who would reap and thresh all the corn throughout the night, saving the farmer a huge amount of labour. But one day someone criticised the way the corn had been stacked, so taking great offence the next night the brownie threw it all over a cliff called Raven's Craig (55.8319, -2.4817; NT699599) and into the Whiteadder Water below. He then left in disgust, never to be seen again. Cranshaws Farm contains an old tower called Cranshaws Castle and a ruined medieval church, but care must be taken to respect people's privacy there. The Raven's Craig is 3km away and can be seen from the road on the opposite side of the river.

55.8354, -2.3644; NT772603; Trailhead: 55.8414, -2.3385; NT789609; 2.3km

11 Eildon Hills, Melrose *

The three rounded peaks of the Eildon Hills are the setting for the well-known story of Thomas the Rhymer and his journey into the land of Faerie. Thomas, who was the laird (lord) of Erceldoune, was sitting under a hawthorn tree by the banks of the Huntly Burn when he saw a lady riding by on a snow-white horse decorated with silver bells. Enchanted by her unearthly beauty he hailed her as the 'Queen of Heaven' and begged her to lie with him under the Eildon tree. But this was no heavenly queen, it was the Queen of Elfland, who willingly obliged him but only after he had pledged himself to her. So now he was in her power and she transformed

herself into a hideous hag and carried him off on the back of her horse into the Underworld. After a dark and terrifying journey under the Eildon Hills they eventually arrived in a fair land where the queen once again regained her beauty. There Thomas indulged himself in every imaginable pleasure, but after only three days the Elf Queen, fearing for his safety, asked him to leave. As a parting gift she gave him a tongue that could never lie and the power of prophesy. Henceforth he became a famous poet and prophet known as True Thomas or Thomas the Rhymer. Thomas of Erceldoune (Earlston) was a real person who lived in the 13th century. The ruins of his tower (55.6359, -2.6813; NT572382) can still be seen just on the edge of the village of Earlston and the inscribed Rhymer's Stone now marks the location of the Eildon Tree (55.5940, -2.6914; NT565335), where Thomas met the Elf Queen.

The Eildon Hills themselves were said to have once been a single hill, cleft in three by an evil spirit doing the bidding of the 13th-century wizard Michael Scott. This seems an unlikely tale because a much earlier Roman fortress nearby was called Trimontium (Three Hills) so perhaps Michael Scott's name was grafted onto an earlier creation legend. An Iron Age Celtic hillfort on the summit of Eildon Hill North was thought to be in use by the Romano-British kingdom of Gododdin and a Roman signal station. It is the largest hillfort in Scotland and has signs of settlement dating back to the Bronze Age. Another story centred on the Eildon Hills is that of a horse trader called Canobie Dick who, unable to sell his horses at market, sold them to a mysterious old man who paid in ancient gold coin. Curious about the old man and his money Dick was eventually

led by him to a secret door in a small hill known as the Lucken Hare (due to its shape like a crouching hare). Inside he found a host of warriors fast asleep who were being provided horses by the old man. Eagerly eyeing a mound of golden treasure, he was then given the choice to either draw a sword or blow a horn, and hastily making the wrong decision by blowing the horn the warriors awoke and beat him senseless. Some say that the old man was Thomas the Rhymer, still doing the bidding of the fairies, while others say that King Arthur and his knights lie sleeping under the hill. The Lucken Hare (55.5794, -2.7218; NT545319) is now known as Little Hill and lies on the southwest edge of the Eildon Hills, which are said to be so full of gold that the sheep grazing there have yellow teeth!

A circular walk from Melrose crosses all three hills while those who are less energetic can view them from Scott's View (55.6002, -2.6468; NT593342), named after Sir Walter Scott who made the tale of Thomas the Rhymer famous. The view takes in Old Melrose, the site of St Cuthbert's 7th-century monastery and a staging post on the sacred journey from **Iona** to **Lindisfarne**. A modern pilgrimage route called St Cuthbert's Way leads from Melrose Abbey across the Eildon Hills and on to Lindisfarne. Another portal into Elfland can be found at the Piper's Grave (55.6293, -2.4316; NT729373) near Ednam. This small mound that may be a Bronze Age burial site, was where a man went in the hope of learning to play the fairy pipes, but he disappeared and was never seen again. A mossy stone slab on top of the mound now marks the spot.

55.5875, -2.7078; NT554328 (Eildon Hill North); Trailhead: 55.5957, -2.7202; NT547337; 2km

12 Merlindale, Drumelzier *

The broad valley of the river Tweed known as Merlindale features prominently in the life and death of Myrddin Wylt, the Scottish Merlin. The valley is dominated by a hill that is topped by the shattered ruins of medieval Tinnis Castle, originally a hillfort called Dun Meldred that Myrrdin is thought to have visited. Myrrdin was a Druid of the old religion and is said to have debated theology in this valley with St Kentigern (see **Traprain Law**), but when he foresaw his own death it is claimed that he received the sacrament from Kentigern over a stone now known as **Merlin's Altar Stone** (55.6080, -3.3396; NT157357). This large flat-topped stone juts out from an embankment beside a lane just opposite Altarstone farm and it was probably a pagan altar where sacrifices were performed in what was then the dark wood of Celidon (Caledonian Forest) that covered the landscape. A broken off part of this stone now forms a small altar in **Stobo Kirk** (55.6256, -3.2993; NT182376) where the pagan-looking altar is flanked by late-medieval grave slabs, one of which depicts a Scottish chieftain. To one side is a stained-glass window portraying Merlin being baptised by St Kentigern. Stobo Kirk is thought to be built on the site of Kentigern's 7th-century chapel and before that an ancient pagan temple site.

Shortly after this event Myrrdin is said to have been ambushed and killed beside the river Tweed by some local shepherds, dying a druidic triple death by being beaten senseless and then falling off the bank to be impaled upon fishing stakes with his

head under water. Myrrdin was buried nearby, not far from the Powsail Burn (now Drumelzier Burn). The grave is virtually unmarked (55.5966, -3.3756; NT134345) and is located by a thorn bush. An old rhyme states that:

When Tweed and Powsail meet at Merlin's Grave,
Scotland and England shall one monarch have.

This prophesy came true when, soon after the Powsail Burn flooded, James VI of Scotland ascended to the throne of England. A more impressive marker can be found a few hundred metres downstream beside the Tweed. This megalith is sometimes known as **Merlin's Stone** (55.6049, -3.3677; NT139354. Trailhead: 55.5995, -3.3605; NT143348; 850m) and is claimed by some to mark the real site of his grave. A fairy path is said to lead from Tinnis Castle through a purpose-made gap in the wall of Drumelzier Haugh farm directly to this stone.

The spirit of the mighty river Tweed which flows through the valley was thought to take human lives on a regular basis, but one day it miraculously gave life when it reputedly made the Baron of Drumelzier's wife pregnant while he was away on crusade! The resulting baby was affectionately known as 'Tweedie'.

After visiting **Hart Fell Spa** to see where Myrddin Wylt lived as a wild man of the woods, Merlindale is the perfect location to explore the final chapter in the life of this mysterious figure.

55.5960, -3.3638; NT141344 (Tinnis Castle); Trailhead: 55.5947, -3.3705; NT137343; 500m

13 **Our Lady's Well, Stow**

Thought to be one of the oldest recorded Christian sites in southern Scotland, this recently restored roadside well once had an attached chapel which displayed an ancient wooden statue of the Blessed Virgin. The statue was recorded by the 8th-century monk Nennius who said that it was brought to this spot by King Arthur himself. In medieval times the well became an important place of pilgrimage and a sanctuary. A stone near the well bore the imprint of a foot said to have been left by a visitation from the Blessed Virgin, but it was later broken up for road building. The path to the well passes an old packhorse bridge and follows the Gala Water beside the A7 road to Edinburgh. Despite the nearby traffic, the well in its circular stone enclosure remains a sacred and tranquil spot.

55.6852, -2.8681; NT455438; Trailhead Parking: 55.6900, -2.8628; NT458443; 700m

14 **Tamlane's Well, Selkirk**

The roadside spring known as Tamlane's Well was the site of a famous episode from the Scottish medieval ballad of Tam Lin (also known as Tamlane). Tam Lin was trapped in the fairy realms but he was able to visit Carterhaugh woods near the place where the Yarrow and Ettrick Waters meet (55.5314, -2.8970; NT434267) – a place where he was reputed to seduce young women. A local girl named Janet heard the rumours and went there willingly, becoming pregnant with his baby. Tam Lin then asked Janet to rescue him, but she was told to wait until she saw the fairy company ride by on their horses the next day, which was Hallowe'en. Tam Lin would be near the back riding a white horse and she was to pull him from his horse and not let go, whatever happened. She did as instructed and clung onto him as he assumed a number of terrifying shapes, including an adder, a bear, a lion and a red-hot iron bar. Finally he turned into a burning coal and Janet cast him into the well where he resumed his human shape, free at last. Water still flows into a stone trough beneath the spring and the words 'Tamlane's Well' can be seen etched into the stone.

Another fairy well, known as the **Cheese Well** (55.5916, -3.0218; NT357335. Trailhead parking: 55.6001, -3.0631; NT331345; 3km) can be found high on Minch Moor. Travellers passing over the moor would stop at the well and make an offering of cheese or pins to the fairies there for safe travel. The well lies beside an old drover's road (now a long-distance footpath, the Southern Upland Way) near the summit of Minch Moor (55.5869, -3.0189; NT358330). Fairies are thought to live inside the hill and after dancing they would sometimes leave fairy rings in the grass that local people would superstitiously avoid. The whole area is now surrounded by an extensive forestry plantation called the Elibank and Traquair Forest. A 3km hike uphill through the forest from Traquair leads directly to the well where a good flow of water issues forth forming the Plora Burn, which flows down the hillside to the River Tweed below.

55.5318, -2.8929; NT437268

15 Cleeves Cove, Dalry

Small caves that pepper the walls of Cleeves Cove were said to be entrances to Elfhame, the land of the fairies – so claimed the witch Bessie Dunlop in her 16th-century trial for witchcraft. She said that on Hallowe'en the fairies would ride out of them astride mouse-sized horses with their golden hair streaming in the wind. Bessie gained many of her insights from an ambassador from Elfhame called Thome Reid, who some say is none other than Thomas the Rhymer (see **Eildon Hills**). She once also saw a fairy rade (ride) crossing Restalrig Loch (55.9605, -3.1620; NT275747) in Edinburgh.

Cleeves Cove is now a remote little wooded gulley through which the Dusk Water flows. The caves in the side wall feel like mysterious portals to the Otherworld. They are quite easy to scramble up to and caving enthusiasts can head deep inside the hill down the dark passages.

55.6915, -4.6793; NS316474; Secret/Secluded; Trailhead: 55.6904, -4.6770; NS318473; 300m

16 St Fillan's Well, Kilmacolm

On the edge of a field under a rocky over-hang lies the healing well of St Fillan where the water was said to cure children of rickets. The well lies not far from a ruined church to which it was once attached. The 8th-century St Fillan has numerous sites associated with him including **St Fillan's Pool**, **St Fillan's Chair** and **St Fillan's Cave**.

55.8869, -4.5853; NS384689

17 Turnberry Point

Standing on the cliffs at Turnberry Point a man called William once heard a mermaid singing on the rocks below. Enchanted by her melodious voice he went down to find her but her song now seemed to come from the waves. Getting in his boat he followed her far out to sea until suddenly a storm blew up from the direction of Ailsa Crag and took poor William's life. Afterwards fishermen of the area were always taught to beware the mermaid's song. Turnberry Point is reached by walking along an idyllic sandy beach to

the cluster of rocks just off the headland and it is best explored at low tide.

The prominent, pyramid-shaped island of **Ailsa Craig** (55.2523, -5.1169; NX019997) is clearly visible far out to sea and legends have grown up around how it came into being. In one version the island was a pebble that fell though the goddess Cailleach's pocket when she was creating the islands of Scotland, while in another it was a rock thrown by the Irish hero/giant Fionn mac Cumhaill at his Scottish rival Benandonner. Further north up the coast lies the stately home known as **Culzean Castle** (55.3547, -4.7893; NS232102; £££ popular). Caves dating from the Iron Age below the castle on the shore were thought to be home to the fairies and one day a fairy boy came to the castle gate begging for a cup of ale for his sick mother. The laird had the butler fill the boy's cup but after emptying the whole barrel into it the cup was still not full. On opening another barrel, however, the cup was immediately filled. Years later when the laird was held captive in a foreign prison, the fairy boy appeared and repaid the laird's earlier generosity by helping him to escape. The caves can be viewed by scrambling along the shore beneath the castle walls at the start of Culzean Bay.

55.3238, -4.8479; NS194069; Trailhead Parking: 55.3103, -4.8338; NS202054; 2km

18 Strathaven Fairy Mound

In a secluded spot by the banks of the Avon Water stands a natural outcrop of rock known as Strathaven Fairy Mound, thought to be home to the fairies and a portal into Fairyland. The idyllic riverside setting in which the mound sits can only be reached by scrambling over a couple of barbed wire fences and across fields, but this does not deter locals who still come here and walk three times around the mound for good luck.

55.6620, -4.0581; NS706428; Secret/Secluded

19 Arthur's Seat, Edinburgh

The majestic rocky hill known as Arthur's Seat dominates the skyline of Scotland's royal capital. It is not known how Arthur's name came to be attached to the hill but Arthur and his men are still said to lie sleeping beneath it. Until recently, some followed the May Day morning custom of washing in the dew on top of Arthur's Seat and then going down to make a wish at **St Anthony's Well** (55.9504 -3.1622; NT275736), which lies near the foot of the hill. Nearby, Calton Hill (55.9556, -3.1824; NT262742) was thought to be a fairy abode and according to 17th-century legend, a boy used to enter a door and play his drum for the fairies every Thursday. Only those with second sight, however, could see the door.

Arthur's Seat is an extinct volcano and the landscape of Lothian is characterised by these volcanic plugs which have been worn down over millennia. Other examples include **Traprain Law**, Bass Rock, now a bird sanctuary out in the Firth of Forth, and Castle Rock (55.9486, -3.1999; NT251734) upon which Edinburgh Castle now stands. Castle Rock was once an ancient fortress and during the 6th century was known as Din Eidyn. At one time it was the capital of the kingdom of Gododdin, a Brythonic -speaking Celtic people whose exploits are recorded in an epic poem called *Y Gododdyn*, the earliest text ever to record the name of Arthur.

55.9441, -3.1619; NT275729; Popular, Trailhead: 55.9509, -3.1703; NT270737; 1.4km

20 Roslin Glen **

Made famous by Dan Brown's *Da Vinci Code* **Rossyln Chapel** (55.8554, -3.1599; NT274630; ££ very popular) sits perched above a mysterious lush green valley known as Roslin Glen. This extensive wooded valley through which the North Esk flows, hides mysterious rock carvings, ancient trees, old wells and curious caves.

The chapel itself contains a wealth of esoteric stone carvings, including over a hundred green men whose faces peer out from their surrounding foliage. These are said to draw upon the green energy of the glen below. The chapel is full of such mysteries about which whole books have been written, and the stone puzzle that is Rosslyn Chapel continues to draw thousands of tourists from all around the world each year. Directly north of Rosslyn Chapel the twin-humped hill of **Arthur's Seat** can be seen in the far distance. This has led to speculation of a 'Roseline' meridian that runs through the chapel, connecting the two sites. The chapel also lies *exactly* on a sacred axis connecting **Bamburgh Castle** with **Iona** abbey leading to further speculation of a geomantic significance to the chapel's placement.

Many paths lead down into the glen but a path just beyond the chapel is one of the best and easiest to access. It soon passes by a couple of very **Ancient Chestnut Trees** (55.8564, -3.1542; NT278631), which are hidden away to the left of the path. These 'grandmother' and 'grandfather' trees are often chosen as ritual sites and places to connect with the nature spirits of the glen. Just beyond them is another ritual site, a clearing flanked by yew trees, located beside a path that descends into the depths of the glen. Various routes can be explored from here, criss-crossing the side of the gorge (look out for an ancient face carved into the rock) before reaching a narrow riverside path at the bottom. From there you should be able to spot the dark square opening of **Wallace's Cave** (55.8566, -3.1508; NT280632; secret/secluded) on the opposite side of the river. This cave, where Scottish hero William Wallace is reputed to have hidden from the English, can be reached from a path that descends from Gorton House (55.8562, -3.1492; NT281631). The cave itself has an incredible resonance for chanting or drumming, then just below and beyond the cave are some ancient and mysterious rock carvings in the cliff face.

Not far from Rosslyn Chapel, **Roslin Castle** (55.8528, -3.1598; NT274627; part private) sits on a promontory overlooking

the glen where the river North Esk makes a sharp hairpin turn. It is said to be haunted by a black dog whose baying can sometimes be heard at night. A black knight and a white lady also haunt the castle and its cellars are said to contain a hidden treasure. Around the back of the castle is an ancient yew (55.8525, -3.1600; NT274627; secret/secluded), which those in the know come to honour and venerate.

This is just a taster of the mysteries of Roslin Glen – you could spend many days exploring its secret places and delving into its numerous mysteries.

Trailhead: 55.8562, -3.1574; NT276631

21 Traprain Law, East Linton *

The rocky volcanic plug known as Traprain Law stands out starkly from the surrounding landscape. It was once the capital of the Romano-British kingdom of Gododdin and has been an important ritual centre since Neolithic times. It is crowned by an Iron Age hillfort and on the very summit is a rocky outcrop from which a slice of rock has broken away leaving a narrow gap. This is the **Maiden Stone** (55.9639, -2.6694; NT583747) and squeezing into the gap is said to confer fertility and good fortune on any young woman who passes through it while touching both sides.

Traprain Law is also connected to the birth of St Kentigern, the Christian rival of the pagan Myrrdin. Kentigern's mother Teneu was the stepdaughter of King Leudonus who had his capital at Traprain. Teneu was seduced against her will by a young prince and became pregnant. Accused of adultery she was to be killed by being pushed off the cliffs, but she survived the fall and was instead cast adrift on the sea in a coracle. Drifting across the Firth of Forth she washed up on the far shore and gave birth to Kentigern. They were then found by St Serf who nicknamed him Mungo (dearest) and he was raised to become a great churchman. He became counsellor to King Rydderch Hael of **Alcluid** and was a great enemy to paganism, taking steps to exterminate the old religion wherever he could find it. He was said to have been responsible for the battle at Arderydd where Myrrdin and the Gododdin were defeated (see **Hart Fell Spa**) and in Christian legend Kentigern is even supposed to have given the sacrament to Merlin shortly before he was killed (see **Merlindale**).

The Gododdin eventually moved their capital to Din Eidyn (Edinburgh) before they were finally defeated and paganism in the north came to an end. They also had a fortress at Eildon Hill North (see **Eildon**

Hills), a magical place that was seen as an entrance to the fairy realm.

Just south of Traprain Law can be found a megalith known as Loth's Stone (55.9585, -2.6771; NT578741). Once said to mark the location of the grave of King Loth, the founder of the kingdom of Lothian, it has now been relocated to the edge of a field. In the nearby town of East Linton **St Baldred's Well** (55.9915, -2.6540; NT593778) is a small ivy-covered holy well dedicated to the 8th-century St Baldred who came over from **Lindisfarne**. He is

remembered in many coastal features in the local area including St Baldred's Cave (56.0515, -2.6366; NT604844) by Seacliff Beach, St Baldred's Boat (56.0560, -2.6246; NT611849) a nearby rock and St Baldred's Cradle (56.0235, -2.5831; NT637813), a rocky outcrop on the shore south of Ravensheugh Sands. Finally, ruined St Baldred's Chapel (56.0770, -2.6414; NT601873) is located on Bass Rock, which is now a seabird sanctuary and can only be reached by boat as part of a birdwatching tour.

55.9634, -2.6726; NT581746

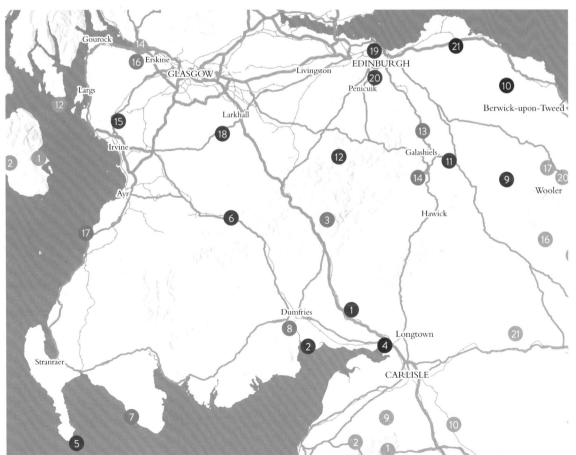

CENTRAL SCOTLAND

This region stretches from Argyll in the west to Perthshire in the east and includes many islands rich with folklore and magic such as Iona, Jura and Arran. Long sprawling lochs punctuate the landscape, overlooked by remote moorland, and there are green wooded glens where prehistoric peoples built enigmatic structures, and where fairies, Celtic saints and the heroes of old once roamed.

On the Isle of Arran is a fairy glen on the lower slope of a mountain named for its fairy inhabitants, while on Machrie Moor the Irish hero and giant Fionn mac Cumhaill (Fingal in Scots-Gaelic) is associated with the prehistoric monuments found there. He used nearby King's Cave as a base for hunting expeditions with his gigantic dog Bran.

The goddess in the form of the Cailleach Bheara is said to wash her clothes in the Corryvreckan whirlpool between the islands of Scarba and Jura and her body is made manifest in the Paps of Jura, conical hills reminiscent of breasts.

On the sacred island of Iona, fairies have long dwelled within its hills and mounds although Iona is most closely associated with St Columba and the early Celtic Christian church. Visitors can see the hill where St Columba communed with shining beings and also bathe their face in the Well of Age, Iona's very own fountain of youth.

On the mainland, the natural stone fortress at Dunadd has links to Ossian, son of Fingal, who left his footprint embedded on a stone there as he leapt from hill to hill. Nearby is Kilmartin Glen where a huge concentration of prehistoric standing stones, stone circles, cairns and rock art can be found.

Further east in Stirling the Rock of Dumbarton towers over the river Clyde. It was here that the ancient fortress of Alcluid endured for centuries, ruled by legendary kings and closely associated with Myrddin Wylt, the Scottish Merlin. Also in Stirling is Aberfoyle, home to a remarkable 17th-century minister who collected local fairy lore and other supernatural beliefs and compiled them into a manuscript. His own life and untimely death have become inextricably tied to legend, with many believing he was taken by the fairies and is still held in their subterranean realm within Doon Hill.

The fairies are also found within the mountain of Schiehallion near Fortingall. They look favourably on those with musical talent, but woe betide any who spoil their songs as they echo through caves that act as portals to their hidden halls.

AYRSHIRE, ISLE OF ARRAN

1 Fairy Glen, Brodick

A small mountain stream cascades down through the forest of the Fairy Glen. Its source is near the summit of Sithein (55.5479, -5.1737; NR998328), the old Scots-Gaelic name for a mound or hill where fairies (*sith*) live – evidence that the place has long been associated with them. People still leave offerings to the fairies on a little altar where the footpath through the woods crosses the stream in the Fairy Glen. From the summit of Sithein you can look out across Lamlash Bay to an isle known as Holy Island. With a long tradition as a spiritual retreat, it is the location of the cave and well of **St Molaise's Hermitage** (55.5226, -5.0769; NS058297). The cave also contains some original Viking runes – graffiti left by passing Vikings long ago. Now a Tibetan Buddhist retreat, there are colourful statues and paintings of Tibetan deities dotted around the island which is served by regular passenger ferries from Lamlash £.£. (55.5353, -5.1245; NS029312) in the summer.

55.5603, -5.1473; NS016341; Trailhead Parking: 55.5557, -5.1437; NS018336; 700m

2 Machrie Moor, Ballymichael

Machrie Moor, on the west side of the Isle of Arran, is covered with a scattering of prehistoric stone circles, standing stones, cairns and hut circles. One of these stone circles, which has a double ring of concentric granite stones, is known as Fingal's Cauldron Seat. It was believed to have been constructed by the Irish hero and giant Fingal who cooked his meals in a massive cauldron within the circle and tied his huge dog Bran to a stone nearby (possibly the holed stone in the outer circle). Fingal also spent time living in **King's Cave** (55.5260, -5.3534; NR884309. Trailhead Parking: 55.5040, -5.3401; NR891284; 3.3km) on the nearby coast while out on his hunting expeditions. Before the 20th century, this cave was recorded as having hunting scenes of hounds, deer and armed men carved into the walls and several enigmatic carvings are still visible alongside more modern graffiti. Today the cave is more famous as the place where Robert the Bruce reputedly hid from the English.

On the opposite side of Arran near Whiting Bay, the **Giant's Graves** (55.4767, -5.0981; NS043246. Trailhead Parking: 55.4820, -5.0923; NS046252; 1.3km) are megalithic

chambered tombs that were once covered by mounds of earth. Some say the giant Fingal himself is buried there and that the numerous prehistoric monuments on the island were raised in memory of local inhabitants slain by Fingal and his band of warriors who were known as the Fians (*Fianna* in Irish).

55.5399, -5.3159; NR908323 (Fingal's Cauldron Seat); Trailhead Parking: 55.5451, -5.3380; NR895329; 1.7km

ARGYLL

3 Ariundle Oakwood, Strontian

A remnant of ancient Caledonian forest, the Ariundle oakwood covers an extensive area to the north of the Strontian River. Explore the fairy-haunted woods by following a path known as the 'Fairies Road' (56.7184, -5.5285; NM841640) that leads down to the town of Strontian (56.6961, -5.5724; NM813617) on the shore of Loch Sunart. Strontian is the anglicized rendering of the Scots-Gaelic *Sron an t-Sithein* which means 'The Fairies Nose', referring to the promontory that juts out into the loch. The local blacksmith's shop in Strontian was reputedly once frequented by a household spirit known

4

northeast of the village of Inverinan. The Falls of Cruachan (56.3946, -5.1142; NN078268) that once flowed down from Ben Cruachan and filled Loch Awe have now been harnessed to create a hydroelectric power station. The wedge of land opposite the power station was said to be a fairy haunt, and anyone who sat on a fairy mound near Creag Thulach (56.3800, -5.1305; NN068252) could incur the wrath of the fairies. In the nearby village of Kilchrenan a child was once abducted by the fairies and taken to a fairy mound in Nant Wood but his father retrieved him by ploughing a furrow all around the mound. Nant Wood is now part of the Glen Nant National Nature Reserve (Trailhead parking: 56.3962, -5.2107; NN019272).

56.4268, -5.1318; NN069304 (Ben Cruachan summit); Trailhead: 56.4066, -5.1165; NN078281; 3.3km

5 Corryvreckan Whirlpool, Jura

The island of Jura has associations with the Celtic crone goddess the Cailleach Bheara, the ancient goddess of the land. She used to wash her clothes in a huge swirling whirlpool known as the Corryvreckan which lies in a deep channel between the islands of Jura and Scarba. There the seas boil as the tides rush in and out creating dangerous swirls and eddies that inexperienced sailors avoid, especially in rough weather when the Cailleach is said to be 'washing her clothes'. The Corryvreckan is best viewed from the south coast of Scarba island or from a boat trip, but the adventurous can enjoy an overview of the Gulf of Corryvreckan from An Cruachan on the northern tip of Jura. The islands to the north of Scarba were said to have been created when a basket full of rocks being carried by the Cailleach burst open and fell into the sea. The goddess also reveals her presence towards the southern end of Jura where the twin peaks known as the **Paps of Jura** (55.9024, -6.0042; NR498749) are said to represent the breasts of the Goddess. These are best viewed from neighbouring Islay (55.9132, -6.1348; NR417766).

56.1432, -5.7125; NM694007 (An Cruachan); Trailhead: 56.0704, -5.7461; NR669927; 11km

6 Dog Stone, Dunollie Castle

The ruined tower of Dunollie Castle £ (56.4265, -5.4846; NM852314) was once inhabited by a glaistig, a female household spirit who came out at night to help with chores, although she could also be moody

as a 'glaistig' and her child. They liked to move the blacksmith's tools around at night and make a lot of noise, until one night the blacksmith waited in hiding and crushed the glaistig's skull with his hammer.

On the opposite side of Loch Sunart, the mountain of **Beinn Iadain** (56.6398, -5.7658; NM691561. Trailhead: 56.6297, -5.8166; NM660551; 5km) was said to be occupied by fairies whose realm could be entered through a portal known as the Black Door. One day the fairies stole a mother and newborn child from a farm at Rahoy (56.6392, -5.8511; NM639563) on the shore of Loch Teacuis. After being taken through the Black Door she refused to eat the fairy food as she knew that to do so would mean she could never leave. That night she appeared to her husband in a dream and told him to tie three knots in her wedding kerchief and leave it at the Black Door. This he did, the portal opened, and she was able to escape.

Another woman was captured by a giantess hag who lived on the mountain, perhaps a memory of the hag goddess the Cailleach. She is said to have gripped the woman as tight as 'ivy round a tree', and in anger the woman cried "I wish it was a bag of shit you held in your arms!". At this the giantess momentarily loosened her grip and the woman was able to escape.

Parking: 56.7108, -5.5542; NM825633

4 Ben Cruachan & Loch Awe

The ancient Caledonian crone goddess, the Cailleach Bheara, was believed to have lived on the sacred mountain of Ben Cruachan overlooking Loch Awe and Loch Etive. Loch Awe stretches for over 35km from Ford in the southwest to Kilchurn Castle in the northeast and was said to have been created by the Cailleach Bheara when she kicked away rocks, releasing all the springs that flow into the valley. In another version of the tale, she fell asleep while collecting water from a magical spring on Ben Cruachan and, forgetting to replace the slab that covered it, flooded the valley below. In remorse she turned to stone, creating a rock formation known as Creag na Caillich, 'Old Wife's Rock', which is thought to be the rock formation in Glen Etive (56.5987, -5.0234; NN144492).

The waters of Loch Awe are said to be inhabited by a water monster known as the Big Beast of Loch Awe. Featuring twelve legs and shaped like an eel or a horse, on winter nights it can be heard breaking up the ice that covers the lake. Another mythical beast said to inhabit Loch Awe is a water bull that can only be killed with a silver shot. Good views of both Loch Awe and Ben Cruachan can be had from Creag an Fhithich (56.3289, -5.2122; NN015198)

and put dust in people's food. Nearby, a tall natural column of rock known as the Dog Stone is where Fingal used to tie up his giant dog Bran. Acoording to the story, as Bran circled round the stone, the rope wore the grooves visible around the base and sometimes his howls can still be heard at night.
56.4235, -5.4835; NM852311

7 Dun Bhuirg, Mull

The romantic ruin of the Iron Age broch known as Dun Bhuirg was once believed to be home to the fairy folk. A woman who lived nearby was tired of her chores one day and wished that the fairies were there to help her. Immediately her home was overrun by the little people who proceeded to perform all her tasks. Worried that the fairies would require some form of payment, she shouted "Dun Bhuirg is on fire!" and all the fairy folk immediately rushed back home. Circular stone foundations and a few low stone walls are all that now remain of the broch, which sits on a green mound beside Loch Scridain near the remote tip of the Ardmeanach peninsula. It is reached by a 6km drive down a rough track followed by a 600m walk but the remote and enchanted atmosphere of the place make it well worth a visit.
56.3581, -6.1755; NM421262; Trailhead: 56.3618, -6.1697; NM425266; 600m; Nearest Parking: 56.3729, -6.0865; NM477275; 6.5km

8 Dunadd & Kilmartin Glen *

The impressive rock fortress of Dunadd dominates the landscape for miles around. It was said to have been the capital of the Scots-Gaelic kings of Dalriada who were crowned after placing their foot in the inauguration stone on the summit, and this long, foot-shaped depression has many legends attached to it. According to one, Ossian, the son of the Irish hero Fingal who was living in Dunadd, was hunting on a hill above Kilmichael when a stag turned

8

8

9

on him so he leaped to Rudal Hill and from there to Dunadd to escape, leaving his footprints where he landed. Another legend says that Dunadd is a fairy fort and that the footprint is known as the Fairy's Footmark. To reach the inauguration stone you must pass through two massive natural stone ramparts looming like craggy cliffs. The stone itself contains the footprint, a cup mark that was said to have been created by Ossian's knee, some faded ogham script which some have interpreted as spelling out the name of Ossian's father Fionn, and also a faded Pictish carving of a boar. All of these are, however, modern copies as the originals have been covered in artificial stone to protect them from erosion.

Not far from Dunadd, the Scodaig Stone (now lost) was said to bear the hoofprint of the legendary Irish Queen Scota's horse. She was reputed to be the daughter of an Egyptian pharaoh who was brought to Ireland by her husband Mil Easpaine. He was the founder of the Celtic Irish race who defeated the Tuatha de Danaan, the Irish fairy folk, and conquered Ireland. Scota is said to have given her name to the Scots people, an Irish tribe who invaded what is now known as Scotland and settled at Dunadd.

Nearby Kilmartin Glen contains a huge number of prehistoric monuments including 13 isolated standing stones, 11 arrangements of stones, 2 stone circles and numerous burial cairns, some with stone cists. Some of the stones are decorated with cup marks, incised images and spirals and there are also extensive rock-art sites where cups, rings and a huge abundance of other designs are cut into the living rock. Highlights of the glen include Kilmartin Linear Cemetery (56.1246, -5.4951; NR828979), Temple Wood Stone Circles (56.1236, -5.4987; NR826978), Ballymeanoch Standing Stones (56.1113, -5.4857; NR833964) and Achnabreck Cup and Ring Marks (56.0606, -5.4435; NR857906).

56.0861, -5.4786; NR836936 (Dunadd Fort)

9 Iona **

The holy island of Iona, off the southwest tip of Mull, is one of the most sacred and magical places in the whole of the British Isles and a place of pilgrimage for centuries. Dozens of early Scots, Irish and Norwegian kings and clan chieftains are buried in the precincts of the monastery that was originally founded by St Columba in the 6th

9

century. Some say that Iona was originally sacred to the Druids and was viewed as an otherworldly island akin to the fairy realm of Tir na Nog. These fairy folk are still thought to dwell on the island, hidden within its hills and mounds.

Arriving by passenger ferry from Fionn-phort, Mull, you dock at the small settlement of Baile Mòr, Iona's only village, which has a selection of inns and B&Bs. Before you reach the famous abbey, stop off at **St Oran's Chapel** (56.3344, -6.3929; NM285244), the oldest remaining building on the island. This is a quiet place of reflection that com-memorates Oran, a saint who was voluntarily buried alive at the site in order to appease supernatural forces that were preventing the abbey from being built. Next comes the restored medieval **Iona Abbey** (56.3351, -6.3916; NM286245; ££) with 8th-century Celtic crosses and set into its walls is a tiny external chapel known as **St Columba's Shrine** (56.3350, -6.3919; NM286245). St Columba was one of the first Irish mis-sionaries to bring Celtic Christianity to the British Isles. He was believed to be buried under where the shrine now sits and the site was thought to be so holy that kings vied for position to be buried near it.

Towering over the abbey is Iona's tallest hill known as Dun I. On the northern edge

of its summit is a miraculous spring-fed pool known as the **Well of Age** (56.3418, -6.3965; NM284252. Trailhead: 56.3411, -6.3910; NM287251; 500m). Bathing your face in its healing water at sunset was said to restore youth and bring renewal. The Well of Age is also known as a visionary site and a place of pilgrimage. Another place to receive visions is a circular enclosure almost 1km southwest of Dun I known as **Cobhain Cuildich, 'The Hermit's Cell'** (56.3379, -6.4088; NM276249; secret/secluded) that resembles the stone foundations of a shepherd's hut. Many people have reported having mystical experiences there.

Returning to Baile Mòr and following the road south along the coast and then inland you soon come to a farm on the left called Sithean. The name means 'Fairy Mound' and next to the farm lies **Sithean Mor, 'The Large Fairy Mound'** (56.3270, -6.4143; NM272237) while a smaller rocky mound on the opposite side of the road is called **Sithean Beg, 'The Small Fairy Mound'** (56.3278, -6.4154; NM271238). In Abbot Adomnán of Iona's *Life of St Columba*, it is recorded that one of Columba's acolytes saw the saint at Sithean Mor (also known as Cnoc nan Aingeal, 'Hill of Angels') communing with white shining beings who descended from the sky. According to

9

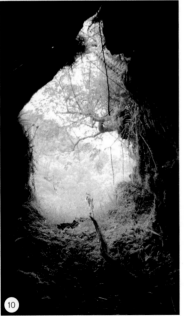

folklore fairy music can often be heard emanating from the mound and one man who went to join the fairy revelry left an iron fish hook stuck in the door so he could escape again. Rituals were also once performed on and around the mound, with cattle being driven between two fires on Beltane and horses being ridden clockwise around the mound on St Michael's Eve.

At the southern tip of the island lies **St Columba's Bay** (56.3092, -6.4268; NM263217) where the famous white-and-green Iona marble can be found washed up on the shore. Pieces of pure green serpentine, which are known as mermaid's tears, can be worn as talismans or good-luck charms and are said to protect the wearer from drowning. The bay is divided into two beaches, Port na Curaich to the east, where St Columba is first said to have made landfall, and Port an Fhir-bhreige to the west which is covered in ancient cairns. On the shoreline people have arranged the pebbles into many amazing sculptures including labyrinths and Celtic crosses. There are many more mysteries to uncover on the sacred isle of Iona, including sacred springs, ringing rocks, tales of selkies (seal people) and household spirits known as 'gruagachs', so it is best to stay overnight and spend the time to fully take in the landscape and explore its mysteries.

The island of Staffa, 8km north of Iona and just 1km across, is composed almost entirely of hexagonal basalt columns. Its shoreline is peppered with caves composed of these magical-looking columns, the most famous of which is **Fingal's Cave** (56.4314, -6.3416; NM324350; boat tour from Iona ££££) where the Irish hero and giant Fingal is thought to have sheltered. Identical basalt columns also make up the famous Giant's Causeway in Northern Ireland and the two sites are connected by legend. A giant called Torquil MacLeod is said to have carried a piece of the Giant's Causeway across the sea in a sack and dropped it to form Staffa, while Fingal is said to have created a causeway connecting the two sites so he could fight his Scottish enemy Benandonner.

Parking: 56.3239, -6.3648; NM302231 (Fionnphort, Mull); Foot Passenger Ferry to Iona £; No Cars Allowed

10 Lochan Uaine
Fairy Loch, Inverbeg

Up on the hillside, above the main road that skirts Loch Lomond, lies a hidden fairy loch with deep greenish-blue water – a colour said to have been created by the fairies dying their clothes. The loch is entirely surrounded by lush green forest and also has a small 'fairy' cave by its banks that can be sheltered in. No paths lead to the loch, the only way to find it is to park by the A82 and then walk up through the forest.

56.1579, -4.6767; NS338993; Secret/Secluded; no paths 200m

11 Mingary Castle

Perched on the shore of Loch Sunart where it flows into the Sound of Mull, Mingary Castle is a medieval keep that once contained a cup reputedly stolen from the fairies. The butler boy from Mingary Castle entered a nearby fairy mound one day and saw the fairies drinking from a magical cup that would instantly fill with any liquid requested. After being passed the cup, he asked it to be filled with water which he then threw over the candles, plunging the room into darkness. He fled with the cup but only managed to escape the fairies by running to the shore and up the back steps of Mingary Castle. The steps, which were added to the castle in the late 16th century, are still there and can be accessed from the shore, but the castle itself is now only open for private rentals and functions.
A sea monster with two humps and flippers was spotted from Mingary Pier (56.6886, -6.0938; NM494626) in 1965 and legends of a water monster are also associated with nearby Loch Shiel (56.7907, -5.5752; NM817722).

56.6928, -6.0802; NM502631; Private

12 St Blane's Monastery, Bute

Located near the remote and rugged southern tip of the Isle of Bute, the ruins of this ancient Celtic monastery lie within a circular enclosure of ancient stonework. The monastery was one of the earliest in Britain and still contains the foundations of ancient monks' cells. It was founded in the 6th century by St Blane, a monk born on Bute who travelled Scotland converting the Picts to Christianity and performing miracles. A circular stone enclosure within the monastery has an uncanny

reputation and is known as the **Devil's Cauldron** (55.7375, –5.0370; NS094535). It once contained a magical old pine tree, a sprig of which placed under the pillow at night was said to induce prophetic dreams. Within the monastery is also an old stone well with water that was reputed to cure sterility. It was also known as a fairy well but it is now unfortunately covered by an iron grille. St Blane's Monastery in its secluded location evokes the ancient past when Celtic saints walked a land still filled with magic and mystery.

55.7368, –5.0368; NS094534 (Fairy Well); Trailhead Parking: 55.7334, –5.0390; NS092530; 500m

13 St Columba's Well, Southend

Near the very tip of the remote Kintyre peninsula the holy well of St Columba is located at Kiel Point where the saint made landfall after crossing from Ireland, which lies just 30km offshore. When Columba stepped onto Scottish land he is said to have left the imprints of his feet on the rock, and these can still be seen just a few metres away from his well. The well itself lies under a rocky overhang in the dark cliff face and is full of offerings of coins and shells. Further north, by Campbeltown Loch, at a secret **Cave Shrine** (55.4216, –5.5428; NR758198; low tide only. Trailhead parking: 55.4169, –5.5638; NR745194; 2km) on Davaar Island there is an image of the crucifixion painted onto the cave wall. The loch itself was the site of an encounter with a dragon that was said to live on Kildaloig Hill to the south. A brave man taunted the troublesome dragon which then chased him across the loch and into a barn that had been filled with hay. Escaping out of the back door the man set the barn alight and the dragon was killed.

55.3082, –5.6682; NR673076; Trailhead Parking: 55.3083, –5.6719; NR670077; 200m

STIRLING

14 Alcluid, The Rock of Dumbarton

This massive outcrop of volcanic rock guarding the entrance to the river Clyde was an impregnable fortress and the Dark Ages capital of the kingdom of Strathclyde

(14)

(15)

where Brythonic (Welsh) speaking people held out against invasions by Scots-Gaels, Picts, Angles and rival British kingdoms for hundreds of years. They finally succumbed to a Viking invasion in the 9th century after a four-month siege by 200 ships.

The fortress was known as Alcluid to the native Britons and Alt Clut, 'Rock of the Clyde' to the Scots-Gaels, who also called it Dun Breatainn, 'The Fort of the Britons'. It was ruled by many kings over the centuries, notably Dyfnwal Hen 'The Old', Tudwal ap Clinog, Clinog Etin, Rhydderch Hael and Gwyddno Garanhir 'Crane Legs'. Many of these characters feature in the folklore of Wales and Lowland Scotland with Tudwal, Clinog, Rhydderch and Gwyddno each possessing one of the Thirteen Treasures of Britain that were later collected by Merlin (see **Bardsey Island**). Gwyddno is also said to be king of the sunken lands of the Cantre'r Gwaelod (see **Sarn Cynfelyn**) while Rhydderch features heavily in the stories of both Myrddin Wylt, the Scottish Merlin (see **Hart Fell Spa**) and St Kentigern (see **Traprain Law**).

Rhydderch was reputedly married to Merlin's sister Languoreth (or Gwenddydd), and Merlin stayed at Alcluid on several occasions. One famous incident occurred when Rhydderch accused Languoreth of being unfaithful. He had one of his servants steal her wedding ring from her lover and toss it into the Clyde and then asked her to produce it to confirm her faithfulness. In desperation she asked St Kentigern for help and he miraculously caught a fish in the Clyde, cut it open and produced the ring. The ring and the fish now feature on the coat of arms for Glasgow.

One legend tells how the twin peaks of Dumbarton Rock were created by the Devil when he dug the stone out of Dumbuck Hill and threw it after St Patrick when he departed for Ireland. Nowadays it is owned by Historic Scotland and most of the visible fortifications date from the 18th century; the only trace of the earlier fortress is the steep imposing rocks themselves. However,

many sculptures from the Dark Ages period of Alcluid can be found in **Govan Church** (55.8646, -4.3130; NS553659; restricted opening times) including Norse hogback tombs, Pictish stones, and the sarcophagus of St Constantine. Govan is one of the earliest Christian sites in the whole of Scotland, dating back to the Roman era.
55.9360, -4.5629; NS400744; £

15 Doon Hill, Aberfoyle *

In the 17th century a minister from Aberfoyle, the Reverend Robert Kirk, went about his parish collecting information about fairies and other supernatural beings from local people and those with second sight. His research was compiled into a manuscript entitled *The Secret Commonwealth of Elves, Fauns and Fairies,* finally published in 1815 at the behest of Sir Walter Scott. In it, he describes the fairies as ethereal beings 'somewhat of the nature of condensed cloud and best seen in twilight'. Although they dressed and spoke like human people and performed human activities like dancing, feasting, and crafting, they could pass through small

(15)

cracks or holes in the ground as if they were made of air. They feasted upon the 'foison' or life force of food and they lived in mounds from which they would travel on the nights of Beltane and Samhain.

Robert Kirk used to take walks on nearby Doon Hill and he reputedly met with the fairies there. One day his lifeless body was found on the hill, but people said this was a simulacrum created by the fairies and that they had abducted the real Robert Kirk for revealing fairy secrets. A footpath known as the Doon Hill Fairy Trail now winds about the hill, passing through an enchanted forest

(15)

that covers a hillside studded with unusual 'fairy mounds'. The summit is crowned by a natural fortress that looks like a fairy fort and at the centre of a clearing is a large pine tree often covered with ribbons and other brightly coloured offerings. This central tree is seen as an entrance to the Otherworld and the place where Robert Kirk disappeared and indeed still may be trapped.

Before serving at Aberfoyle Robert Kirk was a minister at **Balquhidder Church** (56.3580, -4.3716; NN535209) and at the back of the graveyard there is a mound where the fairies used to dance. Also in the churchyard is the grave of the famous Scottish hero Rob Roy.

Aberfoyle sits by the gateway to the Scottish Highlands, with the Trossachs and Loch Katrine a little further north. On the left-hand shore of the loch, not far from the Trossachs, lies the remote **Coire na Uruisgean, 'The Dell of the Urisks'** (56.2380, -4.4493; NN482077. Trailhead: 56.2299, -4.4206; NN500067; 2.8km; no path at end), a gathering place for these fairy-like and forlorn, goat-legged creatures.

Fairies of a different kind can be found at **Bogle Knowe** (56.1688, -4.2792; NS585996. Trailhead: 56.1677, -4.2645; NS594995; 1.2km; no path) a mound located in woodland on the shores of the Lake of Menteith, east of Aberfoyle. The fairies here, presumably boggles, haunted the Earl of Menteith and constantly asked him for work. He tasked them with building a rope from sand, which created the peninsula of Arnmach (56.1725, -4.2940; NN576001) jutting out into the lake.

56.1711, -4.3768; NN525001; Trailhead: 56.1721, -4.3884; NN518002; 800m

16 St Fillan's Holy Pool, Tyndrum

A deep pool in a bend of the river Fillan has been a sacred site since St Fillan baptised converts there in the 8th century. It gained a reputation as a place of healing and an elaborate ritual was carried out in order to effect a cure. After bathing, the sick person had to walk three times around a cairn, drop nine stones into the pool and then leave behind a section torn from clothing worn near the afflicted body part. The upper part of the pool was reserved for women while the downstream part was for men. It is still possible to bathe in the pool today, as people have done for centuries, with only the sound of the traffic on the nearby A82 breaking the sense of tranquillity.

56.4225, -4.6763; NN350288

16

17

FIFE

17 Castle Campbell, Dollar

Built on an outcrop of rock connected to the hillside by a narrow isthmus, Castle Campbell is set in a wild, romantic landscape amongst lush woodlands and bordered by streams cascading down the hillside through verdant gullies. One of the enchanted streams is known as the Burn of Sorrow after a princess who was imprisoned in the castle for falling in love with someone inappropriate. It is perhaps this same princess who now haunts the spring known as the Maiden Well (56.1939, -3.6611; NN970013) located north of Castle Campbell in Glen Queich, a fairy-haunted pass through the Ochil Hills

17

to Glendevon. At the small spring beside the path a woman of unearthly beauty was sometimes said to materialise from the mist. At his 21st birthday party, the Laird of Castle Campbell's son Edwin vowed to capture the woman of the mist or die in the attempt, and drunkenly set off up the valley. On reaching the Maiden Well he brazenly summoned the woman and on his third attempt she appeared but the experience paralysed Edward, all the life force drained from him and he died.

Above the Maiden Well a hill called Maiden Castle (56.1948, -3.6603; NN970014) was known as a fairy dwelling. One day a piper walking though Glen Queich heard music coming from the hill. He went to investigate and was led inside the hill where the fairies made him play his pipes for two days before allowing him to leave. Returning home to Glendevon he was astonished to find that 100 years had passed back home and that his disappearance had passed into local legend. A path still runs though the enchanted Glen Queich to Glendevon but it is now flanked by forestry plantation and the Maiden Well is little more than a wet patch beside the track.

56.1750, -3.6747; NS961993; £

18 Dunino Den *

Behind Dunino Kirk lies a hidden canyon covered in mysterious rock carvings. A deep water-filled well lies beside steep, narrow stone steps that descend into the canyon and down to a green glade where the Dunino Burn trickles around bulbous rock formations. The glade has become a neo-pagan shrine with an altar, brightly coloured offerings decorating the trees and coins jammed into crevices in the rock walls. Some rocks are carved with Celtic knotwork designs and mysterious faces, and below one is a small cave barely high enough to crawl into. A carved footprint on Pulpit Rock, above the stone steps, may be of ancient origin and could be a royal inauguration site similar to **Dunadd**. Sometimes known as Druid's Den, Dunino has associations with ancient Druid worship and it is possible that Dunino Kirk was built above it in order to Christianise the site.

56.2884, -2.7445; NO540109; Trailhead Parking: 56.2890, -2.7430; NO541109; 150m

19 St Fillan's Cave, Pittenweem

In an alleyway called Cove Wynd leading down to Pittenweem harbour there is a metal door decorated with an iron Celtic cross inlaid with semi-precious stones. This is the entrance to the mysterious St Fillan's Cave, a natural sandstone cavity containing a shrine, an altar and a dripping well of flowstone where water collects in a natural basin. A 'secret' passageway at the back also leads up to the abbey. St Fillan was said to have lived as a hermit in the cave in the 7th century, reading his manuscripts in the darkness by the light that emanated from his hand. In later years people were left overnight in the cave in order to cure lunacy and the dripping well, too, was thought to have curative properties. The cave was later used by smugglers and then as a storage room but it has now been restored as a chapel to St Fillan. Ask for the key to the gate at the café on the high street.

56.2133, -2.7275; NO549025; Locked – request key

Scotland's central sacred mountain, known in Scots-Gaelic as *Sidh Chailleann*, 'The Fairy Hill of the Caledonians', was thought to be inhabited by fairies who lived in secret tunnels within. One such entrance to their subterranean realm was the cave known as Uamh Tom a'Mhòr-Fhir, 'Cave of the Great Man of the Bushes' (56.6543, -4.1093; NN707533. Trailhead: 56.5992, -4.0596; NN736471; 8.5km; secret/secluded) located at the foot of Schiehallion by some remote shielings near the Allt Mòr stream. This cave was said to lead directly into the fairy realm but when anyone entered the rock would close up behind them and they would be unable to turn back. The fairies were sometimes heard singing there and one man who helped with the melody of one of their songs was rewarded by having his hunchback removed, while another who was not so musical was punished with an extra hump on his back. The entrance to the cave is hard to find and the only path to the shielings is a long, arduous hike from Fortingall, so the cave remains remote and mysterious. Fairies from the districts all around such as Glen Lyon, Rannoch and Strathtummel, used to attend a yearly gathering on Schiehallion presided over by Queen Mab, the Fairy Queen, dressed all in green with golden hair.

PERTHSHIRE

20 St Fillan's Chair, Dundurn, Comrie

On top of Dundurn Hill lies a natural outcrop of rock known as St Fillan's Chair where people either sat or lay down on a flat slab of rock to cure rheumatism and spinal problems. Also, near the foot of the hill is a ruined chapel (56.3867, -4.1010; NN703235) and St Fillan's Holy Well (56.3828, -4.0934; NN708231) that local people visited each Lammas (August 1st). Dundurn sits in a valley west of Comrie that is surrounded by a stunning vista of mountains.

56.3838 -4.0936; NN708232; Trailhead: 56.3862, -4.0980; NN705235; 800m

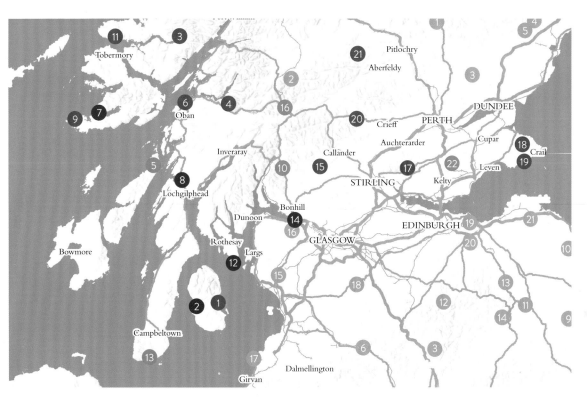

Fortingall is famous for its yew tree (56.5982, -4.0510; NN741470) that, at 5000 years old, was thought to be the oldest living tree in Britain and a place of pagan worship far older than the church it stands beside. The Fortingall Yew now stands in a walled enclosure in the churchyard. In a field opposite the yew tree is a Bronze Age mound, Carn nam Marbh 'The Mound of the Dead' (56.5974, -4.0527; NN740469), where local people gathered on Samhain to perform a pagan fire ritual, while in a field to the east are three Stone Circles (56.5977, -4.0454; NN745469) that also hint at ancient pagan worship. Just west of Fortingall, on the road to Glen Lyon, is a healing well known as the Iron Well (56.6043, -4.0849; NN721477) due to its iron-rich waters.

South of Fortingall is Loch Tay (56.5738, -4.0840; NN720443), said to be inhabited by a water bull that would sometimes mate with the fairy cattle that lived on the slopes of Ben Lawers (56.5450, -4.2209; NN635414). One of the best vantage points for Schiehallion is Queen's View (56.7160, -3.8586; NN863598) on the opposite end of Loch Tummel.

56.6672, -4.1002; NN713547 (Schiehallion summit); Trailhead Parking: 56.6762, -4.0363; NN753556; 4.9km

22 Scotlandwell

Robert the Bruce, in search of a cure for his leprosy was said to have come to Scotland's most renowned healing well, 'Fons Scotae' or Scotlandwell. It is located on the pilgrimage route to St Andrews and many have taken its waters over the centuries in the hope of a cure. The well was restored in Victorian times, when a gabled roof and iron grille were added, and cool, healing waters still flow strongly from the artesian spring in the centre of Scotlandwell village, not far from Loch Leven.

56.2005, -3.3155; NO184016

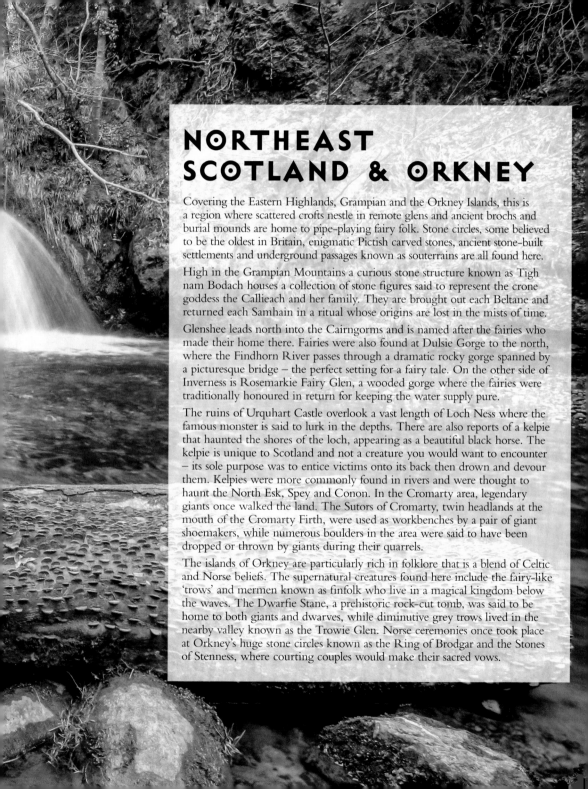

NORTHEAST SCOTLAND & ORKNEY

Covering the Eastern Highlands, Grampian and the Orkney Islands, this is a region where scattered crofts nestle in remote glens and ancient brochs and burial mounds are home to pipe-playing fairy folk. Stone circles, some believed to be the oldest in Britain, enigmatic Pictish carved stones, ancient stone-built settlements and underground passages known as souterrains are all found here.

High in the Grampian Mountains a curious stone structure known as Tigh nam Bodach houses a collection of stone figures said to represent the crone goddess the Callieach and her family. They are brought out each Beltane and returned each Samhain in a ritual whose origins are lost in the mists of time.

Glenshee leads north into the Cairngorms and is named after the fairies who made their home there. Fairies were also found at Dulsie Gorge to the north, where the Findhorn River passes through a dramatic rocky gorge spanned by a picturesque bridge – the perfect setting for a fairy tale. On the other side of Inverness is Rosemarkie Fairy Glen, a wooded gorge where the fairies were traditionally honoured in return for keeping the water supply pure.

The ruins of Urquhart Castle overlook a vast length of Loch Ness where the famous monster is said to lurk in the depths. There are also reports of a kelpie that haunted the shores of the loch, appearing as a beautiful black horse. The kelpie is unique to Scotland and not a creature you would want to encounter – its sole purpose was to entice victims onto its back then drown and devour them. Kelpies were more commonly found in rivers and were thought to haunt the North Esk, Spey and Conon. In the Cromarty area, legendary giants once walked the land. The Sutors of Cromarty, twin headlands at the mouth of the Cromarty Firth, were used as workbenches by a pair of giant shoemakers, while numerous boulders in the area were said to have been dropped or thrown by giants during their quarrels.

The islands of Orkney are particularly rich in folklore that is a blend of Celtic and Norse beliefs. The supernatural creatures found here include the fairy-like 'trows' and mermen known as finfolk who live in a magical kingdom below the waves. The Dwarfie Stane, a prehistoric rock-cut tomb, was said to be home to both giants and dwarves, while diminutive grey trows lived in the nearby valley known as the Trowie Glen. Norse ceremonies once took place at Orkney's huge stone circles known as the Ring of Brodgar and the Stones of Stenness, where courting couples would make their sacred vows.

PERTHSHIRE

1 Dun Shith, Spittal of Glenshee

On all sides stark mountain peaks overlook Glen Shee, the 'Valley of the Fairies'. It has long been considered a fairy haunt: the name *shee* is derived from the Gaelic *sith*, meaning 'fairy'. Until as recently as the 19th century the human inhabitants of the glen were sometimes referred to as *Sithichean a' Ghlinnshith*, the 'Elves of Glen Shee'. At Spittal of Glenshee, a small settlement in the valley, an ancient standing stone sits atop a mound behind the village church. This is known as Dun Shith, the 'Hill of the Fairies'. These fairies were said to have eventually been driven away from the glen by the arrival of the railways and the noise of the steam trains.

Glen Shee also has links to the Scots-Gaelic hero Finn mac Cumhaill (Fingal) and the Fianna, his band of warriors. One legend tells how Diarmid, a member of the Fianna, died after fighting a great boar on the mountain Ben Gulabin overlooking Spittal of Glenshee. His body is said to rest below a mound surmounted by four squat stones that is still known as the Grave of Diarmid (56.8147, -3.4477; NO117701).

Spittal of Glenshee has historically provided shelter for weary travellers passing through the surrounding mountains, with the first hostel or 'spittal' founded there by monks in the 10th century. Today the area still welcomes travellers who come to experience the great outdoors. However, in this remote and dramatically situated glen the fairy folk and heroes of old can still make their presence felt, especially in the dark of winter when heavy snows cut off access to the outside world.

56.8147, -3.4617; NO108701

2 Tigh nam Bodach, Cashlie

In a remote location beyond Loch Lyon a twice-yearly seasonal ritual has taken place at the shrine of Tigh nam Bodach since time immemorial. A low, turf-roofed stone structure houses a number of river-worn stones of vaguely humanoid shape, which are brought out and placed in front of the shrine on Beltane. There they stand and keep watch over the land until they are returned to the shrine's interior at Samhain to see out the winter months. The figures are said to represent the Bodach (old man) and the Cailleach, the Celtic crone goddess who presides over the land and brings about the changing seasons. Great misfortune is believed to fall upon anyone who disturbs these figures outside of their ritual times. Tigh nam Bodach is reached by a long walk along the northern edge of Loch Lyon, then by crossing the Allt Meurain stream and walking up Gleann Cailliche to this intriguing and enigmatic shrine. It sits beside the Allt Cailliche stream that flows down through the valley.

56.5484, -4.6360; NN380427; Secret/
Secluded; Trailhead: 56.5403, -4.5197;
NN451415; 9km

3 Vanora's Mound, Meigle

A low grassy mound in Meigle churchyard is reputed to be the burial place of Queen Guinevere, wife of King Arthur, who is known locally as Vanora. It was once believed that any woman who walked over the mound would become barren, perhaps an echo of Guinevere's own childless state. The true occupant of Vanora's Mound remains a mystery but in previous centuries an elaborately carved Pictish stone, Vanora's Stone, once adorned it. This and others found in the vicinity, including early Christian crosses and grave markers, form a remarkable collection now housed in the adjacent Meigle Museum £ (56.5875, -3.1621; NO287445). Vanora's Stone depicts what is usually described as a figure in a lion's den, but local legend states that this is an image of Vanora herself, about to be ripped to pieces by wild dogs as punishment for her unfaithfulness to Arthur.

56.5881, -3.1620; NO287446

ANGUS

4 River North Esk, Gannochy

A kelpie once haunted a pool in this river. He was a shapeshifting creature who could appear as a man with dripping wet hair, but more commonly took the form of a black horse. In Scottish folklore kelpies liked to entice the unwary to climb on their backs before plunging into the depths of their watery lairs to drown and devour their victim. However, those quick enough to slip a bridle over a kelpie's head could gain control over the creature. The North Esk kelpie, enslaved this way, was compelled to build a castle for the Laird of Morphie and imprisoned in the laird's stables. One day a housemaid took pity on the kelpie and slipped off its bridle to feed it. With a wicked laugh the kelpie leapt from the stable and issued a curse declaring that the Laird of Morphie would never prosper while the kelpie still lived:

"Sair Back and sair banes
Drivin' the Laird o' Morphie's stanes!
The Laird o' Morphie shall never thrive
As long as kelpie is alive."

The prediction came true and not a trace of Morphie Castle now remains. Reputedly, only one example of the kelpie's handiwork can still be seen – huge fingerprints impressed into the surface of the Stone of Morphie (56.7555, -2.4645; NO716627), a tall standing stone said to have been thrown by the kelpie that now stands incongruously by the entrance to a modern working farm. The river North Esk flows through a narrow gorge known as the Rocks of Solitude (56.8448, -2.6761; NO588727; 2.5km), accessed via a trail from Gannochy Bridge. Here the river rushes over waterfalls surrounded by mossy rocks and overhung with trees – a fitting environment for otherworldly water beings.

56.8284, -2.6560; NO600709
(Gannochy Bridge)

from nearby, and feeling jolly he repeated the phrase. Immediately he was swept up into the air and found himself in a fine wine cellar surrounded by fairies. They all made merry and drank and drank until he eventually passed out. He was awoken the next morning by the servants and, finding his fairy companions gone and unable to get away, was dragged before the owner of the wine cellar. This was none other than the King of France, who fortunately was amused by the fabulous tale and sent the lord home with the silver cup as a memento of his adventure. The stone fortress of Duffus Castle now lies in ruins after its abandonment in the 18th century, but the cup remained with the family for many generations, known to all as the 'fairy cup'. Further to the east is **Urquhart Stone Circle** (57.6609, -3.1924; NJ289640), its few remaining stones set on the summit of a small hill surrounded by farmland. They were also known as the Deil's Stanes, and it was believed that the Devil would appear to anyone foolhardy enough to walk around the circle three times at midnight. The stones' proximity to a crossroads, another uncanny location in folklore, must have further enhanced their association with dark forces and midnight rituals.

57.6878, -3.3616; NJ189672

7 Midmar Kirk Stone Circle, Echt

A complete prehistoric stone circle lies within Midmar Kirk churchyard, pre-dating the 18th century church by a few thousand years. It is of the type known as a recumbent stone circle with one large stone lying flat on the ground. The circle's rough stones stand in stark contrast to the neat rows of carved headstones and manicured grass in this curious mixture of old and new religions. To the west, just outside the village of Tarland, is **Culsh Earth House** (57.1376, -2.8198; NJ504054; bring a torch), an Iron Age souterrain. It was called the Pecht House after the belief that the Picts, who were often equated with the fairy folk, once dwelt there. These structures are usually curved tunnels cut into the ground and lined with megalithic blocks. No one knows what they were used for and speculations range from mysterious rituals to the more prosaic storing of supplies. The walls of Culsh Earth House incorporate two cup-marked stones, which suggests this souterrain had some spiritual aspect. The low passageway leads to a dark inner chamber some 14m from the entrance. Within this shadowy, womb-like space it is easy to envisage a portal to an otherworldly realm.

57.1483, -2.4984; NJ699064

5 White Caterthun Hillfort, Tigerton

One of the most spectacular Iron Age hillforts in Scotland, White Caterthun features massive stone walls reputedly built by a giant witch in just one morning. She only stopped work when her apron string broke while carrying a particularly large stone that tumbled down the hill. Local tradition also claims the fort is inhabited by fairies who live within the hill. The oval defensive walls of the fort would once have stood several metres high but even in their current ruinous state they look impressive amongst the heather cover-

ing the hillside. There is also a boulder on the western slope with prehistoric cup marks carved into its surface.

Parking: 56.7841, -2.7344; NO552660

GRAMPIAN

6 Duffus Castle

The lords of Duffus Castle had in their possession a silver cup said to have been acquired long ago by one of their forebears after an adventure with the fairies. He had been out walking when a great wind blew up and he heard a cry of "Horse and Hattock!" come

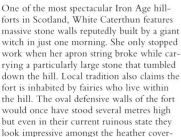

8 St Mary's Well, Inchberry

At one time St Mary's Well was renowned for its healing properties and its waters considered beneficial for whooping cough, sore eyes and joint diseases. A healer called Dame Aliset is once said to have used the well water to cure a sickly fairy child, and although she asked for nothing in return the fairies were so grateful they blessed the water of the well with the power to restore lost youth in those who bathed there. The pointed stone canopy of the well is set into the outside wall of a burial ground and chapel (now a private mausoleum and closed to the public). Below is a basin and shelves that once held the 'miraculous stones' mentioned in a 19th-century account; these were hollowed out to form vessels to hold the healing water. Different stones were used for different parts of the body and the healing ritual involved turning the vessels three times widdershins (counter-clockwise). In front of this structure is the spring itself, flowing into a small pool now concealed beneath metal grating. St Mary's Well was once a place of pilgrimage with people travelling from as far away as the Western Isles to seek a cure, but it is now seldom visited, tucked away on the outskirts of a quiet village, surrounded by fields and woodland.

A short distance to the northeast at **Portgordon** (57.6663, -3.0157; NJ395645), local fishermen regularly saw a merman swimming out in Spey Bay. He was said to have unusually long arms, curly grey-green hair and a swarthy complexion. To see him was considered a bad omen and the boats

would always return to shore after a sighting for fear of some misfortune befalling them. The river Spey (57.5505, -3.1402; NJ318517), which runs near Inchberry to Spey Bay, was said to be plagued by a kelpie which took the form of a white horse. Once a year it would claim a victim by enticing someone onto its back before plunging into the river to drown them.

57.5815, -3.1329; NJ323551; Trailhead: 57.5780, -3.1561; NJ309548; 2km

HIGHLAND

9 Bruan Broch

This Iron Age broch was known locally as the fairy mound of Bruan. One New Year's Eve two men passing by were astounded when, through an opening into the mound, they saw scores of fairies dancing to pipe music. They crept closer and watched for a while, one of them keen to join the dance but the other remaining cautious. Eventually the cautious man set off home, thinking his companion would soon grow weary but the next day there was no sign of him and no sign of any entrance into the broch either. Nevertheless, the cautious man did not give up hope and recalled that mortals taken into Fairyland could be rescued on the anniversary of their disappearance. Sure enough, a year later the door to the broch opened once more and he could see his friend inside. Putting an iron stake into the doorway so that it could not close, the man called out to his friend that it was time to come home, but he replied that he was still waiting for his dance! He refused to believe

a year had passed outside and had to be dragged away from the dance by his brave and loyal friend, who returned them both home safely. Today Bruan Broch stands alongside the A99 road, a stony conical mound surrounded by a stone wall.
Nearby is the **Hill o' Many Stanes** (58.3285, -3.2050; ND295384) covered in numerous stone rows laid out in the unusual fan-like arrangement unique to Scotland. Gold was said to be buried beneath the standing stones and many were dug out over time. However, it was considered bad luck to disturb them and one man who took a stone to make a lintel over a kiln was horrified when it magically burst into flames, forcing him to return it to its original spot. Despite the warnings, around 200 stones are now all that remain from the 600 originally spread over the flanks of the hill.

58.3387, -3.1798; ND310395

10 Creag Mhòr & Creag Bheag, Isauld

The two steep hills of Creag Mhòr and Creag Bheag were said to have been formed by a band of imps under the control of the magician Donald Dubhuail Mackay. Sir Donald Mackay was a real person, by all accounts a thoroughly unpleasant individual, who reputedly learned his dark arts directly from the Devil. He tricked the Devil into taking his shadow instead of his soul and also gained a host of imps or fairies who were set to work performing tasks around his land in the manner of brownies or hobs. Mackay then instructed them to drain a loch in order to find buried treasure. After digging a deep ravine they threw the soil into heaps, creating Creag Mhòr (58.5399, -3.7334; NC991626) and Creag Bheag on either side of the Achvarasdal Burn. However, their work was interrupted by the area's presiding Cailleach (old crone) who cried out and the imps immediately vanished. A furious Mackay hit the Cailleach with a spade with such force her head

split in two and she turned to stone. Now known as **Clach Clais an Tuirc** (58.5448, -3.7343; NC991631; 2.2km along trail) she remains there still, a squat standing stone with a long gash on the top.

A few kilometres southeast, **Loch Shurrery** (58.4889, -3.6432; ND043568. Trailhead: 58.4976, -3.6434; ND043577; 1km) was home to a *tarbh uisge*, a water bull. This supernatural beast was sometimes seen to emerge from the loch, shake himself and give a great bellow before mating with the local cows. Water bulls lack ears and the offspring of their unions, identifiable by their short, cropped ears, were much prized by cattle breeders.

Where the Forss Water flows out of Loch Shurrery was an island once the scene of a 'need-fire' ceremony. The cattle of the district had become infected with a plague after a local crofter, despite dire warnings, had taken soil from a fairy mound. In an elaborate ritual to drive out the infection, every fire in the district was extinguished and then a new fire created on the island. This fire had to be ignited using only friction generated by revolving a piece of wood within a hole cut in a wooden crosspiece

erected on a frame. The men revolving the wood were to wear only wool and no iron. At first the need-fire did not ignite as an old witch had kept some embers burning, but once these were extinguished it ignited easily. The cattle were then driven through the smoke and the plague was eradicated. Loch Shurrery lies in a remote and isolated location. The only access track crosses the Forss Water but the whole area is clogged with reeds so it's now hard to see where the island could have been.

58.5429, -3.7407; NC987629 (Creag Bheag); Trailhead Parking: 58.5602, -3.7504; NC982648; 2.5km

11 Dulsie Gorge & the Findhorn River, Redburn *

One of Scotland's longest rivers, the Findhorn is wild and inaccessible for long stretches making it the perfect habitat for the fairies who are said to dwell along its banks. A glimpse of one of its most dramatic spots can be had at Dulsie where the river passes

through a narrow rocky gorge spanned by the arched 18th-century Dulsie Bridge. A knoll close to Dulsie was believed to be a gathering place for the fairies, although its exact location is now unknown. There is a small parking area close to the bridge with spectacular views of the bridge and gorge, while a steep track leads down to the river itself.

Parking: 57.4503, -3.7815; NH931414 (Dulsie Gorge)

12 Dunnet Bay

A cave beneath Dwarwick Head in Dunnet Bay is said to contain a great treasure trove belonging to a mermaid. She fell in love with a local fisherman and wooed him with jewels and gold that had been salvaged from ships sunk out in the Pentland Firth. However, she became jealous of his flirtations

with human women so she lured him to the cave where she sang him to sleep. According to folklore they are still both there in the hidden cave below the waves, far away from the temptations of pretty girls.

The magician Donald Dubhuail Mackay (see **Creag Mhòr and Creag Bheag**) set his imp familiars to work in Dunnet Bay, tasked with weaving ropes out of sand to make a bridge to cross the Pentland Firth. Although they managed to weave one rope it broke halfway across the water. The imps were angry at being given such an impossible task, and would have turned on their master had he not transformed himself into a black horse and galloped away to safety. The white sandy beach at Dunnet Bay sweeps along the coastline for over 3km and is today popular with holiday makers and surfers.

To the south side of Dunnet Bay **Sibmister Broch** (58.5760, -3.4373; ND165662) sits atop a grassy hillock known as the Cairn of Sibmister. The mound itself was said to be a fairy knoll and a man once entered a doorway into the mound that led to a hall full of dancing fairies. He joined in the dance but a fellow reveller warned him not to accept any of the food or drink that was offered. He stayed for a dance or two before leaving, but on returning home was informed he had been missing for a year and a day. He also learned that had he accepted the fairy food then the fairies would have kept him there forever. It was not long afterwards that he went missing again, this time for good – probably having given in to the temptations of the fairies.

Parking: 58.6226, -3.3670; ND207713 (Dwarwick Head)

13 Fairy Hillock, Wick

Lying alongside the Wick River this low grassy hillock with a prehistoric cairn at one end was the scene of a fairy encounter in 1895. Two men used an incantation to summon the fairy queen who appeared dressed in white surrounded by dancing fairies. A black shape also manifested and challenged the men, asking: "Who art thou?". Panicking, one of the men shouted, "In the name of all that is sacred, depart!". At this all the fairies disappeared and the men escaped. Today the Fairy Hillock can be seen from a path on the opposite side of the river that leads from the centre of Wick.

58.4490, -3.1247; ND344517; Trailhead Parking: 58.4429, -3.0950; ND361510; 1.9km

14 Loch Morlich, Aviemore

A mound on the shores of Loch Morlich was a *sithean*, a fairy gathering place and home to a fairy king known locally as Big Donald. People passing by the mound could often hear Big Donald playing his bagpipes and one day a quick-thinking man threw his cap onto the mound exclaiming "This is yours: that is mine!". His cap disappeared and in its place was a tiny set of bagpipes. He put them in his pocket but on arriving home found nothing but a reed stalk and a puffball mushroom. The location of the mound is lost but there are extensive woodland walks and a sandy shore to enjoy in the Glenmore Forest Park around Loch Morlich, surrounded by the majestic Cairngorm mountains.

In the Ryvoan Pass, high above the Glenmore Forest Park Visitor Centre, lies a green fairy lake known as **An Lochan Uaine** (57.1755, -3.6550; NJ000106. Trailhead: 57.1675, -3.6927; NH977097; 3km). It is surrounded by ancient Scots pine trees and the trackway eventually leads into Abernethy Forest, a rare survival of the ancient Caledonian pine forest. Northwest of Loch Morlich, a smaller lake known as **Loch Pityoulish** (57.2054, -3.7883; NH920141) was said to be haunted by a kelpie that would entice its victims by appearing as a fine black horse decked in silver saddle and bridle on the

shore of the lake. A group of boys spied the horse one day and caught hold of the reins, but it immediately plunged into the water. The only boy to survive had to hack away at his own fingers with a knife to free himself from the supernatural beast.

Further northwest is **Granish Ring Cairn** (57.2173, -3.8102; NH907155; secret/secluded. Trailhead: 57.2116, -3.8222; NH900148; 1.4km) where a druidic ceremony reputedly took place to choose ancient Pictish kings. The ritual involved the raising of spirits who would name the successive king and utter prophesies concerning their reign. The last king to be crowned there was told of the coming of St Columba who converted the Picts to Christianity. Even when the site was no longer used the magic of the ring cairn endured

through the centuries and it was believed to be unlucky to remove any stones. One stone was used as a lintel for a cattle byre but the cows refused to pass under it so it was eventually restored to its rightful place. The cairn lies on the opposite side of a railway line and can be difficult to locate.

Parking: 57.1654, -3.7230; NH958096

15 Loch Ussie, Maryburgh

According to legend, the spirit of Loch Ussie could be consulted in matters of divination if a question was spoken aloud from the shore. Silence meant that the answer was yes, but if the question was followed by

-4.5066; NH502583) with Fingal's Well at its centre. This well was said to have been covered with a large stone by Fingal after he drove out the inhabitants of the fort. The Brahan Seer had prophesied that should the stone ever be removed that the waters of Loch Ussie would seep out of the well and flood the surrounding countryside to such an extent that ships could sail all the way to Strathpeffer. Today no trace of the well remains but the gleaming vitrified walls of the fort make the climb up the hill worthwhile.

Several water spirits haunted the **River Conon** (57.5521, -4.4560; NH531539) flowing south of Loch Ussie. The first was a kelpie, the water horse of Scottish legend, which lured the unwary to drown in the swirling, murky pools south of Cononbridge. Another water spirit took the form of a ghastly woman dressed in green, with a scowling face and bony fingers that she would point at her victims. If they resisted and tried to cling to safety, she would simply drag them under to drown. There are also strange tales of a 'king otter' that lived in the river Conon, distinguished from ordinary otters by his pale colour and large size. If caught he would grant a wish in return for being released, but if killed and skinned his pelt would render the wearer immune from bullets and sharp steel.
57.5775, -4.5080; NH501569

16 Munlochy Clootie Well

The act of tying clootie ribbons to trees growing near wells to bring about healing is an ancient tradition. The sick person would usually dip a rag or item of clothing in the water and rub the afflicted part of their body before tying it to a branch close to the well. As the fabric rotted, the ailment would ease. It was also believed that removing someone else's clootie would take on their ailment. The Munclochy Well is little more than a spring pouring into a small stone trough yet the trees all around are hung with hundreds of brightly coloured ribbons, rags and banners in an ever-increasing display that has, unfortunately, got out of hand creating quite an eyesore. The well is dedicated to St Boniface but it's likely there was a pre-Christian guardian or deity honoured here originally.
57.5527, -4.2736; NH640536

17 Rosemarkie Fairy Glen *

An enchanting series of pools, waterfalls and a rushing stream passing through lush

the sound of snarling or groaning, or ripples were seen in the water, the answer was no. A holed stone belonging to the Brahan Seer, a prophet born locally in the 1600s, is said to lie at the bottom of the lake. The Seer used to peer through the hole, seeing into the future to gather his famous prophesies. However, should anyone attempt to drain the loch to recover the stone it will overflow and drown the town of Strathpeffer. Loch Ussie is an uncanny place and claims persist of distressed cries echoing across the water on dark nights, and that no fish can live in the lake or any birds fly over it. Overlooking Loch Ussie is the Iron Age hillfort of **Knock Farril** (parking: 57.5899,

17

woodland make a journey into Rosemarkie's Fairy Glen an otherworldly experience.
Fairies are said to inhabit this glen and in
return for their help in keeping the water
clean a well-dressing ceremony was once
held here. Local children decorated a spring
and a pool in the glen with flowers in honour of the fairies. It was also at Rosemarkie
Fairy Glen that the author R. Ogilvie
Crombie encountered elves in his book
The Gentleman and the Faun. Today people
leave all kinds of offerings to the fairies and
nature spirits of the glen, including a tree
trunk studded with coins that have been
hammered into it.

Fairies were also found at nearby **Cha-
nonry Point** (57.5738, -4.0943;
NH748556) where they once tried to build
a bridge across the Moray Firth to link For-
trose with Ardersier. However, when people
came to watch and offer advice, the fairies
were offended so abandoned their work and
left. The famous magician Michael Scott
also attempted to cross the firth, using his
imps to build a causeway of sand. They too
were thwarted after a shepherd called for
God's blessing and the imps all fled.

To the south near Avoch, the **Craiguck
Well** (57.5494, -4.2085; NH679531; private
land) is a natural spring issuing forth from
below a rock set into a wooded bank.
Traditionally locals would come here on
the first Sunday in May (close to Beltane) to
gather bottles of water for healing purposes,
a practice that continued well into the 19th
century. Although the well lies on private
land and permission should be sought from
the nearby farmhouse, the trees surrounding
the well are still hung with clootie ribbons
left by people who have taken the time to
seek it out.

57.5937, -4.1247; NH730579; Trailhead
Parking: 57.5926, -4.1175; NH735578; 1km

18 Sutors of Cromarty *

17

The Scots-Gaelic word *soutar* means shoe-
maker and the twin headlands of North
Sutor and South Sutor which guard the
entrance to the Cromarty Firth were said
to have been workbenches for a pair of
shoemaking giants. Although the giants

had a headland each, they shared only one set of tools which they would throw back and forth across the firth. Other tales claim the headlands themselves were once giants who were turned to stone for some now forgotten transgression. There are also said to be hoof-prints embedded in rock on each side of the Sutors, left there by the magician Michael Scott's horse as he leapt over the firth to escape a group of imps who were hounding him.

On the rocky shore of South Sutor, the **Dropping Cave** (57.6799, -4.0031; NH806673; low tide only; 1.5km from South Sutor Viewpoint) is a small sea cave from which sailors have reported seeing blue lights shining. The cave was said to be the haunt of a mermaid who was sometimes seen sitting near the entrance combing her long golden hair. Once she was captured by a sea captain who only released her when she granted him three wishes. The first was for the safety of him and his friends while at sea; the second for good fortune in all his endeavours; and the third was that he should win the love of a certain young woman. Shortly after releasing the mermaid, he encountered his intended and she was so overawed by his tale she did indeed fall in love with him and they were married within the year.

A little further south lies **St Bennet's Well** (57.6588, -4.0257; NH792650. Trailhead: 57.6593, -4.0419; NH782651; 1.4km) a natural healing spring where offerings of clootie ribbons were tied to the hawthorn tree growing overhead. A rough stone trough known as the Fairy's Cradle was once located nearby, close to a chapel dedicated to St Bennet. A suspected fairy changeling would be laid in the cradle in the hope this would compel the fairies to return the stolen human child. Today both chapel and Fairy's Cradle are long gone but the spring still issues forth fresh healing waters.

57.6781, -4.0019; NH807671 (South Sutor viewpoint)

19 Urquhart Castle, Loch Ness

A 'water beast' was first recorded in Loch Ness as early as the 7th century when it was encountered by St Columba. The beast would have attacked and killed a follower of St Columba but fled when the saint made the sign of the cross and commanded it to leave. More recent reports of a monster inhabiting the fathomless depths of Loch

Ness first began to attract worldwide attention in the 1930s, with numerous sightings and even photos.

The loch was also home to a kelpie, the murderous water horse of Scottish legend that would drown those foolish enough to climb on its back. Once a man encountered the kelpie in the form of a beautiful black horse with a fine bridle, but knowing what it truly was he took out his sword and slashed, cutting off a small brass hook attached to the bridle. This brass hook was later used by a local man named Willox in a healing charm, along with a glass hemisphere given to one of his ancestors by a fairy. The charm involved putting first the glass and then the hook into a basin of water, then rotating them three times while invoking the Holy Trinity. This gave the water the power to heal any ailment and the 'Willox Ball and Bridle' was much respected in the local area.

Loch Ness has long been considered an uncanny place and according to legend it was created when a woman, distracted by her crying baby, forgot to put the cover back on a well. The water rose rapidly, drowning well and valley to form the 40km long lake seen today. Hordes of tourists still flock to the shores of Loch Ness today, hoping to catch a glimpse of the elusive 'Nessie' and prove once and for all that the beastie really exists. Good views of the loch are to be had from the battlements of the atmospheric Urquhart Castle, a ruined medieval fortress picturesquely sited on a headland overlooking a vast stretch of the loch backed by majestic mountains.

57.3242, -4.4420; NH530286; ££ Popular

20 Dingishowe, Upper Sanday

This conical grassy mound, also known as Dingy's Howe, marks the gathering place of the local fairy folk on Midsummer's Eve. A

fiddler named Tam went into Dingishowe to play for the fairies but on emerging from the mound after a night spent with the fairies, he found fourteen long years had passed in the mortal world. Excavations have revealed that the rough turf conceals the remains of an Iron Age broch that sits amid sand dunes on a narrow strip of land connecting Deerness with the east mainland. The location is a truly liminal place, caught between land and sea, making it an ideal fairy haunt.

58.9147, -2.7873; HY547033

21 Dwarfie Stane, Quoyness *

A unique prehistoric tomb carved into a huge 'erratic' glacial bolder has, according to local folklore, been a home to both giants and a dwarfish 'trow'. The massive rectangular slab of sandstone sits in a bleak moorland valley overlooked by steep cliffs known as the Dwarfie Hamars because sounds echoing off the cliffs were thought to be the voices of dwarves. At some point in the distant past, the entrance and two small chambers with bed-like shapes were carved into the solid rock. This is said to be where a giant and his pregnant wife slept until one day they were imprisoned there by a rival. The male giant then gnawed a hole in the roof of the rock to escape, which was still visible until filled with concrete in the mid-20th century. The dimensions of the tiny inner chambers and the name of the stone would rather suggest an inhabitant of dwarfish rather than gigantic stature.

Norse settlers to the area brought tales of trolls and dwarves – which became Orkney's trows or fairy folk – who were thought to inhabit the nearby **Trowie Glen** (58.8794, -3.3224; ND238998; 600m walk from the Dwarfie Stane; no paths), a narrow, rocky valley where a stream cascades down numerous small waterfalls. Locals usually avoided the place, but one summer evening a man called Mansie from the seaside village of Rackwick walking home across the moors found himself drawn irresistibly towards the Trowie Glen. A small crowd of peedie folk (small trows only a foot tall) appeared and took him to a cave in the glen leading into a beautiful hall of rich tapestries and carpets where a fairy dance was taking place. Mansie met the leader of the trows who offered him some heather ale, which Mansie drank and then joined in the dancing. Enjoying himself, Mansie took out his clay pipe and filled it with tobacco, which fascinated the trows, but as soon as he lit it and blew out

smoke all around him they started to faint then suddenly all disappeared. Mansie found himself back in the glen sitting by a rabbit hole, all alone.

According to an Orcadian folktale, the Orkney, Shetland and Faroe Islands were formed from the teeth of a monstrous sea serpent called Mester Stoor Worm as it died, having been defeated by a farmer's son called Assipattle. However, Hoy and the small neighbouring Island of Graemsay (58.9297, -3.2906; HY258054) have their own creation legend concerning a giant who dropped a basketful of soil. He was envious of the fertile soil found on Orkney and wanted to bring some home with him to Caithness, so he dug out great quantities to fill up his straw basket. The holes this

left behind filled with water to form the Stenness and Harray lochs. As he set off, a large clod fell out creating Graemsay, then the strap of the basket broke and all the rest of the soil tumbled out to form Hoy.

58.8845, -3.3143; HY243004; Trailhead Parking: 58.8888, -3.3165; HY242009; 500m

22 Ring of Brodgar, Finstown *

The huge Neolithic stone circle and henge known as the Ring of Brodgar was a favourite venue for young couples' betrothal ceremonies in centuries past. It was referred to as the 'Temple of the Sun'

while the 'Temple of the Moon' was the title bestowed on the **Stones of Stenness** (58.9942, -3.2080; HY306125), a short distance to the southeast. Both stone circles were visited in turn by couples in a ritual performed at New Year when prayers would be offered to Odin that the lovers might keep their promises to each other. The ceremony culminated at the Stone of Odin, a standing stone with a hole through which the couples would hold hands and make their pledge. It was also said that any infant passed through the hole would never suffer from palsy in old age. Unfortunately, the stone was destroyed in 1814 by a farmer who was annoyed with the number of people trespassing on his land to reach it, but the jagged stone circles of Brodgar and Stenness can still be visited.

The prehistoric chambered cairn of **Maes Howe** (58.9966, -3.1883; HY318127; popular; check opening times) lies just east of the Stones of Stenness. This large grassy mound conceals stone-built passages and chambers and is aligned with the winter solstice so the central chamber is illuminated at sunrise. According to folklore it was home to a *hogboy*, a creature not unlike an English hob or boggart, who dwelt in the *haug* (burial mound) and kept a watchful eye over local farmsteads. These beings were treated with the utmost respect in case they decided to

wreak havoc. Scratched onto the stones inside Maes Howe is a collection of Norse runic graffiti that includes a carving of a dragon and references to buried treasure. Further east still is **Cuween Hill Cairn** (58.9974, -3.1081; HY364127; bring a torch. Trailhead: 58.9986, -3.1002; HY368129; 500m), regarded as a fairy hill and an entrance to the fairy realm. The chambered tomb was built using a similar design to Maes Howe but on a smaller scale, and when it was excavated a number of human bones and dog skulls were found interred there. While visitors flock to Maes Howe, Cuween Hill Cairn is more often over-looked, but its dark, serene interior retains a magical otherworldly atmosphere.

Fairies were once seen dancing around the **Broch of Burrian** (59.0326, -3.2067; HY308167) on Christmas Day but vanished as soon as they realised they were being observed. A carved Pictish stone was found in the ruined broch where tumbledown stone walls crown the grassy mound. All across the Orkney islands ancient mounds and brochs were believed to be inhabited by bands of trows and fairies, solitary hogboys or dwarves – a belief that some still hold.

59.0015, -3.2298; HY294133; Popular; Check opening times

23 Skara Brae & Bay of Skaill *

Near the unique Neolithic settlement at Skara Brae overlooking the Bay of Skaill, people kept watch for marauding finfolk who would come ashore to raid the mill at Skaill. The finfolk are Orkney's merpeople: female finwives had the traditional fish tail and long golden hair while the ugly finmen were said to be exceptionally strong. They were greedy for gold and silver and would often steal from coastal farmsteads. Most of all they liked to kidnap pretty young humans and take them to Finfolkaheem, their kingdom below the waves. Finwives sometimes preferred human husbands to finmen, to avoid a life of servitude. While exploring the cluster of amazingly well-preserved, stone-built houses at the semi-subterranean village of Skara Brae it's easy to imagine their inhabitants telling tales around the fire on dark Orcadian nights. Skara Brae is part of the 'Heart of Neolithic Orkney' World Heritage site which also includes the **Ring of Brodgar**, Maes Howe and many of the other fascinating prehistoric sites found in Orkney.

59.0487, -3.3418; HY231187 (Skara Brae); ££ Popular

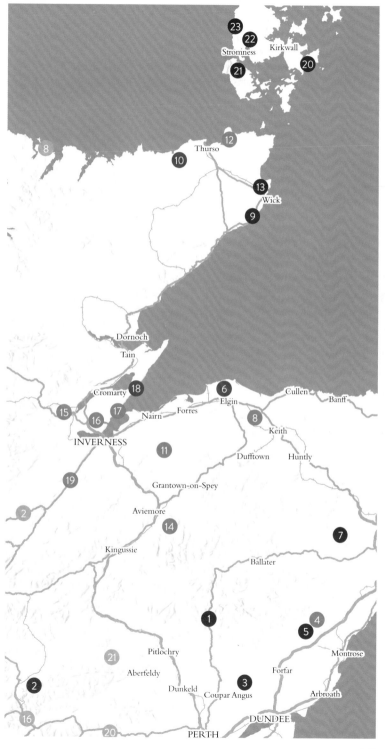

NORTHWEST HIGHLANDS & WESTERN ISLES

The Northwest Highlands of Scotland are one of the most wild and rugged parts of the country with a long Atlantic coastline exposed to gales, storms and raging seas. Here you will find Sandwood Bay, known as the 'Land of the Mermaids' and the hugely impressive Smoo Cave where witches were said to have blasted a hole in the ceiling, letting in a magical waterfall. Inland are lochs inhabited by monsters and fairy folk, and Loch Maree also has a mysterious 'Island of the Druids' where ancient rituals were performed until relatively recent times.

Travelling over the bridge from Kyle of Lochalsh we reach the Isle of Skye, popular with tourists due to its stunning otherworldly scenery. From the Fairy Pools by the Cuillin Hills to the Fairy Glen near Uig the whole island is awash with legends of the fairy folk. In Dunvegan Castle you can still see a fairy flag and fairy cup, one gifted and the other stolen from the fairies. Travelling down to Bracadale we pass by numerous Iron Age duns and brochs. Many of these were thought to be fairy dwellings and several have fairy stories attached to them.

The landscape of Skye was said to have been created in ancient times by the crone goddess the Cailleach battling with her enemies. The Cuillin Hills were thought to have been raised by a spear cast at her by the sun god, while the huge rocky pinnacle known as the 'Old Man of Storr' was said to be a giant turned to stone.

Across the wide channel known as the Minch lie the Western Isles, also known as the Outer Hebrides. The inhabitants of these isles lived on the very edge of the known world on virtually treeless islands exposed to the worst of the Atlantic weather. They are inhabited by Scots-Gaelic people and many of them still speak the language. The long archipelago of islands, from the Butt of Lewis in the north to Berneray in the south were thought to have been created from the body of a huge nine-headed giant who was slain by a liberating hero. The Outer Hebrides also have mermaids, the wild hunt and fairies in abundance but to reach these islands it is necessary to negotiate the dangerous waters of the Minch where malicious water fairies known as the Blue Men of the Minch caused boats to capsize. The Outer Hebrides' most famous attraction, the Callanish Stones, contain Scotland's best known stone circle and Callanish folklore features giants turned to stone, ancient rituals, a fairy cow and a 'Shining One' who walks the avenue of stones at midsummer.

1

HIGHLANDS

1 Coille Loch an Draing, Midtown

A remote forest of ancient twisted birch trees was home to Gille Dubh, the Gairloch Fairy. This helpful spirit was described as having black hair and being clad in leaves and moss, but despite his kindly nature local chieftains decided that they could not allow such a heathen creature to live on their land so they went to hunt him down in his forest home. Despite their best efforts they were unable to find him but from that day forth he was never seen again.

Coille Loch an Draing, in northwest Wester Ross, is located on the side of a hill beside the loch it is named after. It is reached by a long walk from the hamlet of Midtown overlooking Loch Ewe.

57.8431, -5.7489; NG775898; Secret/ Secluded; Trailhead: 57.8060, -5.6694; NG820855; 7km

2 Dundreggan Fairy Knoll

Next to Dundreggan Farm in Glen Moriston is a circular mound that was thought to be both a fairy dwelling and the burial place of a dragon that was slain by the legendary hero Fingal (Fionn mac Cumhaill) and his giant dog Bran. Dun means 'fort' and this mound, a medieval motte now covered in earth and grass, is the 'Dun of the Dragon' and gives its name to the village of Dundreggan. The fairies who inhabited this knoll had a reputation for kidnapping the mothers of newborn babies so they could act as wet nurses to fairy children. Many a man in the local area was heard to lament his lost wife but one was lucky enough to hear his spouse sighing in the wind and after throwing his knife in that direction she fell safely to the ground, able to escape the fairies' clutches owing to their aversion to iron. Another woman and her baby were rescued from the mound itself by a priest who sprinkled holy water on the dun and blessed it. A noise like thunder was then heard, the moon came out from behind a cloud and the mother and baby were found lying on the surface of the mound.

57.1919, -4.7662; NH329146

3 Isle Maree, Talladale *

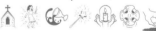

Within the archipelago of small islands in Loch Maree lies Isle Maree, an ancient burial ground that has been called the 'Island of the Druids'. Unlike the other islands in the loch that are characterised by heather, bracken and Scots pine, Isle Maree is entirely covered in a dense woodland of oak that was thought to have been planted by the Druids. The island also contains a 'Druid Circle', a circular formation of stones that has a channel running through the centre of it. It is said that bull sacrifices were performed on this island until the 17th century and perhaps the animals' blood ran into this channel. The Druid Circle lies at the centre of a wooded graveyard with old gravestones dating back to the 11th century. Two of these ancient graves are said to contain a Norwegian princess and her lover who met a tragic end.

Two other mysterious locations on Isle Maree are now lost. One is the 8th century hermitage of St Maelrubha who the isle and the loch are thought to be named after. The other was a sacred spring which was said to cure lunacy. After being taken to the spring to drink the waters, the unfortunate sufferer was then rowed three times around the island in a boat, and each time was dunked in the loch. The ritual was presided over by a hereditary well-guardian who officiated on the island. Near to the location of the now lost spring are the remains of a tree that is studded with old coins dating back to the Victorian era. This 'money tree' was once a sacred oak where people made prayers and tied offerings by the well for wishes and healing. Take care not to remove anything from the island though, as bad luck is said to befall any who do so.

Next to Isle Maree is the much larger island of Eilean Sùbhainn and in the centre is a small lochan that contains another tiny island. The **Queen of Fairies Island** (57.6900, -5.4859; NG923720; secret/secluded) – an island within an island – is a magical place where the Queen of Fairies is said to hold court. Eilean Sùbhainn lies within the Loch Maree Islands National Nature Reserve,

a wild place where nature is still firmly in charge. The loch is backed by high mountains whose lower slopes are covered in native Scots pine forests and the islands can only be reached by private boat hire. Ask at the Loch Maree Hotel in Talladale (57.6752, -5.4986; NG914704).

57.6935, -5.4731; NG931723; Accessible by Private Boat Only

2

3

3

3

4 Isle of Muck, Port Mòr

The last recorded mermaid sighting in the British Isles is said to have occurred off the Isle of Muck. She was seen by an old fisherman in 1947, combing her hair while sitting on a floating herring box just offshore. A rock pool near the southern tip of the island is still known as **Mermaid's Pool** (56.8242, -6.2351; NM417783) so it was perhaps near here that the mermaid was sighted. Also, near the southern tip of the island a strange fairy encounter once occurred. Two young boys out foraging on the shore found a metal tin which they tried to open with a stone. As they hit it two tiny fairy boys appeared dressed in green and asked them what they were doing. The boys then noticed a small boat offshore containing a tiny fairy woman who asked them to come aboard but they were afraid and so she came ashore and gave them loaves of bread the size of walnuts, which they ate and enjoyed. The three fairies then departed in their boat, telling the boys to return home once they had seen them disappear beyond the rocky islet known as Dubh Sgeir which lies at the entrance to Port Mòr harbour. Soon afterwards the boys' sister found them sitting on the shore, still gazing out to sea. Suddenly the spell was broken and the boys started trembling with fear.

The Isle of Muck, a small island only 4km in length, is reached by ferry from the neighbouring island of Eig or by infrequent direct ferry from Mallaig that also stops at the islands of Rum, Eigg and Canna. Excellent views of Port Mòr harbour and the rocks of Dubh Sgeir (56.8264, -6.2216; NM425784; fully visible at low tide) are to be had from the Iron Age fort of Caisteal an Duin Bhain on a headland southwest of Port Mòr. From there you can explore the remote, rocky shoreline where these unusual encounters are thought to have taken place.

56.8276, -6.2275; NM421786 (Caisteal an Duin Bhain); Trailhead, Port Mor Pier: 56.8322, -6.2244; NM424791; 1.6km; Ferry from Mallaig Harbour 57.0074, -5.8266; NM677972; £ No cars allowed; Infrequent service so check before travelling

5 Lochan Sgeireach, 'The Fairy Lochs', Shieldaig

These small lochans south of Shieldaig are known locally as the Fairy Lochs and are nestled between surrounding hillocks, one of which is called **Sithean Mòr, 'The Large Fairy Mound'** (57.6802, -5.6727; NG811715). These enchanted blue lakes are reached by a trail from Shieldaig, which passes by Sithean Beag, 'The Little Fairy Mound' (57.6853, -5.6789; NG807721). Sitheans are ancient abodes of the fairies in the Scots-Gaelic lands and seen as portals to their Otherworld realm.

57.6768, -5.6783; NG807711; Trailhead Parking: 57.6888, -5.6828; NG805725; 1.7km

6 Loch Morar

Morag, the water monster of Loch Morar, was once more famous than the Loch Ness Monster. Like Nessie, she was sometimes described as a black hump-backed beast with a long neck, but this shapeshifting creature has also occasionally been seen as a beautiful mermaid with blonde hair. Belief in this female spirit of the loch probably dates back to ancient times when she was seen as the embodiment of its waters. It was said that her banshee-like wailing, sometimes heard at night, predicted a death in one of the local clan families.

Loch Morar is a large inland loch over 16km long that is surrounded by mountains. At its western end is an archipelago of islands and its only access road is a small lane from Morar to Bracara.

56.9723, -5.7900; NM697931

7 Sandwood Bay, Blairmore

Known by some as the 'Land of Mermaids', Sandwood Bay lies near the remote northwestern tip of Scotland not far from Cape Wrath. It was a place of frequent shipwrecks where the spirits of the ocean would take the lives of those from the land. Frequent sightings of these ocean spirits included beautiful mermaids with long reddish-yellow hair, blue-green eyes and yellow skin, as well as a wild hairy beast with a devilish grin and a powerful tail that was spotted near Cape Wrath (58.6257, -4.9990; NC259747). Sandwood Bay is flanked by an idyllic stretch of golden sand that few visit owing to its remote location and the long hike to reach it.

58.5380, -5.0598; NC219651; Trailhead Parking: 58.4909, -5.0999; NC194600; 6.7km

8 Smoo Cave, Durness *

A plunging underground waterfall and flowing stream lend a magical atmosphere to this most impressive of Scottish caverns which was seen by some as an entrance to the Otherworld realm of Faerie. Smoo Cave is one of Scotland's largest caverns with a massive gaping mouth out of which the Smoo Burn flows. Inside are smaller chambers where a waterfall drops through a hole in the ceiling above. This hole was said to have been created by the Devil and a coven of witches who blew a hole in the ceiling to escape when they heard a cock crow and realised that the sun was rising.

58.5637, -4.7205; NC418671; Tour ££, but free access as far as waterfall chamber

SKYE

9 Dunscaith Castle, Tokavaig

The Irish hero Cu Chulainn used to tie his dog Luath to a pillar of rock just outside

Dunscaith Castle when he came back from hunting. The castle itself was home to his lover and tutor Scathach, hence Dun Scaith, 'The Fortress of Scathach' (see **Fairy Pools**). The site is now occupied by the ruins of a medieval castle which guards the entrance to Loch Eishort and has an impressive backdrop of the Cuillin Hills on the other side of the loch. This later medieval castle, said to have been built by the fairies in a single night, sits upon a dark rocky outcrop that is cut off by the tides each day but could once be reached by a short bridge. The large natural pillar of rock where Cu Chulainn tied his dog is known as Clach Luach, 'The Stone of Luath' and can still be seen in front of the castle.

57.1366, -5.9759; NG595120; Trailhead: 57.1347, -5.9670; NG600118; 600m

10 Duns of Bracadale *

Ancient, fortified duns were often seen as fairy abodes and entrances to their Otherworld realm. In Bracadale are some of the largest and best-preserved Iron Age duns on Skye and many have legends attached to them. **Dun Beag** (57.3602, -6.4257;

NG339386), the biggest and most impressive of them, is a circular broch, its walls still standing over 2m high. It was seen as an entrance to the Otherworld. **Dun Taimh**, south of Bracadale, was reputedly saved from destruction by Murdo MacLeod who prevented his workmen from taking the stone to help build his new cattle shed. A crowd of fairies met with Murdo on a hill by the sea to thank him for saving their home, rewarding him with a herd of white cattle that came out of the sea and filled his new shed. Dun Taimh is the most magical and atmospheric of the duns and still feels fairy-haunted to this day. Nearby **Dun Garsin** (57.3629, -6.3903; NG360387) did not fare so well. Fairies used to dance around Dun Garsin in the moonlight but after a local farmer took some stones to build his cattle shed the fairies left and were not seen again.

57.3441, -6.3843; NG363366 (Dun Taimh)

11 Dunvegan Castle

The home of the MacLeod clan since the 13th century, Dunvegan Castle is a place replete with legends about the MacLeod's

dealings with the fairy folk. On display inside the castle are the fairy flag and the fairy cup, both of which have many tales attached to them. The fairy flag was thought to have been a gift from the fairies and its magical property was to ensure victory in battle three times. It has already been used twice, in 1490 and 1580, but has yet to be flown a final time. The flag is also cursed, so that any pregnant woman or animal that sees it will instantly give birth. Common to the various stories concerning the flag's origin is that it was given by a fairy woman to a member of the MacLeod family. In one version it was gifted to a MacLeod knight after an encounter with a fairy woman while on crusade. According to another, a MacLeod baby was found wrapped in the flag by a fairy woman who was singing him a lullaby in old Gaelic. The lullaby she sang survives to this

day. The most romantic tale is that of a MacLeod chief who married a fairy bride. After giving birth to their first child, she told him that she must return to Fairyland and so they parted by what became known as the **Fairy Bridge** (57.4705, -6.5414; NG278513) and the flag was her parting gift. The small stone-built bridge can still be seen just north of Dunvegan Castle. It could be speculated that all three stories are connected, that the fairy bride was met on crusade and the baby wrapped in the flag before she departed by the Fairy Bridge. The origins of the fairy cup are similarly mysterious. One story tells how it was stolen from the fairies who lived in **Dun Osdale** (57.4242, -6.5969; NG241464), an Iron Age broch not far from Dunvegan Castle. A member of the MacLeod clan watched the fairies dancing there one night but was discovered when he sneezed. He was then dragged inside the mound where the fairies encouraged him to join the revelry. However, he avoided drinking from the fairy cup that was passed to him and instead ran away with it. The cup was later taken to Dunvegan Castle for safekeeping. The Gaelic-style wooden cup is ornamented with silver and gems.

57.4484, -6.5901; NG247490; £££ Open May – October

12 **Fairy Glen, Uig** *

An otherworldly landscape of strange rock formations and ancient forests of hazel has become known as the Fairy Glen. At its centre stands a huge flat-topped column of rock called Castle Ewen that some believe is a fairy dwelling. People push coins into cracks in a cave below it so the fairies will grant their wishes. All around this tower of rock people have made stone sculptures including spirals and labyrinths where rituals are sometimes performed.

57.5827, -6.3257; NG415629 (Castle Ewen); Trailhead Parking: 57.5847, -6.3330, NG411632; 800m

13 **Fairy Pools &
the Cuillin Hills** *

A series of deep pools filled with crystal-clear mountain water, the Fairy Pools are supplied by a stream that cascades down from the Cuillin Hills. A series of small falls connect these magical turquoise pools set against the striking profile of the Cuillins, and the hills feature in one of the Skye's ancient creation legends. The Cailleach Bheur, the

hag goddess of winter, used to dwell on the moors of Skye, particularly near a hill that is named after her called Beinn na Caillich (57.2374, -5.9766; NG601233). She was in conflict with the god of spring who was unable to overcome her, so he called upon the sun god who threw a spear at her. Where this spear landed the earth became molten and rose up, forming the Cuillin Hills. The first to inhabit the Cuillins was a goddess named Scathach. She was challenged by the Irish hero Cu Chulainn who fought with her long and hard. Realising that neither could win the battle they eventually made peace and became lovers, living at **Dunscaith Castle**. Scathach is pronounced 'Skyah' and she could be seen as the embodiment and protectress of the island of Skye. The mystical peaks of the Cuillins Hills are among the most magically charged and atmospheric features of Skye and the stream that rises there and fills the Fairy Pools seems to carry down their magical energy.

The **Cuillin Hills** (57.2415, -6.2348; NG446247) can be reached by continuing on the footpath past the Fairy Pools.

57.2504, -6.2582; NG432257 (Fairy Pools); Popular, Trailhead Parking: 57.2500, -6.2731; NG423257; 1km

14

14

15 Old Man of Storr, Portree *

The immense rocky pinnacle known as the Old Man of Storr is said to be an old man who was turned to stone after an encounter with some giants. The old man (bodach) was travelling with his wife, the old woman (cailleach), and after walking away from the giants they turned around to look at them one last time and were turned to stone. The smaller stone representing the old woman has since collapsed but the immense Old Man of Storr still stands. Detached from the adjacent rocky escarpment, it is surrounded by many other rocky pinnacles in an other-worldly landscape. Another version of the tale says that the Old Man himself was a giant, turned to stone by the gaze of Balor of the Baleful Eye, the mythical leader of the evil Fomorian race from Ireland.
The pinnacle of the Old Man of Storr is visible for miles around and has become an iconic image of Skye, but to truly appreciate its immense size it is worth hiking up to it for a closer look. The nearby Storr Mountain (57.5071, -6.1832; NG495540) is said to be where the Celtic hag goddess the Cailleach used to hang out her clothes to dry.

57.5075, -6.1747; NG500540; Popular, Trailhead Parking: 57.4994, -6.1581; NG509530; 2.7km

16 Tobar na h-Annait, Kilbride

Kilbride, 'The Church of Bride' is sacred to St Bridget and to the Celtic goddess Bride, the goddess of spring, who can be viewed as the Celtic mother goddess in her youthful aspect. The Cailleach, the goddess as old crone, was said to bathe in a fountain of youth each spring on a magical island and be reborn as Bride. In Kilbride can be found Clach na h-Annait, 'The Stone of the Mother' (57.2098, -5.9936; NG589202) and Tobar

16

14 Loch Sheanta & the Quiraing

A fantastical jumble of craggy rocks peeling away from an immense escarpment of cliffs, the **Quiraing** (57.6398, -6.2703; NG452691. Trailhead parking: 57.6283, -6.2916; NG438679; 2km) commands stunning views over the coastal lowlands and the ocean. A steep scramble takes you to the grassy plateau on the Quiraing known as 'The Table' (57.6413, -6.2745; NG450693), which used to be visited each summer by a white fairy cow. The fairest young woman in the district was chosen each year to milk the cow, which gave the sweetest milk they ever tasted. All went well until one year a tinker assaulted the woman and, donning her clothes, went to take the milk for himself, but the cow was not fooled

and tossed him into Staffin Bay where he drowned. From that day the cow was never seen again. Natural amphitheatres between the rocks of the Quiraing were thought to be fairy gathering places and the whole area has a magical and spirit-haunted feel.
Near the foot of the Quiraing, just north of the village of Digg, lies a small magical lochan known as Loch Sheanta. The lochan was believed to be sacred and ill-luck would befall anyone who fished in it or cut wood from its shores. At the western end of the lochan is a sacred spring that was used for healing. Invalids would circle the spring three times sunwise before drinking the water and leaving an offering of rags, coloured threads, pins or coins.

57.6479, -6.2402; NG471699 (Loch Sheanta sacred spring); Trailhead Parking: 57.6468, -6.2430; NG469698; 600m

na h-Annait, 'The Well of the Mother'. The former is a prehistoric standing stone while the latter is a natural spring with a millstone on top so the waters appear to rise below the hole in the millstone. Newly-wed brides were traditonaly taken to the spring to ensure their fertility. The standing stone is said to be magically protected and one man who removed it to use as a lintel suffered all kinds of disturbances until it was returned.

57.2092, -5.9937; NG589202

WESTERN ISLES

17 Beinn Mhòr, South Uist

The remote and inaccessible mountain of Beinn Mhòr was home to a fairy woman known as a *loireag*. She oversaw all aspects of cloth-making including spinning, weaving, and then softening the stiff material – a stage known as waulking. The latter was a communal activity where women soaked then kneaded the cloth while singing waulking songs. The loireag was known as the 'Fairy of the Waulking' and she would come down to the villages and punish anyone who sang out of tune. She was also mischievous and would steal milk from peoples' cattle. One man cried out in the name of St Columba to separate the loireag from his cow, but she then just ran away laughing.

There are no paths either on or leading up to Beinn Mhòr so it is best appreciated from one of the nearby villages that the loireag used to visit.

57.2587, -7.2951; NF808310; No Paths

18 Stinky Bay, Benbecula

On this island between North and South Uist, a small inlet known as Stinky Bay was the site of an unusual mermaid encounter in the 19th century. The mermaid was small, only about the size of a three- or four-year-old child, but with unusually developed breasts. She was swimming about in the bay, watched by an interested crowd of local people when a boy threw a stone and hit her. The next day her body was found washed up on Culla Beach (57.4588, -7.4012; NF762538) and people came from far and wide to look at her before she was given a burial. There are conflicting accounts of where she was buried, some say in the churchyard at Baile nan Cailleach (57.4588, -7.3947; NF766538) while others say it was on the nearby headland. Stinky Bay is named for the abundant seaweed growing there.

15

Baile nan Cailleach was also the scene of an encounter with the *sluagh*, the wild hunt. Two men were sitting in a longhouse one evening tending calves when in rushed two dogs with jewelled collars. Outside voices could be heard calling them and the men rushed out and saw a ghostly procession up in the sky with dogs and hawks prepared for the hunt. They heard a sound like the tinkling of innumerable silver bells, then the huntsmen called out and rode on. Some thought the hunters were elves, riding to their Land under Waves far out in the western ocean. They were known to fire elf shot at the unwary and carry off their souls to join the hunt. People would keep their west-facing windows locked up or barred with iron to prevent the sluagh from firing their fairy arrows through them.

From the same region come tales of a *bean-nighe*, a spirit who washed the shrouds of those about to die and was known as the 'washer-woman' or the 'washer at the ford'. If captured, she could be forced to grant three wishes. A follower of Clanranald of the Isles was travelling home one night to the island fortress of **Dun Buidhe** (57.4679, -7.3490; NF794545; no path) when he encountered the washer-woman. Seizing hold of her he demanded his three wishes. He asked for his home town to

17

18

have plenty of seaweed (for fertilizer), to have his chosen wife, and to know who the shroud was for. The shroud turned out to be for his master the Clanranald chief who subsequently fled the island in a boat. It is not known exactly where the encounter took place but Dun Buidhe sits in a lake just northeast of Baile nan Cailleach and is reached by a narrow isthmus. Perhaps the granting of the man's wish is responsible for all the seaweed in Stinky Bay!

57.4466, -7.4023; NF760524

19 Valley Island, North Uist

The islands of the Outer Hebrides were said to have been formed from the body of a nine-headed giant. He lived on an island called Stack Rock and used to raid the surrounding lands, abducting young women until the betrothed of one of the women rode a water horse over the waves and killed the giant. He first cut off eight of the giant's heads, which formed the small islands between North Uist and Harris including Vallay, Pabbay (57.7739, -7.2312; NF891880), Berneray (57.7182, -7.1825; NF915816), Killegray (57.7406, -7.0834; NF976836) and Taransay (57.8989, -7.0169; NB028009). On Vallay two standing stones known as

Leac nan Cailleacha Dubha – 'The Stones of the Old Black Crone' – were said to be a pair of witches who were killed and turned to stone for stealing milk. The island features stunning sandy bays and can be reached by a long walk across the sand at low tide. Berneray is accessible by bridge and the other islands that were formed by the giant's heads can be viewed from the shore or from the ferry that passes between Berneray Dock (57.7027, -7.1802; NF915799) and Leverburgh (57.7671, -7.0261; NG012863) on Harris. According to the legend, the remainder of the giant's body formed the mainland from Lewis down to Barra, the ninth head became the Butt of Lewis (58.5156, -6.2608; NB519664) and his feet created South Berneray (56.7861, -7.6330; NL561802).

57.6636, -7.3840; NF790765 (Leac nan Cailleacha Dubha); Trailhead: 57.6362, -7.3974; NF780735; 4.7km; Low Tide Only

20 Dun Bhuirgh, Harris

The rocky remains of an Iron Age fortified dwelling are scattered around the summit of this small, remote mound which was known to be a fairy dwelling. At one

time a woman from the local village fell in love with one of the fairy men. Her father, enraged by the union, went over to the dwelling and stuck his iron knife in the secret door to the mound. The fairies, repelled by iron, were trapped inside until one day a local sailor sat on the mound to rest. He could hear sounds of lamentation coming from within the mound but could find no door until he discovered the knife and pulled it out. Immediately the fairies came rushing out joyously and the Fairy Queen gave the sailor an enchanted quern-stone that could grind out salt whenever he said a magic word. Salt was a valuable commodity in those days and eventually the quern was stolen from the sailor by an avaricious sea captain. However, not knowing the magic word to stop the quern grinding the captain's boat filled with salt and sank. The quern is said to be grinding out salt to this day which is why the sea is so salty.

57.8369, -7.0006, NG033940; Trailhead: 57.8394, -7.0078; NG029943; 500m from road; No Paths

21 Callanish Stones, Lewis *

The most impressive and well-known stone circle in Scotland, the Callanish Stones (Calanais in Gaelic) form not just a circle but a shape like a Celtic cross. A double row of stones forming the shaft of the cross points due north, and rows of single stones point east, west and south from the central circle of stones, which itself contains a huge central stone and the remains of a later chambered tomb. All the stones are Lewisian Gneiss, one of the oldest rocks in the world formed 3 billion years ago, which gives them a pale, shimmering appearance. The stones are known in folklore as the Fir Bhreig, 'The False Man' and were believed to be giants who were turned to stone by St Kieran. They were used for ritual purposes until recent times with people gathering there on Beltane and at midsummer (the summer solstice). Couples would meet there to exchange betrothal vows and even consummate their marriages to ensure a happy future. On Midsummer's Day it was also said that the mysterious 'Shining One' would walk the avenue of stones, heralded by the call of a cuckoo from the Celtic Otherworld. Some say that the large central stone came to life on this date and would become the Shining One, but this is more likely a reference to the sun god and a solar alignment. During a period of famine, a magical white fairy cow is said to have appeared out of the sea and made its way to the Callanish Stones where the locals milked it and

avoided starvation. The cow's milk was so plentiful it would fill every container but when a witch brought a sieve instead of a bucket the supply of milk was exhausted. After that the cow disappeared and was never seen again. Another curious story relates how the stones of Callanish were brought over in ships by a priest-king and his attendants who wore feathered robes. Most of the stones were erected around 5,000 years ago and remarkably the majority are intact and still standing, protected over the years by the surrounding peat. Sea levels have risen over time and the stones now stand just 250m from the sea loch, outside the village of Callanish. The Callanish Stones form part of a entire ritual landscape with other impressive stone circles and standing stones nearby, notably Callanish III (58.1957, -6.7242; NB225327) and Callanish II (58.1946, -6.7291; NB222326), which are both a little over a kilometre away and much less visited than their more celebrated neighbour.

Parking: 58.1957, -6.7435; NB213328; Popular

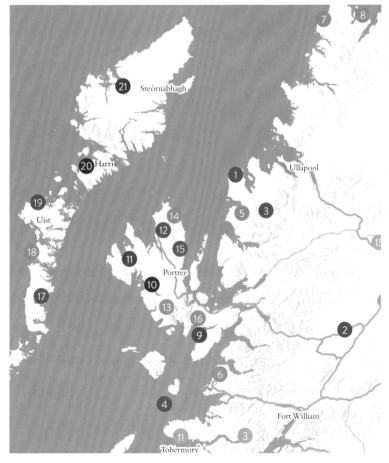

PLACENAME INDEX

PLACES BY CATEGORY

Cleeves Cove
Cley Hill
Clun Forest
Coille Loch an Draing
Cold Pixies Barrow
Cottingley Beck
Creag Mhòr
Cusop Dingle
Cwm Mabws
Cwm Pwca, Clydach Gorge
Devil's Jumps
Dingishowe
Doon Hill
Duffus Castle
Dulsie Gorge & the Findhorn River
Dun Bhuirg, Mull
Dun Bhuirgh
Dun Shith
Dunadd & Kilmartin Glen
Dundreggan Fairy Knoll
Dunnet Bay
Dunraven
Duns of Bracadale
Dunscaith Castle
Dunvegan Castle
Dwarfie Stane
Edin's Hall Broch
Eildon Hills
Elbolton Hill
Eveling's Rath, Hardknot Pass
Fairies Cave, Whitbarrow Scar
Fairies' Well, Tregenna
Fairies' Hole
Fairy Church
Fairy Cross Plain, Fryupdale
Fairy Glen
Fairy Glen
Fairy Glen, Borrowdale
Fairy Hillock
Fairy Holes, Forest of Bowland
Fairy Pools
Fairy Steps
Frenni Fawr
Glastonbury
Goblin Combe
Godshill
Guy's Cliffe
Harmby Fairy Well
Howk
Humberstone
Iona
Isle Maree
Isle of Muck

Janet's Foss
King Arthur's Cave
Lady's Well
Lewcombe Church
Llyn Barfog
Llyn Cynwch
Llyn Fawr
Llyn Gwyn
Llyn y Dywarchen
Llyn y Fan Fach
Loch Morlich
Lochan Sgeireach 'The Fairy Lochs'
Lochan Uaine Fairy Loch
Lud's Church
Maiden Castle
Malvhina Spring
Mingary Castle
Mitchell's Fold
Moel Arthur
Mount Snowdon
Mulgrave Woods
Mull of Galloway & The Rhins
Nine Stones Close
Nithsdale
Ogmore Castle & Arthur's Stone
Ogo Hole
Olchon Valley
Osebury Rock
Pennard Castle
Pentre Ifan
Pin Well
Pistyll Rhaeadr & the Berwyn Mountains
Rosemarkie Fairy Glen
Sandwick Rigg
Sarn Cynfelyn
Schiehallion
Sennen Cove
Simon's Nick
Simonside Hills
St Anne's Well
St David's
St Euny's Well
St Mary's Well
St Milburga's Well
Stinky Bay
Stony Littleton Long Barrow
Strathaven Fairy Mound
Tamlane's Well
Thirst House Cave
Trencrom Hill
Treryn Dinas
Troller's Gill
White Caterthun Hillfort
White Mare Crag & Roulston Scar

Willy Howe
Worlebury Hill
Ystradfellte and the Vale of Neath

Pixies & piskies
Bellever Tor
Cold Pixies Barrow
Dartmeet & The Dart Valley
Fice's Well
Mên-an-Tol
Oakery Bridge
Piskey's Hall Fogou
Piskies House
Piskies' Well
Pixies' Parlour Sharpitor
St Agnes' Well 'The Pixie Well'
Swincombe Rocks
White Lady Falls, Lydford Gorge
Willy Wilcox Hole
Wind Tor
Winsford Hill
Wambarrows

Mermaids & other ocean spirits
Cemaes Head
Church Ope Cove
Doom Bar
Dunnet Bay
Isle of Muck
Llanwnda Church
Llyn Fawr
Loch Morar
Marden Church
Mawgan Porth
Poldhu Cove
Rostherne Mere
Sandwood Bay
Sarn Cynfelyn
Skara Brae & Bay of Skaill
St Audrie's Bay
St Govan's Chapel
Stinky Bay
Turnberry Point
Zennor

Water spirits of rivers, lakes & springs
Ben Cruachan & Loch Awe
Betws y Coed
Fairy Glen & the River Conwy

Black Mere
Caerphilly Castle
Castle Campbell
Dartmeet & The Dart Valley
Dozmary Pool
Ebbing and Flowing Well
Llyn Barfog
Llyn Fawr
Llyn Tegid
Llyn y Fan Fach
Loch Morar
Merlindale
Mingary Castle
Mount Snowdon
Ogmore Castle & Arthur's Stone
Peggy's Well
Pentre Ifan
Pistyll Rhaeadr & the Berwyn Mountains
Plynlimon
River North Esk
Rostherne Mere
Schiehallion
Stinky Bay
Urquhart Castle, Loch Ness
Wharton Tarn
White Lady Falls, Lydford Gorge

Hobs, brownies & household spirits
Arbor Low
Boggle Hole
Caerlaverock Castle
Caerphilly Castle
Cley Hill
Doon Hill
Edin's Hall Broch
Fairy Cross Plain, Fryupdale
Hob Holes
Hob Hurst's House
Hobthrush Hall
Lindisfarne
Mulgrave Woods
Obtrusch Roque, Low Mill
Rosewall Hill Mines
The Written Stone
Thirst House Cave
Thor's Cave
White Mare Crag & Roulston Scar
Worlebury Hill

Merlin
Alcluid, The Rock of Dumbarton
Alderley Edge
Dinas Emrys
Hart Fell Spa
King Arthur's Cave
Lochmaben Stone
Merlin's Hill
Merlindale
Merlin's Cave, Bardsey Island
Pentre Ifan
St Levan's Stone
Stonehenge
Tintagel

Arthur and other legendary heroes
Alcluid, The Rock of Dumbarton
Alderley Edge
Aquae Sulis, Bath
Arthur's Seat
Arthur's Stone
Arthur's Stone
Avebury
Badbury Rings
Blencathra
Bwlch y Groes
Cadbury Castle
Caerleon
Carne Beacon
Castell Dinas Bran
Castle-an-Dinas
Cerrig Meibion Arthur
Clun Forest
Coetan Arthur
Dinas Emrys
Dog Stone
Dozmary Pool
Dunadd & Kilmartin Glen
Dundreggan Fairy Knoll
Dunraven
Dunscaith Castle
Eildon Hills
Eveling's Rath, Hardknot Pass
Frenni Fawr
Glastonbury
Guy's Cliffe
Gwâl y Filiast (Arthur's Table)
Hartland Point
Heltor
Iona
King Arthur's Cave
Llyn Barfog
Llyn Llech Owain
Lud Well

Lud's Church
Machrie Moor
Moel Arthur
Mount Snowdon
Nine Stones Close
Ogmore Castle & Arthur's Stone
Our Lady's Well
Pendragon Castle
Pistyll Rhaeadr & the Berwyn Mountains
Rock of Harlech
Sarn Cynfelyn
Scotlandwell
Sewingshields Crags
Spindlestone
St David's
St Govan's Chapel
Tenby & Caldey Island
The White Mount, Tower of London
Tintagel
Traprain Law
Treryn Dinas
Trethevy Quoit
Vanora's Mound
Wayland's Smithy

Celtic saints & miracles
Alcluid, The Rock of Dumbarton
Callanish Stones
Carreg Pumsaint
Castell Dinas Bran
Castle Howe & Bassenthwaite Lake
Eildon Hills
Frenni Fawr
Glastonbury
Holyhead Mountain
Holywell Cave
Iona
Isle Maree
Jesus Well
Lindisfarne
Llanddwyn Island
Llanwnda Church
Llyn Gwyn
Marden Church
Merlindale
Merlin's Cave, Bardsey Island
Nevern & Carn Ingli
Pennant Melangell Church
Reynard's Cave, Tresilian Bay
St Agnes Beacon
St Anthony's Well

St Beuno's Well
St Brannoc's Well
St Canna's Chair, Llangan
St Clether's Well Chapel
St Columba's Well
St Cybi's Well
St Cybi's Well
St David's
St Fillan's Cave
St Fillan's Holy Pool
St Govan's Chapel
St Levan's Stone
St Margaret's Well
St Medana's Well
St Michael's Mount
St Milburga's Well
St Nectan's Glen
St Nectan's Well, Stoke
St Seiriol's Well
St Teilo's Well
St Trillo's Chapel
St Winefride's Well
St Winifred's Well
Tenby & Caldey Island
Traprain Law

Christianised pagan sites
Alfriston Church
Bailey Hill
Brent Tor
Bungay Church
Carn Brea
Devil's Arrows
Dragon of Linton
Dunino Den
Glastonbury
Godshill
Hope Bagot Holy Well
Isle Maree
Kilgwrrwg Church
Knowlton Henge
Lewcombe Church
Lindisfarne
Little Walsingham Shrine
Llandeilo Graban Church
Llanfeugan Church
Merlindale
Midmar Kirk Stone Circle
Nevern & Carn Ingli
Pennant Melangell Church

Roche Rock
Roslin Glen
Rudston Monolith
Schiehallion
St Blane's Monastery
St Brannoc's Well
St Mary's Well
St Michael's Mount
St Teilo's Well
Stevington Holy Well
Whitwick Holy Well
Ysbyty Cynfyn Churchyard

Norse & Anglo-Saxon mythology
Abbots Bromley
Adam's Grave
Alcluid, The Rock of Dumbarton
Castle Howe & Bassenthwaite Lake
Devil's Humps
Devil's Jumps
Dowsborough Hillfort
Dwarfie Stane
Fairy Glen, Borrowdale
Grimsbury Castle
Grimspound
Long Meg and Her Daughters
Mulgrave Woods
Ring of Brodgar
Roseberry Topping
Sandwick Rigg
Simonside Hills
Stanton Drew Stone Circles
Thor's Cave
Wade's Causeway
Wayland's Smithy

Wild Hunt & otherworldly hounds
Avebury
Blyborough
Bredon Hill
Bungay Church
Cadair Idris
Cadbury Castle
Carn Kenidjack
Clun Forest
Crockern Tor
Cromer Cliffs
Dewerstone Rock

LANDSCAPE GLOSSARY

C = Cornish
N = Norse
W = Welsh
S = Scots
SG = Scots-Gaelic

aber (W) - estuary, river mouth or confluence of water

allt (SG) - stream

barrow - artificial mound, usually over a prehistoric burial chamber

beck (N) - stream

bedd (W) - grave

ben (S) - mountain or high hill

beinn (SG) - see ben

brae (S) - hillside or uplands

broad - lake

broch (S) - Iron Age circular stone tower on mound

burn (S) - stream

butt - mound that a target is placed in front of is for archery practice

bwlch (W) - mountain pass

bwrdd (W) - 'table' of rock

cairn - pile of rocks, sometimes covering a grave

cairn circle - circular arrangement of stones marking a prehistoric burial

cadair (W) - 'chair' rock formation

carn (C) - see cairn

carnedd (W) - see cairn

carreg (W) - stone

castell (W) - castle

cerrig (W) - stones

cist - prehistoric burial chamber lined with stone

clach (SG) - stone

clapper bridge - simple bridge made from large stone slabs

clootie (S) - strip of fabric

coetan (W) - see dolmen

coille (SG) - woodland or forest

coire (SG) - a hanging valley or hollow in a mountainside

corrie - see coire

combe - short valley or hollow in a hillside

craig (W/SG) - rocky cliff or crag

crannog (SG) - artificial island, usually used as a dwelling

creag (SG) - see craig

cup & ring mark - form of prehistoric rock art carved into stone

cwm (W) - see combe

dale (N) - valley

dinas (C/W) - fortress

ddinas (W) - see dinas

dolmen - prehistoric tomb with a large flat stone supported by upright ones

dun (SG) - fortress

dyke - embankment and ditch

eilean (SG) - island

fell (N) - barren hill or mountain

ffynnon (W) - spring or well

fogou (C) - stone-lined underground

passage or chamber of unknown purpose

foss (N) - waterfall

gill (N) - ravine or narrow valley

gleann (SG) - see glen

glen (S) - long, broad valley

gorge - narrow, steep-sided canyon, usually with water running through it

haug (N) - see howe

head - the uppermost end of a valley

head - high promontory extending into the sea

henge - prehistoric circular or oval earthwork enclosure with inner ditch

hillfort - Iron Age defensive enclosure on hilltop

holm (N) - small island

holt (N) - wooded hill

howe (N) - small hill or mound, sometimes covering a burial

hut circle - remains of a prehistoric round house

kirk (S) - church

knock (S) - see knoll

knoll - small rounded hillock

knowe (S) - see knoll

law (S) - hill

llyn (W) - lake

loch (S/SG) - lake

lochan (SG) - small lake

long barrow - long linear mound built over a prehistoric

burial chamber

maen (W) - stone

megalith - large stone, particularly when used in a prehistoric monument

men/mên (C) - stone

mere - shallow lake, pond or wetland

moel (W) - bare hill

moor - uncultivated upland area usually covered in heather

motte - mound that was once the site of a (usually Norman) castle

mull (S) - promontory or headland

mynydd (W) - mountain

nant (W) - stream

ogham stone - stone inscribed with Celtic ogham script

pistyll (W) - see spring

porth (W) - portal or gateway

porth (W/C) – harbour, cove

pound - enclosure

quoit (C) - see dolmen

rhaeadr (W) - waterfall

rigg (N) - ridge

ring - circular earthwork

ring cairn - stone or earthwork prehistoric ritual monument

ring fort - prehistoric circular defensive construction

sarn (W) - causeway

scar (N) - rocky crag

sithean (SG) - mound or hill associated with fairies

spring - natural emergence of water from an underground source

standing stone - megalith placed vertically in the ground

stane (S) - stone

stone circle - standing stones in a circular arrangement

tigh (SG) - house

tobar (SG) - well or spring

tolmen - holed stone

tom (SG) - round hillock

topping - summit of mountain or high hill

tor - hill or rocky peak

tor enclosure - Neolithic stone enclosure surrounding a tor

trilithon - megalithic structure of two upright stones with a third forming a lintel

tump - small hill or mound

uamh (SG) - cave

well - a spring, usually one that collects in a man-made stone basin or similar construction

well - deep shaft created to access underground water

well-house - stone structure built to house a well

ynys (W) - island

Magical Britain
650 Enchanted and
Mystical Sites

Words:
Rob Wildwood

Photos:
Rob Wildwood

Additional research & writing:
Bryony Whistlecraft

Editing:
Anna Kruger

Layout & design:
James Pople
Tina Smith

Illustrations:
Dan Bright (symbols)
Yannick Dubois (Celtic
Wheel of the Year)

Proofreading:
Bethany Williams

Distribution:
Central Books Ltd
50, Freshwater Road
Dagenham, RM8 1RX
020 8525 8800
orders@centralbooks.com

Published by:
Wild Things Publishing Ltd.
Freshford, Bath, BA2 7WG

Contact:
hello@
wildthingspublishing.com

Author acknowledgements:
With thanks to all the friends who helped me on my journey to explore Magical Britain: Alphedia Arara, Esté Cann, Bryony Whistlecraft, Jennifer Hunter 'Feather', Felicity Fyr le Fay 'Flame', Alison Gillies, Deborah Skye & Luminous, Sunshine Tresidder, Phylis Jean 'Dancing Hands', Kate Ray 'Hare Girl', Brian Taylor, Jay & Kestrel Oakwood, Leaf McGowan, Armorel Hamilton, Poppy Ferguson, Sarah Brockbank.

Bibliography / Further Reading:

Albion: A Guide to Legendary Britain, Westwood,
Ancient Stones on Old Postcards, Bird,
Argyll Folk Tales, Pegg,
Arthur & the Twrch Trwyth, Isaac,
Atlas of Magical Britain, Bord,
Between the Realms: Cornish Myth & Magic, Straffon,
Bredon Hill: A Guide to its Archaeology, History, Folklore & Villages, Hoggard,
Britain's Holiest Places, Mayhew Smith,
Celtic Legends of Pembrokeshire, Rhys,
Celtic Sacred Landscapes, Pennick,
The Earth Goddess: Celtic and Pagan Legacy of the Landscape, Straffon,
Echoes of the Goddess: A Quest for the Sacred Feminine in the British Landscape, Brighton & Welbourn,
Enchanted Britain, Alexander,
The Enchanted Land: Myths & Legends of Britain's Landscape, Bord,
Fairy Sites, Bord,
Folklore of Prehistoric Sites in Britain, Grinsell,
Folk Stories from the Lake District, Walker,
Folk Stories from the Yorkshire Dales, Walker,
Folk Tales from the North York Moors, Walker,
The Guide to Mysterious Iona & Staffa, Holder,
The Illustrated Encyclopaedia of Fairies, Franklin,
The Land of the Green Man, Carrington,

The Lore of Scotland: A Guide to Scottish Legends, Westwood & Kingshill,
The Mabinogion, Davies,
Magical Places of Britain, Wildwood,
Myths & Legends of Cornwall, Weatherhill & Devereux,
Myths & Legends of Wales, Roberts,
Mysterious Britain, Bord,
Mysterious Wales, Barber,
The New View Over Atlantis, Michell,
On the Trail of Merlin in a Dark Age, Crichton,
Orkney Folk Tales, Muir,
Oxfordshire Folk Tales, Manwaring,
The Power of Centre, Biltcliffe & Hoare,
The Quest for Merlin, Tolstoy,
The Real Middle Earth: Magic & Mystery in the Dark Ages, Bates,
Scottish Folk Tales, Geddes & Grosset,
Scottish Myths & Legends, Hamilton,
The Secret Commonwealth of Elves, Fauns & Fairies, Kirk,
Somerset Folk Tales, Jacksties,
The Spine of Albion, Biltcliffe & Hoare,
The Sun & the Serpent, Broadhurst & Miller,
Tales of the Dartmoor Pixies, Crossing,
The Travellers Guide to Sacred Scotland, Lines,
The Witchcraft & Folklore of Dartmoor, St Leger-Gordon,

Other books from Wild Things Publishing